Asahel Nettleton:
Sermons From the Second Great Awakening

Taken from the original handwritten
manuscripts of the
Rev. Asahel Nettleton
(1783-1844)

With an Introduction
by Dr. Tom Nettles
and a Preface
by Bennet Tyler

International Outreach, Inc.
P. O. Box 1286, Ames, Iowa 50014

International Outreach, Inc.
P. O. Box 1286, Ames, Iowa 50014
(515) 233-2932

Portrait of Asahel Nettleton on the
front cover reproduced courtesy of
The Connecticut Historical Society,
Hartford, Connecticut.

Copyright © 1995 by International Outreach, Inc.

ISBN 0-9641803-3-2

ASAHEL NETTLETON: SERMONS FROM THE SECOND GREAT AWAKENING

Contents

Foreword...*i*
Introduction..*v*

Part I, Sermons

1. Professing Christians, Awake! (Romans 13:11)................*1*
2. The Contemplation of Death (Deuteronomy 32:29)..........*9*
3. Indecision in Religion (I Kings 18:21)............................*17*
4. The Death of the Righteous (Numbers 23:10)................*25*
5. The Destruction of Hardened Sinners (Proverbs 29:1)...*30*
6. Rejoice Young Man (Ecclesiastes 11:9).........................*40*
7. Seek Ye the Lord (Isaiah 55:6)......................................*53*
8. Genuine Repentance Does Not Precede Regeneration (Jeremiah 31:19)..*60*
9. Discerning Between the Righteous and the Wicked (Malachi 3:18)..*74*
10. The Unclean Spirit (Matthew 12:43-45)......................*84*
11. Abandoned by God (Matthew 13:58)..........................*93*
12. The Wise and the Foolish Virgins (Matthew 25:2).......*97*
13. The Final Judgment, Part I (Matthew 25:31-32)........*103*
14. The Final Judgment, Part II (Matthew 25:31-32).......*114*
15. The Demands of Discipleship (Luke 9:57-62)............*122*
16. Many Now on the Earth Are Greater Sinners Than Those Who Are in Hell (Luke 13:1-6)...............................*127*
17. The Certain Destruction of All Who Do Not Seek Salvation Rightly (Luke 13:24)..*133*
18. A Sermon for Children (Luke 18:16)............................*140*
19. Regeneration (John 1:12-13)......................................*143*

20. Despisest Thou the Riches of God's Goodness?
    (Romans 2:4)..150
21. Gospel Warfare (II Corinthians 10:4).......................158
22. The Mortification of Sin, Part I (Galatians 5:24)........168
23. The Mortification of Sin, Part II (Galatians 5:24).......175
24. The Counsel and Agency of God in the Government of
    All Things (Ephesians 1:11)...180
25. The Perseverance of the Saints (Philippians 1:6)........191
26. All Men Commanded to Pray (I Timothy 2:8)..............205
27. The Judgment of the Great Day (Jude 6).....................212
28. The Wicked Standing Before the Judgment Seat
    (Revelation 20:12)...220
29. Notes on Theology..226

Part II, Sermons

Preface by Bennet Tyler...245
30. Sinners Affectionately Entreated to Enter on the
    Christian Pilgrimage (Numbers 10:29)..........................247
31. The Sin and Consequences of Being Ashamed of
    Christ (Luke 9:26)...261
32. The Parable of the Lost Sheep (Luke 15:3-7)..............278
33. The Parable of the Prodigal Son (Luke 15:11-25).......290
34. The Danger of Hypocrisy (Matthew 25:1-8)................303
35. The Great Salvation (Hebrews 2:3)............................312
36. Self-Examination (II Corinthians 13:5).......................323
37. The Rich Man and Lazarus (Luke 16:19-31)...............334
38. The Duty of Fasting and the Manner in Which the
    Duty Should Be Performed (Nehemiah 1:4)...................345
39. Sinners Entreated to Be Reconciled to God
    (II Corinthians 5:20)..356
40. The Government of God a Matter of Rejoicing
    (Psalm 97:1)..371
41. Christ Standing at the Door (Revelation 3:20)............377

42. Religion the Only Source of True Happiness
(Proverbs 3:13)..383
43. The Backslider Restored (Psalm 51:12-13)..................389
44. Total Depravity (Genesis 6:5)......................................394
45. The Way in Which Sinners Cover Their Sins
(Proverbs 28:13)..399
46. The Example of Esau, A Warning to Sinners
(Hebrews 12:16)..404
47. The Sinner Slain by the Law (Romans 7:9)................408
48. Causes of Alarm to Awakened Sinners (Acts 2:37)......412
49. The Burdened Sinner Invited to Christ
(Matthew 11:28-30)..421
50. The Necessity of Regeneration No Matter of Wonder
(John 3:7)..426
51. The Nature and Reasonableness of Evangelical
Repentance (Acts 17:30)..................................432
52. God's Spirit Will Not Always Strive (Genesis 6:3)......439
53. Salvation for the Lost (Luke 19:10)............................445

Part III, Brief Observations & Miscellaneous Remarks

Matthew 27:63..451
II Thessalonians 2:11-12..452
Romans 9:16...455
Luke 23:39-43..456
John 4:29..458
Psalm 73:10..458
Matthew 23:30..459
James 1:7..461
Luke 14:18..461
Luke 9:54-55..464
Luke 9:59..465
I Corinthians 12:6...466

Psalm 119:59-60..*467*
Psalm 94:16..*468*
Matthew 13:25...*469*
Matthew 5:25...*470*
Ezekiel 33:11..*471*

Miscellaneous Remarks

*What answer would you give to the question, How can I
repent, or love God, or become a Christian?*......................*473*
Special Grace...*473*
Thoughts on Revivals..*495*
On professing religion...*499*
The Duty of being tender of the character of ministers......*500*
Decrees of God...*500*
The doctrine of election..*501*
Perseverance of the saints..*505*
Infant Depravity..*505*
The influence of self-interest on human belief...................*506*
Prayer..*506*

the glory of C. we may imagine will more & more appear. There will not be a single xn in wh. there will not be some thing to exhibit the character of C. Through the medium of every xn, Angels will admire the Saviour. That is one object of 1 day of judgment. Christ shall come to be glorified in his saints, & to be admired in all them that believe in that day.

The saints too will be joyful. They will all know before hand, the issue of their trial. Many of them will then have been with C. in heaven for thousands of years. Abraham, Isaac & Jacob & all who have died in the Lord will have already been assured of heaven, for they have long been with C. They have washed their robes & made them white in 1 blood of the lamb. They have long been before the throne of G. serving him day & night in his temple. And their happiness will not be interrupted by the solemnities of the judgment day

A sample of the handwriting of Rev. Asahel Nettleton. This page is taken from the sermon on Jude 6, *The Judgment of the Great Day*. The portion above is printed on page 214 of this book. The Jude 6 sermon is in the best condition of all the Hartford Seminary manuscripts. Many of the manuscripts are fragile, faint, torn, and difficult to read and handle.

**Rev. Asahel Nettleton
(1783-1844)**
From a portrait which appeared in
Bennet Tyler's
*Memoir of the Life and Character of
Rev. Asahel Nettleton, D. D. (1844).*

Foreword

Throughout history the Lord has used men as his instruments for the spread of the gospel in powerful ways. Seldom has he used a man more mightily for the conversion of sinners than Asahel Nettleton. This has been testified in Bennet Tyler's biography, *Memoir of the Life and Character of Rev. Asahel Nettleton, D.D.*, published the same year as Nettleton's death, and more recently in John Thornbury's work *God Sent Revival*. Both witness to the godly character and powerful ministry of Asahel Nettleton.

It was with great joy that I learned this past year of the existence of a number of Nettleton's manuscript sermons at Hartford Seminary in Hartford, Connecticut. The first 28 sermons in this book and the 29th chapter of Nettleton's notes on theology have been taken from these handwritten manuscripts. These manuscripts are part of the Hartford Seminary Library's collection of manuscript materials. Many of them have never been published before. These first 29 chapters have been taken word for word from Nettleton's handwritten manuscripts. Occasionally a subject word (you, your, etc.) has been supplied. Where deletions have been made due to illegible handwriting or a hole in the manuscript, these have been noted with a footnote. Chapter 29 has been edited for publication. Words which appear in italics were underlined in Nettleton's original manuscripts. Double underlined words in the original are in italics and underlined in this work.

Asahel Nettleton was a thorough student of the human heart. He understood the windings and turnings of the depraved heart and knew how to expose its deceits to awaken the sinner to the desperateness of his lost condition. You who seek to do the work of evangelism today: Are you such a student of the human heart? Do you understand how the unconverted heart operates? In his sermon on *Gospel Warfare* Nettleton said: "Preaching mere external morality will never bring one soul to Christ. That preaching which does not aim at the heart, and take hold of the conscience, never attacks the strong holds of Satan."

Nettleton spoke frequently on such subjects as regeneration, self-examination, death, hell, and the final judgment. How often have you either preached or heard sermons preached on these subjects? Three hundred years ago it was common to hear sermons preached on the difference between true and false conversion. Asahel Nettleton frequently reminded his hearers of the signs of genuine conversion and warned those who heard him to beware of thinking they were converted when they were not. How often is this subject preached on today?

Eternity is a constant theme of these sermons. Nettleton continually reminded his hearers that their eternal destination was either heaven or hell. He seemed to echo the message of one of the hymns in his hymn book, *Village Hymns for Social Worship:* "Eternity is just at hand, and shall I waste my ebbing sand?" In the sermon entitled *The Contemplation of Death* he says: "The season of trial is short. It is never to be enjoyed but once. Eternity is written on the wings of every moment. Every sinner is now on trial *once for all*. He is now invited by all the charms of a bleeding Saviour, urged by all the horrors of the second death to enter the ark of safety. He is now called upon to *strive and agonize* to enter heaven. But death closes the scene forever."

Nettleton also preached on the necessity of the conscience being awakened to its danger prior to genuine conversion. He strongly believed that if the sinner was not awakened to his fearful state, he could not be saved. "Those sinners are commonly the nearest destruction who think and care the least about it. Hell is truth learned too late." To the sinner he proclaimed, "The only remedy which can be applied for the salvation of sinners is the gospel. And this remedy never takes effect without alarming and arousing the guilty conscience...Sinner! If you cannot be alarmed, you cannot be saved."

One way usedby Nettleton to alarm the consciencewas tahrough the useofprobing questions designed to pierce the hearts of the unconverted. He frequently asked a series of questions designed to cause his hearers to consider the lost condition of their souls. Questions have the effect of forcing the listener to think. Under the almighty hand of God they can effectually awaken the sinner.

Parts II and III of this work contain sermons, notes, and miscellaneous writings by Nettleton, published by Bennet Tyler in 1845, the year after Nettleton's death. It should be noted that these sermons were edited by Tyler. In some cases Tyler changed words, in others entire sentences have been deleted. Sometimes phrases have been added. The end result, however, is still very faithful to the original manuscripts. Most of what appears in these sections is not found in the Hartford Seminary collection. I do not know if they are still extant. They have been reproduced here as originally published. The preface to the original volume compiled by Tyler appears at the beginning of Part II.

I would like to thank Mr. Tom Newman the director of the

Hartford Seminary Library who granted permission for these sermons to be printed and a special thanks to Mrs. Carolyn Sperl, head of Reference and Interlibrary Loans at the Seminary, whose assistance in working with the Nettleton papers was invaluable. Without their help these sermons would never have been reprinted. I also express my thanks to The Connecticut Historical Society for their permission to use the Nettleton portrait on the dust jacket.

It is my hope that these sermons will be used once again as they were in the 19th century—for the conversion of many sinners. It may be said of the author of them, as it was said of righteous Abel, "Asahel Nettleton, though dead, still speaks." May his words pierce the hearts of sinners today, as they did 175 years ago.

William C. Nichols
International Outreach, Inc.
February 23, 1995

AN INTRODUCTION TO ASAHEL NETTLETON

NETTLETON'S LIFE

On April 21, 1783, Asahel Nettleton was born into the home of a Connecticut farmer, the second child and eldest son of six children. In his youth, he was catechized in the <u>Westminster Shorter Catechism</u>, giving him a mental apprehension of truths which, when God brought the truths home to his heart, greatly increased his effectiveness as an evangelist. In the year 1800, Nettleton became convicted that his life was dangerously frivolous; as a result, he sought to change both himself and his friends. An increasing sense of the wickedness of his heart brought about a corresponding attempt to prove the Bible wrong. He disliked the God he found there, for he knew that such a Holy Being must of necessity condemn him. He wished for God's non-existence.

After Nettleton struggled in spiritual distress for ten months, God's Spirit changed his heart and brought him to embrace the Savior. He did not at first recognize his change as conversion but now found delight in objects which before had "given him so much distress." His views and feelings were the same as those "whom he regarded as the friends of Christ." Now, instead of hoping for God's non-existence, the attributes of the Tri-une Deity appeared lovely and "the Saviour was exceedingly precious." Now, instead of feelings of bitter opposition, he contemplated the doctrines of grace, with delight, and "had now no doubt of their truth." This astounding change, he knew, was "not the result of any effort of his own, but of the sovereign and distinguishing will of God."[1]

In 1805, in spite of pressing hardships, Nettleton entered Yale College, then under the presidency of Timothy Dwight. During his years there he justly gained the respect of his classmates as having unmixed sincerity in his devotion to Christ and earnestness in his desire for the salvation of his friends. Beyond the necessary study of the liberal arts curriculum, he gave his time to theological study and the development of a capacity for spiritual discernment. During a revival in 1807 at Yale, Nettleton was effective as a spiritual counselor. His career at Yale prompted the judgment from Timothy Dwight, "He will make one of the most useful men this country has ever seen."[2]

Nettleton, along with Samuel Mills, envisioned a life of service among those who had never heard the gospel on the mission field. Three factors converged to preclude that possibility for Nettleton.

One, a debt incurred while in school needed to be paid and he felt he must stay until that was done. Meanwhile, his preaching in destitute areas of Connecticut was so effective that leaders of the Congregational church urged upon him the duty to stay. Third, his contraction of typhus in 1822 eliminated all remaining hopes he had of work on the mission field.

In 1812, at the invitation of the pastors of churches, Nettleton began itinerating. Nettleton had seen the effects, and in fact had interviewed some eyewitnesses, of the inordinate affectations of James Davenport in the Great Awakening. He entered into this ministry with several convictions. One, he must do nothing to win affection from or destroy the influence of the settled pastorate. No lasting good could be done without the support and long-term influence of faithful pastors. Two, he would not seek to stir up interest where it was clear the Spirit of God had not preceded him. If he in fact detected a spirit of "enthusiasm" he would work to root it out. He had no fear at all that in his opposition to this type of misguided zeal he was "quenching the spirit." Three, he would not stay where there appeared to be any reliance on him. He felt he could be of no use if a church's anticipation fostered hope and excitement because of confidence in the human instrument, rather than remorse for sin and desire for the favor of God. Four, he believed that those converted during seasons of revival had a fervour for God purer and more sustained than those who made professions in times without general revival. Nettleton made the following observation in 1829.

> During the leisure occasioned by my late illness, I have been looking over the regions where God has revived his work for the two years past. The thousands who have professed Christ in this time, in general appear to run well. Hitherto, I think they have exhibited more of the Christian temper, and a better example, than the same number who have professed religion when there was no revival.... When I look back on revivals which took place ten or fifteen years ago, I have been agreeably surprised to find so many of the subjects of them continuing to adorn their profession. Take the whole number who professed religion as the fruit of these revivals, and take the same number who professed religion when there was no general revival, and I do think that the former have outshined the latter. I have not made a particular estimate, but from what I have seen, I do believe

that the number of excommunications from the latter is more than double in proportion to the former.³

For eleven years Nettleton immersed himself virtually without respite into the cause of revivals. This involved preaching three times on Sabbaths, usually twice, maybe thrice, during the week, and numbers of personal interviews and visits to homes where small but spiritually interested groups would be gathered. This schedule came to a halt in October, 1822, when after visiting a sick person he contracted typhus fever. For more than two years he was unable to engage in any revival activity, but took advantage of the time to compile his Village Hymns for Social Worship. After that time he could engage in far less strenuous activity, was more selective in engagements, and took longer periods of rest between revival efforts. Though the impression of his person was less powerful than before, accounts of his visits to churches still abound with testimonies of the effectual working of the Spirit of God. He traveled not only in New England during these years but also into the South as far as Virginia and South Carolina.

He went to the United Kingdom in 1831, ostensibly to rest, but preached frequently. In addition, he regularly had opportunity, as well as necessity, to distinguish between revivals in America and the more recent impact of the New Measures excitements. One report of the revivals in America concentrated on methods, events, and results characteristic of the New Measures fervor. Nettleton responded, "I am exhausted in my attempts to vindicate our revivals. I can only tell the good ministers here, that I do not, and never did, approve of the practice mentioned in the above letter."⁴

That practice Nettleton had opposed with increasing conviction since 1826. At that time he was drawn into a controversy with Charles Finney. The controversy was never really about methods although that issue first prompted the initial meetings between Nettleton and Finney. Though Finney declared "He could have led me almost or quite at his discretion," there is no evidence in any of Finney's relationships with older, more experienced and wiser people that he had any penchant for being led.⁵

The conflict climaxed at New Lebanon, New York, in July 1827. Nettleton had written publicly opposing the methods employed in Finney's meetings.⁶ Finney responded with a sermon, "How can two walk together except they be agreed?" The conference was arranged by Nathan Beman, a Finney supporter, and Lyman Beecher.⁷ There amidst wrangling, charges and counter charges, and some histrionic posturing on the part of Lyman Beecher,

Nettleton felt strongly the futility of such discussion. Near the close of the meeting, Nettleton read a letter outlining the disturbing practices and the conference approved resolutions rejecting the use of such practices. Finney and his followers, while clearly advocating some of the measures which give rise to these complaints, denied that these measures consisted of such abuses as outlined in the letter.[8] Perhaps, Finney proposed, a resolution against lukewarmness should also be adopted.

Several factors conspired against any satisfactory resolution to this conflict, especially in the dynamics of the New Lebanon Conference. One, the issue continued to be reduced to one of methods and the underlying theological distinctions garnered only brief attention. The orthodox participants, in fact, seemed unaware at this time that distinction in methods arose from radically different theological assumptions. Only in the next few years was the reason for this impasse in the discussion understood more fully. Two, one of Nettleton's chief protagonists, Lyman Beecher, agreed with Finney's anthropology and would soon be visibly aligned with the theological shift voiced in 1828 by Nathan W. Taylor.[9] Three, others who complained against Finney's methods were actually susceptible to many of Finney's theological caveats concerning human responsibility. They were followers of the "consistent Calvinists" Samuel Hopkins and Nathanael Emmons.[10] Four, Finney and his co-adjutants went to the conference fully convinced that the charges against them were false, or, where correct, merely reflected a theological or methodological insight superior to those of their accusers. Finney claimed that after the conference opposition to his revival efforts decreased.[11] He said that the opposition of Beecher and Nettleton was "impertinent & assuming, uncalled for & injurious to themselves, & the cause of God." And besides that, in spite of their efforts Finney could say, "their opposition never made me ashamed, never convinced me that I was wrong in doctrine or practice, & I never made the slightest change in conducting revivals as a consequence of their opposition. I thought I was right."[12]

In 1832, after his return from England, Nettleton joined efforts to conserve the orthodox theology of the past from the destructive force of Taylorism and the dispiriting effects of Finneyism. A vital part of this effort consisted of the founding of the Theological Institute of Connecticut. Nettleton, refusing an invitation to become a regular faculty member, was retained as an occasional instructor. He spent his last years lecturing on evangelism, counselling students, writing letters to friends making observations on the condition of religion in New England and America, and preaching as strength allowed. In May 1844, he died after a lengthy season of suffering and in a great deal of pain. His comforts in Christ, however, outstripped the rigors his calamitous sickness and to the end he continued to affirm that it was "sweet to trust in the Lord."[13]

NETTLETON'S PREACHING

Lyman Beecher described Nettleton's preaching as "highly intellectual" and "discriminatingly doctrinal." Calvinistic doctrines were "explained, defined, proved, and applied," and objections were stated fairly and given clear answers. These traits he opposed to mere declamation or "oratorical, pathetic appeals to imagination or the emotions." Though avoiding a direct appeal to the emotions, his sermons, nevertheless, were "deeply experimental in the graphic development of the experience of saint and sinner."[14]

Examples of this applicatory manner abound in the sermons in this volume. Nettleton's careful, relentless, and "graphic" pursuit to expose every refuge of the unconverted and illuminate the dark corners of their irrational resistance controls his application of the parable of the virgins to unready sinners.

> Another is under deep conviction, and has labored long, and so he thinks he has done much; for a while he feels resolved that nothing shall divest his attention from this great subject. If there is any thing in religion he is determined to find it, but growing faint and discouraged, he concludes that there is no such thing; <u>and so they that were foolish took their lamps and took no oil in them.</u>
> Another equally anxious and distressed for his soul, and casting about to find some relief, catches at every appearance and persuades himself that there is grace in his heart. And not being careful to examine, he settles down on a false hope and sleeps on secure. <u>And so they that were foolish took their lamps and took no oil with them.</u>
> Sometimes the sinner, having long been anxious, and finding no relief, is persuaded and prevailed on to believe that the most probable method to find relief is to profess religion. At length he is resolved to profess religion in hope that grace may thus be given. But the experiment has been followed sometimes with sad disappointment, no love to God, no renewing of the Holy Spirit has followed. Sometimes it has ended in still greater security; and in this

manner <u>they that were foolish took their lamps and took no oil with them</u>.

As Beecher indicated, doctrinal explanations also abound in Nettleton's preaching. And, as in the sermons of Jonathan Edwards, the explanations are couched within searching and sometimes frightening application. But it is such a fright as is designed not to evoke immediate "decision," but an increased sense of utter dependence on the grace of God for salvation. If the preacher gives the sinner any hope other than sovereign mercy, he destroys him and causes him to stop short of that sense of abandonment to both the justice and mercy of God so essential for true spiritual conversion. Rev. Cobb of Taunton, MA, described the effect of his doctrinal preaching in his parish in 1825, soon after Nettleton's debilitating sickness:

> He brought from his treasure the doctrines of total depravity, personal election, reprobation, the sovereignty of divine grace, and the universal government of God in working all things after the counsel of His own will. And these great doctrines did not <u>paralyze</u>, but greatly <u>promote</u> the good work. <u>Never had brother Nettleton such power over my congregation, as when he poured forth in torrents these awful truths</u>. And at no time were converts multiplied so rapidly, and convictions and distress so deep, as when these doctrines were pressed home to the conscience.[15]

His sermon "Regeneration" based on John 1:12, 13 is the consummate example of giving explanation, definition, proof, and application of a doctrine. The doctrine itself determines the type of application that is to be given. In this case, the application consists of a profoundly stark ending of the sermon with a sober assertion of the just verdict of God in the absence of His sovereign choice to display mercy.[16]

No matter how many unregenerate strivings, preparations, and moral actions there may be, or how much knowledge may exist, "after all there must be a new creation." The same power that raised Christ from the dead must be exerted in behalf of the sinner or he will remain dead in trespasses and sins. Nothing can be hoped for to give life other than "the omnipotence of the divine Spirit." Our understanding is darkened, our wills are "perverse and rebellious," our merits gain nothing but "utter rejection," and we are without strength. Neither power nor desire for spiritual mindedness exists. Ministers of God, no matter how skilled, or spiritual, or persuasive, will not change our minds in this matter. "Paul may plant and

Apollos water, but God gives the increase." Schemes of religious effort may be devised "by the ingenuity of man ... to wrest the glory of this work from the hands of the divine Spirit;" but when all is done, it is seen that nothing but "the free sovereign grace and Almighty power of God" can effect this change. "The work is all his; and the glory must and will forever belong exclusively to him."

The necessity of such a work implies the whole system of the doctrines of grace. Divine sovereignty in election and redemption only by Christ as well as human depravity and other doctrines connected with these, all flow from it. "There is one grand, harmonious, and perfect system: and God is the sum — the substance and the glory of all."

Nettleton acknowledged full awareness of the "difficulties incident to the doctrines here laid down." The natural heart, as he knew strained "both to oppose and misconstrue them." It is enough that "the Bible supports them" and, therefore, "our carnal reason must bow. Here our proud hearts must submit." The resister may charge them with "mystery — with inconsistency — with unprofitableness" but in doing so he assails "not man, but God." It stands "written in characters of light" in Holy Scripture, "which were born not of blood, nor of the will of the flesh, nor of the will of man, but of God."

> This is the only birth which can fit us for heaven, "Except a man be born again," etc. We may please our fancies, and gratify our self-righteousness, by adopting loose Pelagian sentiments on this subject; we may remonstrate against such absolute dependence on the grace of God as has now been advocated, but a new heart, and a right spirit will after all be found of such absolute necessity, that without them we must perish forever.17

And there ends the sermon. Intercession with God was not yet done, however, for Nettleton ended his messages with prayer supplicating God for mercies in light of the truths discussed and applied in the sermon. Samuel Miller noted that the closing prayers of Nettleton "were, perhaps, never exceeded for appropriate simplicity, and adaptedness to seal the impressions of the preceding sermon."18

Just as impressively as Nettleton placarded the monolithic foundation of God's sovereign pleasure and unilateral efficacy of his regenerative power, so he urged the immediate and unalterable obligation of all sinners to turn from sin, embrace the cross, and run toward heaven. An impressive array of sermons presses relentlessly on this infinitely important duty incumbent on creatures made in God's image. "Rejoice, Young Man," "Indecision in Religion," and "The Contemplation of Death" give not a moment's rest to the hearer. He indulges in no word of levity and never lets slip a hint of possible respite from the certainty of judgment. He can only strain himself at every point to prove that at judgment we will clearly see that every moment was invested with eternal importance.. "Every act of ours will have some influence on us through interminable ages," Nettleton preached; and, "All things are now ripening for the day when God shall bring every work to judgment, with every secret revealed." No cultural tolerance of age characteristics will impress God at that day. Instead, "without pity, or allowance for the levity of youth, he will condemn and punish for every failure of perfect obedience." Nothing will be considered innocent which has failed to prepare the soul to appear unblemished before God: "All amusements which prepare the soul for the duties of religion are right, and every Christian is bound to engage in them, and those which do not, will be condemned at the bar of God."

Every moment explodes with urgency; but, particularly, seasons of grace (when the gospel was being preached) were auspicious times. Nettleton would say, "The gates of heaven are now standing wide open to the sinner under the gospel. Heaven with all its glories is now brought within his reach." Preaching, therefore, must employ unyielding images of the necessity of finding a repentant heart. The sermon to the young based on Ecclesiastes 11:9 ended:

> Young man, I leave you in the hands of your final Judge. Life and death are now before you and God is witness to your choice. If a bleeding Saviour has no charms for you — if the thunder of his vengeance does not strike terror through your guilty soul; then go on. March on your way rejoicing — trample under foot the Son of God — Sport with eternal vengeance and deny the thunder of his power. Your fair morning will soon be turned into darkness, your course run — your bodies fall in the grave, and your souls into the hands of the living God.[19]

Andrew Bonar felt that this was the great strength of Nettleton, to "deal very extensively, and very perseveringly, in full doctrinal statements opened up and pressed home on the conscience." The combination of preaching and personal work — pulpit, lecture room, and private conversation — gave both power and purity to the revivals under Nettleton. Though sometimes "in a high degree eloquent," his eloquence was not overpowering as was that of Whitefield. Rather, Bonar called it "solemn and impressive,...more instructive, and addressed more to the conscience."[20]

THE REPROACH OF CHRIST

This strength of Nettleton, however, was also his weakness, according to the <u>Biblical Repertory and Theological Review</u>. In an 1844 review of Tyler's <u>Memoir</u>, the periodical called Nettleton "one of the wisest and best men we have ever known" and expressed sincere admiration for the "extraordinary wisdom with which he discharged the difficult duties of an evangelist," gratitude for the "wonderful success with which God crowned his labours," and an acknowledgment of indebtedness for the "fidelity and skill with which he opposed 'new measures' and 'new Divinity.'" In short, the reviewer had "the highest admiration for his character." All this being said, there still was a peculiar lack of proportion in his ministry and his personal spirituality. As a "New England Calvinist," he gave a preponderance of attention to the "psychological doctrines of the Bible, those doctrines which have more immediate relation to the nature and agency of man." The doctrines of depravity, regeneration, divine influence, particular providence in human affairs, and the teachings on decrees and election cut a much wider swath in his preaching than did the more objective doctrines of the gospel. The reviewers wished for more attention to the doctrines of "justification, of faith, of the mediation and intercession of our Lord." Those doctrines assuredly were not denied, nor were they kept out of view, but they were not "allowed their due prominence and power." On the subjects immediately under his attention, Nettleton preached with "singular adroitness and power," but not "in due proportion."[21]

The peculiarity generated by this so-called lack of "proportion" tended to produce misunderstanding.[22] That Nettleton often was misunderstood and his motives and methods misjudged is seen in an interesting reference to him in the diary of Basil Manly, Sr. Manly, an influential Baptist preacher in the deep South, wrote his observations in 1830 during Nettleton's visit to Charleston. Because Manly was at least reticent about the usefulness of the "New Measures" and at most one of their most piercing critics in the South, his reactions to Nettleton deserve attention. The entire entry into the diary says:

> The Rev. Asahel Nettleton, the respected promoter of re-

vivals in the northern states, has been here for some time attempting to produce a religious excitement in the community. His methods are peculiar: and it is said that tho' he takes a great deal of pains to disclaim the idea of being able to do anything, there seems to be an affectation of singularity for the sake of effect, and an air of self-sufficiency about him. From what I have heard, I believe that an unbiased and discerning mind would not fail to be impressed that those motives & sentiments lurk in his bosom, perhaps unknown in some measure to himself. I was prevented from witnessing his exhibitions for two reasons. As there was a revival in our church when he began and the people were coming to our meetings in great numbers my attention was very much taken up - & Mr. Nettleton's meetings were held of evenings, always I believe, on the same evenings of our meetings. His other meetings I did not choose to attend as they were more private, for this reason — As soon as he came here, I was disposed to welcome him, at Mr. Thomas Fleming's in George St. But he sent word that he was lying down, and declined seeing me. Supposing that he might have, at the moment, some good reason for this, I sent up my name and character — under the idea that if he wished to see me, I should afterward receive from him a visit, or a request to call again. But nothing of this kind occurred — & I concluded that he wished to have no intercourse with me. Yet this gentleman publicly complained ... that he had received no attention in Charleston — publicly entreated the citizens, again & again, to call on him at his lodgings, if it were only for <u>five minutes</u>. Said that there was no religion in Charleston — intimated strongly that ministers & people were all in fault — and as I have understood from several has now left the city in disgust — **AMEN** say I. And so may all leave it who behave like him.

I cannot imagine a more regrettable misunderstanding than that entry suggests. Manly's preaching was of the same searching doctrinal character as Nettleton's and his concerns about the dangers of misguided professions of faith in the climate of "revivalism" were just as profound. Manly described his own preaching as not inclining people "to the acts and exercises which are usual at the close of protracted services .... They seem rather disposed to shrink away into retirement; like Peter, to 'go out and weep bitterly.'" R. S. Smith described the impact of Nettleton's preaching as "awfully overwhelming. Men held their breath, and the audience moved slowly away, not to talk of the preacher, but to meditate, to read, and to pray."[23]

Manly warned against periods of "high wrought excitement" and the desires to "make a great show and parade of the converts which we have made." We should do nothing to pollute the church with "unbelievers, unconverted, and graceless persons" who not only will make the church a harlot, but will themselves be hardened beyond the reach of conscience and gospel. Their last estate is truly worse than the first. Likewise, Nettleton's meetings displayed solemnity and people were not "merely excited." They were rather "awakened to a sense of their lost condition by nature," and of their "entire dependence for salvation on the sovereign mercy of God." If any felt they were converted but manifest affections which arose merely from self-love "they were advised to abandon their hopes without delay."[24]

The impact that Manly and Nettleton made on their sympathetic hearers is remarkably similar. Manly is described as a "decided Calvinist" than whom none could "preach the gospel more freely" or "urge sinners more earnestly and successfully to believe in Christ as their Saviour." These doctrines served to "fire his zeal and stimulate the growth of piety in his own soul." Because the increase was of God, Manly was encouraged to "plant" and "water" the heavenly seed.[25] Nettleton "preached with great plainness the doctrines of Calvinism." They were seen as the power of God unto salvation and had no tendency "to paralyze" or harden men "into stupidity." On the contrary, "Sinners were pricked in the heart and brought to repentance" and saints were "quickened and comforted and incited to fidelity in their Master's service."[26] One could not concoct a more sympathetic understanding of these infinitely important issues than existed in the theology and practice of Manly and Nettleton. Those who knew Nettleton more thoroughly point out some of the characteristics that were negatively silhouetted in Manly's brief experience. Nettleton indeed took "a great deal of pains to disclaim the idea of being able to do anything." This led him to take measures that some, including Manly, would interpret as an "affectation of singularity." Smith records that when Nettleton "discovered that a people or individual were trusting to human instruments" he would seem "to be actually rude in disappointing them." On one occasion he walked away from a place when over a hundred seemingly were under conviction and one woman exclaimed that he was as bad as Satan for he had come only to torment them and then "leave them to do as they could." The woman was eventually converted.

Nettleton's caution in asking any others to participate with him in preaching arose from a high sense of responsibility in the dispensing and application of truth. He would rather appear rude than create any sense of obligation toward a preacher with whom he was not well acquainted.[27] This caution, however, should not be interpreted as an "air of self-sufficiency."

Sometimes, his sense of the peculiarity of his call led him to actions that could easily be misjudged. Smith heard him say that he could not labor where there was not already "some religious feeling." Sometimes, however, "on urgent solicitation" he would visit a place to test its readiness.

> We remember one such, where he preached, and preached earnestly, for a few times. They heard him, but that was all, and he left them saying, it was of no use to stay, since it was evident that Christians there could not be brought up to their duty.[28]

If that same scene happened in Charleston, and he indeed "said that there was no religion in Charleston" and put the ministers at fault, his judgment was premature and is to be regretted. At the time, in fact, Manly was experiencing revival in First Baptist Church and, in his diary, records some encouraging cases of conviction and conversion. Nettleton's departure led to an inaccurate "disgust" on Manly's part, and sadly precluded what might have been a relationship that could have benefited Southern evangelicals, particularly Baptists, at a time when the "New Measures" were beginning to take root in their evangelistic practice.

This introduction to Nettleton's sermons is written with the prayer that the salutary impact of Nettleton may again be felt in our day. It is certain that Manly's misunderstanding now has vanished; perhaps our acquaintance with these sermons will foster a renewed understanding this side of heaven that will bring its glories nearer to our perceptions and inject its joys into our assemblies.

[1] Bennet Tyler, Nettleton and His Labours (Edinburgh: The Banner of Truth Trust, 1975) p. 29. This volume was first published in 1844 and was published in Scotland in 1854 with an introduction and occasional notes by Andrew Bonar and also, by him, "Remodelled in some parts." The Banner of Truth edition is a reprint of the 1854 printing in Scotland. This will normally be referred to as "Tyler," but special mention will be made of Bonar when it is clear that the text is a part "Remodelled" by him or inserted on the basis of his own knowledge.

² Ibid., p. 41

³ From a Letter of Nettleton quoted in "A brief sketch of an Argument respecting the nature of Scriptural, and the importance and necessity of numerous, rapid, frequent, and extensive Revivals of Religion, " in Biblical Repertory & Theological Review, January, 1834, p. 124

⁴ Tyler, p. 289.

⁵ Charles Finney, The Memoirs of Charles G. Finney: The Complete Restored Text ed. Garth M. Rosell and Richard A. G. Dupuis (Grand Rapids: Zondervan Publishing House, 1989) p. 204. Hereinafter this will be referred to as Memoirs. One also should consult John F. Thornbury, God Sent Revival (Welwyn, Herts, England, and Grand Rapids. Evangelical Press, 1977) pp. 164 - 179.

⁶ This was eventually published in 1828 along with other letters in a volume entitled Letters of the Rev. Dr. Beecher and Rev. Mr Nettleton on The New Measures in Conducting Revivals of Religion. New York, 1828.

⁷ Beecher's Autobiography records that Beecher said, "Finney, I know your plan, and you know that I do; you mean to come into Connecticut and carry a streak of fire to Boston. But if you attempt it, as the Lord liveth, I'll meet you at the State line, and call out all the artillery men, and fight every inch of the way to Boston, and then I'll fight you there." Beecher eventually signed a truce with the party of Finney and invited him to preach at his Boston church in August, 1831.

⁸ Finney, Memoirs, p. 222. Finney's version of the conference and all its connections is recorded on pp. 216 - 231 as well as valuable footnotes by the volume's editors. These footnotes contain references to related source material. Finney continued to defend the profitableness of his measures with an unusual sense of their virtual divinity. "I have always & everywhere used all the measures I used in these revivals, & have often added other measures such as the anxious seat whenever I have deemed it expedient. I have never seen the necessity of reformation in this respect. Were I to live my life over again, I think that with the experience of more than forty years in revival labors I should under the same circumstance use substantially the same measures that I did then. And let me not be understood to take credit to myself No indeed. It was no wisdom of my own that directed me. I was made to feel my ignorance & dependence & led to look to God continually for His guidance. I had no doubt then nor have I ever had that God led me by his Spirit to take the course I did. So clearly did he lead me from day to day that I never did nor could doubt that I was Divinely directed" (p. 227).

⁹ In his famous address Concio ad Clerum, Taylor rejected the Westminster Confession's doctrine of original sin. Sinfulness is not innate; neither guilt nor necessary predisposition toward sin are innately connected with the human heart, according to Taylor. Sin always is a deliberate moral choice as has no pre-existence to the choice. One always has the power of contrary choice. This theology blended perfectly with the revival techniques of Finney. Nettleton and Taylor were close friends all of their lives,

but Nettleton ardently opposed Taylor's "New Haven Theology."
[10] Again, Finney's representation of their ideas was extravagant, but their alterations in Edwards's theology diminished the direct connection between original sin and the sinner's sinning, and made it appear that each individual's sin arose from the decree and over-ruling providence of God.
[11] Interpretations of the New Lebanon conference from distinctly different perspectives may be seen in Keith J. Hardman, Charles Grandison Finney 1792 - 1875 (Grand Rapids: Baker Book House, 1990) pp. 133-149; and, lain Murray, Revival and Revivalism (Edinburgh: The Banner of Truth Trust, 1994) pp. 225 - 252. That the theological tendencies of Finney were not clear at this time probably contributed to the focus of the discussion on method more than doctrine and also explains some of the support he received from settled pastors who believed the Westminster Confession. Hardman's discussion of Beecher's zeal for the "social order" explains both his initial opposition and eventual friendship (148, 149).
[12] Finney, Memoirs, pp. 239, 240.
[13] For an account of his sickness see Thornbury's God Sent Revival, pp. 220 - 225. Thornbury's book gives a sensitive and engaging portrayal of Nettleton's entire life.
[14] Charles Beecher (ed.), Autobiography of Lyman Beecher 2 vols. (New York, 1864) 2: 363-365 cited in lain Murray, Revival and Revivalism, p. 199.
[15] Tyler, p. 245.
[16] Nettleton's simplicity, clarity, and uncompromising exposition of the doctrine receives strength from the fact that a sermon on the doctrine of regeneration was part of his experience in pointing out his danger by setting in motion a pattern of resistance to the divine sovereignty and attempts at self-righteous justification.
[17] Nettleton preached plainly and simply on this issue and did not want to confuse or appear to compromise his emphasis on the inability of the sinner to make a new heart and the incontrovertible necessity of a divine creative power to bring about the new birth. On this issue, however, he was clearly Edwardsean and distinguished between natural faculties and moral faculties. He would agree with Edwards that the fall brought about a destruction of the "moral" image of God but not the "natural" image. For example, another paragraph of the sermon on regeneration states regeneration involves a physical work in that "there is an actual new creation." God's creative power operates so that "a new spiritual taste or discernment, and principle is implanted by a sovereign creative operation, and not simply a new direction given to the old faculties." It is clear, however, that which is created is spiritual and moral relish, not natural faculties. The sermon on "Indecision in Religion" confronts the unbeliever with the full force of his natural capacities to "choose" for God. "It is not for want of power to alter your disposition or make you willing to repent. You have all the faculties that Christians have. The true penitent has no more natural power than the impenitent. The natural power of the Christian before, and

after repentance is precisely the same." God does not condemn the impenitent for being unable, but unwilling, to repent. That which he lacks is not natural faculty, or power, but desire, "inclination, or disposition to obey his commands." Regeneration, therefore, is a sovereign creative operation in that new motives, holy dispositions, relish for godliness, eyes to see and a heart to pursue the excellent beauty and desirability of holiness as seen in the person and work of Christ are generated where they did not exist; that which did exist, in fact, was the opposite of all these new things (Ephesians 2:2, 3).

[18] Samuel Miller, Thoughts on Public Prayer (Harrisonburg, VA: Sprinkle Publications, 1985; originally published 1849) p. 246.

[19] This closing is virtually the same as that from the sermon "Indecision in Religion." Nettleton at times transported sections from one sermon into another. Jonathan Edwards did the same.

[20] Andrew A. Bonar in his "Introduction" to the 1854 Scots edition of Bennet Tyler, Nettleton and His Labours (Edinburgh: The Banner of Truth Trust, 1975 reprint) p. viii. See also p. 295.

[21] Review of Memoir of the Life and Character of the Rev. Asahel Nettleton D. D. by Bennet Tyler which appeared in Biblical Repertory & Theological Review (October, 1844) pp. 595, 596.

[22] Nettleton has been both misunderstood and misrepresented. Misunderstandings, such as the one now under discussion, often came from the peculiarity of his style, his conscientious resistance to any element of dependence on his person, and some idiosyncrasies in personality and behavior. Misrepresentations arose from these same factors combined with a lack of sympathy with Nettleton's conscience and his unhypocritical concern that many souls were being deceived and churches polluted by the new measures. He has been pictured as jealous, furious, threatened, crabby, backward, mentally incompetent, and the "real loser at New Lebanon."
Sometimes historians seem to consider it a threat to the objectivity of their craft to give credence to the impact that sincere biblical convictions and theological commitments have on the attitudes and actions of formative personalities. As the sermons of this volume should show, Nettleton was driven by a clear vision of the gospel and its exclusive power in the conversion of sinners.

[23] R. S. Smith, Recollections of Nettleton and the Great Revival of 1820 (Albany: Published by E. H. Pease & Co., 1848) p. 42.

[24] Bennet Tyler, Nettleton and his Labours remodelled in some parts by Andrew A. Bonar (Edinburgh: The Banner of Truth Trust, 1975 [first published 1854]) p. 324 - 330.

[25] J. P. Boyce, Life and Death the Christian's Portion, (New York: Sheldon & Co., 1869) pp. 68, 69; Samuel Henderson. Christianity Exemplified (Atlanta: Franklin Steam Printing House, 1870), p. 34.

[26] Tyler, pp. 331, 332.

[27] Smith, pp. 28, 29.

[28] Smith, p. 40.

1

Professing Christians, Awake!

And that knowing the time, that now it is high time to awake out of sleep (Romans 13:11).

The text is addressed to Christians. The language is borrowed from natural sleep in which a person is in a great measure insensible to the objects, and to what is passing around him, but life remains in the body. And thus it is when there is much insensibility to divine things among Christians—they sleep; but life remains in the soul. Language similar is often addressed to sinners; but then the image is borrowed from the dead who sleep in the dust. Hence the exhortation: *Awake, thou that sleepest, arise from the dead, and Christ shall give thee light.*

The wise and the foolish virgins both went forth to meet the bridegroom—and while he tarried *they all slumbered and slept.* But between the two mark the difference. The one has oil in his vessel, but the other has none. One has life, but the other is dead. Our text then is addressed to the Christian who was dead, but is alive again.— To the Christian who is asleep and again bears the image of death. *And now it is high time to awake out of sleep.*

It is proposed to inquire—

I. When the Christian may be said to sleep.

II. Offer motives which ought to induce him to awake.

I . When does the Christian sleep?

1. In general he desires his own case, and begins to consult that, when it comes in competition with duty. Religion is the great business of his life. It imposes on him many duties which are painful and crossing to corrupt nature. Thus the fraternal admonition— *Exhort one another daily, lest any be hardened through the deceitfulness of sin. Thou shalt in any wise rebuke thy neighbor, and not suffer sin upon him* is the command of God. To neglect this and similar duties for fear of incurring reproach, is to indulge in spiritual sloth. You may sit down and rest quietly if you will not disturb your fellow sinners around you with a sight of their sin and danger. This requires no effort. And here thousands resign themselves to rest. Individuals or a church may close their eyes on the conduct of an offender and be silent, and this awful indifference to his soul assumes the name of charity, without lifting a finger to *restore such an*

one in the spirit of meekness. The slothful servant will ever consult his own ease by sinful contrivance to shun duty.

2. As one in sleep is insensible of the objects and to what is passing around him; so in a measure is it sometimes with the Christian. Though not wholly lost to a sense of divine things, yet they make but a feeble or slight impression on his soul. In this frame they go to the house of God, and no wonder they soon forget what they have never felt. Once they saw the glory of God in the face of Jesus Christ, but now they walk in darkness.—Once they had a feeling sense of the worth of souls and could weep over perishing sinners around them. *I beheld the transgressors and was grieved*—but now they can endure the sight almost without emotion.

This unhappy state of mind is further evident from their *conversation.* Once they seemed to be dead to this world—they spake often one to another—their conversation was in heaven. But now their attention is all engrossed with the world; they converse with ease and cheerfulness about the trifles of time, but on the great things of eternity have little or nothing to say. Or, peradventure they speak on these high and heavenly themes—it is in a dull and lifeless manner. They seem to glance over the mind like trifles. They appear not to take an immediate interest in the subject—They feel not the impressive weight of eternal realities. When this is the case they talk like a person in sleep. He knows not what he says.

3. Another mark of this unhappy state of mind is a reluctance to secret *prayer,* which very properly, has been styled the breath of the Christian. Has any one continued long without the spirit of prayer, it is a sign that he is asleep. And if not shortly awaked from this breathless state, we shall be compelled to believe that he is dead. How far these, and similar remarks apply to professing Christians present you will understand me, is best known to themselves. One thing is certain. Sure I am it is not my business to cry peace in the ears of any who are asleep.

But I proceed,

II. To offer motives which ought to induce them to awake. And 1st: Consider *"the time."* My brethren, it is gospel time. Gospel light is risen upon us. And those who do not open their eyes on the glory of this light must remain in eternal darkness and despair. *For if our gospel be hid, it is hid to them that are lost: In whom the god of this world hath blinded the minds of them which believe not, lest the light of the glorious gospel of Christ, who is the image of God, should shine unto them.*

The light of heaven is shining upon us. *And* can you sleep?

Behold, now is the accepted time; behold, now is the day of salvation. It is no time to sleep. It is the day that we shall ever witness. The *day of salvation.*—The business of this day will not suffer you to sleep. It calls on you loudly to awake. Think, my brethren, have you nothing to do for yourselves? Have you no sins to repent of—no evil propensities to mortify? Are your evidences of grace bright enough? Do you love God with all your hearts—and are you perfectly conformed to his holy law? In short, are you willing to die as you are? If you have any thing to do for yourselves, it is high time to awake out of sleep. *Prepare to meet thy God, O Israel.*

Have you nothing to do for your brethren? Is no brother or sister wandering from the path of duty?—Go and in a feeling, friendly manner tell him his fault between him and thee alone. Why hesitate? Delay not. Duty calls. God commands, and love to his soul demands that you go without delay. *If he shall hear thee, thou hast gained thy brother.*

Parents! Where are your children? Are they all brought securely within the ark of safety?—Doubtless you pray with them and for them. But this is not all your duty. Have you ever taught them that they are sinners?—that they must be born again—and are you urging them to *remember their Creator now in the days of their youth?* Were you this day called to part with one of your children, could you rest satisfied that you had done your duty? Have you not one word more of instruction, of counsel or warning for your children before you meet them at the bar of God?—If so, then it is high time that parents awake to a sense of their duty—that *you set your houses in order and prepare for death.*

Again—It is high time to awake because others are up and active about us. The men of this world shame us by their conduct. They rise up early, and sit up late. They plan and execute. Labor, fatigue, and hardship are nothing to them if they can but collect a little of this world together before they leave it. They are laying up treasures on earth, which the moth and rust will soon corrupt. And shall you not be as earnest to lay up for yourselves a more enduring substance—a treasure in the heavens? They are laboring for that meat which perisheth, but you are called to labor for that which endureth unto *everlasting life.* Do you not feel reproved by their conduct, to think that *the children of this world are in their generation wiser than the children of light?*

Again—My brethren, you are on the field of battle. And it is high time to awake, for the enemy is up and active about us. *The prince of darkness* with all the several ranks of evil angels is your enemy. The malice of their legions is directed against the Redeemer's kingdom in this world. War is declared with all saints. And the legions of hell have gone up upon the breadth of the earth. He is already in possession of the hearts of all wicked men. They are his servants. The devil is styled the *prince of this world—The ruler of the darkness of this world. This is the spirit that now worketh in the children of disobedience.*—While you sleep these are all sowing tares and destroying about us. Says the captain of your salvation, *He that is not with me is against me, he that gathereth not with me scattereth abroad.*

Observe; it is not a feeble foe you have to contend with. You are called to wrestle, not merely with flesh and blood, but before the battle is won you will have to grapple and contend with *angelic powers*—with *principalities and powers*. Observe, your enemy is crafty. Snares and temptations are laid thick around you, and unless you are wakeful you will certainly be ignorant of his devices. That moment when you let down your watch the enemy began to come in upon you like a flood. While you slept the *Philistines be upon you.* And I would come to blow the trumpet and sound the alarm. *Awake thou that sleepest. Cast* off the works of darkness and put on the armour of light. Think not to find a bed of sloth in the field of battle. *Awake and put on the whole armour of God that ye may be able to stand against the wiles of the devil. For we wrestle not against flesh and blood, but against principalities, against powers, against the rulers of the darkness of this world, against spiritual wickedness in high places. Wherefore, take unto you the whole armour of God, that ye may be able to withstand in the evil day, and having done all, to stand. Stand therefore having your loins girt about with truth, and having on the breast-plate of righteousness; and your feet shod with the preparation of the gospel of peace; above all, taking the shield of faith, wherewith ye may be able to quench the fiery darts of the wicked.* Awake, then; for your enemies are *many, powerful,* and *crafty.*

Another reason why you should awake is that sinners are perishing around you. While you sleep your example will contribute much to their destruction. Yes, while you sleep the world may now be stumbling over you down to destruction. Little does that ungodly professor of religion think what a train of immortal souls may be following him down to hell. It is a fact not to be concealed that one ungodly professor of religion may do more to prevent the conversion of sinners than many infidels. I know it is most unreasonable that mankind should suffer themselves to be thus forever ruined. It can surely be no consolation to the sinner in hell that he was led there by a hypocrite.

Brethren, is heaven,—is hell a fable? If so then let us treat them as such. Or are they eternal realities? Whence then, this silence, this seeming indifference to the souls of men that your fellow sinners should obtain the one and escape the other. Do you verily believe that within a few days you shall be in heaven, singing the song of redeeming love—or in hell with devils and damned spirits forever and ever. Have you ever described your own danger, and fled for refuge from the wrath to come, and do you feel no concern for the souls of men? Or are there no sinners in this place? Have they all become righteous? Do all profess to know the Lord from the least to the greatest? Is there no prayerless family in this place, on whom God hath declared *he will pour out his fury?* No prayerless youth to whom God hath said, *I will cast thee off forever?*

My brethren, if there be one impenitent sinner among us who is in danger of going into that place of eternal torment, *can you sleep?* One sinner in this house! One inhabitant of hell! Solemn thought! One soul present that will be lost forever. Who can it be? Could you bear to hear the name? *Who among us shall dwell with the devouring fire? Who among us shall dwell with everlasting burning?* Have you not reason to believe that many are now living *without hope and without God in the world? Wide is the gate, and broad is the way, that leadeth to destruction, and many there be which go in thereat: Because strait is the gate, and narrow is the way, which leadeth unto life, and few there be that find it.*

Wherever God designs to pour out his Spirit and to call up the attention of sinners to divine things, he will be inquired of by his children to do it for them. This he has taught us in his Word and often in the language of his providence. It is high time for you to awake out of sleep; for others are awake—sinners at a distance are alarmed—and hundreds are now flocking to Christ. And can you rest? Are there not more souls here to be saved or lost forever? Are they not as precious as ever? And is he not a prayer-hearing God? *Hath God forgotten to be gracious? Is his mercy clean gone forever? And will he be favorable no more?* No, my brethren, *the Lord's hand is not shortened that it cannot save; neither his ear heavy that it cannot hear*—Come then, *ye that make mention of the Lord keep not silence, if ye speak not to warn the wicked; the same wicked man shall die in his iniquity; but his blood will I require at thy hand.*

Brethren, how is your zeal for the salvation of souls compared with that of the Son of God? *He beheld the city and wept over it.—O Jerusalem, Jerusalem.*

> "Did Christ o'er sinners weep?
> And shall our tears be dry?"

How is your zeal compared with that of Paul? *I have great heaviness and continual sorrow in my heart for my brethren, my kinsmen according to the flesh.—Many walk, of whom I have told you often, and now tell you even weeping, that they are the enemies of the cross of Christ.* There is a dreadful storm of divine wrath coming upon the world of the ungodly. *It is high time to awake out of sleep, for their damnation slumbereth not.*

Again—Consider how long you have slept and you will see that it is *high time to awake.*—How many months—And of some may we ask, How many years have you slept in God's vineyard? And still you continue on sleeping away the day of salvation. Let me tell you that *your* sleep is awfully dangerous—If not shortly awaked God in anger will say: *Let their eyes be darkened that they may not see.*

Further; Consider what time of day it is with you and you will see it is *high time to awake.* How long has your sun been up? Your best season is already gone. With some, I perceive, the sun has already passed its meridian. Yes, it is now hastening its rapid descent. *Aged fathers,* Your sun is now casting its last beams upon the mountains. *Yet a little while is the light with you. Work while it is day; the night cometh when no man can work.* If then you have any work to do—any word to leave for your brethren, or your children, they are now waiting to hear. Delay not, for while I am speaking night is coming on. *What soever thy hand findeth to do, do it with thy might; for there is no work, nor device, nor knowledge, nor wisdom in the grave, whither thou goest.*

The believer ought to awake and take a view of the glorious prospect that lies just before him. Come then ye mourning pilgrim—you who have long traversed the wilderness asking the way to Zion—You who have long labored and prayed and groaned to be delivered from the bondage of sin, your struggles for eternal life shall have an end. *Look up—and lift up your head, for behold, your redemption draweth nigh. It is high time to awake out of sleep; for now is your salvation nearer than when you believed.* Nearer than it was last year. Nearer than it was the last Sabbath—nearer than ever, on all the wings of time it flies. This night you may wake up amid the song of angels—and a crown of glory, of eternal life, may be placed on your head.

> "Short is the passage, short the space
> Between my home and me;
> There, there behold the radiant place—
> How near the mansions be!"

Awake then and behold the glorious dawn of a bright new day. *Where the sun shall no more go down: neither shall thy moon withdraw itself: for the Lord shall be thine everlasting light, and the days of thy mourning shall be ended.*

Finally, It is high time to awake, for all who do not awake in time, will suddenly awake in hell. There is great danger of being deceived and thus only dreaming of heaven. The Christian can never sleep sound, but is always disturbed. *I sleep,* says the church, *but my heart waketh.* He cannot sleep long. He will soon be affrighted and wake up awfully alarmed. But others sleep sound. They are at *ease in Zion.* They neither weep for their sins, nor *rejoice in hope of the glory of God.* Their hope of heaven is a pleasant dream which cannot be broken. And here they sink down into a deep sleep.

The Christian church is a net which gathers of every kind. Ten virgins professed to be followers of Christ. Of this number, five only were real Christians. *Many are called, but few chosen.* Many will go to the bar of God with hopes no better than the spider's web. Many who now commune together on earth will never meet in heaven. Many who now appear to us to be real Christians, will, no doubt to our surprise, be found on the left hand of Christ.

The sinner having professed religion with a false hope can hardly be driven to give it up. *The hope of the hypocrite is like the giving up of the ghost. What meanest thou, O sleeper!* If ye will not now awake, by the worth of your soul, I entreat you to fling away your hope of heaven. *For there shall be weeping and gnashing of teeth, when ye shall see Abraham, and Isaac, and Jacob, and all the prophets, in the kingdom of God, and you yourselves thrown out. And, behold, there are last which shall be first, and there are first which shall be last.*

Better fling away your hope, and conclude you are lost than to sleep any longer; for then will you awake in earnest to inquire, *What must I do to be saved? Watch therefore; for ye know not when the master of the house cometh; lest coming suddenly he find you sleeping.—At midnight the cry will be made. Behold, the bridegroom cometh.* Then will there be great confusion. For thousands will be deceived. *Let him that thinketh he standeth take heed.*

These things saith he that hath the seven spirits of God, and the seven stars; I know thy works, that thou hast a name that thou livest, and art dead. Be watchful, and strengthen the things which remain, that are ready to die: for I have not found thy works perfect before God. Remember therefore how thou hast received and heard, and hold fast, and <u>repent</u>. If therefore thou shalt not watch, I will come on thee as a thief, and thou shalt not know what hour I will come upon thee.

And <u>now</u> it is time—*it is high time to awake out of sleep,* because many will be *forced* to awake when *suddenly* they shall *lift up their eyes in hell being in torment.*

2

The Contemplation of Death

O that they were wise, that they understood this, that they would consider their latter end! (Deuteronomy 32:29).

Man has had a beginning but will never have an end. Though the body will die and return to dust, yet the soul will exist ages without end. Whenever we are called upon to mark the end to which we are hastening, we are to take a serious and solemn view of death with all its consequences.

Sometimes the peaceful and happy death of the righteous and the glorious rewards of heaven is the *end* to which we are *pointed* by the finger of God. *Mark the perfect man, and behold the upright: for the end of that man is peace.*

Sometimes the unhappy death and everlasting destruction of the finally impenitent is the *end* which we are called upon seriously to consider. Says the Psalmist, *I was envious at the foolish when I saw the prosperity of the wicked—until I went into the sanctuary of God; then understood I their end.—How are they brought into desolation, as in a moment. Whose end is destruction.—Who are nigh unto cursing, whose end is to be burned. If judgment begin at the house of God, what shall the end be of them that obey not the gospel of God? And if the righteous scarcely be saved, where shall the ungodly and the sinner appear?*

Of similar import is the text now under consideration. The Lord had repeatedly warned the rebellious Israelites, but they would not hear. He had announced an awful penalty to his law—a penalty which could not be repealed; and yet they continued to rebel. Notwithstanding the awful end to which they were already exposed by repeated acts of transgression, they continued to make their *end* still more awful. And, surprising to tell, their sensibility diminished as their danger increased, until the Lord himself exclaimed, *"O that they were wise, that they understood this, that they would consider their latter end!"*

Our text more than intimates a strong aversion in sinners to a serious consideration of their own death and its consequences. Mankind can converse with much carefulness about the trifles of time—they are wise to plan and active to pursue the business of this world. But few, very few, seem to be laying their plans for and making their calculations for the world to come. At times however, the thoughts of death and eternity may startle and alarm; while we hear the thunders of God's law or witness our friends in the agonies of death; yet, how soon all is forgotten?

Others, there are, who form some faint resolutions to reform or become Christians before they die; but ere one short day or hour is past all is gone and forgotten. The subject is dismissed—there is time enough yet. Death and eternity are now viewed at a distance. But his friends assemble around the sinner—they take him by the hand—they tell him: You are *dying*.

Now for the first time he begins to feel that he is mortal. *All men think all men mortal but themselves.* But he is too far gone to make preparation. This solemn statement is whispered in his ear as he nears the very threshold of the eternal world. Such is the reluctance of others that they die without uttering a word about their souls. Friends too are no less reluctant. All are concerned—all active—all anxious for the body; but if anxious for his soul, yet nothing is said—nothing is done.

What reluctance—what backwardness to speak of death and its solemn consequences! Whence is it that mankind will not pause and reflect on a subject of such infinite moment? Whatever may be the cause, the fact is obvious. On all other topics, friends and neighbors can meet and converse with ease and interest, but on death, judgment, and eternity have little or nothing to say. The great end for which we came into being must neither be spoken of nor thought of. Here both the wickedness and folly of sinners are exposed. On all other subjects they seem to have some wisdom and a little understanding, but on this they have neither. *O that they were wise, that they understood this, that they would consider their latter end!*

However reluctant the human heart may be seriously to reflect on death and its consequences, it is yet absolutely indispensable. Otherwise no preparation will be made. God once commissioned a Prophet to cry in tears to all the world. The evangelical Prophet was sent with this message: *The voice said, Cry. And he said, What shall I cry? All flesh is grass, and all the goodliness thereof is as the flower of the field: The grass withereth, the flower fadeth: because the Spirit of the Lord bloweth upon it: surely the people is grass. The grass withereth, the flower fadeth: but the Word of the Lord shall stand forever.*

Philip, king of Macedonia, employed a crier to call at the door of his bed-chamber every morning, "Philip, remember that thou art mortal." Were the sinner seriously to reflect on death, judgment, and eternity for one-half hour every morning and evening, he would soon be astonished at his own stupidity and the folly of thousands around him.

It may be useful to the saint as well as the sinner to become familiar with this subject. "If you cannot face the image, how will you endure the reality." *It is better to go to the house of mourning, than to go to the house of feasting: for that is the end of all men, and the living will lay it to his heart.*

The text leads us to contemplate death and its consequences.

1. It separates soul and body. The soul is the man—It is the only thing we have worth an important thought. It dwells in a clay tenement—subject to dissolution. *We dwell in houses of clay, our foundation is in the dust. They are fearfully and wonderfully made.*

> "Our life contains a thousand springs,
>   And dies if one be gone;
> Strange! that a harp of a thousand strings,
>   Would keep in tune so long."

The body must die and return to the dust. *There is no man that hath power over the spirit to retain the spirit; neither hath he power in the day of death: and there is no discharge in that war. The dust returns to the earth as it was;* and the soul can no longer keep possession, *but must return to God who gave it.*

The soul and the body do not part without a struggle. It is a solemn thing to die. Aside from its consequences it is in itself solemn. Hence it is called *the king of terrors*. What it is to endure the pangs of death we cannot tell. Some, in the hour of death, have told us it is more solemn than they had ever before imagined—that they had ever considered it a very solemn thing to die, but now it appeared indescribably more solemn than ever. But after all that the dying have told, they have never in a single instance told us all. No one has ever returned to describe the last struggle and pang of separation.

Death is an untried scene to all the living. Notwithstanding so many have died in our world and so many are daily and hourly dying around us; yet when our turn comes it will be all new. Though we may have seen many in the agonies of death, yet when our time comes we shall then feel as we have never felt before. And so death will always continue to be new to all who shall die. It will be as new to the last who shall die on this earth as it was to Abel, the first who gave up the ghost.—Consider,

2. Death dissolves all earthly relations. We have tender connections—near and dear relatives. But all these connections must be dissolved. No ties of kindred blood, love and affection are regarded by the king of terrors. When he calls the nearest relations must part—the dearest earthly ties are broken.—The husband is a husband no more. The wife is a wife no more. The parent is a parent no more. The child is a child no more. The brother is a brother no more. The sister is a sister no more. The pastor and his people must part.

> The earthly shepherds dwell in dust,
> The aged and the young,
> The watchful eye in darkness closed,
> And mute the instructive tongue.

3. It strips us of all our *possessions*. Those having large possessions of wealth—houses and lands—silver and gold and merchandise. And all who have much goods laid up for many years, and are now laying up treasures on earth must obey the summons of the king of terrors. *Thou fool, this night thy soul shall be required of thee. Riches profit not in the day of wrath.* He is released of his possessions at once. He is now reduced to a coffin and grave. *We brought nothing into this world, and it is certain that we can carry nothing out. As he came into the world, naked shall he return to go as he came, and shall take nothing of his labour, which he may carry away in his hand.*

Death strips all of their titles—dissolves kings and emperors. All must lay themselves in the dust.

> "Princes, this clay must be your bed,
> In spite of all your towers,
> The tall, the wise, the reverend head,
> Must lie as low as ours."

Visit the land of darkness and on whom do you tread? *The mighty man, and the man of war; the Judge and the Prophet, and the prudent, and the ancient, the captain of fifty, and the honorable man, and the counselor, and the cunning artificer, and the eloquent orator. The grave hath enlarged herself and opened her mouth without measure, and the glory of the nations, and their multitude, and their pomp have descended into it. Man that is born of a woman is of few days and full of trouble, etc. Man dieth and wasteth away; yea, man giveth up the ghost and where is he?*

4. It breaks up all our earthly plans. All our worldly schemes are blasted at once. The worldling, the covetous, and the man of pleasure must stop their calculations. Their purposes are broken off. The rich man says: *I will pull down my barns and build greater; and there will I bestow all my fruits and my goods. And I will say to my soul, Soul, thou hast much goods laid up for many years; take thine ease, eat, drink, and be merry.* But death breaks into his plans. God says: *Thou fool, this day thy soul shall be required of thee.*

The gay and the thoughtless youth is flattering himself with the prospect of future scenes of happiness on earth; but suddenly the stroke of death ends all forever. All our schemes and plans for doing good, however wise and pious and benevolent, are now come to an end. *Also their love, and their hatred, and their envy is now perished, neither have they any more a portion forever in anything that is done under the sun. Whatsoever thine hand findeth to do, do it with all thy might: for there is no work, nor device, nor knowledge, nor wisdom in the grave, whither thou goest.*

5. It puts a period to our probation, our day of salvation. This is not our home. The great errand on which we were sent into the world is to prepare for eternity. It is now the season of trial—the most important that we shall ever witness during the long period of our existence. Every act of ours will have some influence on us through interminable ages. To every soul God has assigned a great and important work. All things are now ripening for the day when God shall bring every work to judgment, with every secret revealed. The gates of heaven are now standing wide open to sinners under the gospel. Heaven with all its glories is now brought within his reach.

At this critical moment the world is presenting all its charms. The path to hell is broad, of easy, and rapid descent. *The lusts of the flesh, the lusts of the eyes, and the pride of life,* and all the fascinating pleasures of sin are now exerting their united influence to try this immortal soul, whether it will yield and go to hell, or, whether it will *resist, deny itself,* and take up the cross, despising the shame. Every hour and every moment is big with consequences. Characters are rapidly forming. The season of trial is short. It is never to be enjoyed but once. Eternity is written on the wings of every moment. Every sinner is now on trial *once for all.* He is now invited by all the charms of a bleeding Saviour, urged by all the horrors of the second death to enter the ark of safety. He is now called upon to *strive and agonize* to enter heaven. But death closes the scene forever. *At midnight the cry is made, Behold, the bridegroom cometh, go ye out to meet him.* Then those that are ready enter heaven and *the door is shut.*

To the impenitent, death closes the door of heaven. It closes it forever. The voice of the Saviour and the sound of the gospel will be heard no more. Ministers will preach and pray no more. No more will they *warn every man night and day with tears.* The sinner will never again be disturbed by the sound of the gospel. No Sabbath will ever dawn upon his guilty head. The doors of the sanctuary will never again be opened and a voice from the mercy seat inviting him to enter will be heard no more.

> "The sacred temple's sounding roof;
> The voice of mercy and reproof,
> Regarded never,"

will lie heard no more forever.

6. *Death seals up our account to the judgment. It is appointed unto all men once to die, and after this the judgment.* At that solemn hour all the duties of religion neglected, all the sins which have been committed, and unpardoned, will remain unpardoned. At death our work for eternity is ended. The account is gone in—it is sealed up— it cannot be altered. At death every thing begins to put on eternity and to wear the aspect of immutability. Now a voice from heaven hath pronounced: *He that is unjust, let him be unjust still: and he which is filthy, let him be filthy still: and he that is righteous, let him be righteous still: and he that is holy, let him be holy still.*

Thus I have attempted to lead your thoughts to the consideration of a few particulars connected with the closing scene of human life. Death separates soul and body. It dissolves all earthly relations. Strips us of all our possessions. Breaks up all our earthly plans. Puts a period to our probation. Seals up our account to the judgment.

I have been preparing the way to address a few words to these bereaved mourners. To the parents, the partner, the brothers and sisters of the deceased, my friends, you have been called to witness the solemn scene which I have but faintly described. E_____ S_____ is no more. But a few days since you saw her sprightly and active— blooming with rosy health. But the fairest specimen of the human form is like the fading flower. *Man that is born of a woman is of few days, and full of trouble. He cometh forth like a flower, and is cut down: he fleeth also as a shadow, and continueth not.*

You followed—you saw her enter the dark valley—and there her spirit took its flight to the unknown world. Her eyes are now closed in the wakeless sleep of death—Till the heavens be no more she shall not awake nor be raised out of her sleep. Death hath dissolved your relation forever. By weeping you cannot bring her back again. You mu*st go to her, but she shall not come to you.*

When our friends die, our duty to them is ended; it remains for the *living to lay it to his heart.* Fail not to bring this warning home to your houses and your hearts. Now the streams of earthly comforts begin to fail, *set your affections on things above, not on things on the earth.*—And *when Christ, who is our life, shall appear, then shall ye also appear with him in glory.*

My fellow mortals—it is a solemn thing to die. When I look around on this assembly, I see none but must die. Though death now appears to be solemn, yet bye and bye it will appear more solemn than ever. These mortal bodies on which you most fondly dote will soon fade and die. Your friends will assemble around you, and take you by the hand and tell you: *You are dying.* O how will you then feel?

All earthly relations in this house will soon be dissolved. Husbands and wives—parents and children—brothers and sisters must all bow to the king of terrors. As the nations which have gone before us are all sleeping in the dust and the living walk over them; so shortly our bodies will all lie in the grave and the living will walk over us. This solemn sound—E_____ S_____ is dead! strikes on the ear of many a gay and thoughtless youth in this assembly. So will it shortly be said of each one of us. The living will call us all by name one after another. He is dead—She is dead—and we shall all be forgotten among the living. And *the places which now know us will know us no more forever.*

There is something solemn in the close of a day—of a week—of a month—of a year.—The present is the last Sabbath and the last day of the year 1837. We now stand, as it were, on an eminence, between the grand division of time. Here, let us pause and take a retrospective glance at the year that is gone. Let us each one ask himself, What report has it born to heaven? According to the course of events thousands and millions of our fellow travelers have gone to their long home. Many of them entered on the year that is past with blooming health, and the brightest earthly prospects—and where are they now? Some with whom we took sweet counsel and walked to the house of God in company—and where are they now?

"The mighty flood, that rolls along.
  Its torrents to the main,
The waters lost can ne'er recall,
  From that abyss again.

The days, the years, the ages dark,
  Descending down to night,
Can never, never be redeemed,
  Back to the gates of light.

Where are our fathers? Whither gone
  The mighty dead of old?
The patriarchs, prophets, princes, kings,
  In sacred books enrolled?

Gone to the resting place of man,
  His long, his silent home;
Where ages past have gone before,
  Where future ages come."

  Had you been among that number where would your soul have been? Let me ask: Have you repented of your sins and made your peace with God?
  One year more is gone out of your day of salvation—One year more you have enjoyed the privileges of the gospel. One year more God has been waiting to be gracious. The sins of one year more you have to answer for at the bar of God. One year less to live—One year nearer to the grave, and to the judgment seat of Christ, and where are you now? One year more you have stood as a barren fig tree in God's vineyard. The voice of mercy: "Spare it a little longer" has prevailed one year more. Her voice is waning feebler and feebler, while the voice of justice is waxing louder and louder, *Cut it down, why cumbereth it the ground.*

    Today attend his gracious voice,
      This is the summons that he sends:
    "Awake, for on this transient hour,
      Thy long eternity depends."

3

Indecision in Religion

How long halt ye between two opinions? (I Kings 18:21).

These are the words of the prophet Elijah. They were addressed to a large concourse of people assembled together on Mount Carmel. Displeased with the character and worship of the true God, they had generally departed from him. But to quiet conscience, they set up and worshipped false gods. Conscience, however, is not so easily pacified. At times it admonishes that all is not well. Whither art thou going and what will be the end of thy course? It led them to hesitate and halt between two opinions. The contest was now to be decided. At the direction of the prophet, the people were assembled. *And Elijah came unto all the people and said, How long halt ye between two opinions? If the Lord be God, follow him: but if Baal, follow him. And the people answered him not a word.*

This sermon is addressed to all the impenitent. No sinner in this place intends to die without an interest in Christ. And yet many do not like to begin a life of religion now. Many hesitate—they halt between two opinions, whether to begin a life of religion now, or to defer the subject a little longer.

Our text calls upon all such to come to a decided choice, to go one way or the other without delay. *If the Lord be God, follow him, if Baal, then follow him.* In the name of God, I come now to treat with you on this subject. *How long halt ye?*

Then let us inquire,

I. Why have you hitherto neglected to come to a decided choice?

II. How long do you purpose to halt?

I. Why have you hitherto neglected to come to a decided choice?

1. It is not for want of power to alter your disposition or make you willing to repent. You have all the faculties that Christians have. The true penitent has no more natural power than the impenitent. The natural power of the Christian before, and after repentance is precisely the same.

It is a clear point. God does not condemn sinners for being unable, but for being unwilling to repent. Let us appeal to facts on this subject. There are some sinners now in the prison of hell. Were they able to repent? Able or not able, the Lord punishes and will punish them to all eternity for not doing it. Is it for the want of power, or for the want of will that he punishes sinners? We had rather say it is for the want of will, inclination, or disposition to obey his commands.

It was not for the want of power that they did not repent. It is not for want of power that you have not yet repented. For you have all the power that you ever will have. You have all that is necessary—and if you had ten thousand times more than what you now have, it would not help the matter, nor make you willing to obey God. An increase of power would not help. Nor—

2. Is it because God requires any thing unreasonable. To repent, believe and obey God is most reasonable. What can be more reasonable than that you should be required to love God? If you were required to love a deformed character, that would be hard. But it is not so. You are required to love a perfect character. There is not a single spot or stain in all God's character. This is the character which you are required to love with all your hearts.

Again, God requires you to repent of sin. What can be more reasonable than this? Is it hard that you should be required to feel sorrow for sin? for that which is odious in itself? If you were required to feel sorrow for some good conduct of yours, that would be hard. But it is not so. You are required only to feel sorrow that you have done wrong.

So then, Why do you not love God? Why do you not feel sorrow for sin? Why do you not love to pray and praise and practice all the duties of religion? Why do you not come out from the world and be separate? Why not come forward and espouse the cause of Christ?

Why have you not done it already? Not because God requires any thing hard or unreasonable. It is more easy and more pleasant to walk in the path of duty, than in the path of sin. It is far more pleasant and delightful to obey the commands of God than to disobey them. Why then have you not done it? Surely not because God requires any thing unreasonable. Nor—

3. Is it because you have not been instructed in your duty. I trust no one can plead ignorance on this subject. You cannot say that you did not know that there was a heaven and a hell—that you did not know it was your duty to repent and become Christians—that you did not know that God required you to love him and to pray to him.

You cannot say that you have not been warned to flee from the wrath to come—that you have not been called upon over again and again to begin a life of religion. You cannot say that the Spirit of God has not been striving with you—that you have never been warned of the awful danger of resisting the strivings of his Spirit.

You cannot say that you have not been warned of the uncertainty of life. You cannot say that you did not know that you were here on trial for eternity—that you must die and go to the judgment seat of Christ—that unless you repent and believe you must lie down in hell to all eternity. You cannot plead ignorance—you have heard the gospel. Why then have you not complied with the terms of salvation? Why then have you not come to a decided choice? Surely it cannot be because you have not been warned. Where is the enemy? Nor—

4. Is it because you have not had time. For what was time given you but to prepare for eternity? Life and death have for a long time been set before you. Sabbath after sabbath and year after year you have been called upon to make your choice. You have found time to sin; but why is it that you have found no time to repent and pray and become Christians? Suppose you had died yesterday, or the last year, you could not have said that you had not had time to prepare for death. The reason then why you have not yet come to a decided choice is not because you have not had time. What can it be? Where is the enemy? Nor—

5. Is it because the subject is not important. The importance of the subject of religion is acknowledged by all. You may feel as though you had some important worldly business to transact. But after all it amounts to nothing. All is vanity. *The fashion of this world passeth away.* After all their labor and sorrow, high and low, rich and poor, meet together and lie down in the grave at last. If you have not been *laying up treasure in heaven,* you have been laboring in vain. Compared with the subject of religion, all other subjects dwindle into nothing.—The world itself will shortly have an end. *The end of all things is at hand. The earth also and the works that are therein shall be burned up.*

But the soul is immortal. Of all that you possess, that alone will survive the ruins of time. *What shall it profit a man, if he shall gain the whole world, and lose his own soul?* Eternal life and eternal death are before you, and will you say that the subject is not important? If the sinner after suffering in hell could then be delivered, the subject would not be so important. Were you condemned to burn in the flames for only a thousand years, how would you feel? What horror would seize you? Would not your case be awful? Should you not be alarmed?

But this is nothing. If the sinner after suffering in hell thousands and thousands of years could then hear the sound of pardon, it would not be so alarming.—We would not be so anxious for him—we would not press him so hard to attend to the subject—we would let him alone. He might then go on. But it is not so; when the soul is once gone, it is gone forever. There is no coming back to enjoy a state of probation. He must suffer while God endures. The reason then why you have not come to a decided choice is not because the subject is not important. Nor,

6. Is it because salvation is not freely offered. Salvation is freely offered. *Ho every one that thirsteth, come ye to the waters; and he that hath no money, come ye, buy and eat; buy wine and milk without money and without price. The Spirit and the bride say, Come. And let him that heareth say, Come. And let him that is athirst, come. And whosoever will, let him take of the water of life freely. Come unto me, all ye that labor and are heavy laden, and I will give thee rest. All things are now ready.* And you are invited, entreated, nay, commanded to accept. This always has been the case; salvation always has been freely offered to you.

The reason then why you have not yet come to a decided choice is not because salvation has not been freely offered. It is now freely offered, it has always been—and depend upon it, will never be more freely offered. Nor—

7. Is it because you intend to die without religion. Though you may labor to silence your fears and to soothe your consciences, yet you cannot always succeed. Though you cast off fear and restrain prayer, yet at times you cannot but reflect that a day of reckoning is coming. At times you cannot but reflect on the shortness of human life—that its pleasures, at longest, are quickly over and gone forever. *Even in laughter the heart is sad, etc.* The things of time are fast fading, and will soon forever retire from our sight.

You know that you must die and go to judgment—Yes, these blooming bodies on which you fondly dote, must fade and die. I well know that you intend to die the death of the righteous. So did wicked Balaam—So did all who are now in hell. Could you now be admitted to those unhappy regions, not one could be found who had made his calculations to come into that place of torment. And you are now treading in their steps.

We know that you do not intend to die without religion. For, were you assured that within a few days you must lie down in eternal sorrows; in the horrors of despair, you would now break out into the cries and shrieks of the damned. Your hearts would pine away in mournful complaint, *Who can dwell with the devouring fire? Who can dwell with everlasting burnings?* It is evident then that the reason you have not come to a decided choice is not because you intend to die without religion. What then can be the difficulty? You

have all the power that you will ever have.—God's requirements are most reasonable.—The terms of salvation will never be altered.—You have had enough time.—The subject is of overwhelming importance.—Salvation is freely offered—it will never be more freely offered. What can be the difficulty? I will now tell you. Say as Esther of Haman, the adversary and enemy is this wicked heart. *You do not like the duties of religion.* These hearts are so wicked that you *will not come to Christ.* This is the true reason.
 1. The reason why we call on you to repent and believe is not because you cannot, but because you will not.
 2. The reason why God will punish you for not obeying is not because you cannot, but because you will not.
 3. The reason why the Almighty power of God is necessary to draw you is not because you cannot, but because you *will not come to Christ.*

The whole difficulty is to be explained by correcting the sinner's views of his own depravity. On the doctrines of grace all the difficulties meet in the same point—*wrong views of human depravity.* Only admit that the sinner never has and never will do what he can, and you will see why we *call*—why *God commands*—why he *will punish—and why his power is necessary to subdue the human heart.*

Man's heart is so wicked that it needs almighty power to make him do what he can—Not what he *cannot.* Many other methods of explaining the difficulty have been attempted, but all have failed—they have never been able to bring the monster to light. Indeed nothing else can hinder your loving God—Nothing else can hinder your sorrow for sin—Your praying and obeying all the commands of God. This is the reason which conscience assigns. This is the reason which God will assign when you stand at his bar.

We have seen the reason why you have hitherto neglected to come to a decided choice. Let us inquire,
 II. How long do you propose to halt? *How long halt ye?* My hearers, this is a question of infinite importance. I come now to treat with you on this subject. Here I would inquire, How long have you put off this subject? How many years have you *lived without God in the world?* How many warnings have you neglected? How long has the Spirit of God been striving with you? How many years have gone out of your own probation? So long God has been waiting to be gracious. What? and you have not yet repented?—Not yet begun to live a life of religion? Then so many years have gone out of your day of probation and nothing is done. So much of the precious day of

salvation you have spent worse than in vain—All this while you have only been hardening your hearts in vain.

Once more we beseech you to make a solemn pause. All warnings hitherto have proved ineffectual. Sometimes, like Felix, you have begun to startle and look about you while the awful realities of eternity are sounding in your ears. For a moment you have been brought upon the point of deciding, but you go away and all is forgotten. *Go thy way for this time, when I have a convenient season, I will call for thee.* The business has ended only in a vain and empty resolution; and the whole serves only to harden.

No decided choice is yet made. Now how long do you purpose to conduct in this manner? We entreat you, my hearers, to decide the business to day. When will you take up the subject of religion in earnest? *How long halt ye?* Our text demands the time. I pause that you may fix the time now.—To help your decision I will suggest the thought that God sees you—Another, that God's Spirit will not always strive—Another, that death is certain and you have no security of life for a single moment.

My hearers, if there is nothing in religion, then renounce it—if the Bible is a farce, then fling it away. But if it be true, as we all profess, why hesitate to obey its precepts now? Being true—*it is tremendously true—the world will be in flames.* How long halt ye?

Ye parents, who never worship God in your families: Our text speaks to you. Your consciences have often been alarmed. At times you have been almost persuaded to adopt the resolution: *As for me and my house, we will serve the Lord.* You have been upon the point of assembling your families and of carrying their wants to the throne of grace and of breaking through all difficulties at once. But hitherto your resolution has failed. Do you not see that you are likely to die as you are? Can you not look forward a little and see that you are going to the judgment seat without once having prayed to God in your families? Do you intend to die as you are? If not, will you decide the point? Go one way or the other. *If the Lord be God, then serve him. How long halt ye?*

Our subject speaks to you who are in the morning of life. The present is a season peculiarly interesting. Many of your companions are alarmed and anxious for their souls. A number we trust, have already come to a decided choice. They no longer halt between two opinions. *They have chosen the good part which shall not be taken away.* They are now ready to *leave all.* No longer do they stand halting between two opinions, whether to pursue the vanities of the world, or to engage in all the duties of religion. They are now about to bid you a long and eternal farewell. At such a season, many anxious thoughts arise in your mind. While you see one and another of your companions leaving you, you cannot but reflect, that you too have a soul to be saved or lost.

Many seem now to be halting between two opinions. On the one hand you are unwilling to leave your sinful pleasures and companions. You are afraid of incurring the displeasure of God's enemies. You are ashamed to have it thought that you have any concern for your soul. You are ashamed to come out from the world, and openly espouse the cause of Christ. You are waiting for each other—You are ashamed of Christ, the Saviour of sinners—Nay, you are even ashamed of the God that made you. On the other, you know that the friendship of the world is enmity with God—that the companion of fools shall be destroyed. You know that the season of your life will soon be over and gone forever—that you must die and go to judgment. You know that the *Spirit of God will not always strive with men*—that your day of grace is limited—that soon you will have passed the bounds of divine mercy. At times these thoughts alarm you. Is it not so, my young friends? Perhaps you are now upon the point of deciding. And so have you been before. Your situation is no better, but is this day worse than ever. How long will you trifle with your soul? How long will you dally with eternal realities? This indecision is what renders your situation so alarming. This is the high road to perdition—it is the path which all the wicked have trod who have gone down to hell before you. They went halting between two opinions and flattering themselves that they should certainly escape the torments of hell. And you are now heading in their steps.

My young friends, God will not be mocked. The business of religion above all others, requires decision. God requires the whole heart. He will have that, or he will have nothing. You are required to break off all your sins—to come out from the world and be separate. You are required to leave all—to take up every cross and to follow Christ *now*. If you halt at this, it will be of no use for you to think on the subject. You are required to endure shame and reproach for his sake. If you halt at this, Christ will have nothing to do with you. If you are ashamed of him, he will be ashamed of you.

You may think to obtain the favor of Christ by giving him a part of your services—by compromising with God. This is sometimes the case with those who feel some concern for their souls. Being ashamed of Christ, they have resolved to be religious in secret, and openly to serve the world. But you will not succeed in this attempt. *No man can serve two masters.* You may in this way, obtain a false hope; but, you will not secure the favor of God. God will abhor all that you do. If you are not willing to engage in all the duties of religion and give yourselves wholly to God, you may stop where you are. The path to heaven is too strait. The righteous who take to themselves the whole armor of God, will scarcely be saved.

Do you fear the reproach of your companions? Are you so weak, and so timid? Think: what is the breath of an enemy of God, to the blast of the soul by the breath of the Almighty? If you fear the frown of a fellow worm, how will you stand in judgment with an angry God? Be entreated to stand halting no longer. Go one way or the other, with all your hearts. Life and death are now set before you, and God is witness to the choice you make.

In view of all that God and religion require, *How long halt ye?* In view of all the scorn and contempt of wicked men, *How long halt ye?*

Finally: If the joys of heaven will not allure—if a bleeding Saviour has no charms for you—if the thunder of his vengeance does not strike terror through your guilty souls; then halt no longer—go on— *Rejoice, O young man in thy youth; and let thy heart cheer thee in the days of thy youth.* Cast off fear and restrain prayer—Trample under foot the Son of God—Resist the strivings of the Holy Spirit—Sport with eternal vengeance and defy the thunders of the Almighty.—But remember, that your fair morning will soon be turned into darkness. When your course is run, your bodies will fall into the grave, and your souls into the hands of the living God.

4

The Death of the Righteous

Let me die the death of the righteous, and let my latter end be like his (Numbers 23:10).

Few men live and die without some seasons of remorse and anxiety. The wicked are constrained to bear testimony in favor of religion. Conscience though it cannot govern, does not cease to admonish. "Whither art thou going? What will be the end?" is her silent, but searching expostulation with many a deluded sinner as he passes down to the gate of death. He loves the ways of sin better than the wages of it, and though he lives, the sinner earnestly desires to die as the saint. As the veil of futurity is drawn aside and he is half convinced that all beyond is reality and fears, he trembles, he exclaims, "Let me die the death of the righteous." The unhallowed tongue of Balaam uttered this memorable sentence. It stands as a testimony of an enemy to that religion which he hates, and for this very reason addresses us with peculiar weight.

Consider,
I. Who the righteous are.
II. Why it is desirable to die as they do.

These are but two distinct classes of men in the Bible. It delineates various shades of character, but it acknowledges but two essentially and radically different—the righteous and the wicked. A man is denominated righteous in the sermon on two accounts:

1. Because he is personally righteous.
2. Because he has an interest in the righteousness of Christ.

1. Personal righteousness and an interest in the righteousness of Christ must be united in the same person. In a qualified sense, that one is personally holy.

2. Interested in the righteousness of Christ. The sinner has no justifying righteousness. Once he sins, he is lost. What if he has a new heart, repents, and loves God, yet this cannot answer for past sins. His own righteousness is still defective. He must have a complete righteousness. Who will dare venture into the presence of God in such a righteousness? Blessed be God, we are not abandoned to this deplorable resort. There is one who *God hath set forth to be a propitiation for our sins*.

II. Why it is desirable to die as he dies.

We are in a world where all men must die. *It is appointed unto men once to die.* Old and young, rich and poor, honorable and despised, the righteous and the wicked, all must die. With some the day of life is protracted to a good old age—they come to their graves like a shuck of corn in its season, fully ripened. With others, the sun sets at noon, and when they promise themselves years, they may not have days. There is no discharge in this war.

But how different is the manner in which our fellow mortals leave this world. Sometimes we enter the chamber of a dying sinner. We see one who has no hope. The day of mercy is closing. The cloud is dark and impenetrable. We witness the last struggle of departing strength, and we involuntarily exclaim with David, *Gather not my life with sinners, nor my soul with wicked men.*

Sometimes we enter the chamber of the dying saint. We feel it a privilege and pleasant thing to be there. The day of grace is passing away, *but the day of glory begins to dawn.* Every cloud is dispelled. We see the body die, but the happy spirit ascends to endless life and glory. We involuntarily exclaim, *Let me die the death of the righteous.*

The righteous die in *peace.* They have made their peace with God. And though they have often on the bed of death clearer views of his amiable and awful perfections than at any other season, yet they have also the sweet consciousness of his favor. It is a view of God that distresses and distracts the mind of a dying sinner; but it is a view of God that calms and tranquilizes the mind of a dying saint. The dying saint has no controversy with his Maker. That controversy has come to an end. He has laid down his weapons of rebelling, and found peace with God through Jesus Christ. He has tasted and seen that the Lord is gracious and tastes it still. Having made his peace with God, he is at peace with himself, and *who is he that condemneth?* Having made his peace with God and his own soul, he is at peace with death. He meets it without terror. The dread destroyer is robbed of its sting. *The sting of death is sin,* and his sin is all washed away. He passes through the dark valley in calm and placid serenity or in holy and rapturous triumph. He faces the last enemy without amazement. His end is peace.

The death of the righteous is *a death of hope. The wicked is driven away in his wickedness, but the righteous hath hope in his death.* The value of a Christian's hope is that it stands the test of the trying hour. When everything else yields, when every earthly tie is parted, when flesh and heart fail, hope strengthens and brightens and ends only in anticipated joys. The objects of the good man's hope when

The Second Great Awakening

he looks into the grave are great and glorious. It is the resurrection of this corruptible body. Though he molder in the dust, his flesh shall rest in hope. It is the lucid and unveiled exhibition of a divine glory. He rejoices in hope of the glory of God. It is a peaceful conformity to the divine image. For he knows he shall be like him—The full possession of the heavenly inheritance, a building of God, an house not made with hands, eternal in the heavens. These he desires; these he expects. This animating hope sustains him and thus he walks through the valley of the shadow of death, he fears no evil, for God is with him, his rod and his staff, they comfort him. Death loses all its hideous horrors, the grave yields its boasted glory.

The death of the righteous is the *consummation of their state here below.* It is the end of all that has been so ensnaring, so debasing in sin. *They rest from their labors. And I heard a voice from heaven saying, write, Blessed are the dead which die in the Lord from henceforth: Yea, saith the Spirit, that they may rest from their labors; and their works do follow them.* The dying saint may look around on the world for the last time, and say with the Apostle, *I have fought a good fight, I have finished my course, I have kept the faith: Henceforth there is laid up for me a crown of righteousness, which the Lord, the righteous judge, shall give me at that day.* Yes, and his work is done. The last tear is fallen from his cheek, the last pang of suffering has rent his own bosom, the last hour of perplexity and fatigue is on the wing, the last conflict is over, and he is now beyond the reach of toils and trials, of temptation and sin. The last enemy is destroyed and with the dread encounter, his warfare is finished.

At death the righteous enter upon their final reward. At the point where time ends, eternity begins. And what evil can come nigh to him for whom Jesus died? Does the law which he has broken denounce vengeance against him? Behold, that law magnified and made honorable in the death of his Redeemer. Is he afraid that the cry of his sins may rise to heaven and reach the ears of eternal justice? In its stead stands the voice of that blood which speaks better things than the blood of Abel. Does the enemy of souls accuse him at the judgment seat? He is put to silence by his great Advocate and Intercessor at the right hand of the Father. Is he afraid that the arrows of divine wrath which smite the guilty will be aimed at him? Before they can touch, they must again pass the body of that Almighty Redeemer, who is the judge of the quick and the dead. Does he shudder and start back from the dominions of the dead, is a scene of awe presented when the curtain between time and eternity is drawn aside? Jesus his Saviour has the keys of death and the grave. The abodes of the dead are a part of his kingdom and he lay in the grave and hallowed it for the repose of the righteous. And before he ascended on high he said to his disciples, *I go to my Father and your Father, to my God and your God.* Enlightened by these discoveries what a majesty there is in the death of a Christian! He partakes of the spirit of that world to which he is advancing; he meets death with a face that looks to the heavens—There he enters—The termination of sin and sorrow is come. It is the commencement of perfect holiness and unmingled bliss.

He is blessed with the vision and fruition of God. He beholds his Saviour face to face. As one of the great assembly of the sons of God, when all the family of heaven are gathered together, not one shall be missed who is worthy of his affection and esteem. Friendship and union will be improved by heavenly purity and heavenly love. He will glorify and enjoy God without imperfection and without weariness. His happiness will be the happiness of perfect moral purity, of perfect holiness, the happiness of angels and Archangels, the happiness of God.

He shall hunger no more, neither thirst any more; neither shall the sun light on him, nor any heat. For the Lamb which is in the midst of the throne shall feed him and shall lead him into living fountains of water, and God shall wipe away all tears from his eyes. Thus to live is Christ—thus to die is gain. *Blessed are the dead who die in the Lord.* Who would not die the death of the righteous?

Practical Remarks.

1. This subject may afford consolation to those who have been bereaved of pious friends—Some we trust of this character—Some have been made mourners by the death of children of an early age, some by the death of parents who taught you the things of God, and heaven, and allured you by their examples to walk in their steps— Some by the death of a husband—a wife. Oh, how is the severity of your trial alleviated by the thought that these beloved friends died the death of the righteous?—if they furnished evidence by their lives and their deaths that they were really holy and interested in the righteousness of Christ. How easily can you give them up? Especially if you can hope that you are walking in their steps. Love it is true, is their pillow of death. In this world you will see them no more. But in a little while that which you have seen sown in dishonor shall be raised in glory, that which was sown in weakness shall be raised in power, that corruption shall put on incorruption, and that mortal shall put on immortality. The prison of the grave cannot long retain

them. *As Jesus died and rose again, even so them also which sleep in Jesus shall God bring with him.* His omniscient eye will watch over every particle of their dust, till that immortal morning when he will fashion their vile bodies like unto his own glorious body. You have lost much and you have a right to mourn; but brethren, think of those who sorrow without hope, who cannot see one ray of hope that their loved ones are not in the world of woe.

Parents, if you would have this consolation warn and instruct your children—husbands, wives, neighbors, etc. that you may meet in heaven. Urge all to frequent and serious self-examination. Be impartial. Are you prepared?

Finally the subject calls on all to live the life of the righteous. Are you ready to say, "Let me die the death of the righteous." The life of the righteous always precedes the death of the righteous.

By all the solemnities of a dying hour—by all the peace and hope and triumph of the dying saint—and all the gloom and horror and despair of the dying sinner, we urge you to begin the life of the righteous. You know you must die. And how will you feel to find yourself sinking into the grave an enemy to God? How will you feel when you see your day of grace closing upon you, when you see the setting sun of your trial for eternity going down in spite of all your entreaties? You must die. Oh thus to enter the invisible world—thus pass the gates of eternity! "Let me die the death of the righteous."

5

The Destruction of Hardened Sinners

He, that being often reproved hardeneth his neck, shall suddenly be destroyed, and that without remedy (Proverbs 29:1).

A stronger indication of a mind unreconciled to God can hardly be conceived than an unwillingness to receive reproof. The humble Christian is always thankful for admonition administered in the spirit of meekness, and prompted by a sincere desire for the welfare of the offender; while the haughty sinner, whose *way is always right in his own eyes,* indignantly rejects it.

Hence, the reasonable precaution of our Saviour addressed to his disciples: *Give not that which is holy unto dogs, neither cast ye your pearls before swine, lest they trample them under their feet, and turn again and rend you.* It is not the best policy to reprove offenders of every description, and on all occasions. Prudence and judgment ought ever to be exercised in the discharge of this duty. Otherwise, the well-meant endeavors of the man who undertakes the unwelcome task of a sensor, will meet with a sad recompense.

Few, when faithfully reminded of their offenses, will evince the placid temper of the pious David, who (doubtless in allusion to the plain, and pointed reproof administered to him by the prophet Nathan) exclaimed, *Let the righteous smite me, it shall be a kindness: and let him reprove me, it shall be an excellent oil.* Most persons, on the contrary, when closely pressed as he was, and to whose consciences their crimes are set home with a clearness which cannot be mistaken *"Thou art the man,"* will give free vent to their rage; and will not scruple to accost their reprover in the libertine language ascribed to the wicked by the Psalmist, *With our tongues will we prevail; our lips are our own; who is Lord over us?*

The spirit which is discerned in the disdainful carriage of individuals of this sort when reminded of their faults, is a striking comment on the just maxims of the wise man. *He that reproveth a scorner getteth to himself shame: and he that rebuketh a wicked man getteth himself a blot. Reprove not a scorner, lest he hate thee: rebuke a wise man, and he will love thee.* Such is the difference which marks the demeanor of the righteous and the wicked when reminded of their faults.

From the passage which has been selected, it is proposed to

contemplate:
I. The care which God has taken for the reproof of offenders. *It is often administered.*
II. The effect of this reproof. *He hardeneth his neck.*
III. The consequences of an incorrigible disposition. *Sudden and remediless destruction.*

I. The care which God has taken for the reproof of offenders. God has made it the duty of his people to deal faithfully with each other. *Exhort one another daily, lest any be hardened through the deceitfulness of sin.* And again, *Thou shalt not hate thy brother in thine heart (Leviticus 19:17).* The expression is peculiarly forcible. The Almighty considers a neglect of brotherly reproof as on a par with the open indulgence of the feelings of anger and resentment. *Thou shalt not hate thy brother in thy heart; thou shalt in any wise rebuke thy neighbour and not suffer sin upon him.* And says our Saviour, *If thy brother shall trespass against thee, go and tell him his fault between thee and him alone.* Brethren, says James, *if any do err from the truth, and one convert him; Let him know, that he which converteth the sinner from the error of his way shall save a soul from death, and shall hide a multitude of sins.*

Further, God has provided for the reproof of offenders by making it a duty of parents towards their children. To attend to the spiritual concerns of children, and to restrain their wickedness is the most important part of a parent's duty. *We have had fathers of our flesh,* says the Apostle, *who have corrected us, and we gave them reverence*—and most persons can adopt his language in relation to their own experience. Yes; and what a load of guilt will rest upon the head of that ungodly child who has despised all the warnings, the entreaties, and tears, and prayers of a pious father, or an affectionate mother, who *travailed in birth again that Christ might be formed in their souls, the hope of glory,* when their own bodies slumber in the dust.

God also reproves sinners by his *providences.* He sends his judgments *abroad in the earth that the inhabitants may learn righteousness.* By the pains we feel, we are admonished that we are sinners; *and warned to flee from the wrath to come.*

By his *Word. All Scripture is given by inspiration of God and is profitable for doctrine,* and for *reproof.* All the invitations, commands, and threatenings, and warnings in the Bible are so many admonitions to sinners.

By his *ministers. Son of man, I have made thee a watchman to the house of Israel: therefore hear the word at my mouth, and give them warning from me. Show thy people their transgression, and the house of Israel their sin.* Hear the injunction of Paul on Timothy: *I charge thee before God, and the Lord Jesus Christ, who shall judge the quick and the dead at his appearing and kingdom; Preach the word; be instant in season, out of season; reprove, rebuke, exhort with all longsuffering and doctrine. For the time will come* (it seems as if, in uttering this prediction the Apostle had an eye upon sinners of our own day); *For the time will come when they will not endure sound doctrine; but after their own lusts shall they heap to themselves teachers, having itching ears.*

But woe to those ministers who do not feel the weight of this charge—and woe to those wincing hearers, who *(having itching ears that will not endure sound doctrine, heap to themselves teachers* that prophecy smooth things, and say *peace, peace* to the wicked, when God hath declared that *there is no peace for them.* Against such preachers and hearers the *anger of the Lord and his jealousy shall smoke, and all the curses that are written in this book shall be upon them, and the Lord shall blot out their names from under heaven. If ye cease to warn the wicked, the same wicked man shall die in his iniquity, but his blood will I require at thine hand.* Mark: the consequence of withholding the warning, is the destruction of both the preacher and the hearer.

By the conviction and conversion of sinners.

By his *Spirit. And when he is come, he will reprove the world of sin, of righteousness, and of judgment. Behold, I stand at the door and knock: if any man hear my voice, and open the door, I will come in to him.* The Spirit is sent to admonish. Its language is, "Sinner, whither are thou going, and what will be the end of thy sinful course? Prepare to meet thy God."

God (sometimes) reproves one sinner by the conviction and conversion of another. Here is one who has been your intimate friend, and companion. Your views and feelings and pursuits and objects of delight, and I may add, your sins too, have been the same. But yesterday he thought and spoke and acted in all respects like yourself. Today he is alarmed at his awful condition. He trembles in view of a judgment to come. Hither to he has been moving merely along with you side by side. But he dares follow you no farther. He has quit your company, and fled. But why? Alas, he finds himself a sinner—He has a soul to be saved or lost forever. This, my friends, is loud preaching to some of you. When near and dear friends begin to forsake and shun you, it is time for you to begin to look about you. This is a silent, but a solemn warning to you to *Flee from the wrath*

The Second Great Awakening

to come.

When you see or hear of a hardened sinner alarmed at his awful condition; it carries with it this solemn admonition. See the end to which you are coming. Though you may think to hold out, yet you cannot endure long. Your stout heart will soon tremble. And all your boasted courage will end in cowardice. See the fearful end to which you are fast approaching. You too must repent or perish.

II. The effect of this reproof. *He hardeneth his neck.*

Allusion is made to the bullock which has repeatedly felt the galling yoke. At length his neck becomes hardened, and he can bear it without feeling or flinching. The sinner never hears a galling reproof without producing some effect. If his heart be not subdued, and changed, he becomes at length more hardened. The child which is often corrected, but not subdued, becomes more hardened.

The sinner under the afflictive hand of divine providence, is always made better or worse. If sickness and pain and the death of friends do not wean him from the world, and drive him to God, they harden his heart. This is the effect of all the judgments of heaven— of all the calamities and miseries of human life. This is strikingly illustrated in the case of Pharaoh, king of Egypt. *Because sentence against an evil work is not speedily executed, therefore the heart of the sons of men are fully set in them to do evil.*

Because God is so good, etc. Thus despising the riches of divine *goodness, and forbearance and longsuffering*—not knowing that the goodness of God leadeth him to repentance, after his hardness and impenitent heart, and with a stiff neck, he perseveres in his course of rebellion, *treasuring up unto himself wrath against the day of wrath and revelation of the righteous judgment of God.* O, the awful reckoning that awaits such offenders!

It is wholly impossible that a person should be frequently and faithfully admonished for his crimes, and yet experience no alteration in his own condition. His rancorous pride will be augmented and his conscience *become seared as with a hot iron. The earth which drinketh in the rain that cometh oft upon it, and bringeth forth herbs meet for them by whom it is dressed, receiveth blessing from God: But that which beareth thorns and briars is rejected, and is nigh unto cursing; whose end is to be burned.*

On this work the sinner may make rapid advances—he may acquire the faculty of silencing the remonstrances of his conscience, and with a stoical apathy, proudly boast that he is superior to the thunders of Sinai. He may resist the mild accents of mercy, and do *despite to the spirit of grace.* He may spurn the offers of a bleeding

Saviour. The darkened heavens—the rending rocks, and the quaking earth may have no effect—to all these he may render himself impervious. But the day *cometh that shall burn as an oven.* Then his stiff neck, and his stout heart will not exempt him from the terrors that shall thrill through the soul of every guilty culprit that shall stand at the judgment seat of Christ.

III. The consequences of an incorrigible disposition.

Sudden and remediless destruction. He, that being often reproved hardeneth his neck, shall suddenly be destroyed, and that without remedy. He shall be punished with everlasting destruction from the presence of the Lord, and from the glory of his power. This is the doom of the incorrigible sinner:

1. His punishment shall have *no end. Where the worm dieth not, and the fire is not quenched. The smoke of their torment ascendeth up forever and ever.* To cut off from Dives the last hope of relief to his torments, Abraham added, *And beside all this, between us and you there is a great gulf fixed: so that they which would pass from us to you cannot; neither can they pass to us, that would come from thence. Whose end is destruction. The redemption of the soul is precious and ceaseth forever.* His destruction is eternal.

2. It is *sudden.* Shall suddenly be destroyed. Thus the Psalmist: *How they are brought into desolation as in a moment?—They are utterly consumed with terror. As the fishes that are taken in an evil net—so are the sons of men snared in an evil time, when it falleth suddenly upon them.* When sinners lose their souls they always lose them unexpectedly—especially those who have been hardened offenders. *When they shall say, peace, and safety; then sudden destruction cometh upon them, and they shall not escape.*

This sentiment is illustrated in the providence of God. The fact is so common that it has become a proverb. The text itself is the result of a wise observation of the conduct of divine providence. It embodies the wisdom of ages. Thus was it with the inhabitants of the old world. They were often reproved by the preaching of Noah, and the by strivings of the Spirit, but they hardened their necks, and heeded neither. *They were eating and drinking, marrying and giving in marriage, and knew not until the flood came and took them all away. They were suddenly destroyed, and that without remedy.*

Thus was it with Pharaoh who was so often reproved by Moses, and by the judgments of God. Conscience was aroused—but as often did he silence her voice,—and harden his neck. At length he was *suddenly* drowned *and went down quick into hell.*

Thus it was with the inhabitants of Sodom. *Righteous Lot* warned them of their danger. The very evening before their destruction, *the men of Sodom compassed the house of Lot around, both old and young, all the people from every quarter.* And Lot went out and reproved them for their wickedness; but they were too far gone to bear it. *And they said: Stand back.* This unwillingness to take reproof marked them out as ripe for destruction. The same night he went out and delivered his last warning to his *sons-in-law. Up, get ye out of this place: for the Lord will destroy this city.* And what was the effect of this alarm? Why they felt just as sinners now feel: *He seemed as one that mocked to his sons-in-law.* So hardened were they that Lot appeared like a fool and his message like an idle tale. They were not frightened by him. They saw no signs of an approaching storm, and heard no distant thunders roar. The morning arose fair as ever; and all was peace and safety. *They did eat, they drank, they bought, they sold, they planted, they builded; but the <u>same day</u> that Lot went out of Sodom, it rained fire and brimstone from heaven and destroyed them all. They were <u>suddenly</u> destroyed and that without remedy.*

Ah! me thinks it is enough to curdle the blood in our veins to think how suddenly the most stupid and hardened sinner in this house may lose his soul. He may and doubtless will, sleep on, until he is awakened by the voice of God: *Thou fool, this night thy soul shall be required of thee.* For,

3. *There is no remedy.* The sinner who continues to harden his neck under reproof cannot be saved. He shall suddenly be destroyed, and that *without remedy,* because it cannot be prevented. Here is a sinner who will not take reproof—the question arises, What shall be done to prevent the loss of his soul? The answer is *nothing.* He is marching forward to eternity and to the pit of destruction with a proud heart and with a stiff neck, and nothing can stop him in his mad career. Such a sinner must go to destruction and no means can prevent it. This is the meaning of our text.

There is no remedy. The only remedy which can be applied for the salvation of sinners is the gospel. And this remedy never takes effect without alarming and arousing the guilty conscience. But, when warned to break off his sins, and to flee from the wrath to come, the hardened sinner says, "He is not to be frightened to heaven." Thus it was with the old world. *Noah, moved with fear, prepared an ark to the saving of his house; by the which he condemned the world.* By his preaching, and by his example, he warned the wicked world of the coming flood. But, they were not to be frightened. Thus it was with the inhabitants of Sodom. The preacher applied the most powerful means, the only remedy to prevent their destruction. *Up, get ye out of this place: for the Lord will destroy thee.* But, they were not to be frightened. *He seemed as one that mocked.* They would not be alarmed. And so there was *no remedy.* What could the preacher do more? Nothing.

Sinner! If you cannot be alarmed, you cannot be saved. If you do not believe that you are under the sentence of death from God's holy law, then you do not feel your need of pardon, and "Ye will not come to Christ that ye might have life." *He that believeth not is condemned already, and the wrath of God abideth on him.* And the sinner who does not feel the awful conviction of this truth cannot be pardoned or saved.

The language of the gospel is "Except *ye repent, ye shall all likewise perish."* But no sinner ever repented without conviction of sin. Even the Spirit of God never interposes to rescue the sinner from destruction in any other way than by arousing his guilty conscience to perform its office. Its genuine effects on the heart are thus described, "And when he is come, he will reprove the world of sin, and of righteousness, and of judgment." But, you are not to be frightened. *When they heard this they were pricked in the heart,* and exclaimed, *Men and brethren, what shall we do?* But you are not to be frightened. *When the commandment came, sin revived and I died;* but you are not to be frightened. The sinner who talks in this strain is either an infidel, or ignorant of the contents of the Bible.

For such a sinner, with such views and such feelings, the gospel contains *no remedy.* To such a sinner, the Spirit of God offers *no remedy. He, that being often reproved hardeneth his neck, shall suddenly be destroyed. And there is no remedy.* The sinner who will not take reproof, *must be destroyed.* The physician, who has exhausted his skill, and tried every experiment upon his patient can only look on and see him die.—So fares it with the incorrigible sinner; you may soothe him in his sins—you may flatter his vanity —But this is only hastening the work of destruction. The only salutary application is, *conviction of sin, of righteousness, and of judgment to come.* But this his proud heart will not endure. Every attempt to rescue him from destruction will be resisted—It will only exasperate. *He that reproveth a scorner getteth to himself shame: and he that rebuketh a wicked man getteth himself a blot.* Therefore, saith the wise man, *Reprove not a scorner, lest he hate thee.*

But, if such be the effect of reproof, me thinks I hear some one say, Then I will not hear the gospel. I will shun all reproof. Answer: A resolution not to take reproof evinces yourself to be one of the very persons described in the text. Whoever objects in this manner, shows his determination to harden his neck at all events. For no one can *shun* reproof, or a preached gospel, without hardening his neck in the most effectual manner. He voluntarily places himself beyond the reach of hope. The man who has drunk poison may say, "I will run. I will shun it." But, he is too late. You have heard the gospel and can never rid yourself of its everlasting obligations. *If they escaped not, who refused him who spake on earth, much more shall not we escape if we turn away from him that speaketh from heaven. They despised all my reproof, therefore shall they eat of the fruit of their own way, and be filled with their own devices. For the turning away of the simple shall slay them.*

From this subject we make the following reflections,

1. The *equity* of the sinner's punishment. He *hardeneth his neck* against reproof, and *brings destruction on himself.* When the Spirit of God comes, and with a "still small voice" whispers conviction to his guilty conscience; and he feels some concern for his soul, he tries not to be alarmed, but to appear above it. He shuns the light of divine truth. He *loves darkness,* and now he shall have darkness enough. God says, *Let their eyes be darkened, that they may not see.*

The sinner says, *peace and safety. Let us alone.* God says, *He is joined to idols, let him alone.* The sinner says, *Go thy way for this time.* God says, *My Spirit shall no longer strive.* The sinner chooses not to be under conviction, and now suppose God's choice and the sinner's should happen to coincide. All can see the equity of his punishment. If he will not lay up treasure in heaven, then he must lay up treasure in hell. And this is done by hardening his own heart. *After thy hardness and impenitent heart thou treasurest up unto thyself wrath against the day of wrath.*

When sinners are lost their consciences will forever reproach them for *destroying themselves. They are made to eat of the fruit of their own ways, and are filled with their own devices. They utterly perish in their own corruption.* By hardening his neck, the sinner, with his own hand, closes the door of heaven against himself.

2. Our subject is full of alarm to the aged sinner. My aged fathers; how long have you lived *without God in the world?* How many warnings have you heard and lost? So many years have you lived, and so many warnings have you heard and lost them all. I now appeal to your own experience. Do you not find that the longer you live, the harder are your hearts? Can you not bear testimony to the truth of our text? O where are you now? Once you enjoyed a season of youth; but alas, it is over and gone forever. Why stand ye here all

the day idle? Your day of salvation is almost gone.

I address you on the very brink of the grave. You are just ready to launch into eternity, and if you are not suddenly saved, you will be *suddenly destroyed, and that without remedy.* You now live at an interesting crisis—the season of a revival. It has an important bearing on the aged in this congregation. O how many younger than yourselves have hopefully entered the kingdom of God before you. In this, you have been often reproved. And are you still out of Christ? Your case is becoming more and more hopeless. The probability, I fear, is a thousand to one that you will be lost. You have no prospect of witnessing another revival in your day. Let the present season slip, and your case may be considered hopeless, and where are you? This very warning *neglected* will render your case more hopeless. The voice of mercy, spare a little longer, waxes feebler, and while the voice of justice is waxing louder and louder.

3. Our subject contains a warning to the young. If *he, that being often reproved hardeneth his neck, shall suddenly be destroyed, and that without remedy:* Then beware how you feel, and how you conduct under reproof. During the present revival how often have you been reproved by preaching, by conversation, by the conviction and conversion of your companions, by the admonitions and by the strivings of the Holy Spirit? How is this season likely to leave you? Certainly not as it found you. If you do not profit by all these warnings, you will be seven-fold harder than when it commenced.

What improvement have you made of all the warnings you have heard? Where are you now? If my preaching does not prove a *savour of life, it will be a savour of death unto death* to your souls. Every warning neglected is rendering your salvation less and less probable; it is making the work of repentance more and more difficult. You are wandering farther and farther from God—plunging deeper and deeper into misery at every step which you advance.

With your own hand, you are now forging those chains which will bind you down in eternal darkness and despair. To you the Saviour calls. *Turn you—turn you at my reproof.*

Because I called, and ye refused; I have stretched out my hand, and no man regarded; But ye have set at nought all my counsel, and would none of my reproof: I also will laugh at your calamity; I will mock when your fear cometh; When your fear cometh as desolation, and your destruction cometh as a whirlwind; when distress and anguish come upon you. Then shall they call on me, but I will not answer; they shall seek me early, but they shall not find me. They would none of my counsel: <u>*they despised all my reproof.*</u> *Therefore,* says God, *they shall eat of the fruit of their own doings. Today then, if ye will hear his voice, harden not your hearts.*

The more stupid and hardened the sinner is the nearer to destruction. Thus was it with the inhabitants of the old world. They never were more thoughtless than just before the flood came. It came when they least expected it. *They knew not until the flood came.* Never was Sodom more stupid than the very night before it was destroyed. The preaching of Lot seemed like an idle tale. They were doubtless making themselves merry with it until the very moment, when the flames of hell took hold of them. Thus it was with the rich fool. He sang the requiem to himself, *"Soul, take thine ease, eat, drink, and be merry."*

And thus it was with all who have gone to hell from under the light of the gospel. They cried "peace and safety" until they were lost. Death came too soon. And they dropped into hell, as into a snare and it closed suddenly upon them. Those sinners are commonly the nearest destruction who think and care the least about it. Hell is truth learned too late. Because there is wrath, beware lest God take thee away with his stroke, and then a great ransom cannot do.

> "Stop poor sinner, stop and think—
> Ere you are aware,
> You'll drop into the eternal lake."

6

Rejoice Young Man...

Rejoice, O young man, in thy youth; and let thy heart cheer thee in the days of thy youth, and walk in the ways of thine heart, and in the sight of thine eyes: but know thou, that for all these things God will bring thee into judgment (Ecclesiastes 11:9).

  The text speaks to those who are in the morning of life. And doubtless the words have already excited their attention. Such language is expressive and solemn. It catches the native feelings of the heart and carries them onward to the highest pitch, but only to disappoint and dash the rising hopes. We have before us a lively picture of the youthful mind: cheerful and gay; and the prospect of a judgment to come: *gloomy and awful.* The wise man views things in their proper and most important conclusion. The preacher had an affecting view of the shortness of human life, that its pleasures at the longest are quickly over and gone forever.
  Though a man live many years, and rejoice in them all; yet let him remember the days of darkness; for they shall be many. He makes a pause and declares the whole amount. *All that cometh is vanity.* Deeply impressed with the subject, he turns his attention to the young whose rising hopes and cheerful hearts seem to contradict the solemn truth.
  Instead of calling upon them to stop a while and reason on the subject, lest they run an awful hazard and gain nothing; for a while he seems to despair of all success. High hopes of present good, and a strong attachment to the fascinating pleasures of sin, which ever pleads for all the joy it brings, baffle every argument which ought to win the soul and lead it home to God.
  What then can be done? At such a crisis we tremble to hear what God will say. The sad case of a gay and thoughtless youth who sees no danger excites the tear of pity. Determined not to yield the point and quit a course so pleasant and delightful to his heart, nothing now remains, but that he make the trial and take the consequences. At the same time this pleasant and delightful course he must and will believe is safe, innocent, and harmless. Then go on and venture the trial with the final judge, when this short course is ended. *Rejoice, O young man, in thy youth; and let thy heart cheer thee in the days of thy youth, and walk in the ways of thine heart, and in the sight of*

thine eyes: but know thou, that for all these things God will bring thee into judgment.

Pain, sickness, and death are the common lot of all and no feeling heart could wish to interrupt the little joys of the present lifestyle, if there is no better portion. But if your present course is not safe, are you willing to hear it called in question? If your souls are in danger of being lost, by the alluring pleasures of what men call innocent amusements, will you now regard a warning from God? Or do you wish, like the others, to be flattered on to destruction?

The season of youth is truly interesting. Characters are now rapidly forming. And the course they bend, the path in which they now tread, in whatever direction it leads, commonly conducts through life, through death and on through eternity. In the morning sow the seeds and whatsoever a man soweth that shall he also reap, life and death are now depending.

Youth is also the season of joy and cheerfulness. Old age may enfeeble the limbs, and long habits of indulgence wear out the sensitive faculties of enjoyment. Such are the evils incident to old age, the years in which they say, I have no pleasure in them. But while the vigor and sprightliness of youth remain, this is the time, the only season, in which men can rejoice and be cheerful in walking in the ways of their hearts and in the sight of their eyes.

This is the time to rejoice. The season of youth can never be enjoyed but once. It is cheerful and gay, but short and quickly over; and when past it is gone, never to be recalled. But heaven, with all its glories, is now brought near at the critical moment, when the world is presenting all its charms. Here then is no standing still. A choice must and shall be made. Man is a moral agent, destined to act for eternity. He shall walk either in the strait and narrow way to life, or in the broad road to death.

But now is the time to rejoice. The youth engage in the giddy scene and rejoice with merry hearts. And not one has yet renounced the hopes of heaven—not one believes that he shall hear the sentence from the judgment seat, *depart.* In their view, all is safe and all is well. Some may begin to startle at extremes and fear excess, but slacken a little the rapid progress and he will still continue the same course without disturbance. He thinks surely there can be no harm in gathering some of the delights and tasting the pleasures of the present season.

But this is not the language and the spirit of the text. It may now be asked, may we not rejoice; may we not be cheerful, must we be stripped of all at once?—It is proposed to point out the course which has the promise of the present life and in which alone you may rejoice with safety.

Rejoice not in iniquity, but rejoice in the truth. There is a virtuous joy. The former has two distinguishing characteristics. It differs from the latter both in its nature and its object. Its nature is holy. It arises from a holy heart. And hence it is declared to be the fruit of the Spirit; which is love, joy, and peace. This is its nature. And no one who rejoices in the truth, can wish for any other recommended in a false disguise.

Whether directly or more remote it always has God for its object. And hence the people of God are frequently called upon to rejoice *in the Lord*. Here is a fountain—a never failing source of joy. All other sources must fail. The things of time are fast fading and will soon forever retire from our sight. We can carry nothing into the future world. That joy and delight which center in present objects is momentary and can never satisfy. *Even in laughter the heart is sorrowful; and the end of that mirth is heaviness.*

The cheerful countenance must fall, and their youthful and blooming bodies, on which you fondly dote, must fade and die. But God remains the same through all changes. Here our hopes may pin. On this rock our joy can firmly rest. *Rejoice in the Lord always, and again I say rejoice.*

Is God the object of this joy? It will then arise from a sense of his all surrounding presence. *In thy presence is fullness of joy.* And those that remember their Creator in the days of their youth, cannot rejoice in forgetting his presence. This joy begins with believing in Christ. The jailer who just before trembled, rejoiced, believing in God. And many youths, who have been seen trembling in view of the judgment to come, on believing in Christ have rejoiced with joy unspeakable and full of glory.

Further, there are particular seasons in which every youth who pays any regard to the glory of God and his own soul will rejoice.

The *Sabbath* is a peculiar season—the day is appointed by God himself for this very purpose. *A day in his courts is better than a thousand. This is the day which the Lord hath made, I will rejoice and be glad in it.*

The time of a revival of religion is another season of peculiar rejoicing. *I have no greater joy,* says St. John, *than to hear that my children walk in the truth.* When Philip preached at Samaria, *there was great joy in that city.* At the repentance of sinners, there is joy in heaven among the angels of God and to all the friends of Zion on earth. And so it would be in this place, were the youth now returning

The Second Great Awakening

to their Father's house. It would then be meet that they should make merry, for this my son was dead and is alive again, was lost, but now is found.

Other particulars might be named, but these are the principal, and the great occasions, on which every friend of God will exercise the most peculiar joy.—Has any youth found his own case described? Does he rejoice in God? Does he feel a spring of joy on such occasions and long for their return? Then he may walk on his way rejoicing. He has the promise of the present life, and shall shortly receive a crown of never fading joy in the life to come.

Whether this course meets the feelings of the heart, or not, the account will doubtless commend itself to every man's conscience. However insipid and worthless the pleasures of such a course may be to others; yet wisdom is justified of her children, who find her ways pleasantness and her paths peace. But if he cannot rejoice in this course in this manner and on these occasions; then there is nothing in which he can rejoice. Nothing in heaven and nothing on earth but the pleasures of sense, or those which he finds in walking in the ways of his heart and in the sight of his eyes. *Let thy heart cheer thee,* etc.

The same may be said of cheerfulness. This is called virtue. It may be so. You may have often heard it asserted, that there is no religion in being gloomy. So be it; and now the guilty conscience will rest easy. But be not deceived,—every command of God is to be cheerfully obeyed. We have nothing to do but duty. And if this be not done with cheerfulness—if it be not pleasant and delightful to the soul, however much sinners may do, God condemns the whole. No duty is done to God. Youth are apt to consider religion as a gloomy subject. Indeed, it may be so to them, while impenitence and guilt cry for vengeance. But even repentance itself is accompanied with a beam of joy. *Son be of good cheer, thy sins be forgiven thee.*

No degree of joy and cheerfulness is forbidden by the Word of God. But every youth is commanded to rejoice in the Lord, and to walk cheerfully on in the path of duty. And whatever may hinder his progress, whether *brothers or sisters, or evil companions,* he is freely and cheerfully to forgive all, and *glory in nothing, save the cross of Christ.* Such cheerfulness is a duty, and without which there is no religion.

But if while he thinks of heaven, his heart goes after the world— the company of the gay and thoughtless, and their delightful scenes, and he is sorrowful to leave them and reluctant to give them up; this is the sorrow of the world which worketh death. This is a gloom in which there is no religion. He must cheerfully leave all or be contented to take his portion in this world. He must cheerfully leave all or with the young man in the gospel, go away from Christ sad and grieved. Let those who have come out of the world, walk cheerfully on in the path of duty. In Christ, you will have peace. But many trials and difficulties may yet await you. In the world you shall have tribulation, but be of good cheer, Christ has overcome the world.

Having pointed out the course in which alone you may safely rejoice and be cheerful, let us now,

II. Turn out attention to the youth in the text. You will now see the reason why God is angry and will bring him into judgment for rejoicing and being cheerful. The young man is not a Christian. He does not rejoice in God—nor in believing in Christ. And perhaps he would be ashamed to come forward before his companions and openly profess his name and espouse his cause. He forsakes his followers, and prefers the company of the gay and thoughtless. He is cheerful and social with his companions; but says little or nothing to them about the great things of eternity and how it will fare with them hereafter. And perhaps he is so far gone, that he is unwilling to have them think that he has any concern with the God that made him. He does not rejoice in the employment and on the day which God has appointed; but prefers another day and a different employment.

He does not rejoice at the repentance of his fellow sinners—To see his companions bid adieu and give a parting hand to all their joy and mirth gives him no delight. Nay, perhaps he weeps a while in secret, to think he has lost his friend. For he's determined not to follow in such a gloomy path, but chooses rather to renounce his dearest friend—and take sides against him and rest contented while the world is on his side. And now since he had no pretensions to religion, he may have gone to such a pitch as to plead one sin as an excuse for another, and think to justify his present conduct, inasmuch as he has become a frank, openhearted, and avowed enemy of God. But however this may be, he is a lover of pleasure more than a lover of God. And he is unwilling to be startled from his dream of pleasure, and is determined not to be alarmed at the trial of his angry judge.

He is now standing without a Saviour, and yet he has a cheerful and a merry heart. *Let thy heart cheer thee.* He can easily be cheerful. He has only to follow the bent of his inclination. He is impatient and cannot endure self-denial. It makes him miserable. Is he crossed in his inclination, he feels himself injured; and will shun a faithful reprover as an enemy.—Take off restraint, and never call him to a sense of duty. Do not awaken his fear or alarm his conscience by pointing him to consequences. But let him alone. And this is all that he wants to complete his present happiness. *Let thy heart cheer thee.* And hence we see that his joy and cheerfulness spring from walking in the ways of his heart and in the sight of his eyes.

To do this, he has only to contemplate and pursue whatever is fair and pleasant to the eye, and on which the imaginations of his evil heart delight to dwell. Regardless of consequences, his inclination is easily caught and governed wholly by the present appearance. A stranger to the pleasures of religion, he seldom thinks of duty and hence he frequently engages in scenes, which to the Christian would have no meaning. And were he asked the reason of his joy and cheerfulness, he would either be silent or blush to tell. He only rejoices without any rational subject in view; and aside from present gratification all would be dull and lifeless, and would cease to have any further meaning.

It is his supreme delight to forget God and this Solomon intimated by continuing his address—*Remember now* thy Creator. The presence of God chills the soul; and should he venture to reflect a moment, it would strike his pleasure dead. He can best amuse himself with trifles amidst the gay and thoughtless, where nothing of God is heard, expect to sport and trifle with his awful name. He can give a merry turn, and get the laugh on religion; but he intends no harm, he is only casting his arrows in sport. And perhaps he may venture to commend religion at a distance; but he would have her to know her place, and not intrude to interrupt and spoil his joy. *He says to God, depart from me, for we desire not the knowledge of thy ways.* All his joy and cheerfulness arise from sensual gratification, or in the indulgence of a carnal heart. And to give a loose to any of its desires is to walk not after the Spirit, but after the flesh—not by faith, but by sight. *But to be carnally minded is death. And if ye live after the flesh, ye shall die.* And so, notwithstanding his cheerfulness, death is inscribed by the finger of God on his very soul and on all its delights while he continues to walk in the ways of his heart.

The ways of his heart may be many. He may change and vary the objects of his delight at pleasure, but the nature of all is the same until he turns to God. But the whole may be included in the broad way to destruction; and thousands can walk together there—and no being but God can hinder their progress. The way is smooth and gently declining. And travelers may join hand-in-hand and with rapid speed march on their way rejoicing with cheerful hearts.

And parents, whose houses are safe from fear, and while the rod of God is not actually upon them, often help them onward. *They send forth their little ones like a flock, and their children dance. They take the timbrel and harp, and rejoice at the sound of the organ. They spend their days in wealth, and in a moment go down to the grave.* Careless and thoughtless they pass along, and seldom think of returning till their youthful days are ended. Their morning is fair and without a cloud. They see no signs of an approaching storm, and hear no distant thunders roar. And they think it strange that any of their companions should escape for life, and be so timid, as not to run with them to the same excess of riot in such a decent and delightful path.

But the youth in the text is determined not to yield, but to make further trial of his pleasures. He is not satisfied, nor will he yet believe that all is vanity. And Solomon supposed he would not be convinced of his folly until he should come to judgment. He may experience checks of conscience at first, but when he has found his way through some difficulties, he gains strength and finds the way more easy. He wishes others would let him alone. He loves darkness and will fly from the light of conviction. But this cannot always be done; and therefore he labors not to be convinced of sin and to come to repentance, but to silence his fears, and to soothe his conscience. You may now hear him plead his cause and defend his scenes of pleasure. And as no one ever yet set himself to prove directly, *that sin is a duty,* he will give his conduct the soft names of harmless and innocent. He will often plead the example of others, and would be glad to prove that his scenes of pleasure are really necessary and enjoined by the word of God. He thinks himself no worse and perhaps not as bad as many others. Indeed he sees little or no cause for repentance. But will this prove his interest in the merits of a Saviour's blood? Were he assured that his pleasures would soon be over—that within a few days he must lie down in eternal sorrows—in the horrors of despair, this guilty mortal would change his scenes of mirth into the cries and shrieks of the damned. His heart would pine away in the mournful complaint. *Who can dwell with devouring fire? Who can inhabit everlasting burnings?* But the case is far different. What if he lives without God in the world? What though he yet stands without the ark of safety? He feels himself too young to be a Christian; and too young to die. He now believes that Christ has spilt his blood to purchase him the pleasures of sin for a season, and the joys of heaven, when his youthful course is ended. Now this and much more is often necessary to ease his conscience and help him onward to rejoice. For should guilt, death, and judgment stare him in the face, it would end his sport at once.

At first sight, one would think it madness for him to rest a moment without the ark of safety. And much more to rejoice and make merry before he has ever fled to Christ for refuge. But he is charmed with his pleasures, and while his soul is in danger, he will, perhaps be angry if you touch his trifles, and attempt to wrest them from his hand. He is willing to regulate his amusements and to conduct them with great propriety, only suffer him to retain the thing itself which is the joy and delight of his heart. This is truly affecting. He cannot be brought to a sense of the worth of his soul, and to see that he is lost and dead in sin. And here he will rest till he views his conduct in the light of eternity.

Little does he know of the deceitfulness of sin. Were it not pleasant to his taste, it would not, it could not be committed. It is easy to see, that an attempt to regulate in a sinful course, might be soothing to the conscience—but death to the soul—gilding the path to allure him quietly down to the chambers of death. *The heart of the wise is in the house of mourning, but the heart of fools is in the house of mirth. The preaching of the cross is foolishness to them that perish.* And he must continue without a Saviour and forever perish unless he is brought to renounce and hate every evil course.

If he pleads for any joy and merriment before he comes to Christ his case is truly alarming. He is pleading for his own destruction. Now God in kindness, but in dreadful language speaks, and warns him where his danger lies. Rejoice, O young man, and be cheerful, but know thou that for this delightful conduct, I will bring thee into judgment. The pleasure taken is the very thing pointed at and condemned by the word of God. It would not be difficult to dissuade him from his present course were it not delightful to his heart. And in this the danger lies. Every step which he advances in the ways of his heart carries him farther and farther from God. The more he indulges in sinful pleasures, the less he fears, and the stronger his habits become. It is nothing strange should he continue in his present course walking in the broad and downward road. It is only walking according to the course of this world. It is nothing strange should he be more hardened in sin and more loath to return at every step which he advances. It is nothing strange should he continue on filling up the measure of his sins with a joyful and a merry heart.

When sinners have for a while defended themselves in their sinful courses, it is common for God to give them up. And for this cause God shall send them strong delusion that they should believe a lie:

that they all might be damned who believed not the truth, *but had pleasure in unrighteousness*. Because God has called and they have refused—now they shall eat of the fruit of their own way, and be filled with their own devices.

Now the season of his youth is over, and he has gained nothing. The evil days draw nigh, when he cannot rejoice and be cheerful in walking in the ways of his heart. But more than half of the human race die and go to judgment before the season of youth is ended. What a vast multitude is here! Take from this number the little company of pious souls, who had forsaken their youthful vanities, who chose rather to suffer affliction with the people of God than to enjoy the pleasures of sin for a season, and who have died in the Lord. And what a vast multitude of youth have gone from their scenes of merriment, to judgment with all their sins upon their heads. How solemn is the text. While their sprightliness and health remain, they will rejoice and make merry until God lays his hand upon them and brings them unto judgment.

But the youth may live after he has spent the best of his days in sin. But shall the Ethiopian change his skin, or the leopard his spots; then may he also do good, who is accustomed to do evil. Taken in this light, how striking are the words of the text. Rejoice O young man, in thy youth.—Spend thy youthful days in vanity, and then you will be confirmed in your sinful course, and afterwards live only to ripen for a more dreadful judgment hereafter.

This is a general truth, with two exceptions. Let the appeal be made to the word and the providence of God and the general truth will be confirmed. The religious revivals of former and especially of later years are known to be generally confined to the young. They have been called at the very time when they were just entering on their scenes of vanity: cheerful, gay, and thoughtless. At the times when their hopes and expectations were raised to the highest pitch, suddenly were they stripped of all. But far more are left to rejoice and make merry, cheerfully filling up the measure of their sin, until wrath shall come upon them to the uttermost. Nor will they truly repent of their folly, until it is too late. But after their hardness and impenitent hearts they will continue to treasure up unto themselves wrath against the day of wrath and revelation of the righteous judgment of God. It will then appear that their better days in which they now rejoice, were wholly spent in gathering fuel for their own eternal torments. But we leave them in the hand of God—After death, comes the judgment.

My young friends, you and I must shortly open our eyes on a

world where all is new. Where every work will appear in its proper light. You have often heard that you are acting for eternity; you will then believe it.

Once more, life and death are set before you. The only course in which you can safely rejoice and be cheerful is now pointed out. And can you wish for any other? Can you wish to rest a moment without the ark of safety? God is calling. He is calling by the death of your companions, and will you not stop your sport, nor regard his voice? What can be more insulting to the majesty of heaven? Christ is calling. And will you not stop your sinful sport to hear his dying groans, and see the wounds which your sins have made? Will you now make him the minister of sin, and trifle with his blood, because he died to save *his* people from their sins? Will you change the day of probation into a scene of vain mirth while your eternal state is depending on this point of time?

Yes, this you will do. But we hope not all. The Spirit of God may convince of sin, of righteousness, and of judgment. If not, we plead with you in vain. One affecting view of the judgment to come would render other arguments useless. The ministers of God are still encouraged to speak, and hold not their peace, from the hope that God has yet much people among the youth.

Within a few years past, many of your age have been called from the height of their joy and mirth, to tremble in view of a judgment to come. Their scenes of mirth were soon turned into mourning, and their joy into heaviness. Nothing could divert them from the solemn inquiry: *What must I do be saved?* Not a smile of joy could be seen, as you can well conceive, while they saw that they were out of Christ and that their eternal all might be lost the next moment. The trifles of time were lost in the awful concerns of eternity.

And so could it be with you, my friends, were the still small voice of God's Spirit to whisper conviction to your consciences. You would then be convinced of sin, of righteousness, and of judgment to come. You would then see that heaven is no place for carnal joy— that you must be born again, or there is nothing in heaven in which you can rejoice. You would then see how awful a thing it is to live without a Saviour—that God out of Christ is a consuming fire—that nothing but the brittle thread of life, supported by the hand of an angry God now holds the sinner from dropping into the flames of hell. *Because sentence against an evil work is not speedily executed, therefore the hearts of the sons of men is fully set in them to do evil.*

If you have never believed in Christ and repented of your sins, you are already under sentence of condemnation. And all the dreadful threatenings contained in God's Word, are now ready to be executed. And should the unseen hand of death suddenly approach and find you as you are, you are gone, and lost forever. Is this a time to rejoice and make merry? You must die and go to judgment.

I well know that you intend to die the death of the righteous; and so did all who are now in hell. Not one had made his calculations to lie down in eternal torments. And you are now heading in their steps. What then are your prospects? I will tell you—

All your resolutions about future repentance are worth *nothing*. Such resolutions are a part of the ways of thine own heart, for which God will bring thee into judgment. They are necessary to quiet the conscience and to help you onward to rejoice. Such a resolution may be made by that person whose heart is now fully set in them to do evil. It is made for the very purpose of escaping the righteous judgment of God, and now he can once more rejoice in sin. Affliction will always bring men to lament it. I speak only of gospel repentance, which loathes sin for what it is in itself. Can any man, can you promise yourselves a heart to abhor the thing which is now the joy and delight of your heart? And such are the things for which God now threatens to bring you into judgment. You may mourn to think that your joyful season will soon be over; and that you are so near to the judgment. But you have no evidence to conclude that you will hereafter hate what you now love. Besides a resolution to become a Christian hereafter, and not this day, is now determinate rebellion against God. You are urged to secure your interest in Christ. And are your hearts now backward; are you reluctant to begin the work this day? Tomorrow will find your hearts farther from God—more hardened in sin, and difficulties will certainly increase, at every step which you advance. But what is your life? Has God showed you, O young man, that he will not bring thee into judgment before another day shall arrive? At such an hour as ye think not, the Son of man will come.

But you may think to obtain the favor of God though you continue to walk in the ways of your hearts. But you will not succeed. The way to heaven is too strait. It is directly opposite, and every step advanced is gained by opposing the desires of the flesh. The righteous, who take to themselves the whole armour of God will scarcely be saved.

Where is the young man who fears the judgment to come? What is the breath of an enemy of God to the blast of the soul by the breath of the Almighty? If you fear the frowns of a fellow worm, how will you stand in judgment with an angry God?

The Second Great Awakening

Seek first the kingdom of God—and then your amusements will regulate themselves. But if you will not do this; while I exhort you to act as those who must give account at the judgment bar of God—suffer me as a fellow mortal bound to appear at the same tribunal, now to tell you. That all amusements which prepare the soul for the duties of religion are right, and every Christian is bound to engage in them, and those which do not, will be condemned at the bar of God. But if you do not repent of your sins and turn to God, whatever course you may take—whatever your amusements may be—turn which way you will, God is a consuming fire. You sport on the brink of ruin.—Can you amuse yourselves with trifles, while the soul is in danger of being lost? You chase a bubble, at the hazard of falling into endless torments.

It is amazing that mortals should play tricks to cheat the soul out of heaven, by calling evil good. Innocent amusements? Where can an enemy of God be innocently employed? If you really believe that you are innocently employed, then you are as willing to meet the king of terrors in this place as in any other as some have done. You can have no objection to being called from this innocent employment, in the twinkling of an eye, to the bar of God. It is both sinful and dangerous to enter on any course when death would find us unprepared. We are as much accountable to God at one time as at another. He allows his creatures no time for vain amusements. We have just come into being, and a few moments conduct decides our eternal state. We are always to remember that God sees us—and do what we will, we can never get out of his sight, or out of his hand. God will not defer the stroke of death, lest the sinner go to judgment unprepared.

Yet many plead the example of the world, which lies in wickedness. They feel safe because they run with the multitude. Others have done so before. My friends, others have gone to hell. The world were sporting in sin, when suddenly they were not only *drowned,* but *damned.* Would you plead the example of the world? Here it is set forth for your warning.

Why are you anxious about your amusements? You cannot long retain them. You are liable to be stripped of all in a moment. Then take them away. And would you not then exclaim—all my joys are gone. *Ye have taken away my gods and what have I more?* If such desponding thoughts arise, your case is truly alarming. If you have now no better portion you are poor indeed—poor indeed, without a Saviour. You are now, in your lifetime, receiving your good things. And this little may be all that you will ever enjoy. Your last day, your last hour will soon come. Were this day to close the scene of your mortal life, what have you gained? Were the judgment now to open to your view, what have you been doing? Where now is the day of salvation? It is gone. Your work for eternity is ended. And the judge pronounces your final doom. But though this day may not be your last, yet all your work is yet to be done. So long as you have lived, so much is gone out of your probation—so much of the day of salvation is over—your best season is almost gone, and nothing is done for God. It will forever remain true, so much of your golden season was spent, worse than in vain. Your past conduct is now recorded in heaven—the account is gone in, and cannot be altered. It will shortly be presented to your view. The joyful scene will now be changed. Every action will now be weighed by the omniscient Judge. Every secret thing will now appear. God will bring to the light of open day the hidden works of darkness, and the secret counsels of all hearts. And should his awful summons find you out of Christ, still the righteous Judge will proceed to the trial on the principles of strict justice. He will now demand the uttermost farthing—absolute perfection. Without pity, or allowance for the levity of youth, he will condemn and punish for every failure of perfect obedience. An idle word, an impure thought, cannot be forgiven. For all those things, O young man, how will your present *gay conduct* then appear? Inattention to the calls of mercy—open comtempt of the voice of God. The noise of mirth in the day of salvation—sporting with the blood of the Son of God. A pleasant jest on religion—a league with the prince of darkness to block the way which leads to heaven and allure your companions onward with a smile down to hell. *Woe unto you that laugh now, for you shall mourn and weep.*

Young man, I leave you in the hands of your final Judge. Life and death are now before you and God is witness to your choice. If a bleeding Saviour has no charms for you—if the thunder of his vengeance does not strike terror through your guilty soul; then go on.—March on your way rejoicing—Trample under foot the Son of God—Sport with eternal vengeance and deny the thunder of his power. Your fair morning will soon be turned into darkness, your course run—your bodies fall in the grave, and your souls into the hands of the living God.

7

Seek Ye the Lord

*Seek ye the Lord while he may be found,
call ye upon him while he is near* (Isaiah 55:6).

Isaiah in this chapter doubtless personates the ministers of Christ. He makes known the great salvation of the gospel, and by the freeness of the offer and the greatness of the blessing, urges all to accept it. Nor can the earnest prophet be satisfied merely with placing before them these motives. He well knew what every minister of the gospel knows, that the design to seek God at some future time is not only common, but usually followed with a final refusal and final ruin. He cannot therefore leave those whom he addresses without pressing upon them the necessity of immediate compliance with his invitation. The great motive by which he does this is that the Lord *may be found,* that *the Lord is near.*

From the text we may remark,

1. That there is some thing in religion of which sinners are destitute. Something is to be *found.* Seek ye the Lord while he may be <u>*found*</u>. If thou seek him, he will be found of thee, but if thou forsake him, he will cast thee off forever.

2. The *time.* While he *may be found.* Every sinner who comes within the sound of the gospel enjoys a precious season. The salvation of his soul *is* possible—Christ *may be found. Call ye upon him while he is near.* There is a season when the *Lord is near.* An implicit declaration of this interesting truth: that there are special seasons of divine influence. A sentiment which the enemies of experimental religion to quiet conscience would gladly deny. That there are such seasons is obvious from facts abroad in the world around us—from the experience of every Christian, and from the general tenor of the word of God. Of this, the text is a striking proof. On this fact the exhortation of the prophet is grounded.

There is a time when Christ will not be found. *Then shall they call upon me, but I will not answer; they shall seek me early, but they shall not find me.* There is a time when the Lord will not *be near.* As it respects the mode of his existence the Lord is always *near.* We can never *go from his Spirit or flee from his presence. For in him we live and move.* From which it is evident that the *nearness of God* in the text must mean something special—He is near with the striving of his Spirit and the glorious displays of his power and grace. Though God is always present, always *near*, yet not in the sense of the text. We are directed to *seek the Lord, if haply we may feel after him and find him*, though *he be not far from every one of us.*

There is a special season of divine influence. The prophet lays hold of this as a motive to raise the attention of every careless, prayerless sinner.—*Seek—call* upon him *now*, for God is near—improve the season, for he will soon depart.

This then is the plain import of the text; that large as the mercy of God is, although he is always ready to pardon the truly penitent, however guilty and however vile, yet there is a time when in a peculiar sense he is *to be found,* when he is *peculiarly near.* In other words, there are seasons and circumstances which are particularly favorable to seeking the Lord and calling upon him which afford peculiar advantages for this work, and when success is easier that at other times.

This is strikingly the fact with respect to those who live in a place where a revival of religion prevails. There the Lord is peculiarly *near*. He appears in his glory to every eye, and makes the way to holiness and heaven a highway.—My design is to apply the text to this subject, and show that a revival of religion affords to those who witness it, great and peculiar advantages for becoming religious.

Religion, I am aware, is never an easy thing to the depraved heart of man. But the difficulties are perhaps never less than in times of general seriousness. At such a time the external obstacles are far less than usual. This may be illustrated in several particulars,

1. One obstacle with multitudes is that they do not and will not think on the subject of religion. In times of prevailing stupidity the things of the world occupy the mind. Now I need not say that no one ever did or ever will become religious who does not think of religion. Says the Psalmist, *I thought on my ways, and turned my feet unto his testimonies.* Without deep and solemn reflection none will ever become religious. The world, with all its concerns, must be driven from the heart of a sinner. And his soul must be full of eternity. His attention must be fixed closely upon this single object. Compared with the everlasting concerns of the soul, all other concerns are nothing with the awakened sinner. Without the renouncing of every idol and breaking off from every sin, seeking with all the heart, we have no prospect of entering the strait gate.

In times of general stupidity how little is said of the concerns of the soul. How little is said about preparation for death, judgment, and eternity. But no sooner does a revival begin than every body begins to talk. Every one has something to say either for or against. At such a time the great subject of religion—the everlasting concerns of the soul are brought forth and held up to the view of all. It now becomes comparatively easy, or rather impossible not to think.

How, within a few weeks past, has it been in this place. What conversation—what interest excited on the subject of religion! At such a time the world has less influence over the mind. The fashions of the world—the amusements of youth, are all laid aside as trifles. And now eternity rises into view. God and Christ and the Holy Spirit, heaven and hell occupy the minds of sinners. Thus one obstacle is removed.

2. At such a time the fear of man is less. This is a great obstacle in the way of many. This will shut out many from the kingdom of heaven. It is recorded of some in our Saviour's time: *Nevertheless among the chief rulers also, many believed on him; but because of the Pharisees they did not confess him, lest they should be put out of the synagogue. For they loved the praise of men more than the praise of God.* They were convinced in their consciences—but their belief did not raise them above the fear of man—they were more afraid of man than of God, and must loose their souls.

Thousands would become religious, at least as they think, provided others would. Should the sinner become anxious in a time of stupidity, he must become *singular*. His friends and acquaintances may all combine against him. The course of the world is downward—He is surrounded with travelers urging him onward in the broad road. The whole current is against him. He must go out from the world and be separate, and bear the scorn and contempt alone.

But in a time of revival, the fear of man is in a great measure removed. Those very friends and acquaintances are now becoming Christians. They have halted. They have forsaken the broad road—many have already gone and others are now returning. *Many are now inquiring the way to Zion with their faces thither ward.* And their language now is: *"Come thou with us and we will do thee good."* Now the sinner may have company. He need not commence the arduous journey alone. He need not bear the shame and reproach alone. It is easy to mingle and bear it in common with others. He need not forsake the company of all former friends for the sake of Christ—He need not break friendship with them for the sake of going to heaven; but if he will not become a Christian, he must break friendship for the sake of going to hell. And thus another great difficulty is now removed.

3. A revival affords peculiar means of grace. A sinner becoming

anxious in time of prevailing indifference wishes to hear something on the subject of religion adapted to his case. He is in darkness and distress and would rejoice to meet some Christian traveler to inquire, *"What must I do to be saved?"* But all around are cold and stupid and dead—he is left to wander alone in darkness and despair.

But now in a revival the case is different. Christians are awake—Their conversation is adapted to his case. Now their prayers ascend to God with more earnestness in behalf of perishing souls. The preaching too at such a season is adapted to the state of anxious souls, and the preacher himself catches the flame and his heart glows with increased ardor for the salvation of souls. Nothing is like it to lead ministers to be faithful. An effectual door is opened, and he finds a thousand new avenues leading to the hearts of sinners. Conferences, and meetings for anxious souls are appointed, and thus the means of grace are greatly multiplied. And not only so, but you have an opportunity of seeing sinners pricked in their hearts and urging, *God be merciful to me a sinner.* Never is so much of God seen as in a powerful revival of religion. *When the Lord shall build up Zion, he shall appear in his glory.*

Careless and hardened sinners are alarmed and bow before him. We now witness the truth of the humbling doctrines of grace. The commandment *comes,* sin *revives,* and *sinners are slain.* By their sighs and sobs he may now hear in awful anticipation the weeping of the damned in hell. In the joy of converts, he witnesses the reality of that great change without which our Saviour declared none can see the kingdom of God. He now hears the commencement of that new song which none but the redeemed can learn.

The Spirit of God does more for sinners at such a time than at others. This will follow from the last particular. It is a fact, that the Spirit of God ordinarily works by means; and by the very means above mentioned. None are better. At such a time we believe there are very few who do not feel more or less the strivings of the Spirit—if there be any impenitent sinners who do not, this bears the dreadful marks of reprobation (divine dereliction). Notice the effects of the influence, and the fact cannot be doubted. Many tell us they have *never felt so before. Who can help it at such a time as this,* say they.

It often happens in a revival that there is another class who feel. I mean some of those who oppose the work with sneers, ridicule, and contempt. Look at their arguments, at the methods taken to run it down.—Look at the characters. Are they humble Christians? Do they bear the marks of those who sigh and cry for all abominations in the land? Tell us whether they be serious praying persons—whether

The Second Great Awakening

what is said and done appears to be out of a sincere regard to the good of souls, the honor of God, and the prosperity of the redeemed kingdom.—I mention this for the sake of discovering the true state of the heart. No my hearers; it is no very uncommon fact that such persons are on the very point of deep conviction. They feel it and are afraid of it—and are compelled to make the desperate struggle against it. Such persons have often been brought to bow, and afterwards have owned and confessed the fact. Whence these anxious looks—these crowds assembling—this deathlike silence—this awful solemnity! God is *near.* You feel his power. *Sinners in Zion are afraid.*

Now, while I am speaking, your consciences are alarmed. The Spirit of God is moving on the mind. My hearers, is it not so? Enumerate the advantages in a revival and compare them with those in time of spiritual indifference, and then tell us whether the sentiment be not true.

But whether it be so, or not, the text must be obeyed, or your soul must be lost. *Seek ye the Lord while he may be found, call ye upon him while he is near.* From our text it is clear that there is a time when the Lord will not be found.

1. It is certain he will not be found after death. Then you may seek, and call and it will do no good. *Then sinners will cry, Lord, Lord, open unto us.* That time is fast hastening—it may be nearer than you are aware. *Thou fool, this night thy soul may be required. For when they shall say, Peace and safety; then sudden destruction cometh upon them. He, that being often reproved hardeneth his neck, shall suddenly be destroyed, and that without remedy.*

2. By those who have committed the unpardonable sin. And this danger is never greater than at such a season as this. Our Saviour declares, *All manner of sin and blasphemy shall be forgiven unto men. And whosoever speaketh a word against the Son of Man it shall be forgiven, but whosoever speaketh against the Holy Ghost it shall not be forgiven him, neither in this world, nor in the world to come.* The Son when slighted, once said, *I go my way, Ye shall seek me, and shalt die in your sins—O that thou hadst known even thou at least in this thy day the things which belong unto thy peace! but now they are hid from thine eyes.*

3. He will not be found by those who have finally grieved away the Holy Spirit. His convincing, renewing, and sanctifying influences may be forever withdrawn. *And the Lord said, My Spirit shall not always strive with man. Woe also, to them when I depart from*

them. Death may come—or the Holy Spirit grieved and provoked may give up the incorrigible sinner forever.

And now permit me, my hearers, to apply this subject to your hearts. There is something in religion of which sinners are destitute. Something must be found. *Seek ye the Lord while he may be found.* You have heard much of late of sinners finding Christ. This is no new thing. My hearers do you know what our text means? Do you know what it is to find Christ? This we do hope is the happiness of a number present. But to all who have never yet found the Saviour, our text is a loud call. You are yet without hope and without God in the world. Do you intend an interest in Christ?—When will you do it? Hitherto you have slept over the concerns of your souls—you have been dreaming of a more convenient season, but that season has not arrived. But stop.—Some of you may now look back to the time when you flattered yourselves that you would attend to this subject, were it not for the influence of the world—the fear of man—the want of company—the loss of friends—the charge of singularity—the scorn and contempt of the wicked world. And did these things prevent you from attending to the concerns of your soul—O unhappy man! It is a wonder that God has spared you—that you are yet out of hell. The time however, has arrived when you can no longer make this plea. Your former excuses have fled. If you will not now attend in earnest to the concerns of your soul, God intends that you shall be stripped, you shall have *no cloak for your sin.*

You may now well remember that in some moment of serious reflection that is past, you sighed and felt the secret wish; O that the Spirit of God might be poured out—that I might witness something of a revival of religion, then would I attend to the subject myself.— Well, that happy period has now arrived. The little cloud has been gathering. Little drops of mercy have already descended. See the Spirit of God descending all around. And though for a season your expectations have been disappointed; yet this spot is no longer like the *Mountains of Gilboa on which there was neither rain nor dew.* The clouds have gone over and they have covered us with awful solemnity; and you hear the sound of *abundance of rain.* Your own neighbors and acquaintances are now becoming anxious for their souls. In deep distress they have sought and, as they humbly hope, have recently found the Saviour. Some parents and heads of families have adopted the resolution; whatever may oppose: *As for me and my house, we will serve the Lord.* They have commenced the worship of God in their families. Your very neighbors are taken. Ye prayerless families—take warning. The Lord is *near. Now* this is your time. Call ye upon him while he is *near.*

Perhaps he has come into your own family. He has taken your partner—your own bosom companion has felt the convicting and sanctifying influences of his Spirit. God has come near to you. You may now fear that, *One shall be taken, and the other left,* yet these fears are not without foundation*...

some of them think that they have found Christ and become a subject of divine grace. How do these things affect you?

Your children are anxious for your salvation. No doubt they are frequently on their knees praying for *your* souls, and will you not *pray* for yourselves? God has come near to you.—*Call ye upon him while he is near.* A brother, a sister or some particular friend of yours is taken. And are you willing to be left? Because your friend will attend to the concerns of the soul, will you forsake them?*...

In all which you hear God proclaiming See*k ye the Lord while he may be found, call ye upon him while he is near.* My hearers, if under these circumstances you will not *seek the Lord;* when will you?— Will you do it when the present revival is over, and none are inquiring: *What must I do to be saved?* Will you when all around you are asleep, and nothing is heard on the subject of religion? Will you when the precious season of youth, and with it all the calls and invitations peculiar to it are over, and gone forever?*...

When the Spirit of God is gone, perhaps never to return, then will you become a Christian? Then will you come *out from the world? Then* will you commence a life of religion, endure the shame, and bear the reproach of a frowning world *alone?* If you are not prepared for all this, then begin a life of religion *now.*

But do you intend to become a subject of the present revival? If so, you must make haste; for the revival is far advanced already.

> "Soon will the harvest close—
> The summer soon be o'er—
> And soon your injured, angry God
> Will hear your prayer no more."

* The final four pages of this sermon are torn, with subsequent loss of about half of each of the pages. Rather than not print the sermon, we have chosen to make this notation and print what is readable.

8

Genuine Repentance Does Not Precede Regeneration

Surely after that I was turned, I repented (Jeremiah 31:19).

Israel had departed from God. In this chapter his restoration is predicted, and the happy effects which would follow described. *They shall come and sing in the height of Zion, and shall flow together for the goodness of the Lord; and their soul shall be as a watered garden; and they shall not sorrow any more at all.*

But this happy season was to be preceded by deep repentance. In the description of the Prophet we behold a vast company assembled, and commencing their journey up to Zion. *Thus saith the Lord; they shall come with weeping, and with supplications will I lead them.* The repentance of Ephraim, a name which here stands for the people at large is thus further described.—In the conviction and conversion of one, we see a specimen of the whole. *I have surely heard Ephraim bemoaning himself thus; Thou hast chastised me, and I was chastised as a bullock, unaccustomed to the yoke: turn thou me, and I shall be turned; for thou art the Lord my God. Surely after that I was turned, I repented; and after that I was instructed, I smote upon my thigh: I was ashamed, yea, even confounded, because I did bear the reproach of my youth.*

In this account, we have, what is commonly called a state of conviction. God had taken him in hand. *Thou hast chastised me, and I was chastised.* But he would not yield, His heart was too proud, and too stubborn to bow. His conduct, he tells us was like that of a bullock unaccustomed to the yoke—wild, unmanageable, and determined not to yield to the hand of its master.

His opposition is so great, he is convinced that he shall never overcome it. In this great work, he shall never assist in any other manner than as a rebel would help his antagonist to subdue himself. The conversion of a sinner like himself, he is convinced, could never be effected by the power of mere moral suasion. No finite power could do it. None but the God that made him, can manage the sinner.

Under conviction of this truth, you hear him say: *Turn thou me, and I shall be turned; for thou art the Lord my God.* He then states what follows: *Surely after that I was turned, I repented; and after that I was instructed, I smote upon my thigh: I was ashamed, yea, even confounded, because I did bear the reproach of my youth.*

His conversion was followed not only with a change of feeling, but with a change of sentiment.—*After that I was instructed.*—When he saw clearly his past conduct, his sins, his stubbornness, and where the difficulty lay, he was perfectly astonished. *I smote upon my thigh.* It is possible! How could I be so stubborn! *I was ashamed, yea, even confounded.* What is here said is true of every sinner who is brought to true repentance. From the words of our text we derive this doctrine, that

Genuine repentance does not precede regeneration. *Surely after that I was turned, I repented.*

Here it may be proper to state that there are two kinds of repentance. One arising from the fear of punishment, and dread of consequences; without either love to God or hatred to sin. Such was the repentance of Saul, of Judas, and others. Such is the repentance of awakened sinners, and all sinners in a greater or less degree. There may be great distress, many tears, and awful forebodings of a guilty conscience in the unregenerate. This may, and generally does precede regeneration. But this is not godly sorrow. *Godly sorrow worketh repentance unto salvation not to be repented of: but the sorrow of the world worketh death.*

There is a kind of repentance which always precedes regeneration, but it is not the repentance which the gospel requires. That repentance which implies no love to God, and no hatred to sin, and nothing but terror and dismay is not commanded. But that repentance which God commands, and which ministers are bound to preach includes both.

That this repentance does not precede regeneration is evident from the following considerations.

1. From the nature of true repentance. This repentance implies love to God. Sin is committed against God, and so the sinner is to exercise *repentance towards God.* This cannot be done without love. And before regeneration there is no love to God. For it is written, *Every one that loves is born of God. A crown of life is promised to them that love him.* But none can have this promise without regeneration; and therefore love to God cannot exist without regeneration. No one feels heartily sorry that he has offended a being whom he does not love. Much less does he sorrow that he has offended a being whom he hates. But all the unregenerate possess carnal minds; *And the carnal mind is enmity against God.*

Genuine gospel repentance flows only from a heart melted into love to God.—*Against thee and thee only have I sinned.*—*Father, I* have sinned against heaven, and in thy sight, is the language of the true penitent.

This repentance implies love to God's law. Sin is a transgression of the law. No one feels sorrow that he has broken a law which he does not love; much less a law which he hates. But the *carnal,* or unrenewed *mind is not subject to the law of God, neither indeed can be.* If then evangelical repentance implies love to God and love to his law, it is not an exercise of a *carnal,* unrenewed heart; for that is *enmity against God, not subject to his law, neither indeed can be.*

2. Repentance has the promise of salvation. *Blessed are they that mourn, for they shall be comforted. The Lord is nigh unto them that are of a broken heart, and saveth such as be of a contrite spirit (Psalm 34:14).* But this cannot be said of any before regeneration. *For except a man be born again, he cannot see the kingdom of God. The sacrifices of God are a broken spirit: a broken and a contrite heart, O God, thou wilt not despise (Psalm 51:17). For thus saith the high and lofty one that inhabiteth eternity, whose name is Holy; I dwell in the high and holy place, with him also that is of a contrite and humble spirit, to revive the spirit of the humble, and to revive the heart of the contrite ones (Isaiah 57:15; also 66:1, 2).*

But this cannot be said of a natural man; *For they that are in the flesh cannot please God.* But repentance is pleasing to God, and has the promise of salvation. If the sinner does repent before he is regenerated, then, they that are in the flesh *can* please God. But the Apostle says they *cannot please him.* A promise of salvation is annexed to repentance; If then he can have the promise of salvation before regeneration, he can be actually saved without it; which our Saviour declares impossible.

If the sinner can exercise repentance without a new heart, so he can every other Christian grace. He can love God, and believe in Christ without a new heart, as well as repent of sin. Regeneration is no more necessary to prepare the sinner to love God aright than it is to repent aright, for without love there is no true repentance.

If he can repent without a new heart, he can exercise faith without a new heart. But that faith which does not imply love is not genuine. *For in Jesus Christ neither circumcision availeth any thing, nor uncircumcision; but faith which worketh by love.* It is no easier to repent aright than it is to exercise faith; for that repentance which is without faith cannot be accepted. *For without faith it is impossible to please him.*

And then it will follow,

4. That regeneration would not be necessary. For if the sinner can

love God and perform all the duties of religion without regeneration, this is all that is necessary to fit him for heaven. Now it is believed that sinners do not love God and the duties of religion, and therefore regeneration is necessary. But if the Christian graces may take place without regeneration, then the ground of this necessity is entirely destroyed. There is no room for such a work. The power of God would not be necessary. For the work is done, and no change is necessary.

That repentance does not precede regeneration will appear from the *nature of regeneration.* View it in connection with repentance. The change in regeneration is expressed by *taking away the heart of stone and giving an heart of flesh. I will take away the stony heart out of your flesh, and I will give you an heart of flesh.* From this it appears that regeneration is the act of taking away a *hard* and *stony heart.* Now, my hearers, this cannot be a penitent heart. If repentance does take place *before* regeneration then the heart of stone is not there. A penitent heart is not a *heart of stone; it is a broken, and a contrite heart.* And God never takes away such a heart. If repentance does precede regeneration it must be the repentance of a *hard* and *stony heart.* This, when compared with the idea of true repentance, would be a contradiction in terms, the repentance of a *heart of stone.—And I will give you an heart of flesh.* This is a broken and contrite heart, a heart susceptible of feeling. It is a penitent heart.

When God *takes away the heart of stone and gives an heart of flesh*—that is regeneration. *When God takes away the heart of stone and gives an heart of flesh* — Then God *grants repentance.* A new heart is a penitent heart. Regeneration is necessary because sinners have hard, impenitent hearts. And this is the glorious effect of the power of God in the act of regeneration. It reduces the rebel into submission. It melts the stubborn heart into repentance. When God regenerates and grants repentance, he does it by *one decisive act.*

Thus I consider the point established, that evangelical repentance does not precede regeneration.

But, by the way, I would remark, that I have not asserted that the sinner is not under obligations to repent before regeneration. That it is not the *duty* of the sinner to repent before God changes his heart, that we have not asserted. It *is* his duty. The question has not been "what is duty?" but what is the fact?

It is the duty of sinners to do many things which they never have done, and perhaps never will do. It is their duty to stop sinning, and to *love God with all the heart, soul, mind, and strength.* This is their duty. And so is it their duty to repent, without delay, but they have never done it, and some never will do it.

By this time, my hearers will perceive a great difficulty in our subject. It is this: If sinners do not repent before regeneration, then you call upon them to do what needs almighty power to accomplish. This difficulty is not peculiar to this text, or to this subject alone. It is the same difficulty which runs through almost every subject which concerns our salvation.

There are many who think they see a great inconsistency and absurdity running through almost every discourse which they hear. "Ministers contradict themselves, they say, and unsay; they tell us to do, and then tell us that we cannot do." This difficulty some of our hearers see and state for themselves; others think they see it, but cannot state it. This difficulty I am calculating to state in all its absurdity, "You sometimes call upon sinners to believe and repent; and then tell them that faith and repentance are the gift of God. You call upon them to do what needs almighty power to effect." My hearers, this is correct. We are guilty of all this absurdity; and the Bible talks just so too.

But further: "We sometimes hear ministers in one discourse inviting sinners and calling upon them to *come to Christ;* and then they will turn about and contradict the whole, by telling them that they *cannot come.*" And what think you of such absurdity, my hearers? What think ye of such preachers?

That some have been guilty of this absurdity we do not, we cannot deny. Your charge is well founded. We dare not contradict it. I well recollect an instance of this kind. A celebrated preacher in one of his discourses once used these words: *Come unto me, all ye that labor and are heavy laden, and I will give you rest (Matthew 11:28).* And then this same preacher in another discourse used this expression: *No man can come to me, except the Father which hath sent me draw him (John 6:44).*

Now what think you, my hearers, of such preaching and of such a preacher? What would you have said had you been present and heard it? Would you have charged him with contradicting himself? But so it was; this great preacher in one of his discourses did say, *Come unto me, all ye that labor and are heavy laden, and I will give you rest,* and in another, *No man can come to me, except the Father which sent me draw him.* And I have no doubt that others have since adopted the same expressions. This preacher, you will remember was none other than the Lord Jesus Christ. And I have no doubt that many ministers have since followed the same example of their

The Second Great Awakening

divine master. And have therefore been guilty of the same absurdity, if such you would call it.

Now, my hearers, which will you do? Will you say that the difficulty can easily be explained, and that Christ is guilty of no absurdity? If you can explain the difficulty in Christ's preaching; then you can explain it with respect to all subsequent preachers. The same explanation which would relieve his preaching from all difficulty; with a little candor would do it in all similar cases. Will you adopt this course and say all is well? Or will you boldly assert that Christ is absurd, and that he contradicted himself? Then you turn infidel at once. You enter the lists with the Son of God, and boldly renounce divine revelation.

Or will you say, I believe that the Bible is the word of God, and that Christ is consistent with himself, whether I can see *how* to reconcile this difficulty or not? I wish you to remember that this difficulty existed in our Saviour's preaching. Nor is it peculiar to a few texts only; the same difficulty runs through the Bible.

This I will now state more at large: The Bible does call upon sinners to repent; and yet considers repentance as the gift of God.

John, the harbinger of Christ, came preaching, and saying: *Repent ye: for the kingdom of heaven is at hand (Matthew 3:2). From that time Jesus began to preach and to say, Repent: for the kingdom of heaven is at hand (Matthew 4:17).* And the Apostles *went out and preached that men should repent (Mark 6:12). God commendeth all men everywhere to repent (Acts 17:30).*

On the other hand repentance is the gift of God. *Then Peter and the apostles answered and said—Him hath God exalted with his right hand to be a Prince and a Saviour, for to give repentance to Israel, and forgiveness of sins (Acts 5:31).* The disciples with one voice *glorified God, saying, Then hath God also to the Gentiles granted repentance unto life (Acts 11:18). In meekness instructing those that oppose themselves; if God peradventure will give them repentance to the acknowledging of the truth (II Timothy 2:25).*

Thus you see, John the Baptist, Christ, and his Apostles, and God himself urged the duty of immediate repentance. And on the other hand they ascribe it wholly to God.

Again—The Bible calls upon sinners to believe in Christ; and yet, considers faith as the gift of God. *Repent ye, and believe the gospel (Mark 1:15). Believe on the Lord Jesus Christ, and thou shalt be saved (Acts 16:31). And this is his commandment, That we should believe on the name of his Son Jesus Christ (I John 3:23).*

On the other hand; faith is the gift of God. *Unto you it is given in* the behalf of Christ, not only to believe on him, but also to suffer for his sake (Philippians 1:29). *For by grace are ye saved through faith; and that not of yourselves: it is the gift of God (Ephesians 2:8); Jesus the Author and the finisher of our faith (Hebrews 12:2). That ye may know what is the exceeding greatness of his power to usward who believe, according to the working of his mighty power, which he wrought in Christ, when he raised him from the dead (Ephesians 1:19).* Here you see, sinners are commanded to believe, and threatened with eternal death if they do not do it. And faith is wrought only by the mighty power of God.

Again: Sinners are represented as being *dead in trespasses and sins (Ephesians 2:1).* We know that we have passed from death unto life; because we love the brethren (I John 3:14). *I know thy works, that thou hast a name that thou livest, and art dead (Revelation 3:1).*

In this situation God commands them to *live. For I have no pleasure in the death of him that dieth, saith the Lord God: wherefore turn yourselves, and live ye (Ezekiel 18:32).* This is the command of God. *Wherefore he saith, Awake thou that sleepest, and arise from the dead, and Christ shall give thee light (Ephesians 5:14).*

On the other hand, the effect is attributed wholly to God. *You hath he quickened, who were dead in trespasses and sins. The Son quickeneth whom he will. The hour is coming, and now is when the dead shall hear the voice of the Son of God, and they that hear shall live.* Again: *A new heart also will I give you, and a new spirit will I put within you: and I will take away the stony heart out of your flesh, and I will give you an heart of flesh (Ezekiel 36:26).*

But on the other hand, God commands the sinner to make a new heart. *Cast away from you all your transgressions, whereby you have transgressed; and make you a new heart and a new spirit: for why will ye die, O house of Israel? (Ezekiel 18:31).*

Again: Sinners are represented as departing from God. And thus God calls, *Turn ye at my reproof (Proverbs 1:23). Turn ye; turn ye, for why will ye die.* Thus saith the Lord, *Repent and turn yourselves from all your transgressions; so iniquity shall not be your ruin (Ezekiel 18:30). Thus saith the Lord God; wherefore turn yourselves and live ye.*

On the other hand, the Bible ascribes this work wholly to God. *Turn thou me, and I shall be turned, for thou art the Lord my God.* And again, in our text; *Surely after that I was turned, I repented.*

In all these passages you see that the Bible calls upon sinners to do what he needs almighty power to accomplish. Now whether I am able to explain this difficulty or not, it is the language of the Bible, I wish you to remember. You have seen that God does command sinners to *repent,* and *believe,* and *make a new heart,* and *arise from the dead.* And those ministers who do not, in his name, call upon them to do the same, do not preach as God has commanded them. You have seen that *repentance,* and *faith,* and a *new heart* are all the gift of God. And whoever does not attribute them wholly to God robs him of his glory, and does not preach the Bible.

Whoever preaches, and is not guilty of all this absurdity, does not declare *all the counsel of God.* Whether he can explain these difficulties or not, every minister is bound to preach in this manner. If he does not call upon sinners to *do all these things;* and when done, if he does not *ascribe the whole to God,* he does not preach the gospel.

I wish my hearers to bear this continually in mind. That whether I am able to explain this difficulty or not, yet I am bound to preach it. I shall take it for granted that all my hearers believe the Bible to be the word of God. And if I should not succeed in explaining these passages to your satisfaction, the difficulty in reconciling these texts lies equally against all who believe the Bible.

This then is the question before us: How can it be proper for the Bible to command sinners to do what needs Almighty power to do for them?—Many methods have been adopted to obviate this difficulty. One says: You must do as well as you can without a new heart, but you must *try* to repent—*try* to love God and the like. But I answer: The Bible says no such thing. God nowhere commands sinners to *try* to repent—to *try* to love him. But: *God now commands all men everywhere to repent.* Nowhere does it say, *thou shalt try to love the Lord thy God,* but it does say, *Thou shalt love the Lord thy God with all thy heart.* This is what God commands. And the sinner *trying* to repent and love God if he does not do it, amounts to nothing. He does not obey the command.—However hard the sinner may labor and toil; yet if he does not repent and love him, he does *nothing* in the sight of God. After all that he has done, he is still threatened with eternal death, as the consequence of his neglect.

It is sometimes said, "That faith is the gift of God, and you must do as well as you can without it." But what says the Bible to one who does not ask in faith? Does it encourage him to ask without? The Bible answers: *Let not that man think that he shall receive anything of the Lord (James 1:7).* But faith and repentance and love to God are duties which the Bible enjoins; and which every minister is to urge on all his hearers. If he does not preach *faith,* and *repentance,* and *love to God,* he does not preach the gospel, nor urge them to do anything which God regards. Do as well as you can without faith? How will he ever exhort to these duties? Will he exhort the sinner to believe *without faith*—to repent without repentance, and to love God without loving him?

How, on this ground, would an exhortation exhort the sinner to do these duties as well as he can without doing them at all; or say nothing on the subject? In order to settle the difficulty it may be proper to inquire, Why is the power to God necessary to change the heart of the sinner? And to this question there are but two answers: Either because the sinner is *unable,* or because he is *unwilling* to do what God commands.

Let us examine the first. By being unable, I mean just what the sinner means: "That he would if he could, but he cannot." Let us proceed on this ground, and what then? Is the sinner not to blame? If God is really such a being as to command the sinner to do what is in every sense impossible for him to do: Is there any ground for that ease which thousands feel when they plead this excuse? If God commands, and will punish the sinner for not obeying, what can be done? If this be the character of God, the sinner who is in his hand is in an awful condition indeed.

Let us advance on the sinner's own supposition. Is this the character of God and are you in his hands, does it become you to oppose and quarrel with Omnipotence? Whatever his character may be, it becomes feeble worms to beware how they contend with God. Do you believe what you say, "that you would if you could, but you cannot obey the commands of God?" Do you verily believe that you are in the hands of such a being; and can you remain at ease? My fellow sinner: Do you still plead that this is your inability? And will you still allow that God is just and righteous in commanding and punishing you for not doing what you cannot do?

Let us try your own sentiment, for if indeed you cannot believe, or repent or make a new heart, I dare not deny the justice of God in your punishment. I acknowledge that God may be just though he has made it impossible for sinners to be saved. Grant that God has made no atonement for some sinners, and yet I frankly own that I can see no injustice here. He has made no atonement for the fallen angels; and yet they have no right to complain. God has made it impossible for them to be saved—*he has reserved them in everlasting chains unto the judgment of the great day.* And still they have no right to complain. Suppose he had done the same by all or any part of the human race, not one would have had any reason to complain. I dare not object even to a limited atonement on the ground of justice.

Suppose God had made an atonement and made it sufficient only for one single soul, and all the rest had been consigned over to endless perdition, yet I can see no injustice in this.

The sinner often pleads his inability as an excuse. Call upon him to attend to the duties of religion, and he will tell you: *faith, and repentance, and a new heart are the gift of God; and what can I do?* This he intends for an excuse,

Grant the sinner his own plea. Grant that God has made it absolutely impossible for him to *repent, and believe, and be saved,* and what then? What right have you to complain? Suppose a sinner has been guilty of a breach of the laws of this state, that he has been guilty of murder, and is committed to prison, bolted and barred. The criminal walks around by the walls, murmuring and complaining that he cannot get out, "that he would if he could, but he cannot." We ask, what then; what if he cannot make his escape?—Why then he must suffer the penalty of a good law. He suffers no injustice—he has no right to complain; unless he can make it appear that he is innocent, he deserves death.

Now suppose the sinner cannot repent, believe, and be pardoned and saved. What then? Why, then he must be lost; awful indeed! What if the sinner is forever lost? No injustice is done. He suffers the penalty of a good law, and that is all. The sinner has broken the divine law. *Cursed is every one that continueth not in all things which are written in the book of the law to do them* is the sentence of that law. And no reason can be given why this sentence should not be executed. Now unless the sinner can make it appear that he has never in all this lifetime committed one single sin, he has no reason to complain if God has made his pardon and salvation impossible.

There is a strange disposition in the human heart to murmur and complain of God because he is just. The sinner thinks it hard and cruel if God will not allow him the privilege of sinning and rebelling against him. And in addition to this he feels as though God was bound to make him repent and love him. And not only so, but if he should stop sinning and begin to love God now; he feels as though God could not in justice ever punish him for one of his past sins. O, what a demand does the sinner make on God! And yet he will not allow that God, can in justice, make any claims upon him. If the sinner cannot repent and believe and love God, he is certainly in an awful condition.

But though I do not allow that you are under any natural inability to repent and be saved, yet I confess I can see no injustice were you to be placed in this awful condition. And I wish you to remember that what you now complain of may very soon be real. Unless you do soon repent and believe, the very thing of which you now complain, you will be obliged to feel. Very shortly, my fellow sinner, you will be beyond the reach of hope. God will by and by make it impossible for you to come out of your prison. This is the case with all in the prison of hell. There they are fastened, and they cannot get out. And it is a wonder of mercy that you are not now there. When you get there, you will have no reason to murmur and complain *that you would if you could, but you cannot get out of the prison of hell.* The great gulf will be fixed, so that, they which would pass from hence *cannot.* This is the condition in which all the finally impenitent will remain forever. And the sinner who is now out of Christ is every moment in awful danger of sinking into the same condition.

But this instance of a criminal bolted and barred and surrounded by the massy walls of a prison I do not admit to be a correct illustration of the state of the sinner. Though the finally impenitent will be forever shut up in this prison, yet this is not the case with sinners on earth. Though I can see no injustice in God's making it impossible for sinners on earth to come out of their prison and be saved; yet there is one point in which this illustration will not hold.

If the prisoner were to be invited and commanded to come out of his prison, while the doors were shut, and bolted, and barred; I confess I can see no propriety in such invitations and commands. The very fact that God does invite, and command sinners to come to Christ is, to me, a convincing proof that the difficulty lies only in the sinner's will. If the sinner were willing to do all in his power, that is the point where common sense would direct us to stop urging him.

This single command, *Turn ye to the strong hold, ye prisoners of hope* is to me a convincing proof that all the bolts and bars of his prison are now removed. Christ has opened the doors of his prison and proclaimed liberty to the captives. God does not command the sinner to break through bolts and bars and massy walls. But this is the case with all who deny the distinction between natural and moral inability. They call upon the sinner to do what they themselves acknowledge absolutely impossible. This I do not admit.

Again—If the prisoner were to be confined and punished without reprieve for all his past sins, that would be perfectly just, and right. Every friend to good government must heartily acquiesce. But if the prisoner were commanded to break through bolts, and bars, and massy walls, and then in addition to all his past crimes were to suffer tenfold punishment for not doing it; I confess I do not see the justice of it.

But it is acknowledged on all hands that those who perish from under the light of the gospel will suffer an aggravated weight of condemnation. It shall be more tolerable for Sodom in the day of judgment than for such sinners. *Of how much sorer punishment shall he be thought worthy, who hath trodden under foot the Son of God. If I had not come and spoken unto them, they had not had sin.* Now the reason why God *invites* sinners to come out of their prison is not because they cannot; but because they will not. The reason why he *commands* them to do it, is not because they cannot but because they will not. The reason why they are to be punished in such an awful manner for not doing it, is not because they cannot, but because they will not. Unwillingness always makes it proper to invite and command. The will and nothing else is the object of command. This and nothing else is the ground of punishment.

Now God does certainly treat the sinner in all respects as though the difficulty was a criminal difficulty. He does treat them in all respects just as he would on the supposition that they were unwilling to do what they could. It is surprising with what little ceremony the Bible treats the inability, and all the excuses of sinners. I believe every one of my hearers must have been struck with this fact. The Bible commands the sinner to remove the difficulty. To *repent, and believe, and make a new heart.* It commands and condemns without ceremony if he does not do it. The Bible speaks just as freely as though it was every whit unwillingness

I will now state what appears to me to be the real difficulty. *The sinner will not do what he can.* I know this is denied by many. They reason in this way—That because the Bible everywhere attributes this change to God; therefore the sinner cannot do it. It is said that if the sinner could produce this change himself, then the power of God would not be necessary.

But this reasoning will not hold. Because the sinner has power to do what God commands, it does not follow of course that the sinner will exert that power. You will easily see that those who adopt this reasoning take it for granted that the sinner will certainly do the utmost in his power to obey God. But if the sinner will not do what he can, there is the same necessity of almighty power to make him willing to do what he *can,* as there would be to make him willing to do, or, rather, do for him what he could not.

This point is illustrated as follows: Here is a child which has departed from his father; He calls upon him to return to him. He has power to run every way; but he will not return to his father. He invites; but no invitation is sufficient. He threatens; but no punishment is sufficient to make the child willing to do what he can.

Now what is the duty of that child? Common sense declares that it is his duty to obey the command. But the child is unwilling. Now does this unwillingness make it improper for the parent to invite, entreat, and command the child to do what he can? If the child *would,* but could not obey the command, I could see no propriety in the parent's conduct. But if the child can, and will not; his unwillingness is no excuse. His unwillingness is the very thing which makes it proper to command. This unwillingness is the very thing for which he deserves punishment. This is plain common sense.

But, says the parent, "I will reveal one secret. You know not how dreadfully stubborn that child is. Though my commands are reasonable, and the child can if he would, yet he is so opposed to me that he never will do what he can. He never will come unless I go and bring him." Here the child replies, "How absurd you talk; You call upon me to do what you say I never will do unless you make me do it." But because he is so wicked that he never will do what he can, he stands murmuring, "What a cruel parent. Now I cannot come, how can I? What a cruel parent! He calls upon me to do what I never shall do: and how can I be blamed?" My heavens, what answer would you make to that child?

This, in my view, is exactly the state of the sinner. Whether we think it a just comparison or not, God does. He says *I have nourished and brought up children, but they have rebelled against me.* All have departed from God and he invites, and entreats, and commands them to return. *Turn ye at my reproof—Turn ye, Turn ye, for why will ye die?* Now what is the duty of sinners? Why it is their duty to obey the commands of God.

Now suppose God to reveal this fact. That the sinner is so opposed to me that he never will do what I command him. I believe all will allow that this is the fact with all who have lost their souls. If so, then it may be with sinners now living, that they never will do what they can. When in hell all acknowledge it again. Does the unwillingness to do what he can make it improper for God to invite and command and punish? Unwillingness in the case of the child is the very reason why every parent would invite, command, and threaten, and punish. In that case, no one but the child would ever think of complaining. And has not God a right to deal with us in the same manner as we deal with others? Yes; you will say, provided I were equally stubborn with that child. There lies the difficulty, my hearers, you cannot believe that you are so wicked that you will not do what you can.

But it is possible that stubbornness in the heart even of a little child might rise beyond the power of mere moral suasion. It is possible that it might rise to such a pitch that no invitations, commands, or threatenings of the parent would overcome it. Unwillingness might arise to such a pitch in the heart even of a little child that it might be necessary for the parent to go and turn him by the strength of his arm. If there may be such stubbornness in the heart even of a little child; or rather, since there is such stubbornness in his heart, that he will not do what he can, though urged by his parent whom he loves with all his natural affection, then is it not possible that the sinner may be so stubborn in the sight of God? God does make the comparison. And do you believe that you are less wicked than a little child?

If this is possible—then it may be possible for sinners to continue for years to hear the invitations, commands, and threatenings of the gospel and never do what they can. Now the only reason why the parent's arm is necessary to turn the child is because it is so wicked that it will not do what it can. If it were willing to do what it could, nothing *special* on the part of the parent would be necessary. Just so I view the state of the sinner. They will never do what he can—And that will always make it proper to call upon them to do it.

On a dying bed confess it—why would one wish to recover if they are not conscious that they have not done what could. Amidst this mountain of evidence we can summon the conscience of the dying sinner. If you hear any one find fault, you may take it for granted that he understands the subject. Ask him to explain these passages and to give a better interpretation.

1. Reasonableness of the command to make a new heart. Every time they (are) command(ed) to love God, repent, or believe, (they) are commanded to make a new heart.

2. Saved wholly by grace. If not repent certainly does nothing which influences God to give a new heart. So we read—*They that are in the flesh cannot please God.* It will take up a whole eternity to praise him for his grace.

3. A reason why Christians should pray for sinners. Sinners will never do what they could do. All hangs on the mere sovereign pleasure of God.

9

Discerning Between the Righteous and the Wicked

Then shall ye return, and discern between the righteous and the wicked, between him that serveth God and him that serveth him not (Malachi 3:18).

The distinction between the righteous and the wicked in this world has by some been denied. This distinction, it has been said, is without foundation. Thus it was among the Jews in the time of Malachi. There were many who spent much time in talking on the subject. While others were assembling for religious purposes, they spent their time in talking against it. These the prophet intimates would band together and exert their wicked influence. To these the Lord has said in the context *You have been stout against me, saith the Lord. Yet ye say, what have we spoken so much against thee?* But this charge they would not admit. They had said nothing against God. *What have we spoken so much against thee?* say they. The Lord answers: *Ye have said, it is in vain to serve God: and what profit is it that we have walked mournfully before the Lord of hosts? And now we call the proud happy: yea, they that work wickedness are set up; yea, they that tempt God are even delivered.* This is what they said. The prophet adds, *Then they that feared the Lord spake often one to another: and the Lord harkened, and heard it, and a book of remembrance was written before him for them that feared the Lord, and that thought upon his name. And they shall be mine, saith the Lord of hosts, in that day when I make up my jewels; and I will spare them, as a man spareth his own son that serveth him. Then shall ye return, and discern between the righteous and the wicked, between him that serveth God and him that serveth him not.*

But notwithstanding this difference is not now discerned and acknowledged, the Prophet assures us that the day is at hand when it will be easy to discern it. The day is coming when they will return to their reason on this subject. That is the day when he will make up his jewels; it is the day of judgment. *Then shall ye return and discern between the righteous and the wicked, between him that serveth God and him that serveth him not,* the Prophet then adds as a reason: *For, behold, the day cometh, that shall burn as an oven; and all the proud, yea, and all that do wickedly, shall be stubble.*

I propose to consider the following heads,

The Second Great Awakening

I. In this world it is sometimes difficult to discern between the righteous and the wicked.

II. At the day of judgment this distinction will be easily discerned.

I. As above, Divine providence does not always make a visible distinction. The wicked are often in great prosperity. *Wherefore do the wicked live, become old, yea, are mighty in power? Their houses are kept safe from fear, neither is the rod of God upon them.* And says David, *I was envious of the foolish, when I saw the prosperity of the wicked. For there are no bands in their death: but their strength is firm. They are not in trouble as other men; neither are they plagued like other men. Their eyes stand out with fatness: they have more than heart could wish. Behold these are the ungodly, who prosper in the world. When the wicked spring as the grass, and when all workers of iniquity do flourish; it is that they shall be destroyed forever.*

Piety is often found in the deepest poverty. *Hearken, my beloved brethren,* saith the Apostle, *Hath not God chosen the poor of this world rich in faith, and heirs of the kingdom which he hath promised to them that love him? The Son of Man had nowhere to lay his head.*

Virtue is sometimes found in irons while vice is exalted on a throne. The vilest wretches on earth have often been the most secure and free from human punishment. The reigns of human government are often held by the greatest enemies to Christianity. From the time of Christ down to the sixteenth century, no vice or wickedness whatever was punished with so great severity as Christianity itself. Many of these persecutors have at the same time, professed the Christian religion. Persecution and persecuted have both claimed God was on their side!

In the primitive ages of Christianity, Christians were charged with the worst of crimes and then put to death as malefactors. The Jews claimed that they were doing their duty in putting Christ to death. *For a good work we stone thee not. We have a law, and by our law he ought to die.* It was the popular opinion which sounded through the streets of Jerusalem. The multitude went *crying out that he ought not to live any longer. Yea, the time cometh,* saith our Saviour, *that whoever killeth you, will think that he doeth God service (John 16:2).*

When Stephen was put to death, the persecuting Saul *gave his voice against him.* It was no doubt the declared opinion of thousands that he ought to die, for the force of his reasoning and the power of his eloquence could be conquered in no other way. It is always to be remembered that those who are violently opposed or persecuted are never allowed to be good men. This allowance cannot be made without self-incrimination. Here is no distinction between the *righteous and the wicked, between him that serveth God and him that serveth him not.*

St. Paul was taken up by those who were peacemakers and determined to preserve the public order. Say they, *We have found this man a pestilent fellow, and a mover of sedition among all the Jews throughout the world, and a ringleader of the sect of the Nazarenes.* Whenever the Apostles entered a place, it was the general cry, *These that have turned the world upside down are come thither also.* They seemed to suffer in almost exact proportion to their labor and their faithfulness. *For therefore we both labor and suffer reproach, because we trust in the living God (I Timothy 4:10). They were a spectacle to the world, to Angels, and to men.* It was their language: *We are made as the filth of the world, and are the offscourge of all things unto this day.* Though it could not be said in behalf of all, yet thousands who joined in the cry against the Apostles, from what they had heard, would be sincere. They would think from the bottom of their hearts that the Apostles were very bad men; and were there no judgment to come, that opinion would never be corrected.

The glorious reformation from papacy was considered as a great calamity by millions. None have taken a more active part in this work than Wycliffe, Luther, Melancthon, and Calvin. And by the great body of the Protestant world, these men have ever been considered as the pious servants of the *most high God.* On the other hand, their characters have been traduced by the whole body of the Romish church as the greatest villains that ever lived. During this reformation thousands have suffered the most cruel martyrdom. All these claimed that they were suffering in the cause of Christ. On the other hand, their persecutors attributed the whole of their conduct to obstinacy, hardness, and wickedness of heart.

In 1572 more than 30,000 Protestants: men, women, and children were butchered in France, within the compass of a few days. The manner in which this news was received at Rome is wonderful. It was immediately decreed that the Pope should march with his cardinals to the church of St. Mark; and in the most solemn manner give thanks to God for so great a blessing conferred on Rome and the Christian world.—It was decreed that a jubilee should be published throughout the whole Christian world, and the cause of it declared to be to render thanks to God for the extinction of the enemies of the truth and church in France. In the evening the whole

The Second Great Awakening

city of St. Angelos was illuminated, and the cannons were fired to testify the public joy.

This and still more was done to give thanks to God that 30,000 whom we call Christians, and they called the enemies of God, were sent into the eternal world. Persecutors and persecuted both claim the God of heaven and the Lord Jesus Christ on their side. Here we do not alike discern and acknowledge the difference between the *righteous and the wicked, between him that serveth God and him that serveth him not.*

In still later times the celebrated Whitefield appeared and set the world on fire wherever he went. Thousands were pricked in their hearts under his preaching and cried out: *What must I do to be saved?* Thousands of these, some of whom are yet seen tottering on the borders of the grave, have pointed to Whitefield as the messenger of God to their souls. On the other hand, thousands were found, some of whom are yet living, who treated him as the greatest villain, and his followers as a set of deluded mortals. *To discern between the righteous and the wicked, between him that serveth God and him that serveth him not,* is reserved for a future day.

And at the present day many are laboring and thousands are praying day and night for the outpouring of God's Spirit, and for what are called revivals of religion. This work has been rapidly increasing in hundreds and thousands of places within a few years past. And thousands give thanks to God and pray day and night that it might spread and fill the whole earth.

On the other hand, many treat revivals, conferences, prayer meetings, sudden conversion, and regeneration with the utmost contempt. More zeal is manifested against them, than against any vice that could be named. Those who preach and pray that this work may go on, feel as though they were engaged in the cause of God; all who speak or write against it may claim that they too are laboring in the cause of God.

Those who think they have experienced religion, it is often said, are no better than others. They see no difference between one man and another, and therefore they will acknowledge none. Many will acknowledge no difference between the righteous and the wicked and therefore they discern none.

But there are real difficulties. To discern between the righteous and the wicked may in some cases be really difficult. Such are the following,

Wicked men may put on the appearance of real Christians. Many whom we really think are Christians, who appear to us to serve God in sincerity, will finally be lost. Many who profess religion are never called to suffer in the cause of Christ, and their hearts are never tried in this world. Many are accounted Christians because they never say or do anything to rouse the enmity of the human heart. They avoid opposition by keeping the world on their side. They are careful never to offend the enemies of God, they are still friends to the world, and so the world will count them as good Christians. *If any man will be a friend of the world, he is the enemy of God,* said the Apostle. But real Christians are imperfect, and the imperfection may be such as to obscure the evidence in their favor.

None have ever suffered so much as those who are the most active in the cause of Christ. *Marvel not, my brethren, if the world hate you. If ye were of the world,* said Christ to his disciples, *the world would love his own: but because ye are not of the world, but I have chosen you out of the world, therefore the world hateth you. Yea, and all that will live godly in Christ Jesus shall suffer persecution,* is the declaration of an inspired Apostle.

Now all who do suffer in this manner will certainly be considered as wicked by those from whom they suffer. Not one ever did or ever will own that he is designing to stab the heart of a child of God. It has always been the practice of sinners, not to oppose religion as such, but to load the characters of its professors with contempt, and then it becomes easy. In this manner those who killed the Apostles *thought that they were doing God service.*

Real Christians have all manner of evil spoken against them. Now this was so certain to follow the Apostles that our Saviour pronounced: *Woe unto you, when all men shall speak well of you!* Neither because this is the case does it follow of course that he is a Christian. Men really wicked may endure the same. And this is what renders it so difficult *to discern between the righteous and the wicked.* In view of the world many who are really righteous share the character of the wicked in common. Christ was called *mad, deceiver, glutton, Beelzebub, and a friend of publicans and sinners.* And all real Christians ever since have shared in that honour with their divine master.

Real Christians are sensible of their own vileness—they feel that they never suffer what they deserve, and are far less anxious about the good or bad opinion of others. The Apostle accounted it a very small thing indeed *to be judged by man's judgment.* The Syrophenician woman was glad to be called a *dog,* if she might in that way obtain mercy. David would not attempt to stop the mouth of Shimei. Says the king to his servants, *let him alone, and let him curse—it may be that the Lord will look on mine affliction, and that the Lord will requite me good for his cursing this day.* This is the character of all true Christians, they *glory in the cross of Christ;* and rejoice that they are *accounted worthy to suffer shame for his name.*

In this world vice is often clothed with honor, and virtue is covered with shame and disgrace. And hence it is often difficult to *discern between the righteous and the wicked, between him that serveth God and him that serveth him not.*

But we proceed to consider,

II. That at the day of judgment this distinction will be easily discerned.

When the Lord *shall make up his jewels, and the day cometh that shall burn as an oven,* saith the Prophet: *Then shall ye return and discern between the righteous and the wicked.*

Their bodies will be different. These vile bodies *will be changed that they may be fashioned like unto Christ's glorious body.* The morning of the resurrection will be a glorious morning to the righteous. *They will be like the angels of God in heaven.* They shall *awake, some to everlasting life, and some to shame and everlasting contempt.* It will be easy to discern them at first sight. Their bodies will be so different, one fitted for heaven and the other for hell.

The righteous will be very joyful when they behold their Saviour. But the wicked will *call to the rocks and mountains* to hide them from the face of their judge. And then it will be easy to *discern between the righteous and the wicked.*

When every secret thing shall be brought to light; *whether it be good or bad,* it will then appear that the righteous have all been anxious for their souls—that they have mourned and wept over their sins. How much they have loathed and abhorred themselves. How much time they have spent on their knees in their closets. How much they have prayed for their enemies—How much for the conversion of sinners—and the very persons by whom they have been persecuted.

It will then appear how little the wicked have prayed, and how little they have done for their souls. It will then appear that those very persons who have been loaded with so much infamy have earnestly prayed for the salvation of their persecutors. It will then appear that at the very time that their persecutors were inventing and propagating their slanders, these persons were on their knees, pleading with God to have mercy on their souls. It will appear that the wicked have done little else in religion than stand still and find fault with the righteous. It will then appear that they have spent their time in trying to destroy their very best friends. It will then appear how heartily the righteous have forgiven all these injuries, and prayed and longed for their salvation. When their love to God and Christ and to the souls of men shall appear, and all the exertions which both the righteous and the wicked have made in religion. Then it will be easy to discern the difference of their hearts. The truth and reality of experimental religion will no longer be doubted.

When the judge shall proceed to make the separation, and shall set the sheep on his right hand and the goats on the left, and shall pronounce, *Come ye blessed, and depart ye cursed.* Then it will be easy to *discern between the righteous and the wicked, between him that serveth God and him that serveth him not.*

And now the righteous and the wicked will be seen to differ in their *character, condition, society, and employments forever.*

The character of the *wicked.* Once the blood of Christ was offered to cleanse them from sin. *But now there remaineth no more sacrifice for sin.* That blood hath been *trampled under foot.* The Holy Spirit has once striven to subdue and change the rebellious heart. But he hath *done despite unto the Spirit of grace;* and the Spirit shall strive no more. *He that is filthy shall be filthy still.*

Every restraint shall now be taken off, and every wicked passion take full possession of the soul. Horror and remorse of conscience will seize on the souls of the damned. The recollection of former sins, abused mercies, neglected privileges, will fill the soul with intolerable anguish. This will be *the worm that never dies.* Conscience will be constrained to acquiesce, and do homage to an avenging God. Whether he will or not, conscience will be forced to acknowledge the reasonableness of God's law and the justice of his own condemnation. Conscience will drive the sinner to own that he chose to ward off conviction, to resist the strivings of God's Spirit, and rather than bow to the humbling self-denying duties of religion while on earth, he chose to lie down in eternal sorrows.

But the character of the righteous will be entirely different. Their hearts have been renewed and sanctified. All malice and guile and envy and all evil passions of every kind are laid aside. Then Christian warfare is ended. No sinful thought, or passion, or temptation shall again disturb the peace of the righteous. *They have washed their robes, and made them white in the blood of the Lamb.* Their souls are calm and serene, and nothing can disturb them. They are at peace with God and have peace of conscience. They have great inward joy and peace, are perfectly conformed to God's holy law, and love him with all their souls. Their souls are united and are now one with Christ—They *are filled with all the fullness of God.* They are now like Christ in soul and body. *For when he shall appear, we shall be like him; for we shall see him as he is.* The wicked will resemble the fallen angels, and the righteous will resemble Christ. *Then shall ye discern between the righteous and the wicked.*

They will differ in their *condition.* The condition of the wicked is dreadful beyond description. *And these shall go away into everlasting punishment.* They shall go away from Christ from saints and angels and heaven and all happiness forever. Now shall they see the heaven which they have lost. Now will they compare the mansions of the blessed with the abodes of the damned. The latter are thus described: *darkness, blackness of darkness, fire, lake burning with fire and brimstone,* and *everlasting punishment;* without one drop of water *to cool their tongues.* All this will take place in *the presence of the holy angels, and in the presence of the lamb.*

But O how different the condition of the righteous: *but the righteous into life eternal.* Into mansions of rest—the holy city—the new Jerusalem—*the kingdom prepared for them from the foundation of the world.* One shall rise to heaven and the other sink down to hell. Then it will be easy to discern *between the righteous and the wicked.*

Their *society* will be different. Not a friend will be found in hell.—None but devils and damned spirits. But the society in heaven will be glorious. Now all the righteous will be assembled. They shall come from the east and from the west and from the north and from the south, and shall sit down with angels, patriarchs, prophets, apostles, martyrs, and all holy beings in the kingdom of God. There the wicked cease from troubling, and nothing shall ever enter to disturb or interrupt their joy.

Now will their employments be different. The wicked will begin to weep and wail and gnash their teeth, when they turn to *go away into everlasting punishment.* And now the company of the redeemed will begin to ascend, God has wiped away all tears from their eyes, and there shall be no more death, neither sorrow nor crying, neither shall there be any more pain; for the former things are passed away. The ransomed of the Lord shall return and come to Zion with songs and everlasting joy upon their heads; they shall obtain joy and gladness and sorrow and sighing shall flee away.

O what weeping and wailing when this glorious throng begin to ascend. The divine Redeemer, archangels, cherubim, seraphim, powers, dominions, general assembly, and church of the firstborn, myriads of angels, and saints of all ages, and nations, an unfading crown, a throne of glory, and rivers of pleasure are now clearly seen by the wicked, departing forever. All lost—lost—forever lost. O the boundless mercy of God to those hell-deserving sinners, now ascending to glory. While others sink down to hell, how will those converts exclaim: *Bless the Lord, O my soul; and all that is within me, bless his holy name. Bless the Lord, O my soul, and forget not all of his benefits.* Praise the Lord, call upon his name, declare his doing among the people, make mention that his name is exalted. And I heard as it were the voice of a great multitude, and as the voice of many waters, and as the voice of mighty thunderings, saying, Alleluia: for the Lord God omnipotent reigneth. Let us be glad and rejoice, and give honour to him: for the marriage of the Lamb is come, and his wife hath made herself ready.

Now the righteous shall shine forth as the sun in the kingdom of their Father, and then all the wicked shall clearly *discern between him that serveth God and him that serveth him not.* Those poor despised ones who have wandered about in deserts, and mountains, and dens, and caves of the earth. Who have had trials of cruel mockings and scourgings;—counted as the filth of the world and the offscouring of all things, shall be gathered out of the dust in which they have been hid in the day when God shall make up his jewels; then their luster will no longer be obscured by the wicked. Then, O, how *will the righteous shine forth as the sun in the kingdom of their Father.* These are they that have come out of great tribulation, who have mourned and wept and prayed and labored and endured shame and reproach in the cause of Christ. These are they that have come out of great tribulation, and have washed their robes, and made them white in the blood of the Lamb.

While the wicked are sinking into the bottomless pit with the howlings of the damned; the righteous will ascend with Christ and all the armies of heaven, shouting the praises of redeeming love. And here the everlasting song begins—

> "See the souls that earth despised,
>   In celestial glories move,
> Hallelujahs big with wonders,
>   Praising Christ's redeeming love,
> Hallelujahs
>   Echo through the realms of light.
> Joy celestial, hymns harmonious,
>   In soft symphony resound.

> Angels, seraphs, harps, and trumpets,
> Swell the sweet angelic sound."

And so shall they ever be with the Lord. Then all the wicked will alter their opinion. All will then wake up and open their eyes. All my hearers—you who now neglect the duties of religion and the concerns of your souls—who cast off fear and restrain prayer—you whom neither the joys of heaven, nor the torments of the damned can now awake—*Then when the great gulf is fixed—Then will you return and discern between the righteous and the wicked, between him that serveth God and him that serveth him not.*

10

The Unclean Spirit

Matthew 12:43, 44, 45. *When the unclean spirit is gone out of a man, he walketh through dry places, seeking rest, and findeth none. Then he saith, I will return into my house from whence I came out; and when he is come, he findeth it empty, swept, and garnished. Then goeth he, and taketh with himself seven other spirits more wicked than himself, and they enter in and dwell there: and the last state of that man is worse than the first.*

In these words our Lord describes the state of the unbelieving Jews. This he does by a parable, formed upon the case of a demoniac. Christ had just healed one possessed with a devil. But the Pharisees, filled with envy, attributed the whole to satanic influence. Our Lord repelled the blasphemous charge and added a most solemn address on the unpardonable sin. At the close of the whole, he drew a representation of the state of that generation. The occasion furnished an example. After the description given in the text, he makes an application. *Even so shall it be also unto this wicked generation.*

This account is also equally applicable to individuals under the gospel at the present day. We shall then consider it as applicable,

I. To the Jews.

II. To sinners under the gospel.

We remark that the description is drawn by an unerring hand. Our Lord knew the hearts of all men. When he cast out devils he knew what took place. Invisible spirits—the powers of darkness were under his control. He cast out the spirits with his word. He selects a case which he thus describes. *When the unclean spirit is gone out of a man, he walketh through dry places, seeking rest, and findeth none.* It is not the man that walks through dry places as some have supposed, but the unclean spirit. This is done contrary to his inclination, and therefore he cannot rest.

Being disturbed, *he walketh through dry, or desert places*—places the most barren and destitute of the water of life, and where there is nothing to oppose his designs—through *dry places,* where there are no showers of divine grace. *Seeking rest.* Being driven from one habitation, he would seek another where he might *rest* in the hearts of men, and there carry on his designs, undisturbed by

Christ. But being pursued by him, he finds himself disturbed—*seeking rest and findeth none.*

Thus when Christ appeared among the Jews, wherever he went he disturbed the powers of darkness. Evil spirits being driven from one habitation would seek another, where Christ was not known. But being pursued, they flee to a different country. Christ appears again; and unclean spirits being pursued by the faithful and successful preaching of the gospel find no rest. The powers of darkness being thus disturbed by the doctrine and miracles of Christ and his apostles, would for a time recede from the Jews and seek rest among the Gentiles; in those dry lands where no water of life had hitherto been found.—

But in the case described, the evil spirit driven from place to place, for a time would again return. *Then he saith, I will return into my house from whence I came out. My house.* The hearts of wicked men, are the common residence of unclean spirits. This is their dwelling place, where they reside and carry on their designs against the Redeemer's kingdom in this world. Wicked men are considered as the property and possession of evil spirits. He works in them, and by them as instruments just as he pleases. They are called his *servants*—his children, and *are led captive by him at his will. This is the spirit that now worketh in the children of disobedience. I will return into my house from whence I came out, and when he is come, he findeth it empty*—a lonesome dreary mansion, without an inhabitant, or any possessor to oppose his entrance. Christ was not admitted, if so it had not been empty—empty of all good, and of many former obstructions, so that now there is room for more evil spirits—*empty, and swept, and garnished;* already prepared for his reception.

On this discovery; *then goeth he, and taketh with himself seven other spirits more wicked than himself, and they enter in and dwell there.* Thus reinforced, the possession becomes strong. *They enter in and dwell there* without disturbance or further interruption. *And the last state of that man is worse than the first.* And so the possession becomes strong, and more dreadful and incurable than ever. Even so was it also in fact with that wicked generation. The powers of darkness driven from place to place, for a time, by the successful preaching of the gospel, and finding no rest, did actually return among the Jews. Their former habitation was indeed empty. The Spirit of God was gone. They had crucified the Saviour, and were abandoned by God himself. *Behold, your house is left unto you desolate.* Evil spirits did actually return and found the hearts of the

Jews empty, and repossessed that unbelieving generation of Jews. And thus they continue to this present day, sometimes more hardened than they were before the coming of Christ and the preaching of the kingdom of heaven among them.—This account is applicable,

II. To sinners under the gospel. It is more particularly applicable to individuals where the Lord appears to pour out his spirit and to revive his work.

Sinners are alarmed and awakened to a sense of divine things. Now the Lord appears in his glory. A solemn awe fills the place. The Lord is coming. The powers of darkness flee at his approach. And one would think they had fled forever—that all were about to become the followers of Christ—But it is not so.

Many are awakened who never entertain well grounded hopes. The sinner is alarmed. He looks around, and all is vanity. He feels himself mortal, acting for eternity and still out of Christ. Surprised at his former stupidity, he breaks off former habits and forms new resolutions of amendment. Vain and trifling conversation appear unworthy of a rational and immortal being. With amazing anguish he looks forward into the eternal world. He is now determined to bid farewell to all sinful pleasures and companions. His attention is caught. He listens with eagerness to the word of God. He now begins to open his eyes on his lost condition. Everything he hears or reads condemns him. His past conduct rises up to his view, his sins stare him in the face. A dreadful sound is in his ear. The thunders of a broken law, and the wrath of an angry God strike terror through his guilty soul. He now begins with all his might to recommend himself to God. And thus for a while he continues to read and pray and weep. An outward reformation has indeed taken place. *The unclean spirit is gone out of the man.* It indeed retires for a time—*resist the devil and he will flee from you.* But the state of his heart remains the same. Christ is not admitted to *dwell there by faith.*

Of this fact, the sinner himself is conscious. He knows that he has no love to God—no love to Christ or the duties of religion, and on this account he is alarmed. An outward reformation is effected while the state of the heart remains the same. And here he remains, resting on future resolutions—on what he is doing and on what he certainly intends to do hereafter. Here he is halting—he is about to prepare himself to go to Christ—preparing to believe—preparing to repent.

Meanwhile the work of God goes on. Others are alarmed. They see and feel that they are lost, and in earnest inquire, *What must I do to be saved?* They are brought to repentance and receive the Saviour

The Second Great Awakening

into their hearts. *Whom having not seen, they love, in whom though now they see him not, yet believing they rejoice with joy unspeakable and full of glory.* The unclean spirit is departed, and Christ has set up his kingdom in their hearts. *Christ is formed in their souls, the hope of glory.* The Spirit of God descends *like rain upon the mown grass, as showers that water the earth. These are indeed times of refreshing from the presence of the Lord.*

But such seasons are commonly short. The Lord is about to depart; and yet many who have been alarmed are still *without hope and without God in the world.* It is now an awful crisis. The awakened sinner will not remain long in his present situation. God has given his word that his Spirit *shall not always strive with man.* A few months commonly decides the point. Heaven and hell are now depending. The seal is now turning. The Spirit of God departs and the sinner is lost forever. The evil spirit *as a roaring lion, walking up and down in the earth, seeking whom he may devour,* now returns to his old abode. On examination he finds his habitation empty—a desolate and dreary mansion. The Spirit of God is gone—the Saviour is gone and no Christian graces adorn the soul. But it is swept from convictions and all serious impressions. In this manner it is garnished and already furnished for the reception, and entertainment of unclean spirits. His heart is completely prepared to welcome and comply with their suggestion.

The dreadful state of this man is often marked. So plainly marked that it cannot but be observed by others. He begins to manifest a reluctance to serious conversation. He carefully avoids those places where he apprehends danger of being interrogated on the subject of religion and the state of his own heart. He is particularly cautious to avoid the company of those who are faithful to the souls of men. The man has fled; not only from serious company and conversation, but a mark still worse, he has fled from the throne of grace.

Persons of this description, sometimes profess to have altered their sentiments on religious subjects. This they do to keep themselves in countenance. For a while their outward conduct is so glaring, they only betray the hypocrisy and deformity of their hearts. Having long felt the gospel way of salvation grating on their consciences, they may indeed manifest the genuine feelings of their hearts. They may now speak out what before they were ashamed to utter. In them is fulfilled the words of Paul, *They received not the love of the truth that they might be saved, and for this cause God shall send them strong delusions, that they may believe a lie and be damned.* Their conduct frequently becomes equally loose with their sentiments. The company which before they avoided as pernicious, they now frequent. They return again to the same course of conduct which before they regarded with abhorrence. Their apostasy is described by the Apostle Peter. *For if after they have escaped the pollutions of the world through the knowledge of the Lord and Saviour Jesus Christ, they are again entangled therein, and overcome, the last end is worse with them than the beginning. For it had been better for them not to have known the way of righteousness, than, after they have known it, to turn from the holy commandment delivered unto them. But it has happened unto them according to the true proverb, The dog is turned to his own vomit again; and the sow that was washed to her wallowing in the mire.* Having long felt the yoke of religion galling to their inclinations, at length they burst the bonds, and brake through former restraints. And to ward off reproof, and keep themselves in countenance, they make it their business to scan the lives of others; and rake together the faults of professing Christians as an excuse for their own abominations.

    The characters here described are commonly the worst of all— the most hardened, and dangerous to mankind. Nor do I recollect an instance of a person of this character, who was ever again alarmed and brought to repentance. *The last state of that man is worse than the first.* This was the case with numbers in the time of Christ and his Apostles. Many, who for a while listened with solemn attention to the instructions of Christ and followed him from place to place, afterwards lost these impressions. Their apostasy was final. *They went back and walked no more with him.*

    This was also the case of many in all places where the gospel is faithfully preached. Such persons cannot but be noticed with mingled emotions of grief and horror, by those who carefully observe the state of congregations in times of special awakenings. This is doubtless the case of some in every revival. My hearers will carefully observe the character described. It is this; where convictions and strong impressions *precede*. These are wholly lost. And great *obstinacy* and awful *stupidity* once *follow*.

    On the character here described we observe: there is no prospect that he will ever be brought to repentance. From our Lord's discourse we have reason to fear that some of those whom he addressed in our text had committed the unpardonable sin. However solemn it may be, we wish that every sinner might be alarmed at the thought that without repentance, all sin is unpardonable. We do not say that the persons described have been guilty of that particular sin. It

The Second Great Awakening

remains in awful suspense. Nothing but deep repentance can decide the point. Nothing but immediate repentance ought to satisfy.—

But aside from this awful consideration, it appears from various passages of scripture, that some kinds of apostasy, when attended with peculiar circumstances of aggravation are equivalent to it. The sacred scriptures furnish examples of those who, in their life time, had already passed the bounds of divine mercy. Before and after the coming of Christ there ever has been a period in the lives of men when they were given up to God to inevitable destruction.

The only ground of hope in the case of sinners lies in the sovereign mercy of God. The only efficient cause of a sinner's being brought to repentance is the influence of the Holy Spirit. The only hope that is left for such characters, therefore, must arise from the exertion of *his power, with whom all things are possible; but of him they are given up. They have done despite to the spirit of grace, and are given up to strong delusions to believe a lie. It is impossible to renew them again unto repentance.* And again, *Ephraim is joined to idols, let him alone.* Such persons have lost their day of grace. They are given over, not only by the Holy Spirit, but by the Saviour himself. This was the case to whom Christ said, "I go my way, and ye shall seek me, and shall die in your sins." This was the awful case with those over whom he wept, and whom he thus solemnly addressed. *O, that thou hadst known, even thou, at least in this thy day, the things which belong unto thy peace!—but now they are hid from thine eyes.* Their day of grace was gone; their eyes were blinded; and their doom was certain.

Again, on the character here described, the prospect is that he will not be alarmed at his danger until he awakes in hell. Such persons are blind to a sense of their danger. The thought that if they repent they shall be saved, satisfies them. But they will not. They think on the subject and that is all. And the thought lulls them fast to sleep, and that is all. The Spirit of God is gone, and they are commonly the last to conclude that their souls are in this awful state. It is true, they may have some flashes of conviction, some sudden pangs of horror, and remorse of conscience and this may continue for a few days; but it will not last; it will soon wear off again, and the whole serves only to harden.

Sometimes, however, apostates have seen their awful condition before the hour of death. Some in their last hours, in all the horrors, and blasphemous rage of damned spirits, have served as monuments of the truth of God's word. And it ought to be regarded as solemn warnings to those who appear to be bending their course towards the same end.

But their destruction is generally more sudden. *When they shall say, peace and safety: then sudden destruction cometh upon them, and they shall not escape. He, that being often reproved hardeneth his neck, shall suddenly be destroyed, and that without remedy.* As it was in the days of Noah, so it is now—*they knew not until the flood came, and took them all away. So shall also the coming of the Son of man be. At an hour when ye think not the Son of man will come.* Generally those who are given up to *hardness of heart,* are also given up to *blindness of mind. Their consciences being seared as with a hot iron, they are now past feeling.*

O, how awful is their state. Nothing can alarm them. On hearing their state described, one would think that the persons might now be seen trembling on their seats. But nothing will move them. It is true; the motives of the gospel are awful and glorious; heaven on the one hand and hell on the other; every principle of self-preservation addressed to the heart in the most striking manner; the doctrines well founded to command belief—simple and easy to be understood. The soul addressed is immortal. Salvation freely offered on the simple terms of faith and repentance. And yet, with all these advantages, the most eloquent speaker may lay out his strength to the best advantage, and perhaps the wretch will laugh when he has done.

Such persons are commonly given over by all serious praying people. If you attempt to give a friendly warning, it will only exasperate. Or, he may afterwards treat you with utter neglect, and behold you with a steady contempt. *He that reproveth a scorner getteth to himself shame: and he that rebuketh a wicked man getteth to himself a blot.* And therefore the direction is: *Reprove not a scorner, lest he hate thee.* Where such obstinacy and contempt are manifest, Christ says to us: *Let them alone.*

In case the Lord should again revive his work, it is not expected that those will be brought in. Those who have been partially awakened and whose convictions have not been wholly lost may again be awakened. But those who have wholly lost their concern and have gone so far as to make light of serious impressions, and whose *last state is worse than the first,* will again be passed over. A second and third revival have been witnessed where characters of the above description have uniformly been left in awful stupidity and hardness of heart. It is clearly manifest from observation as well as from the word of God that there is no prospect that he will ever repent—*For*

The Second Great Awakening 91

the last state of that man is worse than the first.
 It now remains to improve the subject. Are there any persons present whose awful case has been described?—We shall pass them by. There is nothing in the law, there is nothing in the gospel that will move them. Neither the mercies of God nor the terrors of his wrath, neither the joys of heaven nor the pains of hell, can again awake them from their slumbers. Nothing but the Almighty power of God can do it—but of him they are given up. The Spirit of God lets them alone. And could we see and certainly know them, it would be our wisdom and our duty too, to let them alone. *They have trodden under foot the Son of God; and there remaineth no more sacrifice for sin, but a certain fearful looking for of judgment, and fiery indignation, which shall devour the adversaries*—But which will not now alarm them. Hence it becomes a hopeless undertaking for the servants of God to attempt any thing for their recovery.
 Our object in holding up this character to your view, my hearers, is to warn others to *beware*. Though we cannot make them learn their awful danger, yet you may learn something from them. We now hold them up for a warning to you who feel some concern for your souls. It may be useful to point you to the danger which lies but just before you. Here we point you to the rocks on which others have made shipwreck with their souls. These, O sinners, like yourself were once alarmed. They turned to flee out of Sodom to the mountains of safety. But while lingering on the plains, they turned back in their hearts, and have now become pillars of salt. These awful monuments are still to be found in many places where the Lord has lately appeared to revive his work. Whether any of this character are in this place, we do not certainly know. But from my own acquaintance with the last revival, I do know if they will now exercise gospel repentance, they shall certainly be saved. But there lies the difficulty—*they will not.* They may resolve, and resolve again; but they will die the same.
 These persons, if any such there are, will go from the house of God as they came. Instead of calling for their convictions to return, they will labor to silence their fears and to soothe their consciences. Instead of laboring to be convinced of sin, and to come to repentance, they will attempt to justify their conduct, and flatter themselves that they have never been awakened.
 Instead of being alarmed about themselves, and inquiring, *What must we do to be saved?* they may go from this place finding fault with others, and perhaps scanning the lives of professing Christians. Instead of repairing to the throne of grace, and crying for mercy,

they will say in their hearts to the Almighty, *Depart from us; for we desire not the knowledge of Thy ways; for what is the Almighty that we should serve him? and what profit shall we have if we pray unto him?* and no person will be more likely to go away finding fault with this discourse than that very man whom I have described.

Do you feel no concern for your souls, you have awful reason to fear that the case described is your own. There is no safety here. Do you now begin to feel some concern for your soul? Beware then, O sinner, beware of every approach to so tremendous a precipice. It is dangerous—awfully dangerous to resist the strivings of God's Spirit. It is plain from the scriptures, that the Spirit does strive with man, and that he will not always strive. How often with this man, or how often with that man, we cannot tell; but God knows perfectly well. Now to resist the last effort of the Spirit of God on the soul, is what plunges the sinner into this hopeless state.

While the Spirit is striving, the sinner feels himself moved by something, he cannot tell how; he is alarmed; becomes thoughtful and anxious about his soul. But he resists. The Spirit withdraws and he becomes careless again. The sinner flees to some diversions; or misconstrues some doctrines to give ease to his troubled conscience, or pines on some self-righteous plans. No matter how these things may be, he fixes on false ground, and thus finds some relief—The Spirit visits him again, and again. The sinner still resists its motions, until the last time is come.—O, awful crisis.—Once more he moves upon the heart of the sinner. He is now for the last time in the purpose of God made serious! But alas! The wicked heart wards off conviction! The sinner says—depart—depart!—The Spirit bids adieu! And the sinner is gone forever.

11

Abandoned by God

And he did not many mighty works there, because of their unbelief (Matthew 13:58).

And when he was come into his own country, he taught them in their synagogue, insomuch that they were astonished, and said,Whence hath this man all these things? And they were offended in him. But Jesus said unto them, A prophet is not without honour, save in his own country, and in his own house. And he did not many mighty works there, because of their unbelief.

But though they were astonished, they did not allow themselves to be convinced. But to prevent, began to *cavil. Is not this the carpenter's son? Is not his mother called Mary? and his brethren, James, and Joses, and Simon, and Judas? And his sisters, are they not all with us? Whence then hath this man all these things?* They could not object to what he said—they could not question the few miracles he wrought. But as they were prejudiced—and chose to be, they embraced with avidity the only means of perpetrating their prejudices. This was such a sin that the Saviour thought it proper to punish it. He then ceased to preach to them, and withdrew alike his miracles, and the gracious influences of his Spirit.

Doctrine. God often passes by impious sinners and forbears to awaken and convert them as the punishment of some special provocation. This is clearly asserted in the text. If they had not indulged and fastened such malignant prejudices, Christ would have gone on with his ministry and his miracles as in other places. But when he saw their determination not to be convinced, he determined not to convince them and stopped his mighty works. We have evidence of the same point in Matthew 11:20, 21. *Then he began to upbraid the cities where in most of his mighty works were done, because they repented not: Woe unto thee Chorazin! woe unto thee Bethsaida! for if the mighty works, which were done in you, had been done in Tyre and Sidon, they would have repented long ago in sackcloth and ashes. Luke 19:42. If thou hadst known in this thy day, the things which belong unto thy peace! but now they are hid from thine eyes.* Their state is now hopeless—they are never to be converted, but are doomed to destruction.

But why are they given up? It is for their incorrigible prejudice against Christ—for resisting *light* and neglecting salvation. The city stood many years, and a few were converted; but the great body of its inhabitants were never converted to Christianity. This is only the repetition of a similar sentence executed once before upon that nation and recorded in Psalm 81:8 to the end. *Hear, O my people, and I will testify unto thee: O Israel, if thou wilt hearken unto me; There shall no strange god be in thee; neither shalt thou worship any strange god. I am the Lord thy God, which brought thee out of the land of Egypt: open thy mouth wide, and I will fill it. But my people would not hearken to my voice; and Israel would none of me. So I gave them up unto their own heart's lust: and they walked in their own counsels. Oh that my people had hearkened unto me, and Israel had walked in my ways! I should soon have subdued their enemies, and turned my hand against their adversaries. The haters of the Lord should have submitted themselves unto him: but their time should have endured forever. He should have fed them also with the finest of the wheat: and with honey out of the rock should I have satisfied thee.*

There is one sin which whoever commits shall never be forgiven—Deliberately and maliciously speaking evil of the operations of the Holy Spirit—convinced that they are his operations. The sin is unpardonable not because the atonement is insufficient, but because the crime is of such a nature, that God is determined never to grant the criminal that sanctifying influence which he maliciously reviles. Now though there is but this one sin, which prevents the application of redemption in all cases—there may be many which do it in many cases. And this is confirmed by the providence of God.

There are persons of various classes, to but a few of whom is salvation ever sent—in which probably a hundred perish to one that is saved. This is true apparently with respect to those who put off the care of the soul till they become old. There are also a variety of vicious courses, in which few of the whole number who walk in them are ever reclaimed. The word of God and the providence of God warn every youth to flee those lusts which conduct, etc. The prostitute* is in a state the most hopeless of salvation of any this side of the world of despair. Of her house it is said the dead are there— None that go thither return—her guests are in the depths of hell. There is an instance sometimes of the conversion of an intemperate person, but it is the escape of one only in a thousand.

---

* In the original handwritten manuscript, Nettleton wrote "p---------". How far are we today from having such sensitive consciences as this?

Those who imbibe erroneous opinions of a particular description are taught to believe they are true. Where the divinity of Christ, the total depravity of man, the necessity of a change of heart by the Holy Spirit, and justification by faith are denied and disbelieved—there the Holy Spirit seldom interposes to save the soul. They cry peace until sudden destruction cometh upon them.—They sleep on until death opens their eyes to the truth, and to their ruin beyond the grave. I know that those who deny the doctrines named above, deny also that revivals are the work of God—but this is only the consummation of their delusion. They are the last evidence which God designs to give to those who have no pleasure in the truth.—They are an experiential illustration of the doctrine of total depravity and regeneration by special grace.

The awakened feel and confess—the reconciled rejoice and ascribe to God their deliverance. If from this evidence any turn away in disgust after having neglected or perverted the testimony of the Bible—They repeat the crime of Capernaum, Bethsaida, and Chorazin—and except they repent they will become partakers in their doom. It appears from the Bible that kings and philosophers, the wise, the rich and the great are in few instances, comparatively, made the subjects of regenerating grace. The reason assigned by Christ is *even so Father, for so it seemed good in thy sight.*

This does not imply that in leaving them God acts without reason or that their dereliction is not occasioned by their own crimes. And facts strongly corroborate the supposition that it is.—for examine every class from which few are saved, and each is distinguished by some peculiarly provoking sin which God, though a sovereign, chooses to mark with this most fearful token of his displeasure.

For it is not by his law and his gospel—by precepts and penalties only that he encourages obedience and admonishes the wicked. He governs the world in such a manner as to corroborate his Word. He dispenses his Holy Spirit in such a manner as throws the probability of salvation a thousand-fold on the side of a religious education—and such restraints of depravity as such an education secures.

He exercises sovereign grace in such a way that the neglecter of means has not the same ground to expect interposition of grace as he who regards them—nor the prolifigate man the same as the chaste and the temperate—nor the errorist the same as the believer of the truth—nor the infidel as the scoffer.

Objection: This sets aside the decrees. Answer: No, God has decreed to punish for certain crimes.

Improvement by application to various classes of persons,

1. To those who waive all solicitude about their souls and neglect all exertion on account of their belief of the doctrine of total depravity and election. These draw the stupefying conclusion: "I can do nothing and it is useless to try." But you overlook an important fact, that though you cannot merit salvation, you can merit destruction. Though none of your doings conciliate his favor, it is an easy thing to kindle his wrath. The reason why God passes you by, may be this very perversion of his Word. If you can never save yourselves, it does not follow that you may not so neglect and conduct, as to destroy yourselves.

2. The aged are admonished to inquire what they have done and what they have neglected to do. I do not judge your hearts. God forbid that I should say that you have no religion. I only regret that you do not find cause to avow the cheering fact, and set my heart at rest. I can no more decide that you have religion without your own disclosures, than I can decide that you have not. I have great anxiety for you, lest this revival should pass off and leave you in a state still worse.—You have witnessed one revival—Your next stage will be that of the aged, and your next the grave—I verily believe that with many of you, it is the last time.

Our text says, *The conversion of the sinner is a mighty work.* This work may be stopped as a punishment to some special provocation.

12

The Wise and the Foolish Virgins

Five of them were wise, and five were foolish (Matthew 25:2).

This text is called the parable of the ten virgins. It is designed as a correct illustration of the state of the visible church on earth, including all its members of every description.

Then shall the kingdom of heaven be likened unto ten virgins, which took their lamps, and went forth to meet the bridegroom. And five of them were wise, and five were foolish. They that were foolish took their lamps, and took no oil with them. But the wise took oil in their vessels with their lamps.

All professors of religion are divided into two distinct classes, which our Savior denominates the *wise* and the *foolish*.

It is proposed briefly to consider the following particulars:
1. What is required in a true profession of religion.
2. Why some profess, without possessing it.
3. Why are they called foolish.

1. What is required in a true profession of religion. That something is required is evident from the fact that Christ made a distinction. And this arises from the superior worth of the soul to every other object. Proper attention to the concerns of the soul is a mark of superior wisdom, because an interest in Christ is of the highest importance. *The fear of the Lord is the beginning of wisdom. And the wise shall shine as the brightness of the firmament.*

So on the other hand, a neglect of the concerns of the soul is a mark of supreme folly. These in Scripture are denominated *fools* and *foolish*. And so *religion* is denominated *wisdom;* and *sin: folly. And wisdom excelleth folly as far as light excelleth darkness.* The distinction between the wise and the foolish may to our limited view, appear small, in some instances it may not appear at all in this world; yet in the sight of God there is a distinction as wide as that between *light* and *darkness*. And thus they are called "children of light," and are said *to shine as lights in the world*. And are exhorted to *let their light shine that others may see*.

So in this parable, from the distinction in the words of the text, it is evident that our Savior does make a very wide difference between professors of religion.

There is something which the wise take and the foolish do not.

Something too, of such importance that without it, none can enter heaven. Now what this is, it must be of utmost importance to determine. That from our Savior's parable it may easily be determined what it is not. It is evident that the difference does not consist in a difference in external ordinances of the gospel. For the characters described, are represented as all belonging to the true church, the *kingdom of heaven.* All who belong to this visible church, who are admitted members of Christ's visible church, alike profess religion. So that the great difference between a true Christian and a sinner is not that one professes religion and the other does not. For all whomsoever our Savior describes *took their lamps, and went forth to meet the bridegroom.*

Nor does it appear in this, that at the time of their baptism, or public profession, all were *then wise,* and that part have since lost that character. For when they took their lamps *five of them were wise, and five were foolish.* Nor does it appear that at that time, or at any other period, they received a principle of grace which they have since lost. Whatever else the difference may be, it cannot be *that.* It is certain that it must be something which they *have not lost.* They were baptized and made a profession; but that great discriminating quality, our Savior says they never took.

For in a wise profession of religion is implied:

1. A strong attachment to the cause of Christ. Supreme love is required. *For he that is not with me is against me,* says Christ. God requires the heart and without that no offering can be accepted by him. For *give me thine heart* is his plain injunction. Without this attachment, no real service can be rendered to God. *No man can serve two masters: for either he will hate the one, and love the other; or else he will hold to the one, and despise the other. Ye cannot serve God and mammon.* Supreme attachment to Christ and his course is therefore absolutely necessary.

Those who go forth to meet the bridegroom must, in order to meet with acceptance, be sincere. A feigned attachment is disgusting even to a fellow mortal, much more to this heavenly bridegroom. He must really appear to be the *Chief among ten thousand, and altogether lovely.*

2. A willingness to leave all for Christ. *If any man will come after me,* says Christ, *Let him deny himself, and take up his cross daily, and follow me.* "If any man will come after me and hate not his father, and mother, and wife, and children, and brethren, and sisters, yea, and his own life also, he cannot be my disciple." "And whosoever doth not bear his cross and come after me, cannot be my

The Second Great Awakening

disciple." He must be willing to make any sacrifice when the cause of Christ evidently requires it.

Now he is to examine his heart by these solemn declarations of our Savior and see whether he is prepared for all this. In this way he is required deliberately to *count the cost. Lest haply, after he hath laid the foundation, and is not able to finish it, all that behold it begin to mock him, saying, This man began to build, and was not able to finish. So likewise, whosoever he be of you that forsaketh not all that he hath, cannot be my disciple.*

There must be a willingness to renounce the world. *Wherefore come out from among them and be ye separate, saith the Lord. The friendship of the world is enmity with God. If any man will be a friend to the world he is the enemy of God. Be not conformed to this world, but be ye transformed.*

3. A willingness to suffer in the cause of Christ. *If any man will live godly in Christ Jesus, he shall suffer persecution.* He must be willing to endure shame and reproach in the cause of Christ. If he is not prepared for this, he is not prepared to profess Christ.

4. A willingness to engage in all the duties of religion. Without this there can be no evidence of love to Christ or attachment to his cause. *If ye love me, keep my commandments. He that saith, I know him, and keepeth not his commandments, is a liar, and the truth is not in him.* If there be any external duty omitted the world will know it, and Christ's cause will suffer. *Christ will be wounded in the house of his friends.* And so double dishonor will be done to Christ.

If there is any duty which he does not intend to perform, it would not be wise to profess religion. To take on him the name of Christ without even intending obedience would be gross hypocrisy. No one could advise it, unless he intended to dishonor the cause. For in no way can so much dishonor be done to Christ.

5. Faith in Christ. This was required by the Apostles. An empty, speculative faith is not sufficient, *for devils believe and tremble;* but that faith which makes the things of religion real, which governs the whole conduct. *We walk by faith, not by sight.* Faith which brings with it the assent of the heart. Says the Eunich to Philip, *What doth hinder me to be baptized?* He replied: *If thou believest with all thine heart, thou mayest. For with the heart man believeth unto righteousness; and with the mouth confession is made unto salvation.* That faith which worketh by love and purifieth the heart—that overcometh the world.

And then it will follow that *Regeneration* is included, for without regeneration the Bible informs us that there can be no gospel faith.

For saith the Apostle, *He that believeth that Jesus is the Christ is born of God.* Hence it is evident that without regeneration there can be no wise profession of religion; because without it, there can be no gospel faith. Without regeneration there can be no love to God—For it is declared *everyone that loveth is born of God.* And so faith and love are both the fruit of regeneration.

It cannot be wise to profess religion without being born of God because without this change we are informed that nothing is pleasing to God. So then they *that are in the flesh cannot please God. And the carnal mind is enmity against God. It is not subject to the law of God, neither indeed can be.* Without this change we cannot be the friends of God. And without these qualifications we cannot be the children of God.

Those whose hearts are regenerated; unto whom *old things are passed away and all things are become new;* may be said to *take oil in their vessels. Their hearts are established with grace. They are children of light. God, who commanded the light to shine out of darkness, hath shined in their hearts, to give the light of the knowledge of the glory of God in the face of Jesus Christ.* And in this manner alone are they prepared to shine as lights in the world. This is what I conceive to be implied in a wise profession of religion.

Let us inquire:

2. Why so many profess religion without possessing it? *And five of them were wise, and five were foolish.* This is a charitable representation. If one-half who profess religion enter heaven, Christian charity will not be disappointed.

The reasons which may influence to a profession of religion may be various. In the primitive ages of Christianity, persecution and death operated powerfully to guard against the infusion of false professors. It might well be presumed that none but Christians would then be found in the church. But it was not so. Much less can it be expected at the present day. Should the fear of persecution and death attend a profession of religion now, the number of its professors would doubtless be greatly diminished.

The judgment and consciences of men are ever on the side of religion, even while the heart is opposed to its humbling duties. Thus was it in the time of Christ. *Nevertheless among the chief rulers also many believed on him; but because of the Pharisees they did not confess him, lest they should be put out of the synagogue: for they loved the praise of men more than the praise of God.* Had it not been for the fear of being put out of the synagogue, it is intimated many would have professed Christ, notwithstanding it is added; *they loved the praise of men more than the praise of God.* Though such a speculative belief as theirs with such hearts could avail nothing: except for the sake of quieting conscience, many would profess religion and get the same belief and the same hearts.

One reason why many profess religion without possessing it may be, the influence of example. In churches where experimental religion is not required, many often profess without even the appearance of external decency. Where this is the case, many have been known to do it because it has become a fashion. The form of godliness is assumed without a thought of its power. Some have been advised to do it and their conscientious scruples have, in this way, been removed. Others have done it through ignorance; and perhaps without a thought that a change of heart was required. Others have utterly denied the necessity of experimental religion. Some have gone so far as even to ridicule the thing itself, and yet have dared to take the vows of God upon them. And says our Savior, *the foolish took their lamps, and took no oil in them.*

Others again have adopted the sentiment, and their consciences are alarmed at the thought, that a change of heart is necessary to a preparation for heaven. They continue for a long time in a state of anxious concern without finding relief. They begin to inquire whether this change may not take place and yet they be ignorant of it. Being informed that the thing may be possible, in this way their consciences gradually become quiet, *and so the foolish took their lamps, and took no oil with them.*

Another is under deep conviction, and has labored long, and so he thinks he has done much; for a while he feels resolved that nothing shall divest his attention from this great subject. If there is any thing in religion he is determined to find it, but growing faint and discouraged, he concludes that there is no such thing; *and so they that were foolish took their lamps, and took no oil in them.*

Another equally anxious and distressed for his soul, and casting about to find some relief, catches at every appearance and persuades himself that there is grace in his heart. And not being careful to examine, he settles down on a false hope and sleeps on secure. *And so they that were foolish took their lamps, and took no oil with them.*

Sometimes the sinner, having long been anxious, and finding no relief, is persuaded and prevailed on to believe that the most probable method to find relief is to profess religion. At length he is resolved to profess religion in hope that grace may thus be given. But the experiment has been followed sometimes with sad disappointment, no love to God, no renewing of the Holy Spirit has followed. Sometimes it has ended in still greater security; and in this manner *they that were foolish took their lamps, and took no oil with them.*

The wise it is said *took oil in their vessels with their lamps.* This was their wisdom. The state of the heart was the great thing with them. They were peculiarly careful to attend to that. They were convinced that there must be something in the heart which was not there by nature. They dare not go forth to meet their Lord without their hearts well garnished with the Christian graces. However difficult and painful to obtain, they dare not do it. Like the wise man who built his house on the rock—they dug deep, they were willing to search and to be searched until their foundation was settled on the rock of ages.

But not so with the foolish; when they professed religion they never attended thoroughly to the heart. They were too well-pleased with flattery or meeting with unexpected difficulties, and finding the way so straight, they commenced their journey without any grace in their hearts. *They that were foolish took their lamps, and took no oil in them.*

Let us inquire:

3. Why they are called *foolish?* We answer because they were wicked and not essentially different from other sinners. And they were both foolish and wicked for professing religion without possessing it. They were both foolish and wicked because unto the wicked God saith, *What hast thou to do to declare my statutes, or that thou shouldest take my covenant into thy mouth.*

Whosoever shall eat of this bread, and drink this cup of the Lord, unworthily, shall be guilty of the body and blood of the Lord. For he that eateth and drinketh unworthily, eateth and drinketh judgment to himself, not discerning the Lord's body. An empty professor is both foolish and wicked because God hath commanded, *When thou vowest a vow unto God, defer not to pay it; for he hath no pleasure in fools.*

13

The Final Judgment, Part I

When the Son of man shall come in his glory, and all the holy angels with him, then shall he sit upon the throne of his glory: and before him shall be gathered all nations (Matthew. 25: 31, 32).

The doctrine of a future general judgment is fundamental to the Christian system. It is inseparable from the idea of the existence of God as a righteous moral governor. The text is a description of this solemn event. "When the Son of man shall come in this glory, and all the holy angels with him, then shall he sit upon the throne of his glory."

On this subject we shall notice the following particulars:
I. The certainty—
II. The time when—
III. The manner of Christ's coming to judgment.

With respect to the certainty of a future general judgment we allege:

1. The justice of God. This attribute is not fully displayed in this world. Here we often see good men afflicted and bad men prosperous. This inequality loudly proclaims a judgment to come. It is reasonable to suppose that God will take care to reward virtue, and to punish vice. The Bible however settles the point beyond a doubt. *Our God is a rock, his work is perfect—a God of truth, without iniquity, just and mighty is he. It is a righteous thing with God to recompense tribulation.* Verily there is a reward for the righteous. Verily he is a God that judgeth in the earth.

2. The *certainty* of a future judgment may be inferred from our relation to God. We are his creatures and are bound to obey him. If God is a righteous moral governor, he will not suffer his law to be broken, and his authority to be trampled on with impunity. If we are under any law, that law is binding. If that law is binding, there must be a day of reckoning.

The resurrection of Christ is a proof of the general judgment. Thus Paul reasoned in Acts 17:31. *Because he has appointed a day, in which he will judge the world in righteousness by that man whom he hath ordained; whereof he hath given assurance unto all men, in that he hath raised him from the dead.* This proves not only that there will be a day of judgment but that Christ will be the judge. The argument stands thus; Christ while on earth declared himself to be the judge of the world. *For the Father judges no man, but hath committed all judgment unto the Son. For the Son of man shall come in the glory of his father with his angels; and then he shall reward every man according to his work.* The Savior announced his coming in the words of our text. Now if Christ did actually rise from the dead, this establishes the truth of his assertion. For God would not work a miracle to establish a falsehood.

That God will judge the world by Jesus Christ *he hath given assurance unto all men, in that he hath raised him from the dead.* Again, the Apostle declares, *For to this end Christ both died, and rose, and revived, that he might be Lord both of the dead and living.* Christ was ordained of God to be the judge of the quick and the dead. *He shall judge the quick and the dead at his appearing and his kingdom.*

And Enoch also, the seventh from Adam, prophesied of these, saying, Behold the Lord cometh with ten thousands of his saints, to execute judgment upon all, and to convince all that are ungodly among them of all their ungodly deeds which they have committed, and of all the hard speeches which ungodly sinners have spoken against him. The Psalmist has announced his coming in this sublime language: *Our God shall come, and shall not keep silence: a fire shall devour before him, and it shall be very tempestuous round about him. He shall call to the heavens from above, and to the earth, that he may judge his people. Gather my saints together unto me—And the heavens shall declare his righteousness: for God is judge himself. Know thou, that for all these things God will bring thee into judgment. For God will bring every work into judgment.*

In St. Matthew's gospel it is written: *For with what judgment ye judge, ye shall be judged: and with what measure ye mete, it shall be measured to you again.*

Therefore is the kingdom of heaven likened unto a certain king which would take account of his servants. After a long time the Lord of those servants cometh and reckoneth with them. As I live, saith the Lord, every knee shall bow to me, and every tongue shall confess to God. We know him that hath said; vengeance is mine, I will repay, says the Lord. *And again, the Lord shall judge his people.* These passages, with among others decide with certainty that there will be a day of judgment. *As I live, saith the Lord, every knee shall bow.* On this very subject our Savior declares: *Heaven and earth shall pass away; but my word shall not pass away.*

The day of judgment in scripture is called a *great day*—the *day of*

The Second Great Awakening

the Lord—the day of wrath and revelation of the righteous judgment of God.

As a spectator of passing events, the favored disciple saw and described the tremendous scene of this great day. *And I saw the dead, small and great, stand before God; and the books were opened.*

Respecting Christians coming to judgment we proposed to consider:

II. The time when—

This question was once put to our Savior: *Tell us, when shall these things be? and what shall be the sign of thy coming, and of the end of the world?* With respect to the destruction of Jerusalem he answers: *Verily I say unto you, this generation shall not pass, till all these things be fulfilled.* With respect to the day of judgment, he adds: *But of that day and hour knoweth no man, no, not the angels of heaven, but my Father only.* The time of this great event is kept a profound secret. No man is able to discover the day or the hour. No, not the angels of heaven. *It is not for us to know the times or the seasons which the Father hath put in his own power.* For wise reasons he has seen fit to conceal the exact time.

And when he comes to judgment, Christ chooses to come suddenly. *Watch therefore, for ye know neither the day nor the hour wherein the Son of man cometh.* But of this we are certain, that day and that hour are both *fixed. Because,* says the Apostle, he *hath appointed a day in which he will judge the world in righteousness.* The day is *appointed,* it is *fixed* in the counsel of God and it cannot be altered. *Marvel not at this,* says our Savior, *the hour is coming, in which all that are in the graves shall hear his voice, and shall come forth, they that have done good unto the resurrection of life, and they that have done evil unto the resurrection of damnation.*

The *hour* is coming. So very punctual is this great appointment. The solemn *hour* is continually approaching. It draws nearer and nearer every day—and the intervening space will soon elapse. But,

Though we cannot determine the time, yet many things respecting it are *revealed,* and *certain.* It is certain that the day of judgment will not take place until the great work of redemption is finished. This world was created by God as a stage on which to display the glorious plan of redemption. The world and all its inhabitants were created *by him, and for him, and without him was not any thing made that was made.* It is certain that Christ will finish the great work which he has undertaken. Not one whom he designs to save shall ever be lost.

The day of judgment will be deferred until all that were given to Christ shall be called in. *I came down from heaven not to do mine own will, but the will of him that sent me. And this is the Father's will that hath sent me, that of all which he hath given me, I should loose nothing, but should raise it up again at the last day.*

On account of judgment delayed, the Apostle speaks of some who would conclude that it would never begin, saying, *Where is the promise of the coming? For since the fathers fell asleep, all things continue as they were from the beginning of the creation.* Why is not the judgment instantly set, and why are not all the wicked this moment summoned before the dread tribunal of Jehovah to hear their doom? Why has not judgment already taken place and why have not all the wicked on earth been doomed to hell?

If God be just and if ever he intends to do it, how shall we *account* for this long delay? The apostle Peter answers, that the day of judgment is delayed for the purposes of salvation. *And account that the long-suffering of our Lord is salvation.* The final judgment is deferred for the sole purpose of completing the great work of redemption. In the destruction of the old world, and in the salvation of Noah;—in the destruction of Sodom, and the *deliverance* of Lot, it is evident, saith the Apostle, that *The Lord knoweth how to deliver the godly out of temptations, and to <u>reserve</u> the unjust unto the day of judgment to be punished.* He knoweth how to reserve them as in prison, to the day of judgment to be punished. The fact that the day of judgment is deferred is an evidence that the work of redemption is still going on. And this great work will continue until all the elect are gathered in, and there is not another sinner ever to be converted on this earth. This time, whether longer or shorter, is the exact time to which the judgment of the great day will be deferred.

Again, beyond this time it is evident that the day of judgment will not be deferred. When the last sinner whom God ever designs to save shall be converted, then there will be nothing to hinder the day of judgment. The destruction of Sodom must be suspended until righteous Lot was safe. *Haste thee escape thither,* saith the Lord, *for I cannot do any thing until thou be come thither.* But when he was escaped there was nothing to prevent and nothing could prevent the destruction of the wicked. So will it be when the last sinner shall be converted.

That the last general judgment will not be deferred beyond this period is evident from the Revelation of St. John. *And the angel which I saw stand upon the sea and upon the earth lifted up his hand to heaven, and sware by him that liveth forever and ever, who created heaven, and the things that therein are, and the earth, and the things that therein are, and the sea, and the things which are therein, that there should be time no longer: But in the days of the voice of the seventh angel, when he shall begin to sound, the mystery of God should be finished, as he hath declared to his servants the prophets. Whom the heaven must receive until the times of the restitution of all things which God hath spoken.*

Again—the day of judgment will not come until after the millennium. It is predicted (Isaiah 11:9) *that the earth shall be full of the knowledge of the Lord, as the waters cover the sea.* (Daniel 7:27) *And the kingdom and dominion and greatness of the kingdom under the whole heaven, shall be given to the people of the saints of the Most High. Satan shall be bound a thousand years, and cast into the bottomless pit. He shall deceive the nations no more, till the thousand years shall be fulfilled.* During this period: *All shall know the Lord from the least to the greatest.* These predictions, we think, evidently, have not yet been fulfilled.

Again—It is evident that the day of judgment will take place shortly after the millennium. How long after we are not informed. But it is evident that the time will be short. After the thousand years have expired *Satan shall be loosed a little season. And shall go out to deceive the nations which are in the four quarters of the earth.* Here we have described a general apostasy. Here all predictions end. At this point divine revelation closes. The Bible gives us no account of any state intervening this season of wickedness and the judgment day.

Our text declares that before him shall be gathered *all nations*. I propose to consider more particularly the state of all nations *when* Christ shall come to judgment.

1. The number of inhabitants on the earth at that time will be *great*. During the millennial state, the world will become exceeding populous. Those causes which have annually swept from the earth millions of its inhabitants will now cease to operate. We need not mention the famine and the pestilence or the numberless vices which bring on premature death. This single circumstance that *nations shall not learn war any more* will tend greatly to augment population. And this happy period will continue during the millennial state.

The inhabitants of New England double once in 25 years. Now if, at the commencement of the millennium, the inhabitants of the earth should continue to double once in twice that time, or once in 50 years, at the close of the millennium, there would be more than one million of inhabitants on the earth, to one single individual when it commenced.—In other words: If the millennium were to begin this day, at the end of a thousand years it would be found that every single individual had multiplied into more than a million, if they should continue to increase only one-half as fast as they have done hitherto.

The calculation would be moderate to say, that when Christ shall come to judgment, there will be a million of souls where there is one now. Hence it appears that the number of inhabitants on the earth when Christ shall come to judgment will be *very great*.

2. When Christ shall come to judgment the number of Christians will be *comparatively small*. That there will be some Christians on the earth at the coming of Christ is evident from the declaration of St. Paul. Speaking of the whole multitude of believers down to the end of time he says: *We shall not all sleep, but we shall all be changed*. And again, *We which are alive and remain unto the coming of the Lord shall not prevent them when are asleep*.

When Christ comes to judgment there will be a great and a *general apostasy*. This glorious millennial day will be soon succeeded by great moral darkness. The face of things will now be changed. Christians will die off. The Spirit of God will be withdrawn and there will be no new instances of conviction and conversion. *And when the thousand years are expired, Satan shall be loosed out of his prison, and shall go out to deceive the nations which are in the four quarters of the earth, Gog and Magog, to gather them together to battle: the number of whom is as sand of sea.*

The *nations* of the *four quarters* of the earth shall be deceived—and the number of those who shall now turn enemies to Christ is *as the sand of the sea*. Again, the smoke of the bottomless pit shall ascend and darken the world. They will make great opposition to the church of Christ. They are represented as having taken up arms against Christianity. It is said, Satan shall gather them together to *battle, the number of whom shall be as the sand of the sea. And they went up on the breadth of the earth, and compassed the camp of the saints about, and the beloved city*. At length the whole multitude of apostate nations will rise and combine to exterminate Christianity from the earth. Thus the church of God called the *beloved city* will be threatened and surrounded like the house of Lot in Sodom.

When Christ shall come to judgment it will be a time when iniquity shall *abound*. It will be a time of far greater wickedness than was ever known. It will be a time of great worldly mindedness. *As it was in the days of Lot, they bought, they sold, they planted, they*

builded. It will be a time of great *mirth* and *hilarity. For as in the days that were before the flood they were eating and drinking, and marrying and giving in marriage, until the day that Noah entered into the ark. So shall also the coming of the Son of man be.*
It will be a time of great scoffing at religion, and all serious things. Here the church will be in great affliction and distress. Christians will be so hated and ridiculed, so persecuted, afflicted, and tormented that they will expect deliverance only from the immediate appearance of Christ. In this situation they will be looking and longing and praying for the coming of Christ. These expectations being known to the wicked, they will every where make a handle of it. And particularly will they scoff at the notion of Christ's coming to judgment. Now will be fulfilled that declaration of the apostle Peter. *Knowing this first, that there shall come in the last days scoffers, walking after their own lusts, and saying, Where is the promise of his coming? for since the fathers fell asleep, all things continue as they were from the beginning of the creation.*

And now it will be a time of *great security.* Every warning will tend only to harden. *Because sentence against an evil work is not executed speedily, therefore the hearts of the sons of men will be fully set in them to do evil.*

The description will be universally applicable: *That evil servant shall begin to say in his heart, My Lord delayeth his coming; and shall begin to smite his fellow servants, and to eat and drink with the drunken.* In the language of the prophets, the wicked will begin to defy his coming, saying, *Let him make speed, and hasten his work that we may see it.* It is God's time to appear when things are brought to the last extremity.

From certain passages of scripture, some have doubted whether Christ's coming in the clouds of heaven would not be at midnight. *At midnight the cry was made. Behold he cometh! The day of the Lord will come as a thief in the night.*—Others again from analogy and from certain texts, think it will be in a clear, fair day, like that, when for the last time, the sun arose on the cities of plain. It is said: The same day that Lot went out of Sodom, it rained fire and brimstone from heaven and destroyed them all. Even shall it be in the day when the Son of Man shall be revealed. But, my hearers, both are true. A little reflection will show that the sun can never enlighten more than one-half of the globe at once. Day and night always exist on opposite sides of the earth at once.

We have considered the state of the world where Christ shall come to judgment, only as it respects the inhabitants *then living.* In this great event, the dead and the living are all equally interested. *For to this end Christ both died, and rose, and revived, that he might be Lord both of the dead and living.* He is styled the *judge of quick and dead. When the Son of man shall come in his glory, and all the holy angels with him, then shall he sit upon he throne of his glory: and before him <u>shall be gathered all nations</u>.* How vast will be the congregation of the dead! *One generation passeth away and another cometh.* How often the earth changes her inhabitants! For nearly six thousand years this change has been going on. *The grave hath enlarged herself and opened her mouth without measure, and all nations have descended into it.* Of most of this vast multitude there is now, no remembrance. They have long since been forgotten. All this vast multitude will continue to sleep on till the morning of the resurrection. *Man lieth down, and riseth not: till the heavens be no more, they shall not awake, nor be raised out of their sleep.* And so this course will continue. As the nations which have gone before us are now sleeping in the dust and the living walk heedless over them; so within a little while will it be with us. Within a few years all the present generation will die off, and not one single individual will remain. *When a few years are come, we shall go the way whence we shall not return.* A few years, and another generation will succeed. That generation will all die off, and not a single individual will remain. And so it will continue on down to the millennium, and from thence through all he successive generations down to the end of time. So that all the generations that *have* ever lived, or ever *shall* live on the earth, will return to dust except one.—That one, the last generation will be living when Christ shall come to judgment. All the other generations who have ever lived on this earth from the beginning, to the end of time, shall now be sleeping in the dust. When we take into consideration how many millions will then have lived and died, in every age, in every nation under heaven, this world will appear like one *vast graveyard.*

Send forward our thoughts, my hearers, to the time when Christ shall come to judgment. Imagine what will then be the state of all the dead? Some will have just expired and there will not be time to convey their bodies to the grave before Christ shall come to judgment. Others, like Lazarus, will have been dead but a few days, and their bodies will not have time to dissolve. Some have lain in their graves for a few months, others for a few years. Some, whose monuments still remain, have been dead for fifty and some for a hundred years. Perhaps their bones may all be found. The monuments and perhaps

The Second Great Awakening 111

the bones of some who lived during the millennial state may yet be found.

But where are the bodies of those who lived and died before the millennium? Where are the bodies of that generation which lived in the nineteenth century? Where will be the bodies that this day compose this congregation? They will have been dead more than a thousand years; and they cannot be distinguished from common dust. Where are the bodies of those who lived before the flood? Besides those which have been deposited in the earth, how many have fallen and remained on the field of battle—their bones scattered and lost? Thousands have been drowned and lost in the ocean. Many have been devoured by the monsters of the deep. Thousands of human bodies, around their idols in India, are devoured by dogs and vultures and other beasts of prey. Many have undergone a variety of changes, and have entered into the composition of other bodies, such as vegetables of various kinds. Many have entered into the composition of animal bodies, such as into beasts, birds, and fishes, and worms of the dust.

The celebrated Wycliffe, called the morning star of the Reformation, died and was buried. About forty years afterwards, his enemies, to gratify their malice, dug up his bones, and burned them, and to make an effectual end of this good man, cast the ashes into an adjoining brook. Where is his body now?

What, my hearers, becomes of the particles of a body after it is consumed by the flames? True, it cannot be annihilated, but dissolved into smoke, it is taken and driven around the earth by the winds of heaven; and the little handful of ashes which remains goes to fertilize the earth. And yet thousands of human bodies have been consumed in the flames. How many in the destruction of Sodom were consumed by fire from heaven? *God turned the cities of Sodom into ashes.* How many have p*assed through the fire unto Molech?* How many have been burned to ashes on the funeral pile in India— "Ten thousand women annually," says Dr. Carey, "are burned with the bodies of their diseased husbands."

This, my hearers, is briefly the state of the world when Christ shall come to judgment. These are the nations to be gathered. We are almost ready to ask: Can these bodies ever be found? Can their matter ever be collected? Were we left without divine revelation; well might we ask: *How are the dead raised?* And with what body do they come?

But the scriptures and the power of God will solve the question. The resurrection will find them all. This will be the state of the dead when Christ shall come to judgment; but where are the souls which once inhabited these bodies? The righteous when they die pass immediately into glory. *Lazarus was conducted by angels into Abraham's bosom. Paul desired to depart and be with Christ.* To the repentant thief our Savior declared: *To day shalt thou be with me in Paradise.* The moment the soul of a believer quits this tabernacle of clay it joins the general assembly above. Write from henceforth, Blessed are the dead which die in the Lord.

Yet, on the other hand; the moment an impenitent sinner dies his soul is in the world of despair. *The rich man died, and was buried, and in hell he lifted up his eyes, being in torments; while his five brethren were yet on earth.* The inhabitants of Sodom are *suffering the vengeance of eternal fire.* The antediluvians are now *spirits in prison.*

In this manner souls are continually ascending into heaven, and descending into hell. This has been the case from the death of Abel down to the present time. Some have been in heaven and some in hell for hundreds of years. And there they will continue until Christ shall come to judgment. Shortly all the present generation will die and their souls will either ascend to heaven, or descend to hell. And so the souls of all who shall die will suddenly enter heaven or hell, and remain in the world of departed spirits until Christ shall come to judgment.

And now the number of saints in heaven will be greatly increased. The number, the appearance, the employment, and the happiness of the spirits of just men made perfect are thus described: *I beheld, and, lo, a great multitude, which no man could number, of all nations, and kindreds, and people, and tongues, stood before the throne, and before the Lamb, clothed with white robes, and palms in their hands; And cried with a loud voice, saying, Salvation to our God which sitteth upon the throne, and unto the Lamb. And one of the elders answered, saying unto me, What are these which are arrayed in white robes? and whence came they? And I said unto him, Sir, thou knowest. And he said to me, These are they which came out of great tribulation, and have washed their robes, and made them white in the blood of the Lamb. Therefore are they before the throne of God, and serve him day and night in his temple: and he that sitteth on the throne shall dwell among them. They shall hunger no more, neither thirst any more; neither shall the sun light on them, nor any heat. For the Lamb which is in the midst of the throne shall feed them, and shall lead them unto living fountains of waters: and God shall wipe away all tears from their eyes.* This is a description of the intermediate state between death and the resurrection.

But the souls of all unbelievers who have died or shall die, are shut up in the prison of hell with devils whom *God hath reserved in everlasting chains under darkness unto the judgment of the great day.* And here their souls will remain in a state of separation from their bodies, in fearful expectation until Christ shall come to judgment.

This, my hearers, will be the state of the dead when Christ shall come to judgment.

Here, I would pause and reflect; what will then be the state of my hearers, and this whole congregation?

If the final judgment does not come until after the millennial state then these bodies will all have lain in the grave more than a thousand years. And during this period our souls will be gathered *to the general assembly and church of the first born, which are written in heaven, and to God the judge of all, and to the spirits of just man made perfect.* So our souls will *be gathered with sinners.*

In one or both of these companies all our souls will be found. Probably in both. And then some of us will have been in heaven and some in hell more than a thousand years. Solemn thought! Who would not pray with David: *Gather not my soul with sinners.*

14

The Final Judgment, Part II

When the Son of man shall come in his glory, and all the holy angels with him, then shall he sit upon the throne of his glory: and before him shall be gathered all nations (Matthew 25: 31, 32).

In a former discourse from these words it was proposed to consider
I. The *certainly*
II. The *time when*
III. The *manner* of Christ coming to judgment.
The two former have been already considered.
Let us consider:
III. The manner of Christ coming to judgment.
And, 1st. He will come in his human nature. The same body which once appeared on earth will again appear the second time. The same body that was betrayed for thirty pieces of silver—that was arraigned before the bar of Pilate—scourged, spitted on, and crowned with thorns—The same body that was nailed to the cross, and pierced with a soldier's spear, that yielded up the ghost, arose from the dead, and ascended to heaven. This same body that was treated with such indignity will again appear with all the scars of crucifixion.

> "Now resplendent shine his nail prints,
> every eye shall see the wound."

When our Lord ascended to heaven, two angels appeared and spake thus to his gazing disciples: *Ye men of Galilee, why stand ye gazing up into heaven? This same Jesus, which is taken up from you into heaven, shall so come in like manner as ye have seen him go into heaven.* But how immensely different will be this present appearance: Once as a criminal, now as judge of the world.
2. He will come in *his glory. When the Son of man shall come in his glory, and all the holy angels with him, then shall he sit upon the throne of his glory.* A bright splendor will surround the body of the Savior. Such glory as to mortals is inconceivable. Something of this glory has however been witnessed by some of our Lord's Apostles. Peter, James, and John caught a glimpse of this glory on the Mount

of Transfiguration. *They were eye-witnesses of his divine majesty,* and they testify, that *his face did shine as the sun, and his raiment was white as the light.* In what glory did he appear to Saul of Tarsus! His brightness put out the noon day sun. *At midday, O king, I saw in the way a light from heaven, above the brightness of the sun, shining round about me and them which journeyed with me.* So bright was his appearance that *he could not see for the glory of that light.* The vision of this glory caused even the beloved disciple to *fall down at his feet as dead.* This can give us but a faint idea of that glory in which the Son of man will come.

Christ will appear not only in his own glory, but in the *glory of his Father.* The Father will judge the world by him—having committed all judgment to the Son. He is now the *brightness of the Father's glory, and the express image of his person.*

His coming will be like the lightning seen from one end of heaven to the other. *He shall come with power and great glory,*—such glory as will cover the heavens, and darken the sun. In short it is *the glorious appearing of the great God.*

3. He will come in the most public manner. His first coming was unobserved. He was in the world and the world knew him not. But now the whole world shall know it. When he appeared in his glory to the disciples on the holy mount, to Saul, and to the beloved disciple, this too, was not generally known. But now, Behold he c*ometh with clouds, and every eye shall see him.* He will descend *from heaven,* and will be seen coming in the *clouds. Then shall they see the Son of man coming in the clouds of heaven, with power and great glory— He maketh the clouds his chariot, he walketh upon the wings of the wind.*

He will be attended with a *glorious retinue: When the Son of man shall come in his glory, and all the holy angels with him.* Holy angels take a lively interest in the glorious plan of redemption. They announced the birth of the Savior—strengthened him in his agony in the garden—rolled back the stone from the door of his sepulcher and attended him back to heaven. At an instant, he could then command *more than twelve legions of angels. The chariots of God are twenty thousand, even thousands of angels.* These are all ministering spirits, waiting upon him to do his pleasure. *Bless the Lord ye his angels, that excel in strength, that do his commandments, hearkening unto the voice of his word.*

Now the sight of one angel is appalling to the stoutest heart. Witness the scene at the Saviour's sepulchre. *The angel of the Lord descended from heaven, and came and rolled back the stone from the door, and sat upon it. His countenance was like lightning, and his raiment white as snow: And for fear of him the keepers did shake, and became as dead men.*

But when the Son of man shall come in this glory, *All* the holy angels will be with him. All of every rank, whether they be Seraphim, Cherubim, Thrones, Dominions, Principalities or Powers. All that *innumerable company* will appear when Christ shall come to judgment. These shall all attend upon him, *thousand thousands ministering to him, and ten thousand times ten thousand round about him.* These will be his attendants in the clouds of heaven—every one will be busy and active. These are the greater things which Nathaniel should see. *Verily, verily, I say unto you, Hereafter ye shall see heaven open, and the angels of God ascending and descending upon the Son of man.* Thus, my hearers, will the Lord Jesus Christ be *revealed from heaven with his mighty angels.*

Again, when Christ shall come to judge he will be attended by *all the saints in heaven.* The number of saints in heaven will then be very great. St. John in a vision said, *(I) Beheld, and, lo, a great multitude, which no man could number, of all nations, and kindreds, and people, and tongues, stood before the throne.* These are unimbodied spirits—*the spirits of just men made perfect.* Patriarchs, prophets, Apostles, and martyrs, and all who have died in the Lord, will now appear. When on the mount of transfiguration, but two of this number appeared. *And behold, there appeared unto them Moses and Elias talking with him.* But now they shall all come out of that world, at the call of Christ. Thus the Psalmist: *Our God shall come, and shall not keep silence. He shall call to the heavens from above—that he may judge his people. Gather my saints together unto me.* And Enoch also, the seventh from Adam, prophesied saying, *Behold, the Lord cometh with ten thousand of his saints.*

All the souls of the redeemed who died in the Lord, will now descend with him to be reunited to their glorified bodies. Paul speaks of *the coming of our Lord Jesus Christ with all his saints.* What an immense multitude! what a cloud of attendants. Thus with the whole multitude of the heavenly host will Christ descent to judgment.

He will appear *conspicuous. When the Son of man shall come in his glory, and all the holy angels with him, then shall he sit upon the throne of his glory.* Nothing can be more august than the description given of this tremendous day. The Apostle, in vision, saw and described this majestic scene. *And I saw a great white throne, and him that sat on it, from whose face the earth and the heaven fled away; and there was found no place for them.* And thus *every eye shall see him.*

4. When Christ shall come to judgment he will be *heard.* The acclamations of attending angels will be heard. The regions of the air will resound when the armies of heaven shall come. *For the Lord himself shall descend from heaven with a shout, with the voice of the archangel, and with the trump of God.* That moment when Christ shall appear, all the living will have noticed. The armies of heaven will give a shout. The King of Kings has now arrived. "Hark!" the archangels voice proclaiming, "Thou old time shall be no more."

Now the trump of God shall sound. Here description fails. When the *law was given by the disposition of angels* on Mount Sinai notice was given by *the sound of a trumpet, and the voice of words; which voice they that heard entreated that the word should not be spoken to them any more; for they could not endure that which was commanded. And the voice of the trumpet was exceeding loud; so that all the people that were in the camp trembled—and the whole mount quaked greatly. And when the voice of the trumpet sounded long, and waxed louder and louder, Moses spake, and God answered him by a voice—Whose voice then shook the earth.* St. John in a vision describes a *mighty angel, who cried with a loud voice, as when a lion roareth: and when he had cried, seven thunders uttered their voices.* But nothing can equal that thunder which will echo round the world when the archangel shall swell the sound of the last trumpet.

5. Christ will come *suddenly.* God has often declared that the wicked shall *suddenly* be destroyed.—That they shall *be brought into desolation as in a moment.* But now the truth of all such declarations will appear clearer than ever.

God has even chosen to come on the wicked when they feel most secure. Thus when he brou*ght in the flood upon the world of the ungodly*, he had given them sufficient warning, but they would not believe. And now he chooses to wait until they became so hardened that it is said, they *knew not until the flood came, and took them all away.* So when he *turned the cities of Sodom into ashes*, God chose to wait until the wicked were all prepared for so great a doom. Lot must go out and once more cry: *Up, get you out of this place: for the Lord will destroy this city. But he seemed as one that mocked. They did eat, they drank, they bought, they sold, they planted, they builded; But the same day that Lot went out of Sodom it rained fire and brimstone from heaven, and destroyed them all. Even thus shall it be in the day when the Son of man shall be revealed.*

The destruction of the old world, of Sodom, and of Jerusalem are only images and shadows of the day of judgment. From what God has done he would have us know what he will do. It has never yet been God's manner to come out in judgment when the wicked were expecting it, and preparing for it. When he comes to punish, he chooses to take them when they are ripe for it; and then, with surprise. Were the good man of the house to apprehend a thief, or an incendiary, he would choose to detect him in the very act. Thus his crime is proved and his mouth is stopped. So when sinners are talking and laughing and scoffing and sporting in sin all over the earth,—when they are in the midst of their wickedness, and when they least expect it; Christ will come. When the world is thus reveling in wickedness, *Behold he comes.* As the lightning, his glory shall suddenly brake forth. *The day of the Lord will come as a thief in the night.* At the same time, the voice of laughter and singing; the *sound of the timbrel and harp, and the organ,* shall be interrupted by the *Shout,* the *voice of the archangel and the Trump of God.* The mirthful, haughty countenance—the sneering, contemptuous look of those who can blush only at the name of Christ, will at once be changed. *All faces will gather blackness.* In an instant, the wicked, all over the world, will *begin to weep and wail and gnash their teeth.* The sight of the Son of man, coming in the clouds of heaven, will compel them to cry to the rocks and mountains for shelter. O the sight of his face!

But now the righteous will rejoice. *They shall lift up their heads, for behold their redemption draweth nigh. They love his appearing* and the sight of their Savior will banish the fear of their enemies. Surely, I come quickly. *Amen,* will they answer, *Even so, come, Lord Jesus.*

At the same time the *dead will be raised. Before him shall be gathered all nations. The hour has come when all that are in their graves shall hear his voice, and shall come forth.* Every grave will open and all the bones arise. The bones of unnumbered millions scattered over the face of the earth will all come together, bone to his bone. The dust and ashes of martyrs, and all who once perished in the flames, shall come forth. *The sea gives up the dead which are in it; and death and hell deliver up the dead which are in them.* The elements shall be made to deliver up every particle of human dust. The whole creation groaneth and travaileth in pain together. But it shall now be delivered from its long bondage of human corruption.

The height of Carmel, and the bottom of the sea will be no hiding place. The earth, the air, and sea shall all deliver up their dead. The dead, small and great, *shall hear his voice and come forth; they that have done good, unto the resurrection of life; and they that have done evil, unto the resurrection of damnation.* At his call, every bone of all the unnumbered millions of the human race, will *come together, bone to his bone.* At the same time, all the scattered atoms will collect, each into its own body. All that dust shall now return, be arranged and marshaled in its proper place and order, by the same wisdom and almighty power which at *first created man out of the dust of the earth.*

Was there a noise and a shaking among the dry bones in the valley of vision? What will be the noise, and shaking, and uproar, when every bone shall fly through the atmosphere, in quest of its kindred bone. But not one shall be lost, or miss its way, or mistake its place! What apparent wild disorder when clouds of dust shall rise and darken the world! Now all that dust shall assemble a form a vast multitude of human bodies, of both the righteous and the wicked. And now the whole race of Adam appears upon earth at once. A multitude which no man could number, of all the ages and nations and languages. But their bodies will be widely different.

The bodies of the righteous will be *glorious.* Their *weak, vile, corruptible* bodies will be changed, and made *incorruptible, vigorous, spiritual, and glorious.* Their bodies will resemble the body of Christ on the mount of transfiguration. *We look for the Lord Jesus Christ: who shall change our vile body, that it may be fashioned like unto his glorious body.*

With respect to the bodies of the *wicked*, very little is revealed— But that they shall be *incorruptible, immortal* and inglorious. *They shall awake to shame and everlasting contempt.* Their bodies will appear suitable to their character and condition. Destitute of the robe of innocence and the righteousness of Christ, they will possess all the feelings of shame and remorse of one that God hath declared *shall awake to shame and everlasting contempt.*

Now the souls of the righteous will come to take possession of their bodies. All the spirits of just men made perfect will return each to its own former habitation. What must be the emotions of a glorified spirit about to take possession of a glorified body? This is the body which I once inhabited, from which I have long been absent. This is the body in which I sinned, in which I enjoyed a day of salvation. This is that body in which I once heard the sound of the gospel, and felt such a weight of guilt and horror that made me cry out, "What must I do to be saved?" This is that body in which I repented of my sins—and cast myself at the Savior's feet crying, "God be merciful to me a sinner." This is that body in which I first became acquainted with the Saviour, *when old things passed away; and behold, all things become new.* This that body which I dedicated, and presented to God a living sacrifice to be his forever—This is that body in which I endured such temptations and felt such struggles in my Christian warfare. This is that body in which so often knelt in prayer, in which I found sweet communion with Christ. This is that body in which I suffered shame and reproach for the sake of Christ, and now it is raised in his image to go and dwell forever in his presence. Happy union.

Now the souls of all the spirits in prison shall come forth, and take possession of their bodies. Each one will return to its own appropriate body. O wretched habitation. "This is the body which I once inhabited, from which I have long been absent. This is that body in which I sinned—in which I heard the sound of the gospel—this is that wretched body which I fed and clothed with so much care to the neglect of my soul—that body in which I was ashamed of Christ—Which was too proud and stubborn to bow the knee in prayer to God—O that I had never seen you, and could never see you again. Is it not enough to be tormented alone for all the deeds done in the body? Must I again take a dwelling so loathsome, and fitted and *prepared for the devil and his angels?"* Miserable union!

And now all the righteous and wicked have become reunited to their bodies—and stand up on their feet ready to be assembled before the dread tribunal. And now the dead being raised the *living will be changed.* This seems necessary to prepare them to endure the trial of the judgment. Flesh and blood could not endure the sight of the judge, much less bear the trial. Sinners now under conviction of sin sometimes loose all their strength and all their rational facilities. And this, only under a partial view of their guilt and danger—and that too, while hearing the sound of pardon, and the offers of salvation in the gospel. How then could they endure the sight of all their sins, before a frowning judge?

Sometimes the criminal, before an earthly judge, faints and falls back on hearing the sentence of death. If human nature cannot stand before this petty tribunal, much less before the judgment seat of Christ. If sinners are over come with the fear of those, who have power only to kill the body, much less could they endure the fear of him who has power to cast into hell. Their powers too must be such that they can retain what they hear, and recollect all the sins which they have ever committed.

The living must be changed, otherwise the sight would over power their bodies and take away life. All would faint and become as dead men. The sight of one angel which descended, with a countenance of lightning, at the Savior's tomb, struck down a guard of soldiers; and they became as dead men. At the sight of the Savior, Paul fell; and so did the beloved disciple. So that the living must be changed to prepare for the trial.

This change of the living will not be gradual. They will not die, and their souls depart for a season into the world of spirits,—into heaven and hell, and then return. It will be a change much resembling death. The bodies of all the Christians then living will become like the bodies of those which are raised from the dead. They will feel this mortal begin to put on immortality. This will be a mysterious, a wonderful change.

This great change will be sudden, in the twinkling of an eye. The time will probably be about the time at which the dead are raised. It will be at the sound of the last trumpet. *Behold, I show you a mystery; We shall not all sleep, but we shall all be changed, in a moment, in the twinkling of an eye, at the last trump: for the trumpet shall sound, and the dead shall be raised incorruptible, and we shall be changed.*

The bodies of sinners too, will now be changed, and fitted for their destiny. The bodies of saints and sinners all over the earth being raised and changed.—Now the whole multitude shall be assembled before the tribunal of Christ. Before him shall all nations be gathered. *At the end of the world the Son of man shall send forth his angels, and they shall gather together his elect from the he four winds. When the Son of man shall come in his glory, and all the holy angels with him, then shall he sit upon the throne of his glory: and before him shall be gathered all nations.*

And now the fallen angels shall all be assembled. The Prince, and the ruler of the darkness of this world, who has headed the grand rebellion shall now be present with all his followers. For though God hath *cast them down to hell;* yet he *hath delivered them into chains of darkness, to be reserved unto judgment.* These, though they now suffer in hell, as do others, have as yet had no public, formal trial. They are criminals in chains, reserved to the day of trial, when Adam and Eve and all the accusers shall appear together. *And the angels which kept not their first estate, but left their own habitation, he hath reserved in everlasting chains under darkness unto the judgment of the great day.*

And I saw the dead small and great stand before God.—And the judgment was set, and the books were opened.

15

The Demands of Discipleship

And it came to pass, that, as they went in the way, a certain man said unto him, Lord, I will follow thee whithersoever thou goest. And Jesus said unto him, Foxes have holes, and birds of the air have nests; but the Son of man hath not where to lay his head. And he said to another, Follow me. But he said, Lord, suffer me first to bury my father. Jesus said unto him, Let the dead bury their dead: but go thou and preach the kingdom of God. And another also said, Lord, I will follow thee; but let me first go bid them farewell, which are at home at my house. And Jesus said unto him, No man, having put his hand to the plough, and looking back, is fit for the kingdom of God (Luke 9:57-62).

This passage contains a number of incidents in the history of our Saviour, which perhaps occurred at different times. They are all presented in one interesting cluster because they bear upon the same important point.

The first is as follows: *And it came to pass that as they went in the way, a certain man said unto him, Lord, I will follow thee withersoever thou goest.* What led him to express this determination the context will show: *And it came to pass, when the time was come that he should be received up* (i.e. should be put to death, arise from the dead, and ascend to heaven), *he steadfastly set his face to go to Jerusalem.* With the scene of his sufferings full in view, he was not diverted from his purpose. *And he sent messengers before his face: and they went and entered into a village of the Samaritans, to make ready for him.*—to ask whether any of the inhabitants of that village would be disposed to receive and accommodate their Lord and Master on his way to Jerusalem. *And they did not receive him.* But why? The reason is thus rendered: *Because his face was as though he would go to Jerusalem.*

And why should this be made an objection? It will be recollected that there was a dispute between the Jews and the Samaritans about the proper place of worship. *Our fathers,* said the woman of Samaria, *worshipped in this mountain, but ye say that in Jerusalem is the place where men ought to worship.* Hence they held no friendly intercourse—interchanged no acts of kindness. *For the Jews have no dealings with the Samaritans.* Would the Saviour change his course, and go up the hill of Gerizim where stood their own temple, built by Sanballat, then they would receive him. But now their prejudices prevented. *And when his disciples, James and John, saw this, they said, Lord, wilt thou that we command fire to come down from heaven, and consume them, even as Elias did?* This slight, offered to their divine Master, filled them with indignation. And well it might. Their ardent love to him would lead them to feel very deeply every indignity offered to their Lord. And they were for avenging the insult at once. *But he turned and rebuked them, and said, Ye know not what manner of spirit ye are of.*

What a lesson on interaction is this to all the disciples of Christ. If the warm-hearted disciples, James and John, in vindicating the cause of their divine Master might lose a good spirit or intermingle a bad, how does it become others to take heed. James and John were certainly on the right side—On the side of religion—on the side of Christ. In this they were right. Well might they feel a holy indignation. But in their zeal, they unwittingly intermingled a bad spirit, for which they met a solemn rebuke. What a lesson of instruction is this to the ministers of Christ, who are sent to cities, towns, and villages, *as messengers before his face to make ready for him*—to prepare the way of the Lord, by opening their houses and hearts to receive his message of mercy. Should they meet with a repulse through prejudice and pride and unwillingness to receive the Saviour, this may grieve their hearts.

But in vindicating the cause of Christ, and urging sinners to receive him, they must not forget the solemn unction, *Take heed to thyself.* The example of these two ardent disciples is recorded for their instruction. In the ardor of their zeal there may be something noble, but still they may lack *the meekness and gentleness of Christ.* The case before us is truly affecting. That which many would commend as bold and heroic in the cause of religion, may still meet with the divine rebuke—*Ye know not what manner of spirit ye are of.* While ministers are faithfully to deliver their whole message, *whether men will hear or forbear,* yet there are limits beyond which they must not pass. Opposition to the message of mercy may be of such a character, that further effort at this time might be worse than useless. Even Christ would not obtrude himself upon the inhabitants in the village of Samaria. If they were willing to receive him, well; but if not, he would leave them unto their own choice. So now there are limits beyond which ministers need not dispute the point whether sinners shall open their hearts and bid the Saviour welcome. If they choose to receive him, well; if not, the whole responsibility of rejecting the message may be left resting upon their own consciences.

The rejection of Christ by this village doubtless awakened a general murmur of indignation among the multitude that followed him. *But he turned and rebuked them.* I can fancy that, as he once stood upon the deck of a ship, the seas and the waves roaring, and rebuked the winds and the sea saying, *Peace be still* so now he *stilled the noise and the tumult of the people. For the Son of Man* he adds *is not come to destroy men's lives, but to save them.* The destruction of life would not comport with the Saviour's message of mercy to the souls of men. He would rather work a miracle *to save,* or even raise them from the dead. For the rejection of the message of his mercy they must answer at another day, *where he shall come in the clouds, with power and great glory.*

And they went to another village. At this interesting crisis, the silence was broken by the voice of one that followed him. *It came to pass, that as they went in the way* as they turned from that village to go to another, *a certain man said unto him, Lord, I will follow thee withersoever thou goest.* If they will not receive you in this village go to another and I will follow—And if they will not receive you in that, go to another still, and I will follow thither also.—And if they reject you the world over, I am determined to *follow thee withersoever thou goest.* Now this is just as it should be. Without this resolution, no one can be a true disciple of Christ. Let it cost what it may—the loss of father and mother, wife and children, and even life itself! This is characteristic of all who arrive at heaven—*They follow the Lamb withersoever he goeth.* Christ's terms of discipleship are very definite: *If any man come to me and hate not*—comparatively—*his father, and mother, and wife, and children, and brethren, and sisters, yea, and his own life also, he cannot be my disciple.* And what says the Saviour to the man so firmly resolved to follow him? *And Jesus said unto him, Foxes have holes, and the birds of the air have nests, but the Son of Man hath not where to lay his head.* The Saviour would not deceive him. He would have him count the cost of becoming his follower. *Foxes have holes and the birds of the air have nests:* the wild beasts of the desert may find their lairs, where to hide and rest themselves: and the fowls of heaven a place where to lodge, and to lay their young: But the Son of Man who came from heaven *to seek and save lost sinners hath not where to lay his head.*

The rejection of the Samaritans is but a specimen of the treatment which the Saviour meets the world over. *He was in the world, and the world was made by him, and the world knew him not. He came*

The Second Great Awakening

unto his own, and his own received him not. We have all treated the Saviour in the same manner. Though invisible to mortal eyes, he has long stood knocking at the door of their hearts, pleading for admittance. And, hitherto, many in this assembly have ungratefully bid him depart. He has come with all the blessings of salvation in his hand; and urged them upon our acceptance, but ye would not receive him. You have ungratefully bid him depart, *Go thy way for this time—depart from us—we desire not the knowledge of thy ways. What is the Almighty that we should serve him, and what profit shall we have if we pray unto him?* is the language of all these hearts which do not bid the Saviour welcome.

*And he said unto another, Follow me.*This was the language of Christ when he first began to obtain followers. *Walking by the sea of Galilee, he saw Peter and Andrew casting a net into the sea, in the midst of business, and he saith unto them, Follow me. And going on from thence, he saw others* in the midst of business; and he called them and they immediately left all and followed him. He *saw Levi sitting at the receipt of customs*—with his head, and heart, and hands full of business, *and he said unto him, Follow me.* And with what readiness did he comply? *And he left all, rose up, and followed him.* There is something majestic in all this: Follow me. He has a right to say this: "the world is his and they that dwell therein." The same language is addressed to all, who hear the sound of the gospel. To every sinner in this assembly, the Saviour speaks as really as though he were personally present, calling him by name, Follow me, follow me: and every sinner is bound by all the authority of God to take his heart and his affections from every earthly object and place them supremely upon Christ. In this sense he is required without delay, to *leave all, rise up, and follow him.* Without this he cannot be his disciple.

The man to whom the call is made in the text replies, *Lord, suffer me first to go and bury my father.* He resolves to follow him, but begs for a little delay. The call finds him in peculiar circumstances. He is in deep affliction. His father is dead. *Lord, I will follow thee, but suffer me first* to pay the last tribute of respect to a parent.

How many in similar circumstances, resolve to attend to the subject of religion. How many, when summoned around the sick and dying bed of a pious father, or a mother, a brother, a sister, or some dead friend, resolve that they *will* attend to the subject of religion. They sigh and are ready to exclaim, *Let me die the death of the righteous, and let my last end be like his.* Or it may be they are summoned to hear the warning voice of such as have neglected the concerns of their souls and slighted all the calls and melting invitations of the Saviour while in health. The very sight itself or even the tidings of the death of kindred and friends, checks the spirit of worldliness and vanity, and says impressively, *Be ye also ready.* Thousands under these circumstances have felt the littleness of earth with all its concerns, and have resolved that they will attend to the great concerns of the soul. But unhappily as is the case before us, their very afflictions prevent an imme*diate* attention to the subject, and thus the call of infinite mercy is neglected to their eternal undoing.

* This sermon has the following notation at the top: "Mr. N's extemp. Ser. taken by A. Dickinson. Unfinished."

16

Many Now on the Earth Are Greater Sinners Than Those Who Are in Hell

There were present at that season some that told him of the Galileans, whose blood Pilate had mingled with their sacrifices. And Jesus answering said unto them, Suppose ye that these Galileans were sinners above all the Galileans, because they suffered such things? I tell you, Nay: but, except ye repent, ye shall all likewise perish. Or those eighteen, upon whom the tower in Siloam fell, and slew them, think ye that they were sinners above all men that dwelt in Jerusalem? I tell you, Nay: but, except ye repent, ye shall all likewise perish (Luke 13:1-6).

It is extremely natural for mankind to talk and complain much of the sins of others. This we have all had occasion to witness. The fact was the same in our Saviour's day. *There were present at that season, some that told him of the Galileans, whose blood Pilate had mingled with their sacrifices.* The fact to which they alluded was this: A number of Galileans refused subjection to the Roman government. And on a certain occasion, when they were all assembled for the worship of God, Pilate, to enforce the law, embraced that opportunity and sent a company of armed soldiers who slew them and mingled their blood with their sacrifices.

This event was related to our Saviour, doubtless with feelings of self-complacency, which led to the solemn disclosures in my text, from which we remark

1. That some sinners have already perished.
2. They perished through their own fault.
3. The greatness of their suffering is proof of the greatness of their criminality. But,
4. The greatness of their suffering is no evidence that they were greater sinners than those that were spared.

1. Some sinners have already perished. Of this the text is sufficient proof. *Except ye repent, ye shall all likewise perish.* What a vast multitude perished in the general deluge? Not only drowned, but damned: spirits in prison. Sodom perished. It was not a temporary punishment merely, but God hath told us that they were *set forth as examples, suffering the vengeance of eternal fire.* This is also evident from the parable of the rich man and Lazarus. Our Lord

in this gives us a correct view of the invisible world. *The rich man died, and was buried; And in hell he lift up his eyes, being in torments.* Are there few that be saved? *Strive. Because strait is the gate, and narrow is the way, which leadeth unto life, and few there be that find it.*

Compare the character and conduct of multitudes who have died with the declarations of scripture, we shall be compelled to join in the declarations of our Saviour. The fact is acknowledged by all who believe the Bible, that some sinners have perished.

2. They perished through their own fault. God never inflicts undeserved punishment. *The Judge of all the earth will do right.* The very fact of their sufferings is proof that they were sinners, and deserved to die. *Remember, I pray thee, who ever perished, being innocent? (Job 4:7).* The fact that all are sinners shows that all deserve death. But this is not all—even after they had sinned, and deserved death, they might have been saved, if they would. And that they were not, was particularly their own fault. They had the offers of pardon and salvation. God warned them—The old world by the preaching of Noah and the strivings of his Spirit. So Sodom.

But they perished through their own *neglect. They did not repent.* A sinner some times says, "What have I done that I deserve death?" It is not merely for doing—but for *not* doing that the sinner must die. It is on the ground of neglect that gospel sinners perish. *They did not repent. Except ye repent, ye shall all likewise perish. He that believeth not, is condemned already. If any man love not the Lord Jesus Christ, let him be Anathema.* The Bible does not say, How shall we escape if we lie and swear and cheat and steal. But it places condemnation principally on the grounds of neglect. How shall we escape if we *neglect* so great salvation. *But those enemies of mine which would not that I should reign over them, bring hither, and slay them before me. God shall send them strong delusion, because they received not the love of the truth. Taking vengeance on them that know not God, and that obey not the gospel.*

Nor can the sinner plead that he would repent if he could. He is as really, and as highly criminal for not repenting as for his overt acts of sin. *Then began he to upbraid the cities wherein most of his mighty works were done, because they repented not: Woe, woe, woe because they repented not. After thy hardness and impenitent heart treasurest up unto thy self wrath against the day of wrath and revelation of the righteous judgment of God.* When you get to hell conscience will then upbraid...*Nay, father Abraham: but if one went unto them from the dead, they will repent.* Thus all who have perished, perished through their own neglect, because they did not repent.

3. The greatness of their suffering is proof of the greatness of their criminality. Sinners suffer only for their crimes. In this world, God often inflicts punishment far less than the sinner's real desert. It does not equal the crime, but in inflicting punishment God never exceeds the measure of his guilt. God has selected and set forth some sinners of the human race as examples *to those who should after live ungodly.* The old world and Sodom were specimens of this. Their punishment was awful. But awful as it was, we may rest assured that it did not exceed the measure of their iniquity. For in this *the Judge of all the earth shall do right.* In the greatness of their punishment we may read the greatness of their crimes.

But,

4. The greatness of their suffering is no evidence that they were greater sinners than those that were spared. When God inflicts a heavy punishment upon a people, we are apt to conclude that they were greater sinners than others. And should he send any to hell, it is common to conclude that they must have been sinners of the worst kind—such as all would be ready to pronounce monsters in wickedness—This was the opinion of our Lord's hearers. They viewed the destruction of the Galileans in this light. On account of their sufferings they were supposed to be great sinners: greater than those who had escaped these sufferings. But this conclusion was erroneous. Our Saviour replies, *Suppose ye that these Galileans were sinners above all the Galileans, because they suffered such things? I tell you, Nay: but except ye repent, ye shall all likewise perish.*

There were sinners living in Galilee, whose crimes were as great as the crimes of those who had suffered the wrath of heaven. *Suppose ye that these Galileans were sinners above all the Galileans, because they suffered such things? I tell you, Nay.* Sinners who had gone to hell from Galilee were no worse than sinners then living in that place.

Again: The same was true of inhabitants of Jerusalem. *Or those eighteen, upon whom the tower in Siloam fell, and slew them, think ye that they were sinners above all men that dwelt in Jerusalem? I tell you, Nay: but except ye repent, ye shall all likewise perish.* So that sinners who had gone to hell from Jerusalem were no worse than those then living.

Again: Sinners to whom our Saviour preached in Chorazin,

Bethsaida, and Capernaum were as great sinners as those already in hell. This our Lord told them to their face. The inhabitants of Sodom were set forth as *examples, suffering the vengeance of eternal fire.* He told them that they were greater sinners, and would suffer greater punishment than sinners already in hell. *But I say unto you, that it shall be more tolerable for the land of Sodom in the day of judgment, than for you.*

This sentiment was then true in our Saviour's day. Sinners of other countries and other times, who had gone to hell before them, were no worse than sinners then living. Let us bring the warning home to this congregation. Suppose ye that sinners who have died and gone to hell from other places were sinners above all the sinners dwelling in this place? I tell you *nay; but, except ye repent, ye shall all likewise perish.*

To you who have not yet repented of your sins, this subject delivers a loud warning. What think ye of sinners already in hell? Suppose ye that they were greater sinners than yourselves? You are, no doubt, ready to say that they were great sinners, and deserved to perish. But for what crimes were they lost?

Will it be said that their hearts were *totally depraved*? This is doubtless correct. *And God saw that the wickedness of man was great in the earth, and that every imagination of the thoughts of his heart was only evil continually.* The same may be said of sinners now living. The eye of God is fixed upon every sinner's heart. He takes cognizance of every thought and every imagination. They are *all evil, only evil continually.*

They had the strivings of God's Spirit. So you have resisted the strivings of his Spirit. They did not repent. They were favored with many means, with Christ and the Apostles. Were they stupid and thoughtless and not at all alarmed? So you. They were told their danger in very plain terms and they might have taken warning. So you. Did not Noah and Lot and the Prophets and Christ warn? Did not God warn through them? So God warns now in his word, by the same preachers—their discourses are recorded—and the awful end of those who refused these warnings is recorded too. God's evinces the sincerity of his threatenings to you in a manner that sinners in hell had never before witnessed. He sets them forth as examples. Were they not afraid of the wrath of God? (But they) never slighted half the privileges (you have).

The very person who told him of the Galileans were as great sinners as the persons of whom they spoke. They had hard hearts.

*Power. Time enough. Terms reasonable. Not ignorant. Salvation freely offered. Delayed. Presumed.

Infer,

God does exercise sovereign mercy for some sinners out of hell greater than those in. Persons to whom Christ declared the warning in the text were indebted to the sovereign mercy of God. Some quarrel with this truth—but they quarrel with that very mercy which keeps them out of hell.

2. Necessary for all to repent, even the very best.

3. Alarming that sinners now may be heading close upon the heels of some who have gone to hell.

4. What must be the feelings of sinners in hell respecting their companions on earth? I have five brethren; (send Lazarus) that he may testify unto them, lest they also come into this place of torment. When last they see how their companions in sin are coming after them.—Could they be permitted to speak, would they not cry out— not groan in this congregation.

5. Nothing but sovereign mercy keeps sinners in this house from dropping into hell this moment.

Learn,

1. That sinners often talk and complain much of the sins of others when they have never repented of their own sins—they may be greater sinners, every moment in danger of perishing forever. Those who talk and make these complaints are commonly very ignorant of their own hearts.

2. God does exercise sovereign mercy. For when our Saviour delivered this discourse there were some of his hearers who were greater sinners than some in hell. These very persons were indebted to that very mercy every moment.

3. There may be redeemed sinners in heaven who were greater sinners than some now in hell.

4. The chief of sinners may be saved if they will repent.

5. The least of sinners will be lost except they repent.

6. There may be sinners in this house more guilty than many now in hell.

Thousands of thoughts and imaginations which you think little of, may be awfully wicked in the sight of a holy God. Sinners in hell had no love to God and no love to the duties of religion. And the

---

* See Sermon # 3 for an expansion of Nettleton's thoughts here. Since he often spoke extemporaneously, Nettleton most likely filled in here with the outline found there.

hearts of sinners now living are equally depraved. Will it be said that they resisted the strivings of the Holy Spirit? The same may be said of sinners now living. When the Spirit of God has moved upon your heart and conscience and has begun to awake, how often have you labored to silence your fears?

Will it be said that they lived long in sin? The same may be said of many now living. How many years have gone out of your probation? Thousands and millions have died younger than you. Already has your day of salvation been lengthened out beyond that of most of the human race. Many in this house are no doubt older and lived longer in sin than many now in hell.

Will it be said that they sinned against great light? The same may be said of sinners now living. Sinners in this house have enjoyed far greater light than many sinners now in hell. The inhabitants of the old world and of Sodom who are *set forth as examples, suffering the vengeance of eternal fire,* never enjoyed such light as sinners now under the gospel. Never did they hear half the preaching or enjoy half the privileges of sinners in this assembly. Their light was to yours, no more than a taper to the noon day sun. The guilt and punishment of sinners are to be measured by the light rejected. *He that knew his lord's will, and did it not, shall be beaten with many stripes.* Many in this house have known their Lord's will for years and have not yet done it.

Were they so stupid and thoughtless? The same may be said of you. Noah, Lot, and the Prophets warned. So God now the same.

He seemed as one that mocked—How does it seem to you? Are you not going to be frightened to heaven?

God does not always wait for sinners to arrive at the same pitch of wickedness before he destroys them. This should serve as a warning to young offenders. There is no evidence that you will be suffered to go half the length that others have. You are now treading close upon the heels of some who have been lost—far beyond the bounds. You have already overleaped the bounds of God's forbearance with others.

17

The Certain Destruction of All Who Do Not Seek Salvation Rightly

For many, I say unto you, will seek to enter in, and shall not be able (Luke 13:24).

The question was put: Lord, are there few that be saved? And he said unto them, Strive to enter in at the strait gate: for many, I say unto you, will seek to enter in, and shall not be able. Here is an interesting question. A question about salvation. It leads to a useful though an alarming answer. To the question, "Are there few that be saved?" mankind have given different answers. It is a question above the reach of human reason. Whether few or many or any at all will finally be saved are questions that cannot be determined without a revelation from God. Discarding the word of fallible mortals, we (must depend upon) divine revelation. We appeal to our omniscient Saviour. Whatever men may say, the Son of God has declared, *Many, I say unto you, will seek to enter in, and shall not be able.* What proportion of the whole race of Adam will finally be saved or lost, I cannot say, for I have not been told. But one thing is certain, *Many will seek to enter in, and shall not be able.*

Let us attend to the fact asserted.

1. Many have sought and have missed of salvation.

All who exert themselves in religion do in some sense, seek to enter heaven. Even the heathen, who know nothing of the Saviour, are concerned about a future state. They build temples, worship idols, and offer sacrifices. They offer their own children in sacrifice and subject themselves to the most cruel tortures and for what? To atone for sin and to obtain pardon and salvation. All these exertions are demonstrations of anxiety and concern about a future state. Thousands and millions have sought, in this manner, to enter heaven, and have not been able.

With respect to idolaters we have positive declaration, that *they shall not inherit the kingdom of God (I Corinthians 6:9).* For without are *murderers, and idolaters, and whosoever loveth and maketh a lie (Revelation 22:15).*

Cain, as well as Abel, offered sacrifice. *He brought of the fruit of the ground an offering unto the Lord.* And the Lord had respect to the offering of the one and not of the other. Yet both sought, and yet both were not accepted. The Jews in the time of Isaiah offered thousands of sacrifices;—appeared before the Lord in solemn assemblies, and made many prayers. And yet the Lord declares, *When ye spread forth your hands, I will hide mine eyes from you; yea, when ye make many prayers, I will not hear.*

When Christ was on earth, many were punctual in all the externals of religion. They *prayed and fasted and paid tithes of all that they possessed.* In this manner they sought, and yet were excluded, *For,* says the Saviour, *I say unto you, that except your righteousness shall exceed the righteousness of the scribes and Pharisees, ye shall in no case enter into the kingdom of heaven.*

The Jews at the present day; notwithstanding they denounce Christ as an impostor, are punctual in the duties of their religion. They are seeking to enter heaven. And yet Christ told them, *Ye shall die in your sins: for if ye believe not that I am he, ye shall die in your sins.* Thus many *have* sought to enter heaven and have not been able. These you will remember, did not live unconcerned; they were not without thoughts on the subject of salvation.

2. That many will seek to enter heaven, and shall not be able is evident from plain declarations of scripture. At the day of judgment many will be found pleading for admittance into heaven on the ground of their religious duties. *Many will say unto me in that day, Lord, Lord, have we not prophesied in thy name? and in thy name cast out devils? and in thy name done many wonderful works? And then I will profess unto them, I never knew you: depart from me, ye that work iniquity.*

The text itself is a sufficient confirmation of this fact. *Many, I say unto you, will seek to enter in, and shall not be able.* My hearers will notice that the Saviour is not speaking of those who do not, and will not, *think* of religion. He is not speaking of those who sit down and do nothing—But what renders it still more alarming, he is speaking of those who *seek to enter heaven.* They sought and were not able to enter. *Not able* says Christ; but if they sought, why were they not able?

My hearers are doubtless, all ready to answer, because they did not seek aright. This is doubtless correct. Many will seek to enter heaven but will not be able for the same reason. They will not seek aright. Every thing depends on the manner.

Then let us,

II. Point out some of the ways in which sinners may seek, and yet miss of salvation.

1. They do not seek it as a thing of the *first importance.* The

direction is, seek first the kingdom of God. Let it be the first and leading object of your pursuit. Everything else must give way—and lie in subordination to this object. Whatever may come in competition, however dear, you must be able to renounce it without a sigh. *The kingdom of heaven is like unto treasure hid in a field; the which when a man hath found, he hideth, and for joy thereof goeth and selleth all that he hath, and buyeth that field.*

But many who attend to the subject of religion will not seek it in this manner. They will attend to the subject by the bye. They do not make it the *one thing needful*—nor feel its overwhelming importance. The grand maxim of many is seek first the world—and then if you can find time—Though they attend to religion, yet they attend more to the world. All who attend to the subject in this manner, will miss of heaven. *No man can serve two masters: for either he will hate the one, and love the other; or else he will hold to the one, and despise the other. Ye cannot serve God and mammon.*

2. By their own righteousness. Many will trust to what they have done, to what they are doing, and to what they intend to do. It will not be through want of zeal or engagedness in religion; not because they did not do more, but because they trusted in what they did. This was the fatal mistake of some in the time of the Apostles. *For I bear them record that they have a zeal for God, but not according to knowledge. For they being ignorant of God's righteousness, and going about to establish their own righteousness, have not submitted themselves unto the righteousness of God.* They compass themselves about with sparks which they have kindled—But they shall lie down in sorrow. Without feeling that they are sinners, without conviction, without conversion. So the Pharisee, *God, I thank thee, that I am not as other men are, extortioners, unjust, adulterers, or even as this publican. I fast twice in a week, I give tithes of all that I possess.* None can enter heaven on the ground of their own righteousness. *Except your righteousness shall exceed the righteousness of the scribes and Pharisees, ye shall in no case enter into the kingdom of heaven.* Strip off his garments of self-righteousness. Thus did Paul, *Yea doubtless, and I count all things but loss for the excellency of the knowledge of Christ Jesus my Lord.*

3. Many will adopt sentiments which will effectually prevent the necessary preparation for heaven. Many deny the necessity of regeneration. They intend to live moral lives, and do not believe in the necessity of a change of heart. But all who seek to enter heaven, without being born again, will be disappointed. However sincere a person may be in disbelieving the doctrine—however much he may

do to enter heaven without being born again, it makes no difference. The error must be fatal. The Saviour hath repeatedly declared, *Verily, verily, I say unto thee, Except a man be born again, he cannot see the kingdom of heaven.* After all that may be said to explain away this doctrine, it will be found of such pressing necessity, that without it, none can enter heaven.

This, by the way, is one gate which sinners are to enter. Repentance is the gate, and the only gate which leads to the door of heaven. Sinners are commanded *to strive, to agonize, and to enter this gate.* Those which deny the necessity of regeneration may, *seek to enter heaven,* but they never seek to enter the strait gate. It is the command of Christ. *Enter ye in at the strait gate.*

The difficulty of repentance is stated as the reason why many will not be saved; *because strait is the gate, and narrow is the way, which leadeth unto life, and few there be that find it.* Those who do not believe in regeneration do not *even seek to enter in at the strait gate.* All who attempt to climb up some other way will certainly be excluded. They spend their time in idle attempts to widen the gate. Instead of humbling themselves and breaking off their sins and striving to enter by regeneration and repentance will waste their day of salvation by cutting and carving and widening the gate so that all may enter with all their sins, etc.

4. Not in season. Many will seek to enter heaven, but their exertions will be too late. *Afterward came also the other virgins, saying, Lord, Lord, open to us. But he answered and said, Verily I say unto you, I know you not. When once the master of the house hath risen up, and hath shut to the door, and ye begin to stand without, and to knock at the door, saying, Lord, Lord, open unto us; and he shall answer and say unto you, I know not whence ye are.— I tell you, I know not whence ye are; depart from me, all ye workers of iniquity.*

Those who have frequently stilled their convictions, and resisted the Spirit of God are in danger of being too late. *Because I have called and ye refused; I have stretched out my hand, and no man regarded.* Then take heed lest *there be any as Esau, who for one morsel of meat sold his birthright. For ye know how that afterward, when he would have inherited the blessing, he was rejected: for he found no place of repentance, though he sought it carefully with tears.*

But hear the Saviour's word,
"Strive for the heavenly gate,

> Many will call upon the Lord,
> And find their cries too late."

5. Not willing to part with all for heaven. This was case with the young man in the gospel. He came to Christ with the important question, "Good Master, what shall I do to inherit eternal life?" He imagined that he was willing to do any thing, to obtain heaven. *Go and sell all that thou hast.* This tried him—it showed him his heart. It sent him away *sad.* It is recorded of Herod, that when he heard John, he did many things. With respect to the sinner anxious for his soul; doubtless, some one sin prevents him from yielding to the terms of the gospel. Whatever it may be, the sinner must renounce it. He must break off from every sin—it is required to do it on pain of eternal death. *If any man will come after me, let him deny himself, and take up his cross daily, and follow me. If thy right eye offend thee; pluck it out, and cast it from thee: for it is profitable for thee that one of thy members should perish, and not that thy whole body should be cast into hell.* He must part with all his sins, or he must part with heaven. All who seek to enter heaven without renouncing all their sins, seek in vain.

Or it may be some friend or acquaintance with whom the sinner is not willing to part or whom he cannot bear to offend—*Let me first go bid them farewell, which are at home at my house. No man, having put his hand to the plough, and looking back, is fit for the kingdom of God.*

Finally, some seek for a time and then drop the subject. This is often the case in times of revival. For a time they are alarmed; they read and attempt to pray. They struggle with conviction for awhile. Find their hearts so hard, and duties of religion so crossing and painful that they drop the subject—they give it up, and are lost forever.

Those who are about to give it up, commonly do it by taking offense. They do it at almost anything. Thus it was in the time of Christ. They followed him for awhile, but by and by his preaching came *too close.* Then unhumbled hearts could not endure it. *They took offense and from that time many of his disciples went back, and walked no more with him.*
Do not seek as it is a thing of first importance.
Own righteousness
Not in season.
Not willing to part with all for heaven.
For a time and then they drop the subject.

Infer,

1. The danger of a loose sentiment on the subject of religion. If strait is the gate, let us beware how we attempt to widen it. We may succeed in quieting conscience; but we do it at peril of loosing our souls. None will be better than the sentiments which he adopts will make him. What some call liberality, the Bible would pronounce infidelity. No preacher ever made the way to heaven more difficult than the Son of God who said, *Wide is the gate, and broad is the way, which leadeth to destruction, and many go in thereat,* and *Strive to enter in at the strait gate: for many, I say unto you, will seek to enter in, and shall not be able.* If any preacher attempts to show an easier way to heaven than by the strait gate and narrow way of regeneration, you may know that he does not preach the way of salvation.

2. If so, then those who are not yet anxious for their souls may fear that they should yet be among that number. My friends, I must tell you that your fears are not without foundation. Many whose souls are as precious as yours have been lost; many who have been as anxious; many who have done more in religion. It is altogether uncertain how it will terminate. There is no safety here. You may after all lose your concern, and the last state will be worse than the first. And if you drop the duty, or quit now without a new heart, this will certainly be the case.

3. If many seek to enter in and shall not be able, it would not be surprising if some who are considered as the subjects of this revival should ere long turn back. A revival is well described in the parable of several kinds of hearers: Wayside thorns, Stony places, Good ground. Those who have stood out during this revival may be waiting to see how others hold out. Should a number of those who think they have experienced religion by and by turn back, it will not disprove the reality of it in others. Because there was a Judas among the Apostles—had Christ no true disciples? Because the seed fell on stony places does it follow that none fell on good ground?

When one of this description drops the subject and goes back to the world, how common is it for the wicked to speak of it with an air of triumph—*There goes one of your good Christians.* What does this prove?

1) That you who speak in this manner have no religion.
2) That you are glad that others are going to hell with you.
3) That so much the greater the probability that you will be lost, if others have been deceived, you may well imagine there are but few going to heaven. So much greater the probability that you will be lost. Remember this only proves the truth of our text—*Strait is the*

gate, and narrow is the way, which leadeth unto life, and few there be that find it.

4) If the unconverted seek—what will become of those who do not even *seek,* but do nothing? If the unconverted are anxious for their souls—what stupid? If the unconverted pray—what about those who never pray at all? If some have started to flee to the city of refuge—what about those who have not yet taken alarm? If some who have taken alarm *Escape for thy life*—what about those who, after all, look back and become pillars of salt, or are yet sleeping in Sodom?

18

A Sermon for Children

But Jesus called them unto him, and said, Suffer little children to come unto me, forbid them not: for of such is the kingdom of God
(Luke 18:16).

When the Saviour was on earth he took special notice of little children. He once took a little child and set him in the midst of his disciples. From such he taught them the lesson of humility. He felt more compassion for them than many parents now do.

Many parents however, are anxious for their children. It is a comely sight to see them bringing some in their arms and leading others by the hand to the Saviour. And his disciples rebuked *those that brought them*. Though they were Christ's disciples that did it, yet it was wrong and very displeasing to Christ. Mark says, *When Jesus saw it, he was much displeased.* And our text says, *But Jesus called them unto him, and said, Suffer little children to come unto me, and forbid them not: for of such is the kingdom of God.*

The phrase kingdom of God sometimes means the whole church, sometimes the invisible. In either case I think it an argument in favor of the salvation of some little children. I know some have taken it otherwise. As though Christ intended only to designate the character of real Christians, of *such* who possess humble childlike trust, of *such* is the kingdom of God. But this would be no reason why little children should come to Christ, because grown people are converted and saved.

At present, I choose to consider the text as applicable, not to infants, but to little children, such as are present and can attend to what is said. I have chosen this text on their account, and I must invite all the little children in this place to listen and attend to what is said.

When Christ was on earth he called little children to him, and said to their parents, *Suffer little children to come unto me, and forbid them not.* Here I will ask you one question. Why is it necessary for little children to come to Christ? Why is it necessary for such children as you are to come to Christ? This important question I will try to answer. It is because they are born into the world without any sin? No; this is not true. If children were born holy, and without sin, then it would not be necessary for them to come to Christ. Christ tells us he came not to call the righteous, but sinners to repentance. If they were born into the world holy and without any sin, then it would not be proper to have them baptized. When you see them baptized, that is to show you that their hearts are naturally wicked and need to be washed and made clean by the blood of Christ.

The Bible tells us: *That the wicked go astray as soon as they be born, speaking lies. By one man sin entered into the world, and death by sin.* Infants, you know, sometimes die. God who sees and knows all things, views them as sinners. Those who have no sin need not come to Christ. But there are no such persons on earth, "All have sinned." I will now give you a number of answers to the question which I wish you would not forget.

You must come to Christ then,

1. Because you have precious souls. When your bodies die they will be buried, they will not see, nor hear, nor know anything. But your souls will live. They cannot die like the body. When the body dies, the soul goes away into another world. Those that are good will be happy, and those that are wicked will be miserable forever.

Now these souls of yours are very precious. One soul is worth more than all the world. Our Saviour, who knows the worth of our souls, once asked this question: *What shall it profit a man, if he gain the whole world, and loses himself, or be cast away?* Now there is great danger of losing your souls.

2. Because you are sinners. If you were not sinners, then it would not, we told you, be necessary for you to come to Christ. But you are sinners. You have wicked hearts. The Bible says *The heart is deceitful above all things, and desperately wicked. The imagination of man's heart is evil from his youth.* You may sometimes learn the state of your hearts from your words and your actions. The wise man says: *Even the child is known by his doings, whether his works be pure and whether it be right.*

God has commanded children to obey their parents in the Lord. Have you not sometimes disobeyed them? Have you not slighted their advice and grieved their hearts? This is wicked. It is disobeying God. All those children who do not obey their parents, do not obey God. Have you not used bad words, and taken God's name in vain? Then you are guilty, *for the Lord will not hold him guiltless that taketh his name in vain.* Have you never been guilty of telling lies? When you have done wrong, and you are afraid that your parents will find out and punish you for it, did you never tell a lie to conceal it? Children who tell lies are called *children of the devil.* When they die they cannot go to heaven. *All liars shall have their part in the lake which burns with fire and brimstone, which is the second death.*

Wicked children do not love the Sabbath. They feel bad when the Sabbath comes. They some times sport and play and break God's holy day. That too is a great sin. It is breaking God's plain command. *Remember the Sabbath day, and keep it holy.* Wicked children are glad when the Sabbath is gone. Is it so with some of you? Then you have very wicked hearts.

Wicked children do not love to think much about God. *God is not at all in their thoughts.* Wicked children try not to think much about death, and judgment, and God, and Christ, and heaven, and hell. And is not this the case with some of you?

Wicked children do not love to pray to God, and sometimes they neglect it. *They say unto the Lord, depart from us.*

19

Regeneration

But as many as received him, to them gave he power to become the sons of God, even to them that believe on his name: which were born, not of blood, nor of the will of the flesh, nor of the will of man, but of God (John 1:12-13).

The important and simple doctrine taught by these words, is that those who *receive* Christ—who have power given them to become the sons of God and who believe on his name are *born of God*. In other words, every real Christian becomes such by a special exertion of Almighty power to change his heart. The phrase *born of God*—begotten of God, so often used by the writers of the New Testament is figurative. Its propriety, when applied to things of a spiritual nature, arises from the analogy which exists between the beginning of our natural and spiritual existence. Believers are the sons of God and this must be understood in a peculiar sense. All men equally receive their existence and natural faculties from the Creator, and in *this* sense are *all* the children of God. But when the Scriptures apply the phrases *sons of God* and *children of God* to the saints by way of distinction, it must be to point out a relation to God which is not common to all men. This relation is wholly of a new and spiritual nature; and God is the sole author of it, and by virtue of it they are his sons, they are said to be born of him; begotten of him, in allusion to the relation between earthly parents and their children.

The object of this text is to deny that our relation to God as his spiritual children is produced in any way, but by his own special and sovereign power. It was originally adapted to oppose the carnal prejudices of the Jews. For the common opinion was that all who could be counted as the children of Abraham were heirs of the divine promises and entitled to eternal life. This notion was uniformly opposed by Christ and his apostles. Leaving an attempt to ascertain the precise meaning of the phrases *"not of blood, nor of the will of the flesh, nor of the will of man,"* I observe that there were three ways in which individuals became the reputed children of Abraham: *by regular descent; by unlawful connection;* and *by adoption.* Let the method be which it might, the Jews supposed that whoever became a child of Abraham, of course, became a child of God. The celebrated Lightfoot supposes the object of the Evangelist is to cut off the false hopes of the Jews, by denying that *either* method and of course *any* method of becoming the children of Abraham would make them the children of God. Another birth is necessary; a new filiation from above. *They must be born again—born of God.* Whatever may be the particular meaning of the text, the obvious general impression from it, and the one designed to be made by the sacred writer is that all other ways of becoming the sons of God are false and visionary, except that of *being born of him.* It was spoken to meet the prevailing prejudices of the day, and may now be used in the same manner.

Of all subjects, that which respects change from death unto life, is certainly one of the most important, and interesting to us. To have clear and definite ideas here is of great moment. Error on such a fundamental point is awfully perilous.

In one sense all things are of God. He is the Creator and governor of all. All a man's powers and faculties are from God, and all the means of grace and institutions of religion are ordained by him. But when the Scriptures speak of being born of God, they mean something more than that a man is influenced by these means and institutions in the use of his ordinary powers and faculties.—To prevent misconception, I have said that regeneration is the *special work of Almighty power.* Errorists have never dared to deny, directly, that saints are *born of God;* because this would be to renounce all *appearance* of belief in the Scriptures. They have chosen a surer method of propagating their sentiments. While they retain the language of the sacred writers, they have attacked and frittered away their meaning, until regeneration becomes the mere application of an external rite, or a persuasion of mind affected in an ordinary manner and a consequent reformation of morals.

To expunge error serves to illustrate the truth. I shall briefly consider some false notions respecting regeneration and then proceed to illustrate what it is to be born of God.

I need not consume the time in labouring to prove that baptism is not regeneration. Nothing is plainer than that an external rite cannot change the heart. Baptism is only a *sign* or *token* of the saving influences of the Holy Spirit, and is not that work itself. It cannot be the *token of a thing,* and the thing itself at the same time. Both the Scriptures and experience show, that all who are baptized are not regenerated; for in their lives and conversation many who are baptized differ not from the "world which lieth in wickedness." On this, I shall only add the words of an eminent English divine, "This scheme," says he, speaking of regeneration by water baptism, "is the utter rejection and overthrow of the grace of our Lord Jesus Christ." And again, "The vanity of this presumptuous folly is destructive of the grace of the gospel; invented to countenance men in their sins; and to hide from them the necessity of being born again; and therein of turning unto God. But my beloved Christian brethren, *you have not so learned Christ.*"

The absurdity of substituting this and other things of a like nature is so palpable and gross, that it is very likely to be seen and apprehended, where any considerable degree of knowledge respecting the nature of religion exists. There is far less danger from such extravagant notions than from those which are more specious and imposing.

Pelagius in the 4th century first invented and advocated a scheme of regeneration which, with a few modifications, sometimes in the phraseology, and sometimes by partial additions or diminutions, has been the scheme of the great body of all sectaries, who have dissented from orthodox evangelical sentiments.—Authors have appeared in different periods and in various countries, who have brought forward this specious scheme of the new birth, as principally illustrated, or defined by *themselves;* and many whose reading is superficial have been deceived into this supposition. The fact is, that almost the whole system of vague and inadequate notions on this great subject is only the heresy of Pelagius, so universally condemned by the ancient Church, which has now been newly dressed up, after the modern fashion, to secure a better reception.

The fundamental truths of the Pelagian and Arminian scheme, (for they are in substance the same) are these:

(1). That God not only proclaims the offers of grace and salvation to all men alike, but that the Holy Spirit is equally and sufficiently distributed to *all* men to insure their salvation, provided they duly improve the benefits bestowed upon them.

(2). That the precepts and promises of the gospel are not only good and desirable in themselves, but so suited to the natural reason and interests of mankind, that they will of course be inclined to receive them, unless overpowered by prejudice, and an habitual course of sin.

(3). That the *consideration* of the threatenings and promises of the gospel is sufficient to remove these prejudices and reform that course.

(4). That those who thus seriously reflect and amend their lives have the promise of the Holy Spirit, and are entitled to the benefits of the new covenant.

Under this specious statement of fundamental principles which is apt to strike an inconsiderate mind in a favorable manner, the very life and soul of gospel truth is taken away. On this scheme, all men are regenerated alike, originally; all having an equal measure of the Spirit, and the difference between one man and another is to be ascribed wholly to himself; to the improvement he has made of the blessings vouchsafed. And regeneration is a reformation of life, induced by moral suasions, or commenced in consequence of the understanding being enlightened and the affections being moved by divine truth alone. If you ask, how does salvation proceed from divine grace on this plan, the answer is that all the means of improvement are bestowed by God and herein is the grace.

The whole scheme is simply this, God gives faculties and grace to all, and to all alike and thus furnished, they work out their own salvation, being persuaded to do this by the promises and threatenings of the gospel. The dreadful mischief which this extensive and popular scheme has caused springs from its plausibility—from such an appearance of truth, mixed with so many great and dangerous errors.

That the Holy Spirit makes use of the word and many other instruments to bring sinners to Christ, I have no doubt. But that men are naturally so inclined, as to approve of and obey the precepts of the gospel, unless some *peculiar* course of sin or prejudice prevent them, contradicts the whole tenor of the gospel, in which it is a fundamental principle, that by nature we are children of wrath, and that we are at enmity with God and blinded to the light of his truth and dead in trespasses and sins. That the Holy Spirit is communicated to all in a sufficient manner to save them, entirely overthrows the idea of any *special grace,* and makes one man as much *born of God* as another! Our text says that as many as *received Christ, and believed on his name,* were born of God. If so, others who did not, were not born of God, and the undistinguishing influences of the Spirit cannot be maintained.

It is a great stumbling block, in the way of many, that God should give more of his Spirit to one, than another. To remove this subject of prejudice, Pelagius and multitudes ever since, have maintained that all men receive gifts alike, and are alike furnished to work out their salvation. This effectually destroys the new birth, and makes it alike common to every man. On this scheme Judas had as much grace as Paul, Ahab who sold himself to work wickedness, as David, a man after God's own heart. All the difference between them, was owing to the different manner in which they improved their privileges.

I know such doctrine is agreeable to corrupt nature; and the easy reception it has met with ever since it was first preached proves how agreeable it is to carnal reason. But neither the Scriptures nor experience afford us any reason to believe it. I do not doubt that the Spirit of God strives with all men who are not reprobates. I fully admit it. I admit that the promises and threats of the gospel would be sufficient to persuade us to a holy life, if our understandings were neither darkened, nor our affections depraved. But after all this, I deny that common grace makes us the sons of God, or that we are *persuaded to be Christians* without any special divine influence; or that all men receive the same measure of the Spirit.

After all preparatory means—all the promises and threats of the gospel—all the operations of common grace—and all exertions of unregenerate sinners, they must be born of God to become his children. There must be a *new creation,*—a work accomplished by Almighty power—a sovereign—special—supernatural act, like making a world, or raising the dead, as to the power exerted, and without such an act no one can ever see the kingdom of heaven. *Persuasion* is not sufficient to make men new creatures. If the Spirit operates on the minds of men only by setting persuasive arguments or motives before them, be the kinds never so diverse or well adapted to this purpose, yet after all, it depends on the will of man whether any shall be regenerated or not. On this scheme the glory of regeneration would belong to ourselves. It would be uncertain also, whether Christ would have any spiritual seed, as it would depend after all upon the uncertain determination of each individual before whom the motives were set. This then contradicts the Scriptures. God does not confine his operations to setting motives of persuasion before men, *thy people shall be willing in the day of thy power.*

Moral persuasion to a better life confers no new real, supernatural strength to the soul, which may enable it thus to live. No new taste— no new spiritual discernment springs from persuasion. If regeneration comes thus, then a man begets himself, he is born of himself, he makes himself to differ from others. On this plan the Spirit of God has no more to do than Paul or Apollos.

Besides, this is not for what we pray; we pray not that motives may be set before us to regenerate ourselves, but that God would *change* us, *create us anew.* The ancient churches urged this prayer upon the heretics, who denied a *supernatural* work in regeneration, and they felt themselves sorely pressed without.

There is then only one way left for a creature dead in trespasses and sins to rise to life. This is by the power of God which quickens him—creates him anew. Observe in what language sacred writers have chosen to communicate their ideas on this subject: *born of God; begotten of God; quickened; or made alive from the dead; created anew.* If it be said this is figurative language, I agree to it, but if there be any correctness in the figures, the work of regeneration must be the commencement of a new spiritual existence. On any other grounds the language of the Scriptures is of all books the most fancied, unmeaning, and obscure.

You may suppose all the preparation, all the knowledge; motives; morality (in the common acceptation of the term); unregenerate strivings which you please; after all there must be a new creation,—the dead must be *quickened*—believers must be *born of God.* The same energy which brought Christ from the dead—the exceeding great power of the living God must perform the work. This is the apostle's statement, *that we may know what is the exceeding greatness of his power toward us who believe, according to the working of his mighty power, which he wrought in Christ, when he raised him from the dead.*

Indeed, my friends, where else can we look for the origin of such a change as makes believers pass from death to life but the omnipotence of the divine Spirit? Is it our understanding which accomplishes this change? But our understanding is darkened. "The natural man receives not the things of the Spirit, neither can he know them." Is it our will? But we are "prone to evil as the sparks fly upward." Our wills are perverse and rebellious. Is it our strength? Christ died for the ungodly who are *without strength. We are not sufficient of ourselves to think a good thought.* Is it our merits? We merit nothing but utter rejection. *Is it the ministers of God who persuade us? Paul may plant and Apollos water, but God gives the increase.*

Every effort has been made by the ingenuity of man, by palpably erroneous schemes, and by plausible ones, to wrest the glory of this work from the hands of the divine Spirit, and claim the operation for ourselves; at least to share in the honor of it. After all, its origin can be traced only to the free and sovereign grace and Almighty power of God. The work is all his; and the glory must and will forever belong exclusively to him.

It is a doctrine supported by the great light of the Reformation and by the pillars of the evangelical churches ever since: that regeneration is a *physical work.* And by this they mean there is an actual *new creation,* as absolutely so as when the world was created; that a new spiritual taste or discernment, and principle is implanted by a sovereign creative operation, and not simply a new direction given to the old faculties. Such a work being proved, the whole system of evangelical truth; the doctrines of grace; of divine sovereignty; of election; of redemption only by Christ; of human depravity and others connected with them, all flow from it. There is one grand, harmonious, and perfect system: and God is the sum—the substance and the glory of all.

My friends, I am fully aware of the difficulties incident to the doctrines here laid down. I know full well how ready the natural heart is both to oppose, and misconstrue them. But if the Bible supports them, it is enough. Here our carnal reason must bow. Here our proud hearts must submit. Charge them with mystery—with inconsistency—with unprofitableness, O sinner, and you assail not man, but God. Look on his word and read. There it stands; and it is written in characters of light, "which were born not of blood, nor of the will of the flesh, nor of the will of man, but *of God."*

This is the only birth which can fit us for heaven, "Except a man be born again, he cannot see the kingdom of God." We may please our fancies, and gratify our self-righteousness, by adopting loose Pelagian sentiments on this subject; we may remonstrate against such absolute dependence on the grace of God as has now been advocated, but a *new heart, and a right spirit* will after all be found of such absolute necessity, that without them we must perish forever.

20

Despisest Thou the Riches of God's Goodness?

Or despisest thou the riches of his goodness and forbearance and longsuffering, not knowing that the goodness of God leadeth thee to repentance? (Romans 2:4).

Another anniversary has returned where we are called upon to recount the mercies we have enjoyed, and to render a tribute of thanksgiving to God. Our obligations to this duty are too obvious to render proof necessary. The crime of ingratitude is so obvious that an Apostle hath told us, that the very heathen *are without excuse; because that, when they knew God, they glorified him not as God, neither were thankful; but became vain in their imaginations, and their foolish heart was darkened.*

The text which I have read leads us to contemplate,
I. God's treatment of us.
II. Our treatment of Him.

His goodness is manifest throughout all creation. *The invisible things of him from the creation of the world are clearly seen. The heavens declare his glory, and the earth is full of his riches.* The sovereign power of God alone gave us being. It is the discriminating goodness of God which has raised man above the brute creation, *and made him wiser than the fowls of heaven.* That we are rational and immortal beings, and not insects of a day, is owing to his mere good pleasure.

But we speak of temporal mercies, *they are more in number than that we can reckon them up. How great is the sum of them?* They are new every morning and increase with every moment. Thus some of the richest temporal mercies are often overlooked and perhaps entirely forgotten, merely from the fact that they are so common.

Such, my hearers, are the pleasures derived from the organs of sense. The eye is the inlet of a thousand delightful objects. Deprived of this little organ, we should never again behold the countenance of a friend or the beauties of creation around us. Never more should we behold the light of the sun, or read God's message of mercy to man. *Truly the light is sweet, and a pleasant thing it is for the eyes to behold the sun.*

The *ear* too, is the inlet of mercies innumerable. How many agreeable sounds of music; what delightful and easy intercourse of

The Second Great Awakening

friendship had otherwise never been known. But for this organ the sweet sounds of salvation could never have been flowing from the lips of the messenger of mercy to guilty men.

This morning we have already experienced mercies almost without number. These active limbs of ours refreshed and invigorated have been briefly employed in administering to our comfort. How many useful and agreeable movements have they already performed? With ease have we been conducted hither and seated in the house of God this morning.

Had we been blind from our birth, what tribute of gratitude and thanksgiving had been due to the Author of that stupendous miracle which had given sight to all in this house this morning! What cause of gratitude, my hearers, to the Author of that miracle which had this morning for the first time loosed the tongue of the dumb, or unstopped the ears of the deaf! With what interest do we read the little history of the man whose withered limbs had never transported him to the house of God. *He was carried, and laid daily at the gate of the temple—to ask alms of them that entered into the temple.* With eager look the helpless cripple gazes at the multitude whose active limbs had saved them from begging their bread and were conducting them into the temple of God. *And Peter in the name of Jesus of Nazareth took him by the right hand, and lifted him up, and immediately his feet and ankle bones received strength. And he leaping up stood, and walked, and entered with them into the temple, walking, and leaping, and praising God. And all the people saw him walking and praising God.* The whole congregation *were filled with wonder and amazement at that which had happened unto him.*

With what tears of joy—with what emotions of gratitude and thanksgiving did he fly to the instruments of this miracle of mercy and hold them fast in the embraces of his arms. *And as the Canaanite man which was healed held Peter and John, the people ran together into Solomon's porch, greatly wondering.*

My hearers, these wonders of mercy have been enjoyed by us this morning. If the blind, and the deaf, and the dumb, and the lame ever had cause of gratitude and thanksgiving, what are *our* obligations to God this morning? All these mercies to us are but common blessings. And what an ungrateful wretch is that who never feels the importance of such mercy, only by its loss.

We are called upon to render united thanks to God, for his distinguished favours to our state and nation; in particular for the great blessings of peace, internal tranquillity, general health, and fertile seasons—Our thanks are due for meaner things, but these are all the *riches of divine goodness*. In the gift of his Son to our lost and ruined world he has manifested the *riches of his goodness* named in our text. *God so loved the world, that he gave his only begotten Son, that whosoever believeth on him should not perish, but have everlasting life.* God was under no obligation to send his Son to die for rebels against himself. Why then should he come to this earth with a message of peace and good will to man? Why not take on him the nature of angels and extend pardoning mercy to them? It is owing to the riches of divine goodness, my hearers, that the cross of Christ was erected in our world and not in the world of despair. But every mercy is heightened from the fact that we are *sinners*. *God commendeth his love to us in that while we were yet sinners, Christ died for us.*

"He saw the nations dead in sin,
 He felt his pity move.
How sad the state the world was in,
 How boundless was his love."

Every day we live, every breath we draw, renews our obligations to the mercy of God. For every drop of rain which comes to *us,* my hearers, and not to the rich man in hell, we are bound to give thanks to God. A realizing of the sense of our sins would lead us to thank God every day that we are out of hell. *For it of the Lord's mercies that we are not consumed.*

The riches of divine goodness appear not only in the sufferings and death of the Son of God, but in *the melting invitations* of mercy to sinners.—*Ho every one that thirsteth.* In the parable of the *great supper* the invitation is to all. *Come for all things are now ready.* The *riches of divine goodness* (are offered to) the poorest and vilest of sinners. To *us,* my hearers, is the word of this salvation sent. Yes, pardon, peace, and all the treasures of heaven are brought even to our doors and offered to us for nothing. Not only are they freely offered, but even pressed upon our acceptance by every endearing consideration.

Nay, the riches of divine goodness appear in all the warnings of God's word. What a mercy is it that God has not left us to go on in sin without pointing us to its tremendous consequences? Surely every one who is not fully determined to persevere in sin will esteem it a mercy to be told his danger, and to be warned to *flee from the wrath to come.*

The *riches of divine mercy* appear in sending the Holy Spirit *to convince of sin, of righteousness, and of judgment to come.* One would think, that after sinners had rejected the free offers of salvation, God would make no further exertions to save them from deserved wrath. But to all this, he has superadded the strivings of the Holy Spirit. This is God's last effort to save sinners.

Our text speaks of *God's forbearance.* The impenitent sinner who has stood so long idle in God's vineyard has been spared another year. So many years has the Saviour been standing with open arms and with a bleeding heart inviting him to life. So many duties have been neglected, and so many sins committed in the sight of the sin-hating God and yet the sinner has been spared.

Our text speaks of the *longsuffering* of God. If God is angry with the wicked every day, and is determined to punish sin, why is it that we yet live? God, my hearers, is *longsuffering.* No parent ever exercised such forbearance and longsuffering to his own offspring as God does toward impenitent sinners. God has exercised his *forbearance* and *longsuffering* toward us far beyond what he has towards most of the human race—and far beyond some who are lost. The majority of mankind die younger than the most of us who are now in the house of God. Multitudes younger than ourselves have gone to their long home during the year that has past. They have done with Sabbaths and sermons and all the concerns of time. Their day of salvation is over and gone forever. But all the riches of God's goodness and forbearance and longsuffering have been exercised towards sinners in this house and this year. And *why* is this, my hearers? Why has God borne with *us* so long? Our text informs us: it is to *lead us to repentance. Hear, O heavens, and give ear, O earth: for the Lord hath spoken, I have nourished and brought up children.* He has watched over and fed and clothed us. The sun has arisen and wasted its beams upon us. God has been lavishing on us all the blessings of this life. He has opened the windows of heaven and shed around us the light of the glorious gospel *to lead us to repentance.*

II. Our treatment of Him.

Despisest thou the riches of his goodness? Let us consider some of the ways in which this is done. It is done

1. By forgetfulness, or overlooking his mercies. And the very reason why they are forgotten is because they are so common. How is it, my hearers? Have you not enjoyed the uninterrupted use of these bodily organs so long that you have forgotten your dependence on God? *That in him you live, and move, and have your being?* Have you employed your faculties of soul and body in the

service of God? Have you *yielded your members as instruments of righteousness?* Can you adopt the language of that penitent?

> "These eyes that once abus'd the light,
> Now left to thee their wat'ry sight,
> And weep a slient flood;
> These hands are rais'd in ceaseless prayer,
> Oh, wash away the stains they wear,
> In pure redeeming blood.
> These ears, that once could entertain
> The midnight oath, the festive strain,
> Around the sinful board;
> Now deaf to all th' enchanting noise,
> Avoid the throng, detest their joys,
> And long to hear thy word."

Bless the Lord O my soul and forget not all his benefits. Ye are not your own, ye are bought with a price; therefore, glorify God in your bodies and spirits which are his.

2. We despise the goodness of God by forgetting that he is the *Author* of every mercy. *When thou hast eaten and art full, then thou shalt bless the Lord thy God for the good land which he hath given thee. Beware that thou forget not the Lord thy God, in not keeping his commandments, and his judgments, and his statutes, which I command thee this day: Lest when thou hast eaten and art full, and hast built goodly houses, and dwelt therein; and when thy herds and thy flocks multiply, and thy silver and thy gold is multiplied, and all that thou hast is multiplied; Then thine heart be lifted up and thou forget the Lord thy God. And thou say in thine heart, My power and the might of mine hand hath gotten me this wealth. But thou shalt remember the Lord thy God: for it is he that giveth thee power to get wealth, that he may establish his covenant which he sware unto thy fathers, as it is this day. And it shall be, if thou do at all forget the Lord thy God, and walk after other gods, and serve them, and worship them, I testify against you this day that ye shall surely perish. As the nations which the Lord destroyeth before your face, so shall ye perish; because ye would not be obedient unto the voice of the Lord your God. The young lions roar after their prey, and seek their meat from God. The sun ariseth, they gather themselves together, and lay them down in their dens. Man goeth forth unto his work and to his labour until evening. O Lord, how manifold are thy works! in wisdom hast thou made them all: the earth is full of thy*

riches. So is this great and wide sea, wherein are things creeping innumerable, both small and great beasts. There go the ships: there is that leviathan, whom thou hast made to play therein. These all wait upon thee; that thou mayest give them their meat in due season. That thou givest them they gather: thou openest thine hand, they are filled with good. The eyes of all wait upon thee; and thou givest them their meat in due season. Thou openest thine hand, and satisfiest the desire of every living thing. From the highest angel that sings in glory down to the meanest insect that crawls in the dust, all are equally and absolutely dependent on him. *By his spirit he hath garnished the heaven; his hand hath formed the crooked serpent.*

3. We despise the goodness of God when we do not set a just *value* on his mercies. This is the case with temporal mercies.* But this is eminently the case with the great blessings of the gospel. What are the privileges of the gospel, my hearers? Would you learn in some measure the value of the gospel in a civil point of view, cast your eye over the darkness and degradation and cruelties of the heathen world. But for the gospel, you might this day have been bowing down to a stock or a stone. You might have been practicing on your own bodies the most cruel tortures that ingenuity could invent to appease the anger of some cruel demon, or to atone for the sin of your soul. The poor heathen often show more concern for their souls than sinners under the gospel. Yes, my hearers, the very heathen, who come into our country are often thunderstruck with the stupidity of sinners under the gospel.

What think ye would a lost soul in hell give for one Sabbath on earth? I need not tell you, my hearers, that those who neglect the house of God; who disregard the Sabbath; who stay at home this day, to prepare to pamper the body, rather than come to the house of God to render thanks for his mercy; despise the riches of his goodness. Their god is their belly and they stay at home to worship it. Those who pay more attention to the body than to the soul—who will neglect the latter for the sake of the former despise the riches of divine goodness. They are like Esau *who for one morsel of meat sold his birthright.*

Again: Those despise the riches of his *goodness, and forbearance, and longsuffering* who improve them as occasions for sinning. And this, my hearers, we have too much reason to fear that many will improve this anniversary season.

---

* About six lines of handwritten text are illegible at this point due to a large hole in the manuscript.

This day which is appointed for the express purpose of rendering the homage of grateful hearts to Almighty God is awfully perverted. Instead of thanksgiving to God, shall it be made the means of provoking the wrath of heaven? Such scenes of carnal mirth and festivity have been witnessed that far more sin has been committed than at other seasons. Had no such day been appointed, God had not been so highly provoked.

All who neglect the gospel do emphatically despise the riches of divine goodness. Every day they trample under foot the Son of God. Sinners despise the forbearance and longsuffering of God, every moment they are unconcerned for their souls. I make the appeal to your own consciences. My hearers, had God visited this place with the famine or the pestilence, were your friends and neighbors daily and hourly dying around you—would you be so regardless of God? Had God in his providence laid you on the bed of sickness and threatened you with a speedy dissolution, would you have treated him with such ungratefulness? And now, because God has been so good, he has spared you and your families and friends and given you all that heart can wish, will you now for all his mercy venture to provoke him. O the ingratitude of such hearts! *Because sentence against an evil work is not executed speedily, therefore the heart of the sons of men is fully set in them to do evil.* The plain language of such conduct is: "If God had not been so good—if he had not spared me so long, I should not have dared to provoke him as I have done. If God had not been so kind to me, I had not been so regardless of him."

And now, my hearers, let me put the question: How have you improved the mercies of God to you during the past year? Has the goodness of God led you to repent of your sins? Has it made you more humble, faithful in the service of God? Have you been careful for nothing or do you still continue to provoke him because he is so good? Think what Christ has done for your salvation and what returns have you made? Will you this day render him the homage of your hearts? Or will you continue still longer to despise all the offers of a bleeding Saviour? Will you say, *What is the Almighty, that I should serve him? and what profit should we have, if we pray unto him?*

Come, my fellow sinners, one and all, and present your thank offering to the Almighty God in his house this day. And let it be that of a broken and a contrite heart for *all* your sins. And this shall be an *offering acceptable and well pleasing in his sight.* For the *sacrifices of God are a broken spirit: a broken and a contrite heart, O God, thou wilt not despise.* This done, we may say to you all, *Go thy way, eat thy bread with joy, and drink thy wine with a merry heart; for God now accepteth thy works. They that honor me,* says God, *I will honor, but they that despise me shall be lightly esteemed.*

> "Though treasures brought before his throne
>   Would no acceptance find,
> He kindly condescends to own
>   A meek and lowly mind.
> This is an offering we may bring
>   However mean our store,
> The poorest child, the greatest king
>   Can give him nothing more."

21

Gospel Warfare

For the weapons of our warfare are not carnal, but mighty through God to the pulling down of strong holds
(II Corinthians 10:4).

Paul, wherever he preached, met with opposition. This appears in all his epistles. Though, in general, future events were veiled in obscurity, yet one thing was certain—opposition would follow him wherever he went. At his last interview with his brethren in the ministry, he uttered these words: *And now, behold, I go bound in the Spirit to Jerusalem, not knowing the things that shall befall me there: Save that the Holy Ghost witnesseth in every city, saying that bonds and afflictions abide me.*

The same appeared when he preached in the city of Corinth. During his residence in that city we are informed that they not only *opposed* and *blasphemed;* but that *the Jews* actually *made insurrection with one accord against Paul and brought him to the judgment seat.* After his departure from them, opposition still continued, but it now assumed a different form. Though the Apostle had been blameless and inoffensive, arduous and useful in his labors; yet he had incurred the envy and hatred of many. They did what they could to undermine him to lessen his influence and reputation. In this chapter he vindicates himself against their false charges, in a humble and Christian manner. Under all his reproach, Paul preserved a Christian temper.

Now I Paul myself beseech you by the meekness and gentleness of Christ. He had been represented as a person of no influence, mean and despicable in his person. Paul seems to quote the words of his calumniator—*Who in presence am base among you*—as if he had said, "This apostle of yours is a mean, base fellow, when he is among you, how *contemptible* he appears, when absent, see how he *boasts!*"

They impeached Paul's motives and ranked him among the wicked. Some, says he, *think of us as if we walked after the flesh.* To which he replies, *Though we walk in the flesh, we do not war after the flesh.* But though he and his brethren were subject to the infirmities incident to human nature, though they *walked in the flesh,* living in human bodies; yet they *did not war after the flesh.* True, we are engaged in a warfare, but we do not conduct like men of the world. Our contest is entirely different. *For the weapons of our warfare are not carnal, but mighty through God to the pulling down of strong holds.*

From our text we remark,

1. The work of the gospel ministry is a warfare. Every Christian is a soldier, and as such, he is required to take the *breastplate,* the *shield,* the *helmet,* and *sword,* and *to gird on the whole armour of God.* Every Christian is engaged in a warfare with sin, Satan, and the world. But the work of the ministry is eminently a *warfare.* This Paul recognizes in his charge to Timothy. *This charge I commit unto thee, son Timothy, according to the prophecies which went before on thee, that thou by them mightest war a good warfare. Thou therefore endure hardness, as a good soldier of Jesus Christ. No man that warreth entangleth himself with the affairs of this life; that he may please him who hath chosen him to be a soldier.*

That the work of the gospel ministry is a warfare will appear if we consider the following particulars.

1. The enemy which it encounters.
2. The victories which it achieves.
3. And the weapons which are used.

1. The enemy. The world has revolted from God. The grand object of the gospel is to reduce sinners into subjection to Christ. Sinners have not only cast off their allegiance to God, but have gone over to the kingdom of Satan. He is styled *the god of this world.*—The prince of the power of the air—the spirit that now worketh in the children of disobedience. He has established his kingdom in this world. But a kingdom is nothing without subjects. This kingdom is established in the hearts of all sinners. Nothing can be done towards recovering lost sinners to God without invading the kingdom of darkness. The adversary is tenacious of his subjects. Nothing can be done but by the gospel without awakening his jealousy, and arousing his opposition. He will exert his power to the utmost to retain every soul in his kingdom. St. Paul was sent to sinners *to open their eyes, and to turn them from darkness to light, and from the power of Satan unto God.*—They are to be instructed, that they may recover themselves out of the snare of the devil who are taken captive by him at his will—Hence, Christians are said to be *delivered from the power of darkness, and translated into the kingdom of God's dear Son.*

Now the craft, the malice, and power of Satan are very great.

With these every faithful minister will have to encounter. *For we wrestle not against flesh and blood, but against principalities, against powers, against the rulers of this world, against spiritual wickedness in high places.*

Our text speaks of the pulling down of *strong holds*. Satan has many strong holds in his kingdom. A strong hold is a place fortified and prepared for an attack. Allusion is made to a strongly *fortified city*. It is a place of resort where the enemy takes his last *stand; entrenching* himself about the *walls; strengthening* all his *redoubts and ramparts;* and neglecting nothing that might render his fortress impregnable.

This, my hearers, is the description of a human heart. *It is a strong hold.* Here Satan holds his seat. The Saviour considered the heart of a sinner as the devil's palace. It is the seat of his government, which he takes special care to fortify. *When a strong man armed keepeth his place, his goods are in peace.* The heart of a sinner is the devil's *strong hold.*

The ways in which the sinner's heart is *fortified* and becomes the strong hold are many—

1. The devil will do all in his power to keep possession. He is not only strong himself, but he is *armed*. By his subtlety he keeps sinners in peace. He tempts them to the commission of sins and then persuades them that it is not sin. He blinds their minds, and hides from them the sight of their danger. *If our gospel be hid, it is hid to them that are lost: in whom the god of this world hath blinded the minds of them which believe not, lest the light of the glorious gospel of Christ, who is the image of God, should shine unto them.*

So long as the adversary of souls can make the sinner believe that he is not *lost,* so long he knows that he will not feel his need of salvation. He knows that Christ came to save such, and such only, and while he can persuade the sinner that all is well, he knows that he never will come to Christ, and therefore cannot be saved. Christ came to seek and to save that which was *lost,* and were the sinner to see and to feel the solemn truth, he would cry for mercy; he would inquire, *What must I do to be saved?* This the adversary well knows, and therefore, in order the more effectually to fortify the sinner's heart against Christ, he labors to *shut out* the light of conviction, and to keep him in peace. So said our Saviour, *when a strong man armed keepeth his palace, his goods are in peace.*

The devil never awakened a sinner to a sense of his sins, guilt, and danger, but always tries to soothe and quiet him in his sins. If he can but keep him quiet, he knows that he is safe in his possession. And if by any means, the sinner becomes alarmed—he, with all his emissaries, will awake lest they should loose one of his subjects. And now, if possible, he will prevent all intercourse between God and the sinner.

The grand design of the gospel is to bring about a reconciliation to God. This is the business of an ambassador for Christ. He comes *beseeching them in Christ to be reconciled to God.* When the sinner beings to be alarmed, with what opposition does he sometimes meet! He thinks of beginning to pray, of finding a secret place where he can hold intercourse at the throne of grace; but the adversary is always active at such a time. The sinner appoints the time and the place and thinks that he will not, he dare not stand out any longer. The time arrives, but the deceiver of souls helps him to an excuse and tells him that he will be discovered—that some person will see him, or hear him: that he is too wicked, or there is time enough yet. Thus the devil frightens them away from the throne of grace and prevents them from leaving his kingdom. Were they permitted to hold intercourse with Christ and his ambassadors, the devil knows that his subjects would be in danger of revolting from his kingdom. And therefore, he will do every thing effectually to prevent it.

In the great revival in New England 70 years ago, when sinners began to be anxious for their souls, they were watched. Many who were anxious, and felt it their duty to retire in secret and pray, were watched by those who never felt anxious for their own souls.— When a sinner became anxious it was some thing strange, and unaccountable, he must not be left alone, but must be narrowly watched, for surely say they, he is becoming crazy. This is what I have heard related by some aged Christians who were acquainted with the fact.

Sometimes the adversary attempts to fortify the hearts of sinners by stirring up his subjects to soothe and flatter those who are beginning to be anxious. The world will now make many fair promises and pretend great friendship. If this will not answer, to keep them quiet, harsher discipline must be adopted. All manner of evil is spoken against them. They must be considered and treated as enemies. If they attempt to desert the cause of Satan, he will certainly wound them if he can. We read of one, who, on coming to Christ, was *thrown down. And as he was yet coming, the devil threw him down and tare him.* Another very common method for Satan is to *fortify* the sinner's heart by strong and powerful prejudices. These are raised sometimes against the gospel itself, against its doctrines and duties; and sometimes against the minister of the gospel. Thus it was with Christ himself. Some insinuated that he had none but weak and ignorant followers. *Are ye also deceived,* say they, *Have any of the rulers of the Pharisees believed on him? Some said he was a good man: others, nay; but he deceiveth the people.* It seemed as though they could not let him alone. *If we let him thus alone all men will believe on him.* Some spake out plainly, *He hath a devil and is mad, why hear ye him?*

So it was with the Apostles. They *spoke against those things which were spoken by Paul, contradicting and blaspheming.* In order to prejudice the minds of sinners against the gospel, they even followed the Apostles from place to place, *and raised persecution against them and expelled them out of their coasts. As for this sect, we know it is everywhere spoken against.* The Apostles always took the front of the battle. Here their own words, *For I think that God hath set forth us the apostles last, as it were appointed to death: for we are made a spectacle unto the world, and to angels, and to men. We are fools for Christ's sake—being reviled, we bless: being persecuted, we suffer it: being defamed, we entreat: we are made as the filth of the world, and are the offscouring of all things unto this day.* And all this was done for the sake of raising strong prejudices in the minds of sinners against the apostles, and to destroy the effect of their preaching. And thus Satan fortifies the hearts of sinners.

2. Sinners fortify their own hearts. They are in love with sin—It is dear to them as a right eye.—*They hold fast deceit and they refuse to return.* When he hears the curse of God against him, *he blesseth himself in his heart, saying, I shall have peace, though I walk in the imagination of mine heart.—He flattereth himself in his own eyes, until his iniquity is found to be hateful.* It is unpleasant to be awaked and hence they cry yet, *a little sleep and little slumber, a little folding of the hands to sleep. They love darkness rather than light, because their deeds are evil. And every one that doeth evil hateth the light, neither cometh to the light, lest his deeds should be reproved.*

When the devil tries to make sinners believe that they are not *lost,* they try in turn to believe him. When he tries to persuade them not to pray, and suggests some excuse for their neglect; they are glad to find an excuse. When others soothe and flatter and attempt to quiet their fears, and tell them that they need not be alarmed, there is no danger, they are pleased with it. They thought it was a false alarm. They are glad to get others to help fortify their hearts, and so they join with them and help on the work; thus their hearts become strongly fortified against Christ.—

Especially when they hear smooth things from the sacred desk, this is exceeding pleasant and useful and the most effectual means of helping on the work of fortifying the sinner's heart against Christ. They do not like to have their hearts searched and probed to the bottom. Thus saith the Lord, *they have healed also the hurt of the daughter of my people slightly, saying, peace, peace, when there is no peace.* They cry *peace and safety to themselves* and they are pleased to have others do the same. *And,* saith God, *my people love to have it so.*

When others try to prejudice their minds against the doctrines and duties of religion, this too they employ as a means of hardening their own hearts. Often the sinner will listen with eager attention to all the objections and cavils against the doctrines and duties of religion, and will take special pains to remember and repeat them. In this way, he fortifies his own heart, and makes it as strong and stout against Christ as possible.

When the solemn truths of God's word are declared in a clear and convincing manner, sinners are often alarmed. They are sometimes almost convinced, and begin to say, if these things be so, then my situation is truly alarming. Now the method to avoid deep conviction is to obtain some prejudice. If they cannot perpetuate their prejudices against either the doctrines or the preachers of the gospel, they will be in danger of being overcome.

In this situation the sinner will seize with avidity every thing which may help him to condemn others and justify himself. There is no alternative. He must either conquer or fall. If he cannot condemn the messages of divine truth, he feels the awful conviction that he is found even to fight against God. My hearers will notice that the sinner's heart is a *strong hold.* They are stout-hearted and far from righteousness.

It is often the case in times of revival that many effect to despise it. *Their words are stout.* They speak and think and act as though they felt far above it. They affect to despise and treat such things with supercilious contempt. At such a time the sinner often feels his heart swell and rage with opposition. He is most obstinately determined that he will not yield. His very thoughts and imaginations rise against it with desperation. We have an account contained in the context, of towering *imaginations, and every high thing that exalteth itself against the knowledge of God.* These are the enemies and the strong holds which the gospel has to encounter.

We consider,

2. The victories which the gospel achieves. The grand object of the gospel is to destroy the works of Satan in the hearts of sinners.

To bruise Satan under foot. As strong as he is, there is one who is infinitely stronger than he. God is the mighty conqueror. *The weapons of our warfare are not carnal, but mighty through God.* The Lord Jesus Christ is the glorious conqueror.—*When a stronger than he shall come upon him, and overcome him, he taketh from him all his armour wherein he trusted, and divideth his spoils.*

These very persons whom I have described—the most powerful and desperate enemies to the gospel, and especially to all the revivals of religion are *brought down.* Those who have been by universal consent the most unlikely subjects, have been overcome by almighty power.

When the Apostles returned from their first mission, they joyfully exclaimed, *Lord, even the devils are subject unto us through thy name!* To which he replied, *I beheld Satan fall as lightning from heaven.* The sinner with all his objections and cavils, and opposition, is overcome. The proud rebel is brought low. The sinner has lost all his opposition. He is disarmed at once. He feels and acts entirely different. Even his very thoughts are changed and brought into subjection to Christ. By the Almighty power of God this strong hold is *pulled down. Mighty through God to the pulling down of strong holds; Casting down imaginations, and every high thing that exalteth itself against the knowledge of God, and bringing into captivity every thought to the obedience of Christ.* This is the description of a victory over the heart of a sinner. The army of God comes against this strong hold, and attacks it. All the *fortified* places are carried. His towering *imaginations,* and schemes of opposition are speedily taken and destroyed. And every *high thing that exalted itself against the knowledge of God* and was determined never to yield—all the *castles* and *towers* are *sapped—thrown down and destroyed* and the besieging army, carrying every thing at the point of the sword, enter the city, storm and take the citadel. Everywhere defeated, the sinner now submits, and is taken captive by Christ. And thus Satan's kingdom is *demolished* and his whole government destroyed.

Which mighty effects, my brethren, does the gospel produce in the name of Christ? *It is the power of God to salvation unto every one that believeth.* Thus is that prophecy of Isaiah fulfilled, *I will divide him a portion with the great, and he shall divide the spoil with the strong.* And thus is Christ described as a mighty warrior and armed for the field. *Gird thy sword upon thy thigh, O most mighty, with thy glory and thy majesty. And in thy majesty ride prosperously because of truth and meekness and righteousness; and thy right*

The Second Great Awakening

hand shall teach thee terrible things. Thine arrows are sharp in the heart of the king's enemies; whereby the people fall under thee. The sinner not only lays his weapons at the feet of his conqueror, but repairs to his camp; he now cheerfully enlists under his banner. *Thy kingdom come.* This prayer is now answered. *For behold the kingdom of God is within you.*

Consider,

3. The weapons of our warfare. These weapons are not carnal. External violence is utterly excluded. Preachers of the gospel must not adopt the maxims of the world. They must not use such weapons as human wisdom, or human policy would employ. When the ministers of Christ are attacked by the world, and have all manner of evil spoken against them (as Paul and his associates had, who were *accounted as the filth of the world and the offscourging of all things*) in their warfare they *must* not recriminate. That would be using carnal weapons. If they render railing for railing they take the devil's ground and use his weapons.

In this warfare an angel of light would not render railing for railing in his combat with Satan. It would be taking carnal weapons and *he dare not do it. Yet Michael the archangel, when contending with the devil, he disputed about the body of Moses, durst not bring against him a railing accusation, but said, The Lord rebuke thee.* It is the *devil* who is styled *the accuser of the brethren.* Such weapons as these the Apostles never used. Nor, when treating with sinners, did they attempt to *flatter* them into subjection to Christ. Sinners may do many things by being flattered. But in this way *not one* will *ever become a Christian, not one will leave the kingdom of darkness.* The strong hold of Satan can never be pulled down by flattering words. This Paul says he never did, *Neither at any time used we flattering words, as ye know. My speech and my preaching was not with enticing words of man's wisdom.* Paul knew too well that converts made in this way were worthless. *But we preached in the demonstration of the Spirit and of power. That your faith,* says he, *should not stand in the wisdom of men, but in the power of God.*

Preaching mere external morality will never bring one soul to Christ. That preaching which does not aim at the heart, and take hold of the conscience, never *attacks the strong holds of Satan.* Such preaching never was and never will be opposed by the prince of darkness or any of his subjects. The weapons used by the Apostle *were not carnal;* but they were every way opposed to the carnal heart. They wielded the *sword of the Spirit.* They preached the doctrine of total depravity; openly declared that men were *dead in trespasses and sins—by nature children of wrath—the carnal mind is enmity against God: Ye do always resist the Holy Ghost as your fathers did, so do ye.*

They penetrated the sinner's heart, and uncovered his wickedness, and showed him the immutable obligation of the divine law. *Cursed is every one that continueth not in all things which are written in the book of the law to do them.* They proclaimed open war with all sin, even in thought. And when the *commandment came, sin revived, and sinners were slain.* They urged the absolute necessity of *regeneration;* That God would not accept of the doings of the unregenerate. *They that are in the flesh cannot please God.* They urged the sinner to believe on the Lord Jesus Christ. *For without faith it is impossible to please God.—Let him ask in faith otherwise, let not that man think that he shall receive any thing of the Lord.* They urged the duty of *immediate repentance.* However distressed—However deeply pricked in the heart, inquiring *Men and brethren, what shall we do to be saved? Sirs, what must I do to be saved?*

The Apostles never altered their directions, but seemed to take occasion from the greatness of their distress to *press* their consciences with the duty of *immediate* repentance. And whenever the sinner was brought sweetly to submit, they attributed the effect wholly to *God who commanded the light to shine out of darkness.* When the glorious work is done, they hide both themselves and the sinner in the dust. *Neither is he that planteth any thing, nor he that watereth, but God. Born not of blood, nor of the will of man, but of God. By grace—through faith, and that not of yourselves, it is the gift of God.*

These were the weapons with which they drove the sinner out of his strong hold of self-righteous deception and showed him his naked dependence on the sovereign mercy of God. These weapons which the Apostles used—which were *mighty through God to the pulling down of strong holds.* With these they *commended themselves to every man's conscience in the sight of God.* With these, idol temples were demolished—sinners pricked in their hearts, and brought to bow submissively at the Saviour's feet.

These are the doctrines which were preached in the time of the glorious reformation from papacy, throughout the whole Protestant world. These were the weapons used by Luther, Melancthon, Calvin, Crammer, and Knox. They went forth with the sword of the Spirit pressing the consciences of men. They urged the positive declarations of God. Says the celebrated Luther in his discourse delivered at Wittenberg in the height of the reformation, "I had the whole

The Second Great Awakening

body of the papacy to oppose. I preached, I wrote, I pressed on men's consciences, with the greatest earnestness, *the positive declarations of the word of God*—and what has been the effect?—This same word of God has, while I was asleep in my bed, given such a blow to papal despotism as not one of the German princes, not even the emperor himself could have done. It is not I—I repeat it, *it is the divine word* which has done every thing—Had it been right to have aimed at a reform by violence and tumults, it would have been easy for me to have deluged Germany with blood—The devil smiles in secret when he sees men pretend to support religion by seditious tumults; but he is cut to the heart when he sees them in faith and patience rely on the written word." (Mitner, Volume 5, p. 195).

These too are the doctrines which have been preached in the late revivals, in New England. Doctrines which have awakened the enmity of thousands, and have shown sinners their opposition to God. Doctrines which many have opposed with all their hearts, in which contest thousands have been convicted and slain. These are the weapons which have been wielded by the hand of the divine Spirit and have been *mighty through God to the pulling down of strong holds*. These are the doctrines which thousands have embraced, by their own confession, at the very time when they submitted to God and began to love the duties of religion.

With these weapons, my brethren, we must not forget to add the prayer of God's children. Christ is the glorious conqueror. He is thus described as a mighty warrior armed for the field. *Gird thy sword upon thy thigh, O most mighty, with thy glory and thy majesty. And with thy majesty ride prosperously because of truth and meekness and righteousness; and thy right hand shall teach thee terrible things. Thine arrows are shot in hearts of the king's enemies; whereby the people fall under thee.*

22

The Mortification of Sin, Part I

And they that are Christ's have crucified the flesh with the affections and lusts (Galatians 5:24).

Self-denial and mortification of sin are prominent traits in the Christian character. Where this is neglected, painful consequences will follow. Hence discord arose in the churches of Galatia. To settle these was a leading object of Paul in this epistle. The preacher does not palliate. He strikes at the root. They are in danger of forfeiting their Christian character. He enumerates the *works of the flesh, the fruits of the spirit* and then adds; *They that are Christ's have crucified the flesh with the affections and lusts.*

The word *flesh* denotes human depravity. Of this there can be no doubt; for the Apostle himself has thus explained it. *Now the works of the flesh are manifest, which are these: adultery, fornication, uncleanness, lasciviousness, idolatry, witchcraft, hatred, variance, emulations, wrath, strife, seditions, heresies, envyings, murders, drunkenness, revellings, and such like; of the which I tell you before, as I have also told you in time past, that they which do such things shall not inherit the kingdom of God.*

This is the Apostle's own explanation. *These are the works of the flesh. The flesh with the affections and lusts* includes the whole body of sin. The text presents us with an interesting subject. Here is the Christian. Something has been done. Something of great importance has taken place in every Christian. *They that are Christ's have crucified the flesh with the affections and lusts.* To *crucify* and to *mortify* are words of kindred import. *Mortify therefore your members which are upon the earth. If ye through the Spirit do mortify the deeds of the body, ye shall live.*

On the mortification of sin, it is proposed to consider the following particulars,
1. What it implies.
2. Wherein it resembles crucifixion.
3. The means of promoting it.
4. The evidence that the work is begun
5. Inferences from the whole.
6. Motives to engage in the duty.

1. What it implies. It does not consist in the suppression of external acts *merely*. This may be done and yet the heart be in love with sin. The impenitent, through pride of character or fear of punishment, may abstain from external acts of wickedness—They may sustain a fair reputation among men and yet sin may hold the dominion over the heart. This our Lord asserted: *Now do ye Pharisees make clean the outside of the cup and the platter; but your inward part is full of ravening and wickedness.* Nor,

2. Does it imply an entire freedom from all sin. *For if we say we have no sin, we deceive ourselves, and the truth is not in us.* There is a warfare in the hearts of all Christians. *The flesh lusteth against the Spirit, and the Spirit against the flesh.*

But it implies,

1. The indwelling of the Holy Spirit. Christians are said to do that which is done by the agency of the Holy Spirit. *If ye through the Spirit do mortify the deeds of the body, ye shall live.* It implies a prevailing attachment to inward holiness and the things of the Spirit. *They that are after the flesh do mind the things of the flesh; but they that are after the Spirit the things of the Spirit. But ye are not in the flesh, but in the Spirit, if so be that the Spirit of God dwell in you. Now if any man have not the Spirit of Christ, he is none of his. And if Christ be in you, the body is dead because of sin; but the Spirit is life because of righteousness. And,* so in the text, *they that are Christ's have crucified the flesh.*

Again; Mortification of sin implies the subversion of its dominion. A mortified sin is not a reigning sin. Sin does not hold the throne in the heart. Christ holds the dominion. He holds the highest seat in the affections. *Let not sin therefore reign in your mortal body, that ye should obey it in the lusts thereof. Sin shall not have dominion over you.* Sin was once a pleasure and religion a burden. But now it is the reverse. Religion is a pleasure, and sin is a burden. *Grace reigns.* Sin has received its death wound. If it be not dead, yet it is dying.

II. Wherein does mortification resemble crucifixion? Christ was crucified; he was put to death. And sin must die; it must be put to death.

1. The death of the cross was not a natural, but a violent death. This instrument of death was literally a cross of wood. On this the arms of the sufferer were stretched out, his hands and feet nailed fast. And then it was suspended and the body left to sink with its own weight. And so sin must suffer a violent death. It will never die of course. If let alone, it would live forever. It would reign in the

soul to all eternity. It must be *suspected, detected, condemned, and crucified.*

2. The death of the cross was a shameful death. It was considered as the greatest scandal.—Reserved for the worst of criminals. So the Christian who mortifies the deeds of the body will certainly endure shame and reproach. Real Christians take up his cross, and bear it after him—and endure shame and mortification in his cause. Not only so but the Christian condemns himself for all his sins. He charges himself with the very worst sins of which he is guilty. And in the sight of the heart-searching God is frequently found confessing them with shame and confusion of face. Thus the prophet Ezra prayed, *O my God, I am ashamed and blush to lift up my face to thee, my God.* And so Daniel confessed his sins with *confusion of face.*

3. The death of the cross was a lingering death. By loss of blood, the life is gradually exhausted. So it is with the death of sin. It does not die in an instant. At times the Christian imagines that he has gained at once a complete victory over some particular sin or sins. But the conflict returns. The same passion which has slept for months and years may again be roused. Different circumstances present new and powerful temptations. And the believer may be called to the same conflict over and over again. The mortification of one sinful passion may cost you labor, constant watchfulness, and much time. With such lingering slowness is sin crucified, and the victory obtained.

4. Crucifixion is a painful death. The body suspended by its nerves is reduced to one vast wound, till the violence of torment ends in the agony of death. The mortification of sin may be exceedingly painful. This may be one principal reason why it is compared to crucifixion. The process of mortification is often extremely painful. So it is with the mortification of sin. It may cost the believer many tears, and groans, and prayers, and cries to heaven to mortify one sin. It may appear strange to those who never oppose the torrent of their own corruptions and therefore know nothing of it from experience. But Jesus Christ compares it to cutting off a right hand; or plucking out a right eye. *If thy right eye offend thee, pluck it out, and cast it from thee: for it is profitable for thee that one of thy members should perish, and not that thy whole body should be cast into hell.* It may be very hard and painful to break off old sins, but by the grace of God it *can,* and *must* be done, or the soul will be cast into hell.

It may be *universally* painful. Every member, every sense, and the whole body of sin must be attacked. The impenitent, when being

The Second Great Awakening

driven from one sin, fly to another. Not so with the Christian. His warfare is with the whole body of sin. They *put off the old man, which is corrupt according to the deceitful lusts. Knowing this, that our old man is crucified with him, that the body of sin might be destroyed, that henchforth we should not serve sin. And they that are Christ's have crucified the flesh with the affections and lusts.*

The work is so difficult and universally painful that few only thoroughly engage in it. On account of this very difficulty, the way to heaven is called *strait. Because strait is the gate, and narrow the way, which leadeth unto life, and few there be that find it.* Hence the death of sin is compared to crucifixion, because it is *a violent—scandalous—lingering—painful death.*

We proceed to consider,

III. The means of promoting mortification of sin.

1. Feel your absolute dependence upon God. Your need of the influences of the Spirit to take hold and conquer your sins—that without this influence nothing will be done—that you will certainly wax worse and worse. And this will make you afraid to grieve and stifle its blessed influences. And this will lead you to cry: *Cast me not away from thy presence; take not thy Holy Spirit from me.*

2. Avoid temptation.—And especially the company of those who would tempt you to speak or act in an unchristian manner. Beware of the flattering insinuations of friends. They will sometimes flatter your pride, your vanity, and give occasion for corruptions of the heart to arise. Here you need the more caution because the evil comes from a source unsuspected. However well designed or well meant, take everything of this kind as a serious injury to the welfare of your soul. Never listen to flattery—stop your ears and be unwilling to hear. It can do you no good—and every thing which gratifies the pride and corruption of the heart is making work for better repentance.

Impress your heart with a sense of your obligation to God—how much you are bound to do and how little you have done and be ashamed of every neglected duty. Resist the very commencement of evil. Banish sinful thoughts. You are in danger from a single evil thought. If you suffer it to lodge and rest in the heart, you rock a giant. It will soon arise and overpower you.

3. Labor for a still deeper sense of the vanity of the world. All its pleasures and honors within a few days will be over and gone forever. Lower your expectations of worldly prosperity—expect nothing from the world. Be alarmed at an uninterrupted course of worldly prosperity. You are surrounded by temptation, and are in

danger of neglecting your soul. Be afraid of receiving all your good things in this life.

4. Bring clearly to view the great things of eternity. Remember that death, judgment, and eternity are but just before you. Every day imagine yourself on a dying bed, and your body in the grave. Make it real. Know and feel the solemn truth that the hour of death will soon be past, and your soul in heaven or hell.

Remember that God is present. Whenever you are tempted to sin, remember that God sees you—that you can never flee from his presence—that your heart is naked to his view.

5. Carefully attend to all the duties of religion. Never be idle. Maintain daily communion with God. Let no day pass without entering your closet—and calling self to an account—and humbling your soul in the dust for your sins. If at any time you are conscious of having yielded to temptation; let not guilt drive you from your closet. For you know not when it will end. Delay not—go immediately to the throne of grace, with all your sin and guilt fresh in your mind. Tarry not till you feel better, lest you obtain a false peace, and cover your sins, and never repent and lose your soul.

However humiliating, no matter, delay not, go just as you are and tell the Lord the worst of your case. Feel no disposition to justify or palliate your sin in the least, but own and confess the very worst of your case. Some Christians have found much benefit from particularizing their sins. Some of your most heinous sins at times may lie with weight on your conscience. While secluded from the world it might be proper to name them in the presence of God—to dwell on their enormity until the heart is deeply affected, humbled, and broken. Such a particular confession is useful because it is humiliating.

Would you have your sins mortified? Be willing to have others tell you your faults. This is one great object of Christian fellowship, to help on the work of mortification. It is a great privilege to a Christian to unite with those who are faithful. To put himself under the watch of those who will warn him of his danger. And when wandering from the path of duty, will labor to bring him to repentance. This is a great, an inestimable privilege, and is so esteemed by all true Christians. *Rebuke a wise man, and he will love thee (Proverbs 9:8).* Sin is blinding. Others can often discover it when we cannot. And to be warned of our danger is a great kindness. It was esteemed by David. *Let the righteous smite me, it shall be a kindness: and let him reprove me, it shall be an excellent oil, which shall not break my head.*

Would you mortify your sins? Be very careful when you are reproved by a Christian brother—be very careful, I say, and *never take it amiss.* Whether you can see your sin or not, be ready to suspect danger. If you are not guilty it can do you no hurt. And if you show displeasure you are gone. Your best friend meeting repulse will forever after let you alone. You will perish and none will dare venture to help you. *Woe to him that is alone when he falleth; for he hath not another to help him up.* And lest your brethren should neglect their duty, select some particular Christian friend and request him to be faithful, and always *feel* thankful for his admonitions, whether you discover your error at the time or not.

And to the same end, improve the reproaches of enemies. When others speak evil—never retaliate. Be careful how you speak much in your own defense. It can do you no good, and the habit is always injurious. *For what glory is it, if, when ye be buffeted for your faults, ye shall take it patiently? But if, when ye do well and suffer for it, ye take it patiently, this is acceptable with God.* Some faithful friend or some malicious foe must be helpful to us in this work. Bend all your efforts against your easily besetting sin. There be always on your guard, then set a double watch.

And finally,

Cherish those thoughts which are the most opposed to all sin. View the evil nature of sin. It always renders you unhappy—it subjects you to the goadings of a guilty conscience and at times fills the soul with awful forebodings of future punishment. It renders you odious in the sight of God and all holy beings, and fit only for the society of fiends, and actually deserving of eternal damnation.

But above all think what your sins cost the Saviour. Go, my brethren, frequently to that interesting scene. *Now when evening was come, he sat down with the twelve.* Here him relate the sorrowful story: *Verily, I say unto you, that one of you shall betray me. And he took bread, and gave thanks, and brake it, and gave to them, saying, This is my body which is broken for you: this do in remembrance of me. Likewise also the cup after supper, saying, This cup is the New Testament in my blood, which is* <u>shed for you</u>*.*

The scene changes, *And when they had sung an hymn, they went out into the mount of Olives.* Here him declare to his disciples: *All ye shall be offended because of me this night.* Again the scene changes, *And they go to the garden of Gethsemane. Sit ye here,* saith he *to his disciples, while I go and pray yonder.* And he taketh with him three of his disciples, and began to be *sorrowful and very heavy.*

Then saith he unto them, *My* <u>soul</u> *is* <u>exceeding</u> *sorrowful,* <u>even</u>

unto *death*. *Tarry ye here and watch with me*. And he went a little farther and fell on his face, and prayed saying, "O Father, if it be possible let this cup pass from me! nevertheless not as I will, but as thou wilt." There behold his agony; and his sweat; as it were great drops of blood. See the multitude with swords falling down to the ground; and slaves assembling to take him. See him betrayed by a kiss, forsaken by all his disciples—led forth to his trial, and condemned, *scourged,* spit upon. See him taken by the cruel soldiers and dragged into the common hall. See him stripped, and covered with a scarlet robe, and crowned with thorns, with a reed in his hand. See the insulting mob bow the knee before him and pay him mock homage. See him led forth bearing his own cross and fainting under the weight. See him stretched out, his hands and feet pierced through and nailed fast to the accursed tree. See it raised from the ground, and his body suspended between the heavens and the earth.—And there Christian, hangs your Redeemer. There see what your sins have done.

Hear him cry, "My God, my God, why hast thou forsaken me?" and learn what *your* sins have done, and what you deserve. This is that Saviour whom you profess to love, and will you crucify him afresh? Will you not rather *crucify the flesh with the affections and lusts?*—Call to mind your solemn obligations. You have avouched the Lord Jehovah to be your God—You have openly professed Christ before man. This you have done before the world. And will you take on you the name of Christ and go out into the world and betray his cause? Will you wound the Saviour in the house of his friends?—or will you not rather *crucify the flesh with the affections and lusts?*

23

The Mortification of Sin, Part II

And they that are Christ's have crucified the flesh with the affections and lusts (Galatians 5:24).

In the previous discourse I considered,
1. What is implied in the mortification of sin.
2. Wherein it resembles crucifixion.
3. Means of promoting it.

We proceed on the same subject to consider the following particulars:
1. Evidence that the work is begun.
2. Inferences from the whole.
3. Motives to engage immediately in the duty.

As above, 1. Evidence that the work is begun.
1. Tenderness of conscience in regard to all known sin. But is it so with you?
2. Do you above all things desire to be delivered from sin? Do you long to be more holy? Is it your chief care to live a holy life? Are you thankful when others reprove you and in Christian meekness tell you your faults?
3. Do you watch against temptation and steadily avoid it? Do you live as if you were facing toward hell? Are you continually inquiring about your actions, is this sin? Or do you say, "May I do so and so?" If so, then this indicates a bad heart. If there is any doubt about whether something is sin or not the true Christian will flee. On an enemy's ground you would not be so nice about the limits. You would not stand measuring distances to see whether you had barely crossed the line. Rush onward into the heart of the country. Run, till you could see yourself out of reach of danger.
4. Does death appear more desirable, if the consequences may be deliverance from all sin? Leave out of the account the pains of death. Paul said, *I am in a strait betwixt two, having a desire to depart, and be with Christ; which is far better.*

I will go still further and inquire, what is the evidence of progress in this business.
1. Are you more submissive under afflictive providences?
2. Are you more able to bear the reproaches of enemies? Do they

cause less uneasiness? Are you more patient? Do you find it more easy to take a reproof for your sin? Is it easier to forgive injuries? Young converts are apt to talk and make much of what they suffer in this respect. Those low in grace are ever talking and making much of trifles.—The humble Christian thinks of his master and is ashamed.

3. Can you more easily part with the comforts of life at the call of God? Has the work of self-denial become easier? Do you take more satisfaction in acts of charity? If so, this is an evidence that the world has less hold of the heart.

4. Is it easier for you to resist sin in its first motions? Is it easier to stifle it in its commencement?

5. Do you bear prosperity and adversity with greater equanimity? Are you less elated by the former and less depressed by the latter?

6. Is your heart more steadily fixed in the duties of religion? Are you more and more unwilling to leave a religious course?

Finally, do you discover things to be sinful which formerly you thought little of? You may feel that you are less sinful, and yet this is no evidence of the fact—Many think they are growing better, when in fact, they are waxing worse and worse. This is often the case with the impenitent. Bunyan, before his conversion, informs us that for some time he was very strict and punctual in religious duties. He thought that no man in England served God better than himself.

Nor is it decisive evidence either for or against that a person feels that he is growing worse. He may feel he is growing worse and it may be true. Another may feel that he is growing worse, and yet this may be owing entirely to growth in grace. The Christian may discover new sources of wickedness in himself. On that case, things have *always* appeared sinful, now appear more sinful than ever. The same things appear more sinful. Is it so with you?—This is a paradox to some. It is a fact that the most holy men have made the most bitter complaints of their own sinfulness. Job, Isaiah, David, Daniel, and Paul are examples of this. The centurion says, *Lord, I am not worthy that thou shouldest enter under my roof: Wherefore neither thought I myself worthy to come unto thee.* And what was the reply of our Lord? *Verily, I have not found so great faith in all of Israel.* To the Syrophenecian woman, he said, *It is not meet to give the children's bread to dogs.* She readily added, *truth Lord: yet the dogs eat of the crumbs which fall from their master's table.* Witness her deep sense of her unworthiness. Witness our Lord's answer, *O woman, great is thy faith.* The more light and holiness increase, the clearer will be the discovery of sin. It may fitly be compared to a

The Second Great Awakening

person in a filthy dungeon or to one *whose senses have been exercised to discern between good and evil.*
Infer,
1. The life of a Christian is no idle or easy life. We are exhorted to *watch,* and *pray,* and *strive,* and *wrestle,* and *fight.*
2. If mortification is the great business of the Christian, then those who give occasion for our corruptions to rise, do us a real injury. Those who flatter our pride, or our vanity, we are apt to regard as our best friends; but this is a sad mistake. They do us a serious injury. Those who in a serious, solemn, and affectionate manner, warn us of our danger and make us most uneasy with our sins, are our very best friends. These are the persons whose friendship it would be our highest interest to cultivate.
3. If mortification is the great business of the Christian, then we have reason to fear that the number of real Christians is small. How few appear to possess the marks which the Bible gives us of the Christian. How few of whom it can be truly said, *They have crucified the flesh with its affections and lusts.* How many instead of wishing to be told their sins, secretly hate those who do it. These do not bear the marks of a Christian. *Rebuke a wise man, and he will love you. Reprove a scorner, and he will hate you. Strait is the gate, and narrow is the way, which leadeth unto life, and few there be that find it.*
4. From our subject we may see the use of afflictions. It is to help on the work of mortification. Our hearts are such that we cannot bear prosperity. Hence the children of God are often found in the deepest affliction. God corrects in mercy. W*e have had fathers of our flesh who corrected us, and we gave them reverence: shall we not much rather be in subjection unto the Father of spirits, and live? They for their pleasure corrected us, but he for our profit, that we might be partakers of his holiness.*
5. The most desirable situation in life is the most free from temptation. This affords the best advantages to gain the victory over our own sins, and to grow in grace. And yet *riches, honors,* and *pleasures* raise mountains between us and heaven.
6. Infer, the benefit of Christian fellowship to help on the work of mortification. Here *two are better than one, for they have a good reward of their labor.*
I come now to offer motives to engage immediately in this duty.
1. Your present comfort and happiness *demands it.* A double satisfaction arising from it: That of having performed a Christian duty and a clearer evidence of a good estate. Romans 8:10. *If ye*

through the Spirit do mortify the deeds of the flesh, ye shall <u>live</u>. Now if we be dead with Christ, we believe that we shall also live with him. These two are intimately connected. Would you then, on good ground, be delivered from disposing double and painful suspense about an interest in Christ—engage immediately in this duty. The difficulty can be removed in no other way.

Mortification is also attended with inward satisfaction—a calm serenity of soul. Sinful indulgence disturbs and alarms. *The wicked are like the troubled sea when it cannot rest, whose waters cast up mire and dirt. There is no peace, saith my God, to the wicked. Great peace have they that love God's law.*

2. Your own usefulness in the cause of Christ is depending on it. If you refuse to mortify your sins you will also not do good to others. Conscious guilt will always prevent. David prays, *Restore unto me the joy of thy salvation.* II Timothy 2:21. In a great house there by many vessels, *some to honor and some to destruction. If a man purge himself from these, he shall be a vessel unto honour, sanctified, and meet for the master's <u>use</u>, and prepared for <u>every good work</u>.* You must be sanctified—meet for the master's use and meet for every good work.

3. Your safety in the hour of temptation depends upon it. All are more or less exposed to temptation from the world. If you have not been inured to mortification and self-denial you will be found an easy prey. You will be taken by surprise.

4. The honor of religion requires it. Are you afraid of bringing the cause of religion into reproach? Then deal fast with your hearts. All the disgrace drawn upon it by professors of religion is owing to unmortified lust.

If you have fallen because you have suffered your sin to take deep root, it will be hard for others to reclaim you—the unhumbled and unsanctified heart will be found unmanageable—you will continue to stand out, and so bring still greater disgrace on the cause. If all are found guilty of neglecting their own hearts, discipline will run down—others being guilty and so many being guilty, nothing will be done. If we neglect ourselves, we shall neglect others—in this manner churches may run down—and finally run out. Then the candlestick will be removed. Brethren, the honor of religion requires that you engage in this duty.

5. It is a necessary preparation for the day of adversity. There is nothing like it to fit you to bear affliction. If you are not dead to the world, it will be hard parting in the hour of death. If you are dead to

The Second Great Awakening

the world, it will be easy parting. Then you will find nothing to do but to die.

6. Again, think, when tempted to sin, what will be gained or lost by indulgence. Set heaven on the one hand and hell on the other. Weigh the matter well. Think again, what is that commodity for which you are about to barter away your soul? What is that for which you are willing to lose heaven and endure the pains of hell forever? Think what the damned in hell now suffer for that very sin.

Finally, let every sinner in this house take warning—The way to heaven lies directly opposite to every feeling of the natural heart. Sinner—You must part with your sins, or part with heaven. However painful, the work must be done. Christ requires it on pain of eternal death. *For if ye live after the flesh, ye shall die.*

It is reduced to this single point. You must kill, or be killed. *Now* is the time to break off your sins. The longer it is deferred, the greater the difficulty. Sinful habits wax stronger and stronger. Your case will soon become desperate. Let the awful warning of our Saviour sink deep in every heart. *If thine eye offend thee, pluck it out. It is better for thee to get into the kingdom of God with one eye, than having two eyes to be cast into hell fire. Where the worm dieth not, and the fire is not quenched.*

24

The Counsel and Agency of God in the Government of All Things

In whom also we have obtained an inheritance, being predestined according to the purpose of him who worketh all things after the counsel of his own will (Ephesians 1:11).

It is a desirable thing that God should govern the world. All intelligent beings who are delighted with his moral character will certainly rejoice in his universal government. The infinite holiness and purity of the divine character render it infinitely desirable that his government should be complete and universal, extending to all creatures and events; that so nothing might take place which would eventually tarnish the divine glory. Has sin spread desolation through our world, and assaulted the throne of God? It is certainly desirable to hear that the wrath of man shall praise him and that the remaining wrath shall be restrained. Is the prince of darkness, with his followers, grasping at universal empire? It is certainly desirable to hear that the *Lord hath prepared his throne in the heavens, and that his kingdom ruleth over all. And that he doeth according to his will in the army of heaven, and among the inhabitants of the earth: and that none can stay his hand, or say unto him, What doest thou?*

This, then, is a desirable truth which is contained in our text, and to which your serious attention is now invited—*That God works all things after the counsel of his own will.*

In examining this subject, we shall notice—

I. The *Counsel*

II. The *Agency* of God in the government of all things—

God never acts without design, or determination. Thus to act, would be to act without wisdom and with folly. He has a perfect plan, defined exactly according to the counsel of his own will, as asserted in the text. This counsel denotes, his design, purpose, or decree respecting all events. That God has such a counsel or decree we are now to prove. And this is evident both from reason and revelation.

All our knowledge of God consists in a knowledge of his perfections; of his essence we know nothing save this, that he is a Spirit. Whatever perfections God possesses he must possess in the highest degree; otherwise they are not perfections, and such a God would be limited, finite, and no God. A denial or limitation of any of his essential perfections, is, therefore, tantamount to a positive denial of the existence of God; and thus will he find it in God's account who has thus *limited the Holy One of Israel.*

I observe then, that the existence of God cannot be proved by any person who denies the divine decrees. The great argument in proof of the Omniscience of God is derived from effects produced—from the *design* manifest in the works of creation, and from the existence of intelligent beings. The argument is fair and lucid. Where there is a design there must be a designer. The Laws of nature are nothing but God's *fixed* and *settled plan* or mode of operation. And all our knowledge of natural philosophy is nothing but a partial and imperfect discovery of the *great plan and eternal counsel* of the divine will. But we are soon lost in the wide extent and unfathomable depth of that knowledge which is displayed in the works of creation. The whole face of nature bears the most evident marks of *choice* and *plan* in the mind of its author. So that we are forced by every dictate of reason and common sense, to conclude that the eternal God must have a perfect plan worthy of his infinite mind, according to which he governs and disposes all events in the universe. But—if these things do not demonstrate the *design* and *counsel* of God, we have no proof from the works of nature that God knows anything.

But if God is omniscient, he has certainly decreed the existence of all things. Knowledge implies absolute certainty. With respect to the existence of all *past* events, it is intuitively certain that they have taken place. This we know. But God eternally knows this same certainty; otherwise we know what God did not. To say that God *knows all things,* and yet that he does *not know the absolute certainty* of their existence, is a contradiction. But if God *certainly knows* all future events, they are all fixed in the infinite mind with the same certainty as if they were actually past. Whether past or future, the certainty is the same. There can be no *doubt* or *uncertainty* in the omniscient mind. With God nothing can be *probable* or *improbable.* Whatever will not exist, *he knows* will not exist.

But will it be said that with God there is no *past* nor *future,* all is present with him? Granted, just so it is. God *sees at once,* with equal *clearness* and *intuitive certainty* the beginning and the end. *All things* are *present—naked and open* to the omniscient eye. All future events are therefore made *sure* of existence, for God *now sees* them, and *they have been eternally before him!* Although it be true that God views all things as present to his infinite mind; yet it is also true, that *all things are future* to him who is declared to be *"before all things* and by whom all things consist."

The ground, or reason of the existence of any thing must be in the counsel of the divine will. Had God never determined or willed the existence of any thing, nothing could ever have existed. The time, manner, and circumstances of the existence of every event, are all fixed and determined by God. The reason why we exist *now* rather than in the days before the flood, at the birth of Christ, at the Millennial day, or why we exist at all, and worship in the house of God and not in the house of Rimmon, must be because *"God hath determined the times before appointed, and the bounds of our habitation."*

If God has not decreed the existence of future events, neither the existence, nor time, nor manner of such events could possibly be foreknown. The omniscient God views all things as eternally present. Yet, *as he existed before all things,* his knowledge of all things must have consisted in the knowledge of *all future events.*—In thus; He must have had a *present* and *perfect knowledge of all things,* while as yet there was no creature or actual existence beside the eternal self existence of God. He alone has existed from eternity, yet he is eternally omniscient. The *actual existence of all things* must have been *future,* and *known* to be future to the Self-existent, omniscient Jehovah.

But future events must become *certain* of existence *before* their existence can be *certainly known.* Though what is certainly foreknown, is equally certain of existence; yet mere knowledge cannot be the cause or ground of this certainty, but the contrary; in order of nature, absolute certainty is the ground of the knowledge. Now what could be the ground of the certain existence of all events, in their time, order, and perfect harmony; and what could make them eternally the objects of present certain intuitive knowledge in the infinite mind, while as yet there was none of them in actual existence? What, but the eternal *purpose of him who worketh all things after the counsel of his own will.*

But events cannot be known to be future unless they were made so by the divine decree. If the world, or any event could be *certainly* future, with the time and circumstances of its existence, without being made so by the decree of God, then it can actually exist without him; for its existence is certain and necessary, and it *cannot but exist,* when it becomes certainly future.

But if we admit that God barely foreknew that *all things would exist just as they do,* without his determining or decreeing their existence, we need not perplex ourselves to find out the ground or reason of the *certainty* of his knowledge, for on this supposition we are left without any proof of the *existence of God.* For if things exist without the determination or decree of God, then they certainly exist without any cause at all; and infinite knowledge is a mere hypothesis, and which, though it *were real,* could not be the efficient cause of the existence of anything.

Our proof, therefore, of the divine omniscience, is really a consequence inferred only from the previous certainty of the decrees of God. They mutually imply each other and on the ground of reason and argument stand or fall together. If God does not know all things *because he has decreed* their existence, we have no other argument in proof of his omniscience than this, that God knows all things *because* he knows all things.

Again—Infinite wisdom is a moral perfection of God. It is a complex attribute, and implies infinite knowledge, infinite holiness, benevolence, and indeed, like many other general terms, it contains every divine excellence; and comprehends the whole moral character of God.

I observe then, that leaving out the eternal counsel or decree of God, no just conceptions can possibly be formed of his moral character, or of any of his moral perfections. The clear and only obvious definition of infinite wisdom is this—It consists in discerning and proposing the highest and best possible end, and in determining, fixing on, and pursuing the best means, in order to accomplish it. Observe. This is a complex attribute; infinite knowledge to discern the best end and the best means.

This is one part. But there is no true wisdom in *mere knowledge.* Wicked men and devils know what is right; but having no *fixed determination to do it,* their wisdom is mere folly and madness. And without this determination, an increase of their knowledge would increase their folly. God might have infinite knowledge and discern the highest and best possible end, and yet be infinitely unholy, and without one moral excellence.

What then is the other part? What is infinite wisdom? Omniscience discerns without a possibility of mistake; the best means or whole chain of events by which it may be accomplished in the best possible manner. And all this may still be without one *moral* excellence in the character of God.

If God has not *eternally determined* to accomplish all that which omniscience sees best; then he is neither infinitely wise nor infinitely good; unless the foundation of infinite wisdom and goodness consists essentially in a perfect indifference to the existence of the greatest possible good. Would we ascribe the perfection of infinite wisdom to God? *It exists essentially in his fixed and immutable determination* to accomplish exactly, all that which omniscience sees best. An infinitely wise plan is infinitely holy, just, and good. This plan the omniscient God views not with indifference. But in a fixed and immutable determination to accomplish this plan consists, essentially, the infinite wisdom, holiness, justice, and goodness of God.

Is God immutable? By this we mean that he is subject to no change in his essence, and especially in no one of his essential perfections. To attribute to the infinite God one new scheme or alteration which was not laid in his eternal counsel, implies, either that he might have done better, or that he is now altering for the worse. Indeed it cannot be done without attributing a mistake to the Almighty, and denying his immutability, omniscience, and the whole of his moral perfections. "If the foundation be thus destroyed, what shall the righteous do?" But—

2. From the divine testimony we are assured that, "He is a rock, *his work is perfect."* "I know that whatever God doeth, it shall be forever, nothing can be put to it nor anything taken from it." No new thought shall ever enter his eternal counsel. *"The counsel of the Lord standeth forever, the thoughts of his heart to all generations" (Psalm 33:11).* It is formed in the most wonderful, and executed in the best possible manner. *"The Lord of Hosts is wonderful in counsel, and excellent in working" (Isaiah 28:29).* No devices of wicked men, however numerous, can disannul or alter it. *"There are many devices in man's heart; nevertheless the counsel of the Lord, that shall stand" (Proverbs 19:21). "There is no wisdom, nor understanding, nor counsel against the Lord" (Proverbs 21:30).* With infinite ease, and without a possibility of mistake, he views at once the beginning and end. *"He declares the end from the beginning, and from ancient times the things that are not yet done, saying, My counsel shall stand, and I will do all my pleasure" (Isaiah 46:10).*

Thus it is evident from the perfections of God and the direct testimony of his word, that his counsel or decree is eternal and universal, that it is infinitely wise, holy, just, and good. *This counsel shall stand.* We shall notice,

II. The agency of God in the government of all things. God, who is *"great in counsel, is mighty in work."* He worketh all things after

The Second Great Awakening

the counsel of his own will. The agency of God is coextensive with his decrees. *It is universal.* This is contained in the text: *"Who worketh all things."* That his agency is universal, and that he *works all things* after the counsel of his own will *in the natural world* will be disputed by none but an atheistical contemner of divine providence. By the natural world, I mean the whole material universe, or all that is not mind or spirit. If the natural world is not upheld and governed by God, it is neither upheld nor governed at all. Since the universal agency of God in the government of the natural world bears an intimate relation to the government of moral agents; with respect to the former it may be observed—That the providence of God in the natural world is clearly proved by arguing from effect to cause. But this proof rests on the fact that no creature or thing can exist without the agency of God as its primary-efficient cause. But if one thing may come into being or continue to exist without the agency of God, another and another may. To assent this, or that his agency is not universal would be to sap the foundation of all our reasonings in proof of the existence of God from his works. For who could tell whether the divine agency were concerned in this or that, or whether in any thing at all? There is therefore the same proof of the universal agency of God in the government of the natural world as there is of any providence or even of the divine existence.

The whole scheme of natural philosophy is built on the same foundation. Philosophy, like Jacob's vision, says one, "discovers to us a ladder whose top reaches up to the footstool of the throne of God."

That all things take place in perfect accordance with his pleasure, is as certain as it is that nothing cannot produce something. For if nothing in the natural world can take place without it, it certainly cannot take place against the will of God. If the least event can take place in the natural world without the agency of God, all things may. If the Laws of nature do operate without the divine agency, all things are as independent of God as it is *possible to conceive;* as much so as the ruling of the planets is of the energies of man.

The same truth is evident from the word of God. "He upholds all things by the word of his power." "By him all things consist." "In him we live, and move, and have our being." Not a sparrow can fall to the ground, or an hair from the head without his notice. God alone is self-existent and independent. All beings are equally dependent on him. The angels that excel in strength, no less than the meanest insect. By the word of his power all are upheld; by him *all consist, in him all live, and move, and have their being.*

When he created the angels, he created just so many and just such beings as he *pleased.* When he created this world, and the countless living creatures upon it, he formed just so many and just such creatures as he *pleased,* and as would exactly answer his purpose. The same Almighty hand that garnished the heavens, formed the crooked serpent. Neither the angel nor the serpent could say, what has thou made?

The Lord *hath made all things for himself.* For this end they were made, and for this end they are upheld and continue to exist. And this is the song of the angelic host before the throne of God.—*"For thou hast created all things, and for thy pleasure they are, and were created."* And this same end shall be accomplished. For he hath declared, *"My counsel shall stand, and I will do all my pleasure."*

Thus we have seen that all things and beings both in the natural and moral world *were created exactly according to the purpose of him who worketh all things after the counsel of his own will.* That all are equally dependent on his agency for preservation. That he upholds and governs them all as he pleases that they may answer the end for which he designed their existence. That the government of the natural and moral world, which include all creatures and events and necessarily implies universal agency, is also *executed according to the purpose of him who worketh all things after the counsel of his own will.*

The counsel and agency of God as thus represented extend to the actions of moral agents. *Even the wrath of man shall praise him.* What shall we then say? If our *unrighteousness commend the righteousness of God, What shall we say?* Shall we say that God did not design or decree that it should praise him; that if he did, sinners are not free agents?

Have wicked men and devils escaped from the government of God? Have they defeated the plan of infinite wisdom, and carried headlong the counsel of the Almighty? *"The Lord of hosts hath purposed, and who shall disannul it? and his hand is stretched out, and who shall turn it back?" "There are many devices in man's heart; nevertheless the counsel of the Lord, that shall stand."*

But it will be asked; if God has decreed the actions of men, how can they be free? That man is free, and that God has decreed his actions are plain matters of fact. Both are clearly manifest in the word of God.

That we are free in our actions we have as clear and certain

The Second Great Awakening

evidence as we have of our own existence. Every man is conscious that he acts with perfect freedom. That he chooses and refuses is as certain as it is that he exists. Of this every man is conscious. And this consciousness is the highest possible certainty. It is by this that we are certain of our own existence.

That the decrees are accomplished by the free and voluntary actions of men, we have plain, direct scripture testimony. *"And truly the Son of man goeth, as it was determined: but woe unto that man by whom he is betrayed" (Luke 22:22).* *"Him, being delivered by the determinate counsel and foreknowledge of God, ye have taken, and by wicked hands have crucified and slain" (Acts 2:23).* *"For of a truth against thy holy child Jesus, whom thou hast anointed, both Herod, and Pontius Pilate, with the Gentiles, and the people of Israel, were gathered together, For to do whatsoever thy hand and thy counsel determined before to be done" (Acts 4:27, 28). And when they had fulfilled all that was written of him, they took him down from the tree, and laid him in a sepulcher.*

Without shedding of blood there is no remission. Has God offered up his Son a sacrifice for sins, or has he not? Did Christ lay down his life for his sheep, and did he make his soul an offering for sin when the Jews put him to death, or did he not? When they wounded and bruised and crucified him, was he *wounded for our transgressions, and bruised for our iniquities,* or was he not? If the hand and counsel of God was not in it, who will dare say with the Prophet, "The Lord hath laid on him the iniquities of us all?" *Truly the Son of man goeth as it was determined.*

There are innumerable instances in the Scriptures, of God's determining and foretelling the voluntary actions of men. There is not perhaps, a single prediction in the Bible, which is not an instance of this. The conduct of Cyrus, in taking Babylon, was foretold long before his birth. After these words; "declaring the end from the beginning, and from ancient times the things that are not yet done, saying, My counsel shall stand, and I will do all my pleasure"; as a proof of this declaration, we are referred to this very fact, the calling of Cyrus, in the following words. *"Calling a ravenous bird from the east, the man that executeth my counsel from a far country; yea, I have spoken it, I will also bring it to pass; I have purposed it, I will also do it."*

God told Abraham that he would bring his seed from Egypt into the land of Canaan, after four hundred years, which event depends on innumerable voluntary free actions of that people, and of others. The same might be said of the predictions respecting the Persian,

Grecian, and Roman empires; and indeed of all the predictions that have been fulfilled. All were fixed and certain, yet they could not be accomplished without them.

The facts then are certain; man is free, and yet God has decreed his actions. Now whether we can perceive *how he is free,* or not, the facts are clear and plain; and these we are bound to admit. Further, it is not in our power to conceive of higher free agency, than of acting voluntarily. The child knows and feels that he is accountable for his voluntary actions, and for no other. Though many theories have been adopted respecting the question, "In what does free agency consist?" yet in the common affairs of life, no man or child ever mistook the point.

Free agency does not consist in a power to act either without or against volition and choice. Neither does it consist in a power to act independently of God; for if he should withdraw his agency we could neither choose nor act at all.

Man is a free agent in this sense only, that he is the subject of volitions. Whatever bodily powers he may loose, while volition or choice remain, man is a free moral agent. And nothing can possibly destroy free agency, which does not at the same time destroy volition or choice. Willing or choosing is certainly an exercise of free agency in the sight of God. It is also an exercise of the highest freedom of which it is possible for us to conceive.

But there is a difference between volition and its cause. They are as distinct as any other cause and effect. Now whatever may be the cause of volition, it cannot effect free agency. Volition is an effect of which God is the efficient cause; yet the agency of God and the act of the creature are perfectly distinct. The creature's act in exercising choice is not God's act, it is his own and constitutes him a free moral agent. Neither is causing volition any part of the creature's act. Indeed, if it were it could not be free, unless freedom and criminality consist in an act previous to volition, which act must be involved previous to volition, which act must be involuntary, for a volition cannot be the voluntary cause of itself.—

According to this representation man may be free in all his actions, and yet God may work in him both to will and to do. And this the Apostle asserts. *"For it is God who worketh in you both to will and to do of his good pleasure,"* or just as he pleases. He doeth his will in the army of heaven, and *among the inhabitants of the earth,* and none can stay his hand. *He worketh all things after the counsel of his will.*

The child is conscious that he is accountable for his voluntary actions, and for no other. Free agency consists in voluntary action. At the same time, it is asserted that, *God works in you both to will and to do. The king's heart is in the hand of the Lord, as rivers of water: he turneth it whithersoever he will.* God has the hearts of all in his hand, and he can turn them whithersoever he pleases, without destroying free agency in the least.

The Jews were commanded to go up out of their land, thrice in the year to appear before the Lord. Yet God promised that their enemies should not, at such times, *desire* their land. *"Neither shall any man desire thy land, when thou shalt go up to appear before the Lord thy God thrice in the year."* While the Jews were leaving their land nearly destitute of inhabitants, why did not their enemies take possession of it? The opportunities were frequent, and fair. But this they did not. And this God promised, *Neither shalt any man desire thy land.* If God had no power to control their hearts, no such promise could be made. Neither could they have done it, without they had contradicted what God had said and made him a liar.—

But if God cannot control and govern the hearts of men, he cannot have a moral government. At least he is not the moral governor of our world; and his government of this world consists only in governing dead matter. Neither can his government here be complete; for whatever man does is interrupting the government of God. If the minds of men are uncontrolled by God, he cannot completely govern any thing that comes within the reach of man. God may govern the distant planets, but he cannot completely govern the world.

Wicked kings and emperors have stained the earth with the blood of martyrs, and countless millions of the human race. And yet the Christian world have ever been taught to acknowledge the hand of God in the death of their friends. But in the case before us, would not such conduct be an impious affront to the Almighty!

Surely it would if the *king's heart* is not in the *hand of the Lord.* But, *the living may know that the Most High ruleth in the kingdom of men, and giveth it to whomsoever he will, and setteth up over it the basest of men (Daniel 4:17).* "And that there is an appointed time to man on the earth." The extermination of the wicked Canaanites was accomplished by the voluntary actions of men. But it was a heavy judgment inflicted by the hand of God. *God drove them out.* It was God *who smote great nations, and slew mighty kings; Sihon, king of the Amorites, and Og, king of Bashan, and all the kingdoms of Canaan.*

To deny the agency of God on the hearts of men, is to renounce Christianity. *It is the Spirit that quickeneth, the flesh profiteth nothing.* Sinners cannot be delivered except they are *drawn by the Father; and made willing in the day of his power; according to the purpose of him who works all things after the counsel of his own will.* Christians are *kept by the power of God through faith unto salvation.*

God may operate on the hearts of all men just as he pleases, and yet they be free. It is by admitting this truth only that we can pray for ourselves and others, that God would turn the hearts of sinners to himself, and grant them repentance unto life—that he would make us vessels of mercy, and not of wrath fitted to destruction.

Amidst all the confusion, darkness, and disorder which sin has introduced into this world, it is a *ground of strong consolation* to the pious mind, that God is on the throne—that he sees the end from the beginning, and hath said, *My counsel shall stand and I will do all my pleasure.* That God *who worketh all things after the counsel of his own will,* hath declared that, *All things shall work together for good to them that love God, to them who are the called according to his purpose.* You are therefore entreated to *work out your own salvation with fear and trembling; for it is God who worketh in you both to will and to do of his good pleasure.* And thus you may *rejoice in the Lord always—for all things are yours,* God is every where present. On the right hand and on the left, he is working. In all things you may hear the voice of the presiding Divinity, proclaiming to you that *all is well. God reigns and all is well.*

25

The Perseverance of the Saints

Being confident of this very thing, that he which hath begun a good work in you will perform it until the day of Jesus Christ
(Philippians 1:6).

These are the words of St. Paul. The inspired Apostle speaks with confidence. His language is plain and definite. *Being confident of this very thing, that he which hath begun a good work in you will perform it until the day of Jesus Christ.*

With respect to this *good work,* two things claim our attention:
I. The work itself.
II. The certainty that it will be finished.

I. The work itself. It may be observed, that it is not the work of *conviction.* This commonly precedes the good work, and is the effect of divine influence, and hence some have concluded that it must be a good work;—It being the effect of a good cause. But this is not true. For as every effect is distinct from its cause, the one may be good and the other bad. That the devils continue to exist is owing to Divine agency. And God will forever cause the wicked to feel the weight of his wrath; and yet this holy and righteous act in God will produce no virtue or good work in the damned. Felix may tremble, and Judas despair; but this is no virtue in them. God may cause the terrors of hell to seize on the most hardened sinner, and he may die in despair; but this bears no resemblance to the good work in the text.

In itself consider, there is no good in the fear of hell. That this is not the good work intended in the text is further evident from the fact that it does not always remain. The good work will go on in spite of all opposition. But conviction is often of short duration.

It is a fact, not very uncommon in times of special awakenings, that sinners tremble, and have awful forbodings of future, endless punishment, and then fall asleep again, more secure than ever. The work of conviction, being often of short continuance, is, therefore, not the work intended.

2. Is it any thing that can be found in the natural man? For, *Every imagination of the thoughts of the heart is only evil continually.* He is by nature depraved; *and unto every good work reprobate. A corrupt tree cannot bring forth good fruit.* And hence, good works

are declared to be the effect of a new creation. Says St. Paul, *We are his workmanship, created in Christ Jesus unto good works, which God before ordained that we should walk in them.* This good work then, is regeneration, or the *new creature. If any man be in Christ, he is a new creature.* This is the foundation—the beginning of the good work.

In this we may observe,

1st. The work is God's. The new creature is his workmanship. Man, who is the subject of this work, remains an active, moral agent; but, as it respects the cause he is wholly passive. *He is born, not of blood, nor of the will of the flesh, nor of the will of man, but of God.* In this work, God displays his sovereignty. *Of his own will begat he us, with the word of truth.* Before the formation of light, we are informed, that, *darkness was upon the face of the deep. And the Spirit of God moved upon the face of the waters. And God said, Let there be light: and there was light.*

Before this good work, the sinner remains in darkness, *and loves darkness rather than light.* Nay, *every one that doeth evil hateth the light, a*nd opposes it with all his heart. But, says the Apostle, *God who commanded the light to shine out of darkness, hath shined in our hearts, to give the light of the knowledge of the glory of God in the face of Christ.*

As in the former case, the invisible things of him from the creation of the world, *are clearly seen,* especially his *eternal power;* so from this workmanship we learn, *what is the exceeding greatness of his power toward them that believe;* it is *according to the working of his mighty power, which he wrought in Christ when he raised him from the dead. And you hath he quickened, who were dead.* God alone can raise a soul from the death of sin, to a life of holiness. He must breath upon the slain; or they will never draw the breath of everlasting life.

2. God not only begins, but carries on this good work. Many who acknowledge that God begins the work, seem to forget that his power is equally concerned in carrying it on. They talk and reason, as though God in a sovereign manner began this work; and then left it in the hands of the creature, to perform it or not. But, if it were depending primarily on the Christian, it would instantly cease.

Is the love of God shed abroad in his heart? *It is by the Holy Ghost.* Does he continue in the exercise of faith? It is because he is kept by the power of God. He is the author and the finisher of faith. Does he exercise any Christian grace?—*Love, joy, peace, longsuffering, gentleness, goodness, faith, meekness, temperance;*

The Second Great Awakening

these are the fruit of the Spirit. The branch cannot bear fruit of itself.

Respecting his vineyard, it is said, *I the Lord do keep it; I will water it every moment.* Does the good man walk in the path of duty? *His steps are ordained of the Lord.* He cannot take another step without being led. As well might he begin the work himself as put forth another holy exercise.

Whatever one may *say* on this subject; yet he cannot make a rational prayer without feeling and acknowledging this fact. Not one Christian walks without being led. *As many as are led by the Spirit of God, they are the sons of God.* Says St. Paul, *I follow after, if that I may apprehend of Christ Jesus.* It is here evident, that the same power which began, is necessary to continue the work. The same truth is contained in the text, *that he which hath begun a good work in you will perform it.* The beginning of this good work is regeneration; that which follows is sanctification.

Let us now attend to the

2. Proposition. Which is the certainty that the work will be finished, or the final perseverance of the Saints—And this may be predicated,

1st. On the *Covenant of Redemption.* As the covenant of works was made with the first Adam, and all his posterity; so the covenant of grace was made with Christ, the second Adam, and in him with all his chosen seed. *Now to Abraham, and his seed were the promises made, he saith not, unto seeds, as of many; but as of one, to thy seed, which is Christ. All the promises of God are in Christ, yea, and Amen,* to the glory of God. This covenant includes all that will ever be saved. And says the Apostle, *we are saved,* and called, with an holy calling; not according to our works; *but according to his own purpose, and grace, which was given us in Christ Jesus before the world began.* And again, *according as he hath chosen us in him, before the foundation of the world, that we should be holy.* And Christ says, *All that the Father giveth me shall come to me; and him that cometh to me I will in no wise cast out.* This covenant *is ordered in all things, and sure.* It depends on no conditions to be performed by man. God has engaged to *cause* them to persevere. *I will, and you shall.* The promise *is yea, and Amen.* The everlasting covenant, which the living God hath sworn shall never be removed, runs thus; *They shall be my people, and I will be their God. And I will give them one heart and one way, that they may fear me forever. And I will make an everlasting covenant with them, that I will not turn away from them to do them good; but I will put my fear in their hearts, that they shall not depart from me.*

Here God who cannot lie, declares in the strongest manner, that those who are included in this covenant, *shall not depart from him, and that he will never cease to do them good. The mountains shall depart, and the hills be removed; but my kindness shall not depart from thee, neither shall the covenant of my peace be removed; saith the Lord that hath mercy on thee.*

2nd. The *love* of God is engaged for their security. The unmerited—the eternal love of God moved him to begin this work. Hence he declares, *I have loved thee with an everlasting love: therefore with loving kindness have I drawn thee.* And again, *The mercy of the Lord is from everlasting to everlasting upon them that fear him.* And thus we hear the Apostle exulting in God's immutable love—affirming, that nothing in the *heights above,* nor anything in *the depths beneath,* nothing *present,* nor anything *future,* nor *life* nor *death itself, should be able to separate them from the love of God.*

3. The *power* of God is engaged on the behalf of those who are begotten again to a lively hope. *They are kept by the power of God through faith unto salvation.* Christ says, *My sheep hear my voice,—* and then affirms, *I give unto them eternal life; and they shall never perish, neither shall any pluck them out of my hand. My Father, which gave them me, is greater than all; and none is able to pluck them out of my Father's hand.* He who has all power in his hand, and whose kingdom ruleth over all, hath declared by the mouth of his servant, that *All things shall work together for good to them that love God, to them who are called according to his purpose—For whom he did foreknow, he also did predestinate to be conformed to the image of his son—Moreover whom he did predestinate, them he also called: and whom he called, them he also justified: and whom he justified, them he also glorified.* Here is a chain which all the powers of darkness cannot break. *They that trust in the Lord shall be as Mount Zion which cannot be removed, but abideth forever.*

4th. The *intercession* of Christ for his people affords another evidence of the same truth. Their glorious advocate, who ever liveth to make intercession for them *will thoroughly plead their cause.* Our ascended Redeemer is not a mere petitioner, who may, or may not succeed. He is always heard. For he has fully performed the conditions of the everlasting covenant. And to all its blessings he has a previous right. In his intercession, every believer is interested. His plea is always valid. *Who, then, shall lay any thing to the charge of God's elect?—Who is he that condemneth?* And further, Christ

The Second Great Awakening

has pledged his faithfulness. For we cannot forget the great errand on which he came from heaven to earth. He says, *I came down from heaven, not to do mine own will, but the will of him that sent me. And this is the Father's will which hath sent me, that of all which he hath given me I should loose nothing, but should raise it up again at the last day.*

Now, if Christ whom they were given, became responsible for them to the Father at the last day, as these words clearly import, he will doubtless *loose nothing.*

The same truth is further evident from this—*Union* to Christ. He is the *living head,* believers are *the members of his body, of his flesh and of his bones.*—And the *fullness of him that filleth all in all.* As it is written, Christ *is our life—Your life is hid with Christ in God.* The life of one is the life of the other; *for he that is joined to the Lord is one spirit,* and therefore, absolutely inseparable. By reason of this union the life of Christ, and the eternal life of the believer are equally certain. And no other meaning can I affirm to that heart cheering declaration of Christ to his disciples, *Because I live, ye shall live also.*

Respecting this truth, we may further allege, the *promises* of God to his children. *He that believeth shall be saved.* The expression is unqualified, and the promise absolute.

Here it may be proper to consider a very common mistake on this subject. And that is of correcting the word of God by making all the promises conditional, by adding—if we continue to believe—if we do our duty—if we are not wanting on our part, etc. Now this is inverting the order of the text; and subverting the whole of God's work at a single stroke. For if we continue to believe, do our duty, and are not wanting on our part, God has nothing to do. The work is wrested from his hand, and the creature undertakes alone.

If these are the conditions on which we are to receive the promise of salvation; then, there is not an absolute promise in the Bible. For such conditions cannot be performed till death. And hence, it would be absurd to talk of promises on this side of the grave. For the conditions must be performed before the promise can be claimed. As well may the infidel claim the promise before he believes, as the believer before his death.

Again, on such conditions all will be lost. If salvation is suspended on condition that we do our duty—that we be not wanting on our part; then all will be lost. For if we do our duty, we shall keep all the commands of God—and if we are not wanting on our part we shall henceforth be absolutely perfect. After the performance of such conditions there would be no necessity for God to carry on the work of sanctification.

What shall we then say? If we do as well as we can, may we not claim some promise of divine assistance? My hearers, such language is common; but cannot be found in the Bible. And if it could, not one soul would be saved on this ground. If the assistance of the Spirit of God is necessary in order to enable the Christian to do his duty, on what conditions does God grant that assistance? You will remember that every good work is the fruit of the Spirit. God begins, and carries on the work. On what conditions, then does he do it? None whatever. If we make the perseverance of the Christian depend originally on himself; he will never advance a single step.

And as for those who make such conditions to be performed first by the Christian; it is no wonder that they imagine that some may fail and be lost. On such conditions they may, and they certainly will, all be lost. While looking at the Christian, and the conditions which he would perform, St. Paul would say, *his strength is weakness. I have no confidence in the flesh.* But when looking at the Christian, and the work which God had undertaken, he would say: *I am confident of this very thing, that he which hath begun it will perform it until the day of Jesus Christ.*

While considering the promises of God to his children, your attention, my hearers, is directed to one important fact, which, may God grant you never to forget. It will be granted, on all hands, that if God has made one promise to carry on this work, he will certainly do it. There is, either some connection between your believing now, and your final salvation or there is not. If there is not, if God has made no such promise, the fact that you now believe is no evidence that you will not be lost. The fact that the jailer rejoiced believing in God was no evidence that he would not be in hell the next day. All who believed on the day of Pentecost may now be in hell. You may rejoice in a revival, because sinners are brought out of darkness into marvelous light;—but this is no evidence that they will not dwell in the blackness of darkness forever. This day there may be joy in heaven over *one sinner* that repenteth; and tomorrow, that sinner may be in hell. And you, my hearers, believing in Christ, may rejoice with joy unspeakable and full of glory, and your sins may now be actually forgiven and yet, this is no evidence that you will not, for all your sins, suffer the pains of hell forever.

My brethren, is there no connection between your believing now and your salvation? Where will you look for consolation? Will you begin to form resolutions? These can afford you no evidence of

The Second Great Awakening

safety for a moment. you may now say, *Though I should die with thee, yet I will not deny thee.* But look at Peter, and learn that your own strength is perfect weakness. *He that trusteth in his own heart is a fool.*

If you have ever seen the depravity of your own heart, and your absolute dependence on the sovereign, unmerited grace of God, where can you find *an anchor of the soul?* Nowhere can the Christian look for salvation with the least confidence without adopting the language of St. Paul in the text. If he cannot say that he is confident of this very thing, that God will perform the good work wherever he begins it, he certainly can have no confidence that he shall be saved. Whatever hope or consolation he may derive from any other source, it is all vain confidence and mere delusion.—And granting that God has actually begun a good work, yet if he has made no absolute—unconditional promise that he will never leave it unfinished; then, no Christian on earth has the least evidence that he shall be saved. *Men and brethren, what shall we do?* The *Christian* may be lost. He stands in jeopardy every hour. Has God made no promise? For the stranger without the covenants of promise, is without hope and without God in the world.—*But the foundation of God standeth sure.* Wherever he has begun a good work in the believer, he has *sealed it with that Holy Spirit of promise, which is the earnest of his inheritance.* And the Father of mercies hath declared that *he will confirm them to the end—and preserve them to his kingdom.—That the righteous shall hold on his way, and be stronger and stronger.—That though he fall, he shall not utterly be cast down, for the Lord upholdeth him with his hand.—That they shall not depart from him.*—Yes, God hath repeatedly declared, that he *will never;* no *never leave them nor forsake them.*—And hath he said, and shall he not make it good?

These promises, with many others, are unconditional and absolute—*yea and Amen.* These promises—let Christians exult in the cheering thought! These promises were made by him that cannot lie; to which he has annexed his most solemn oath; with this professed design, that *every sinner, who has fled for refuge to lay hold on the hope set before him, might have strong consolation. Which hope he has as an anchor of the soul, both sure and steadfast.*

If God is immutable; if there be any validity in his promises, the true believer shall certainly persevere.—Rejoice then ye feeble followers of the Lamb. The basis of your confidence and consolation is *firm* and *strong.* You have the utmost reason to conclude with St. Paul, that wherever God begins a good work, he will certainly *perform it until the day of Jesus Christ.* For the Only Wise God who has once laid the foundation of this good work in regeneration, will never leave it unfinished. No; it shall never be said by his enemies; here God *began to build, but was not able to finish.*

Having considered the evidence in favor, let us attend briefly to some of the principal objections against this doctrine—And to this it is objected—

1. That if Christians believe this doctrine, no matter how they live, their salvation is certain, they cannot be lost. Reply: That none will be deceived, we dare not affirm. Some, who now imagine themselves to be Christians, may be lost. This will no doubt be the case with thousands. But this objection has nothing to do with the doctrine we have advanced. Which is, that the true Christian will certainly persevere. Then the objection involves this absurdity. If we shall certainly persevere, no matter how we live, we shall certainly persevere, whether we persevere or not.—If it be true that the righteous *shall* hold on his way, no matter if he stop, or even go back—Nor,

2. Is the objection that the *belief* of this doctrine tends to make the Christian careless, less absurd. The formal professor, the self-righteous, the hypocrite and all who esteem the service of God weariness and are building on the sand, may think to find some relief in this doctrine. That this will not be the case we do not assert.—But the temper of heart which is necessary to give evidence of a gracious state is such, that no one who has it, can be careless. The objection involves this absurdity. I have evidence that I love God and the duties of religion; and now since I shall *certainly continue to love* God and the duties of religion, I care nothing about the honor of God or the duties of religion.

This objection, if made sincerely, is like to prove that the objector himself has no religion; and that he would willingly throw it off as an intolerable burden. No one who feels disposed to make this objection can possibly have evidence that the good work is begun in his soul; but, on the contrary, this disposition itself is a probable evidence against him. And besides, there are many zealous Christians who yet firmly believe this very doctrine. I adduce St. Paul as an example. Says he, *I am persuaded that neither life nor death shall be able to separate us from the love of God.* And again, in the text, he declares his *confidence* on this very subject.

3. To this doctrine is objected that passage in the 6th chapter of Hebrews, *For it is impossible for those who were once enlightened, and have tasted of the heavenly gift, and were made partakers of the*

The Second Great Awakening

Holy Ghost, and have tasted the good word of God, and the powers of the world to come, if they shall fall away, to renew them again unto repentance.

To this it may be answered,

1. It wants proof that these were Christians, for nothing is said regarding their love, faith, etc., and if they were not Christians, their case, had they been actually lost, would be no objection to the doctrine. Again, if they were Christians, and if they had actually fallen, it proves too much. For David and Peter fell and repented again; but this passage says, it is *impossible* to renew them again to repentance. By granting the objector his whole argument, it will plunge him into a difficulty, from which I trust, he will not be able to extricate himself. How is it that David and Peter fell and repented again; when this passage says that it would be impossible?

Again, it is only a supposition, therefore it can prove nothing. it barely states what would be, *if they shall fall away.* But should the objector feel disposed to push the inquiry still further, and ask: "Though it does not prove that any will be lost, yet, granting that they were Christians, does it not prove that the thing is *possible,* and St. Paul was fearful that they would be lost, for if he was persuaded otherwise why should he attempt to startle them by the supposition?"

Answer: St. Paul was persuaded differently and yet did speak in this manner. He adds; But *beloved, we are persuaded of better things of you, and things that accompany salvation; though we thus speak.* This whole passage taken in connection, falls on the other side of the question. For St. Paul here declares his full persuasion that his Hebrew brethren had experienced something which was infallibly connected with their final salvation.

It is objected,

4th. We read of Hymeneus, Alexander, Demas, Saul, Judas, and others who have apostatized. Answer: This conduct proves that they were never Christians. Their case will be found the best comment that can be given on that passage, I John 3:6. *Whosoever sinneth hath not seen him, neither known him.* And again, *They went out from us, but they were not of us; for if they had been of us, they would no doubt have continued with us.* This proves that they were not Christians, for if they had been, it is said there could be *no doubt* of their perseverance.

And finally, to end the contest, when the wicked shall be all assembled on the left hand of Christ, at the day of judgment, there will not be found one Christian whom Christ did acknowledge.

Though it now is pled in behalf of Saul, of Judas, and others, that they were once real Christians; and when they shall stand up and plead for themselves that they have prophesied, and even cast out devils, and in the name of Christ done many wonderful works; yet on the other hand, Christ will say, *I profess unto them, I never knew you; depart from me, ye that work iniquity.*

This doctrine, let it be observed, is either true or false. I shall therefore dismiss the objection with a short contrast. On the one hand it is positively asserted; and on the other it is positively denied. On the one hand: *He that believeth shall be saved.* On the other; he may be lost. On the one hand: *Verily, verily I say unto you, he that believeth hath everlasting life, and shall not come into condemnation*—On the other; he may be condemned. On the one hand: *There is therefore now no condemnation to them which are in Christ Jesus*—On the other; they may be condemned. On the one hand: *The gospel is the power of God to the salvation of every one that believeth*—On the other; some will be lost. On the one hand: *Whosoever liveth and believeth in me, shall never die. Believest thou this?*—On the other; no, we do not believe it.

This doctrine being established, salvation is wholly of grace from first to last. And the believer is taught to put no confidence in his own strength or resolutions. It rests wholly with God whether any shall persevere and be saved, or fall and be lost. Though you are weak and feeble, the Almighty hath said, *I will never leave thee, fear not; I am thy shield, and thy exceeding great reward. What God hath promised, he is able also to perform.* When the powers of earth and the gates of hell united assail the believer, menacing his destruction; then, the *Name,* the promises, the oath and the attributes of Jehovah are a *strong tower,* an impregnable fortress; and conscious of his own inability, he runneth into it and is safe from every attack.

The doctrine being established, we draw the following inferences:

1. We see why the angels rejoice at the repentance of one *sinner.* If angels did not believe this doctrine, they could have no ground on which to rejoice. They must wait until the sinner gets to heaven. The true penitent will certainly arrive safe to the mansions of the blessed. A firm belief of this doctrine lays the only foundation for joy in heaven over his repentance. If angels did not firmly believe this doctrine, their joy would be unfounded. Their language would be: "That sinner has truly repented, he is now a child of God—an heir of heaven—But, whether he will ever reach this happy place—whether

The Second Great Awakening

he ever sings with us in glory is a matter of great uncertainty. He may yet become a child of the devil—and an heir of hell. What a joyful thing it would be, if we knew that he would certainly arrive safe at heaven. Could we know this we might now tune our harps and sing glory to God in the highest—But since we have already been disappointed—and devils and damned spirits are now triumphing over some, at whose repentance we once rejoiced, it is best to wait and see how they hold out."

"Ye angels," says the adversary, "Ye angels" say they, "ye may now suspend your harps—let your joy be turned into mourning—*victory is ours.*" What think ye, my hearers, has there been any joy in heaven over some who are now in hell? If they so rejoiced at the news of his repentance, what messenger shall carry back the mournful tidings that the sinner is lost? If angels did not believe this doctrine, they could have no solid ground on which to rejoice. But now their joy is well-founded. At the repentance of one sinner, a new accession is made to their number. On this ground, angels can safely rejoice over one sinner that repenteth.

2. It is a great thing to be a Christian. If this doctrine were true, the state of the Christian would be no better than the state of the sinner. He could be no more certain of salvation than the sinner. Though he may be a Christian today, he can have no evidence that he shall be a Christian tomorrow, or the next moment. He may be a Christian one moment, and a sinner the next. But it is not so. When we look upon a Christian, what do we see? An inhabitant of another world—a child of God—an heir of heaven.

3. A revival of religion is a joyful thing. If this doctrine is true, here is grounds for rejoicing in a revival of religion. And here we read that when Philip preached at Samaria there was great joy. But on the other hand, if this doctrine is not true, all who believed on the day of Pentecost may now be in hell. If this doctrine is not true, you my hearers, may rejoice in a revival because sinners are brought out of darkness into marvellous light; but this is no evidence that they will not dwell in the blackness of darkness forever.—But if it is not so, when God has begun a good work, he will perform it until the day of Jesus Christ. Being confident of this very thing, how joyful to behold sinners flocking to Christ. Him that cometh unto me—All who truly repent of their sins, will certainly meet in heaven.

If this doctrine is true, then there may be such a thing as the full assurance of hope in this life. But if this doctrine is uncertain, the best Christian must be uncertain of heaven. It is surprising that some who deny this doctrine will yet say that they are certain of heaven.

This is plainly absurd. If I admit that one sinner may fall away and finally perish, then another and another may.

I remember a short conversation on this subject. A person who denied this doctrine was manifesting his joy in believing. He was interrogated on the subject, Why do you rejoice, my friend, do you think there is any certain connection between your believing now and your final salvation? He perceived if he answered in the affirmative, he must admit the doctrine, and so he replied in the negative. The question arose again, if there is no certain connection between your present belief and your final salvation, why then do you rejoice? He replied: Because my sins are forgiven. Why rejoice because your sins are forgiven? You say you have no evidence that you are not to suffer in hell for your sins after all. Why rejoice because your sins are forgiven? Why, if I am faithful, if I persevere to the end, I shall be saved. Answer: Very true, unless you persevere you cannot be saved. But what reason have you to conclude that you shall persevere? What makes you so confident that you shall be saved? Do you trust in your own resolutions? No—Well, what then? What reason have you to think you shall persevere? Do you trust in the stability of your own will? Do you think that you are a person of such decision, such stability and firmness that when you undertake the work that you shall go through with it? Is this the reason that you have to think that you shall persevere and be saved?—No. Well, what then? What reason have you to think that you shall be faithful—that you shall persevere and be saved?

If God is not first faithful to you, you will not be faithful to him.—and my hearers, he could see not reason why he should rejoice—he could find no rest for the sole of his foot until he was driven back on the ground of our text. *Being confident of this very thing, that he which hath begun a good work in you, will perform it until the day of Jesus Christ.*

And my hearers, what confidence have you that you shall persevere? Do you trust in anything short of the sentiment in the text—you trust on a broken reed—you build on the sand—There is depravity enough in your hearts to sink you to hell if the Lord leaves you one moment. And if you have not seen it, you have never yet seen your own hearts, nor been thoroughly awakened. If you have not felt this awful truth, you have not been driven out of yourselves—not yet left the strong hold of self-righteous deception—not yet fled for refuge to lay hold on the hope set before you.

5. It follows from what has been said, that salvation is entirely of grace, from first to last. The believer is taught to place no confi-

dence in his own strength or resolutions. It is of free, rich, and sovereign grace, that he has been renewed in the temper of his mind; and the same grace which begun the work, has engaged to carry it on to perfection. However weak and feeble the Christian may be, the Almighty has said, "I will never leave thee"—"Fear not—I am thy shield, and thy exceeding great reward." And what God has promised, he is able to perform. When the powers of earth and the gates of hell combined, assail the Christian, menacing his destruction; then the name, the promises, the oath, and the attributes of God, are a strong tower—an impregnable fortress; and conscious of his own weakness, he runneth into it and is safe. *The righteous man dwelleth on high,* out of the reach of every evil. *His place of defense is the munitions of rocks,* immutable as their solid foundations, inaccessible their lofty ridges.

Those who live near to God in the lively exercise of grace, and bring forth the fruit of the Spirit, can, with confidence, take hold of the promises. Those exceeding great and precious promises, to which God has annexed his oath, were made that such persons have strong consolation. But others can derive no consolation from this doctrine, or any of the promises of God. You may have been the subject of powerful conviction; and yet be lost. Like the stony ground hearers, you may have received the word with joy; and yet you may be lost. If you bring forth no fruit, and have long been apparently declining; you have great reason to question; not the truth of the doctrine; but did the seed sown fall on good ground? You have great reason to fear that the good work is not yet begun.

And let the true child of God take warning. He has never promised that you shall not fall into sin. But in that case he has engaged to correct you. Your communion with God will be much interrupted. This is sometimes the case with his children—Their persuasion of an interest in the everlasting covenant has been terribly shaken, if not lost for a season, so as to wound their hearts with the keenest anguish; till, after great watchfulness, many prayers and tears, they have again been indulged with the smiles of his countenance, and the joys of his salvation. The frowns of a Father will be hard to bear. For correct them he will, but not disinherit them. This is a part of his covenant with his children: *If they break my statutes, and keep not my commandments; then will I visit their transgressions with a rod, and their iniquities with stripes. Nevertheless, my lovingkindness will I not utterly take from him, nor suffer my faithfulness to fail.*

But as for the professor who can live long without sweet intercourse at the throne of grace, and can quietly enjoy the good things of this life, and is not awfully alarmed; it is a mark of rejection—if he is not severely corrected before he dies, it will be because he is not a child of God—*Woe to them that are at ease in Zion.*

Say to the righteous, it shall be well with him. Christians, ye know not what ye are—Heirs to an eternal inheritance, reserved in heaven—*Heirs of God.* And it doth not yet appear what you shall be; but, if it be true that you are *now* the sons of God, we *know that when he shall appear, you shall be like him; for you shall see him as he is.*

Shortly will you join the company of angels, and unite in the song of the redeemed. For God has undertaken your deliverance. All heaven was moved at your repentance. Angels are now acting with joyful expectation to see the work completed, *Being confident of this very thing, that he which hath begun a good work in you will perform it until the day of Jesus Christ.* Amen.

26

All Men Commanded to Pray

I will therefore that men pray everywhere (I Timothy 2:8).

There is no duty in Christianity, the practice of which Christ and the Apostles press upon us more frequently than prayer. Amidst all the absurdities and heresies which have sprung up in the Christian world, we know of none who have dared to deny the duty of prayer. Whatever diversity of sentiment may have existed, whatever disagreement there may be in other respects, yet all are agreed in this, that prayer to God is a plain and undeniable duty.

It is unnecessary to multiply quotations from sacred writ to establish the general proposition. The passages are numerous. Therefore, while the *heart* may be opposed to it, on the side of the duty under consideration I shall have the *conscience* of every person in this audience. Our text inculcates this duty. And Christ spake a parable to this end: *that men ought always to pray and not to faint.* It is taken for granted that all my hearers believe that prayer is a duty.

The subject has many parts on which we might dwell with profit; but for the sake of clearness, I have selected the two following:

It is proposed to inquire,

I. What prayer is.

II. Whether this duty is binding on all men without exception. Our ideas on a subject of such importance ought not to be loose and general; but clear and specific.—

What is prayer? It is defined to be: *An offering up of our desires to God for the things agreeable to his will, in the name of Christ, with confession of our sins and thankful acknowledgements of his mercies.* I know not of a more scriptural and correct definition than this.

For our satisfaction let us briefly examine it by the light of revelation. Our offering up of our desires to God. God is the only object of religious worship. It is written: *Thou shalt worship the Lord thy God, and him only shalt thou serve.* It is one of the most distinguished acts of religious worship. It is therefore to be addressed to God only. Thus saith the Psalmist, *trust in God at all times, pour out your hearts before him.*— For things agreeable to his will. This is the confidence, says the Apostle John, *which we have in him, that if we ask anything according to his will, he heareth us. Thy will be done.*

Thus that prayer which is acceptable, which is heard and answered, must be *an offering up of our desires to God for things agreeable to his will.* This is plain; for God cannot grant things which are not agreeable to his will, nor accept of prayer contrary to his known will.

In the name of Christ. And thus our Saviour told his disciples, *Verily I say unto you, Whatsoever ye shall ask the Father in my name, he shall give it you.*

With confession of our sins. Thus the Psalmist, *I acknowledged my sin unto thee, and mine iniquity have I not hid. I said, I will confess my transgression unto the Lord, and thou forgavest the iniquity of my sin.* And again, *he that confesseth and forsaketh his sins shall find mercy.—And thankful acknowledgment of his mercies.* Thus the Apostle: *Be careful for nothing; but in everything by prayer and supplication with thanksgiving let your requests be made known to God.* But what claims special notice is in the beginning; at the first setting out.

Prayer is the offering up of our <u>desires</u>. And these desires must be for things agreeable to his will, etc. Without the desires of the heart there is no acceptable prayer.

It is a plain case. A person comes to you with all the appearance of friendship, and with an air of solemnity requests a favour at your hand—your company at such a time and place, and at the same time you know that he does not *desire your presence.* Every person present would despise the request from his heart. And will God, who looks on the heart, and knows perfectly every thought—will the Omniscient God *who is of purer eyes than to behold iniquity,* will he accept at your hand a sacrifice of solemn mockery? With all the appearance of friendship, sincerity, and solemnity, without the desires of the heart; *it is iniquity, even the solemn meeting.*

For example: the command of God is, *love your enemies. Pray for them that despitefully use you, and persecute you.* Now if any person attempts to pray to God who does not from his heart freely forgive all his enemies, and desire their temporal and eternal welfare, that person does not pray for his enemies. God will not hear such a sinner. Hear the words of Christ. *So likewise shall my heavenly Father do also unto you, if ye from your heart forgive not every one his brother their trespasses.*

Take another example: we are commanded to pray for the prosperity of Zion. Whoever then does not rejoice to see sinners brought to repentance—who does not desire to see them profess the name of Christ and openly espouse his cause in the face of a frowning world;

God will not hear his prayer. In short, *whoever regards iniquity in his heart, the Lord will not hear him. But it is written, he will fulfill the desire of them that fear him.* And again, *the desire of the righteous shall be granted.*

Thus it appears that our definition is agreeable to the word of God. The substance of it is this. We must offer up our desires to God—to God only—for things agreeable to his will—in the name of Christ—confessing our sins, with thanksgiving.

It is important to keep in sight this view of the duty of prayer while we consider the following proposition. Let us inquire,

II. Whether it is the duty of *all men* to pray.

Many Christians seem to think that there is a difference of opinion existing on this subject. Some divines and private Christians have been accused of maintaining that it is not the duty of unregenerate men to pray. I know not whether this accusation is strictly just. It is however strongly suspected that the difference of opinions to which we have adverted, consists rather in the manner of stating it, than any real disagreement of ideas.

However, if there be any among us, who think, or maintain, that it is not the duty of *all men* to pray, I beg their attention to the following considerations:

1. The duty of prayer is not limited in the scriptures. Christ spake a parable to this end that *men* ought to pray. Thus also, *pray always—pray without ceasing.* And a multitude of other passages which might be easily adduced. Here are no limitations; no excuses; no permission to dispense with the duty granted to any individual of the human race. You may just as well say that the scriptures do not command all men to love God—to fear him or to obey him, as that they do not command *all men everywhere to pray.* These commands all stand on the same basis—they have the same universality. All men are equally dependent on God and equally bound to obey him.—But,

2. If the scriptures do not command the unregenerate to pray; then it is no sin in them *not* to pray. But hear the word of the Lord. *The wicked, through the pride of his countenance, will not seek after God.* And punishment is threatened against those who neglect this duty. *Pour out thy fury upon the heathen that know thee not, and upon the families that call not on thy name. Destruction unto them, for they have not cried unto me with their heart.* Other passages might be adduced; but it will not be disputed that God will punish the wicked for neglecting to pray. And if this be a plain fact, which none will deny; it is equally plain that their neglecting to pray is a sin. If

then, the impenitent are charged with guilt and threatened with punishment for neglecting to pray; can it be questioned whether it be their duty to pray?

Once more; Is it not the duty of all men to become Christians? And if it be their duty to become Christians and that without delay, then it is their immediate duty to perform all those acts which are essential to the Christian character. Among these is prayer. If then it is the *duty* of all men, without delay, to become Christians; and it is the indisputable duty of Christians to pray, then it is the immediate duty of all men, whether unregenerate or not, to pray.

But there are several texts of scripture which are brought forward, in support of the opinion that the unregenerate ought not to pray. These merit a candid discussion. These passages are the following: *The sacrifices of the wicked are an abomination to the Lord, but the prayer of the upright is his delight. He that turneth away his ear from hearing the law, even his prayer is an abomination. The sacrifices of the wicked are an abomination, how much more when he bringeth it with a wicked mind. The plowing of the wicked is sin. Whatsoever is not of faith is sin.*

The person who should not believe it is the duty of the unregenerate to pray, would say that these texts point out his prayer as a peculiar abomination and if this be the case, he ought not to be guilty of such abomination. This reasoning, as we shall have occasion to show, is partly true and partly erroneous.

On the other hand, such as have an aversion to this duty are glad to lay hold of these texts, and pervert them in order to find an excuse for their neglect—"If our prayer is an abomination," say they, "then it is our duty to refrain from prayer"; and thus if they but avoid one abomination, their consciences become quiet, though they run directly into another.

Before I proceed to examine the texts under consideration, I beg leave to premise some plain principles which will not be denied. You will grant that God commands all men to love him—That he commands them to repent and believe and that whatever they do he directs them to do it for his glory. Now unless these plain commands may all be dispensed with, it will follow that when God commands men to pray, he commands them to do it with penitent, believing, and obedient hearts. This is a plain, simple command. *Every* one may understand it.

Now, there are three courses a person may take, he may either refuse to pray at all; or he may attempt to pray with an impenitent, unbelieving heart; or he may pray with a penitent, believing heart.

You will easily see that if he prays in an impenitent, unbelieving manner, he does not obey the command of God. There are two wrong courses, and but *one* right one. The simple command of God is, *Let him ask in faith.* Any thing then, but obedience to this plain command is disobedience.

From this brief view of these obvious principles, let us return to the texts under consideration. And here it is not my design to evade or explain away the meaning of God's word. These texts, my hearers, are not dark and mysterious. They speak plain truth. When the Bible asserts, *The sacrifices of the wicked are an abomination to the Lord*— it means just what it says.

These texts, when viewed in their proper light, afford some of the most demonstrative proof in all the Bible of the total depravity of the unregenerate. They are not to be considered as they sometimes are, as making out that the prayers and sacrifices of the wicked are more abominable than the rest of their conduct. This is what the Bible does not appear to declare. But they are to be taken in this light: While men are impenitent and unreconciled to God, what they regard as their very best acts, are an abomination in his sight. Even the sacrifices and prayers of the wicked, which *they* consider as the real worship of God, *he* considers as an abomination. *The very plowing of the wicked,* says God, is *sin.* And the plain reason is, that when these things are done without any love, or regard to the glory of God, they are not obedience to his commands. His commands are all to be obeyed from the heart, and with such feelings as God has enjoined.

If then, the very acts which, among men, are deemed acts of worship—of what is esteemed the very best part of the character of the wicked be an abomination, which God has again and again expressly asserted; there is no difficulty in deciding whether the rest of their conduct is an abomination in his sight. This presents such a view of the depravity of the human heart as cannot be explained away. So deep and extensive is it, that even the sacrifices of the wicked are an abomination.

These passages, therefore, which are brought forward to show that the unregenerate ought not to pray, do not support any such conclusion. They go to establish one point—the awful depravity of the unregenerate. This is the least that can be made of them. But I do not view them as intending, by any means, to declare that the sacrifices and prayers of the wicked are *more* abominable than the rest of their conduct. Though they are frequently regarded in this manner, I apprehend they support no such conclusion. The object of the sacred writers appears to be this, to prove that the very fairest and best acts of the impenitent, as they are viewed by men, are abominable in the sight of God. And if this be the case with such acts, plainly it must be with all others of a moral nature.

When persons, then, under pretense of avoiding abomination in the sight of God neglect to pray, they have no right to expect that their conduct will be approved. Nor have they any right to conclude, that refraining from prayer is less abominable in the sight of God, than it would be to pray with an impenitent heart. God has made no such declaration in his word. And we have no scales to weigh sins, and determine which are the most enormous. There is, therefore, no grounds for that case which many persons feel who live in the neglect of prayer.

They say that they have wicked hearts and that it is an abomination for them to pray with such hearts.—Granted—just so it is.—But what then, it may be an abomination equally heinous, and for ought I know more so, not to pray at all. Do not expect then, that one abomination will be accepted by God as an excuse for another.

"But," says one, "what must we do then? You tell us we must neither neglect prayer, nor pray with impenitent hearts; both are abominations to God—You leave us no choice. We expose ourselves to the curse either way." This statement is not correct. You have a choice left, and that is to pray as God commands you—Why are you not willing to choose what God has commanded?—Why do you wish for any other course than the plain simple one which he has pointed out?

It is true, you have no choice between neglecting prayer; and praying with an impenitent heart. You have no right to choose either. It is your duty to choose obedience to his plain command. The path of duty is *plain, direct, and single;* while there are many ways which lead to destruction. My hearers, you are to choose none of these ways.—"But, if to neglect prayer is sin; and to pray with an impenitent heart is sin—I wish to know which of these sins is the least."

Why do you ask such a question as this? What right have you to be balancing between sins to see which you shall choose, when your duty is plain before you? It is of no consequence to you to have this question answered. Your path is plain: you must pray with a penitent heart, or you must be lost.—But if you insist upon having your question answered; I must say I am unable to answer it. God has not given it in trust to his ministers to weigh sins.

Of this we are certain—to neglect prayer or to pray with an impenitent heart is abomination to God—Both are disobedience—

Both subject us to the curse of the law—Both ways lead down to hell. Of what consequence to the poor soul who walks in them to destruction is it, to be informed whether the roads are of unequal length, when they both conduct him with the same certainty to the bottomless abyss? It is enough for us to know that salvation can be found in neither of these ways. It is enough that the path of duty is plainly pointed out.

"But I *cannot* pray with a penitent and believing heart, I do not possess such a heart; and I cannot renew my own heart." Let me ask you, my friends, if there is any obstacle to prevent your praying as God has commanded, but the want of a proper disposition? Do you love God? Then you will pray aright. Now will God, who commands you to love him, accept it as an excuse for neglecting this duty, that you hate him? This is your very criminality.

You say you have no disposition to pray. What a confession is that! This is your very guilt. God commands such a disposition. You plead your guilt—your desert of condemnation as an excuse for not doing what God commands. Will he excuse your disobedience because you do not possess the disposition he commands?—Not at all.

The reason why creatures sin, is because they have not the disposition to obey God's commands. Does he excuse them on this ground?—Let the *myriads in hell witness!* And can you expect, because you have not a penitent heart, that is, because you are wicked that God will excuse you from praying as he has commanded? This is equally contrary reason to common sense and the word of God.

"But the ground you take leaves only one way for the sinner, and cuts off all hopes of safety in any other." True. This is the very thing I aim at. To cut off all hope of safety in your present case is the grand point of this discourse. The ground I have taken is, that obedience, and *that* only is acceptable to God—that we are bound to do what God commands and not to expect safety in any other course.* It is your duty to do what God commands.

Let every sinner in this house *hear and tremble;* or obey the voice of God—*Repent, therefore, of this thy wickedness, and pray God if perhaps the thought of thine heart may be forgiven thee*—Amen.

---

* The top 2/3 of the final handwritten page of the manuscript is torn and missing at this point.

27

The Judgment of the Great Day

Unto the Judgment of the great day (Jude 6).

The Apostle, announcing the certain destruction of the wicked in his day, illustrates his subject by facts. Among others, he alludes to the example of the fallen angels. These criminals as yet, had no formal trial; but they were reserved in chains until all things were ready for this solemn event. *And the angels which kept not their first estate, but left their own habitation, he hath reserved in everlasting chains under darkness unto the judgment of the great day.* That will take place, *When the Son of man shall come in his glory, and all the holy angels with him, then shall he sit upon the throne of his glory: And before him shall be gathered all nations.*—Unto this day are they reserved.—It is *the judgment of the great day.*

I come now to notice some of the particulars in which the day of judgment will appear to be a great day. The judge will be *great*. The Son of man will appear in his *own glory,* and in the glory of *his Father.* His glory will cover the heavens. It is the glorious appearing of *the great God.* He will be seated on a *great white throne,* as emblematic of his majesty, dominion and power. *And I saw a great white throne, and him that sat on it.*

The concourse will be *great.* Christ will call all the inhabitants out of heaven to attend him down to this world. He will call all them living on the earth, and all the dead out of their graves, and summon *all nations before him.* Every intelligent being of which we have ever heard, of every rank and grade will be there. In short, all the inhabitants of three worlds: heaven, earth, and hell will be there. It is a great day which must excite the attention of so many worlds. Heaven and hell will be emptied of all their inhabitants, to attend.

It will be a day of *great transaction.* When a case of life and death is to be tried, we now consider it as a matter of great importance. A case of life and death, it is now saying everything. But souls are to be tried. Everything is now to be settled finally and forever. It is a decisive day.

Again—It will be a *long day.* Time will now have come to an end. *And the angel, which I saw stand upon the sea and upon the earth lifted up his hand to heaven, and swear by him that liveth for ever and ever, that there should be time no longer.* Now the present state

The Second Great Awakening

of things shall be ended. The sun, and moon, and stars shall all disappear. These shall all be darkened and disappear. It will be an end of all happiness to the wicked, and God will no more cause his sun to rise on the earth. There will be no further use for these luminaries. The seasons of the year will now cease to revolve; Day and night will cease to return. This alternate season of labor and rest will be of no further use. The bodies of saints and sinners are all fitted for a far different state of things. When sinners return from the judgment of the great day, they will no more return to their houses and families and farms and other employments.

The description of that great city Babylon is now literally true of the whole world. *And the voice of harpers, and musicians, and of pipers, and trumpeters, shall be heard no more at all in thee; and no craftsman, of whatsoever craft he be, shall be found any more in thee; and the sound of a millstone shall be heard no more at all in thee; And the light of a candle shall shine no more at all in thee; And the voice of the bridegroom and of the bride shall be heard no more at all in thee (Rev. 18:22). The sun shall be darkened, and the moon shall not give her light, and the stars shall fall from heaven, and the powers of the heavens shall be shaken: And then shall appear the sign of the Son of man in heaven: and they shall see the Son of man coming in the clouds of heaven with power and great glory.* Though time will then have come to an end, and days and months and years will be known no more; yet *duration* will remain. A succession of events will continue for ever.

We cannot determine how long the day of judgment will be; but the transactions of that day, we may well conclude will continue for thousands of years as we now calculate time. The powers of saints and sinners may then be greatly enlarged; they may be able to recollect and communicate ideas with far greater faculty than at present. Yet, suppose the world to stand seven thousand years. It is calculated that there will be more souls to be tried than there are seconds in seven thousand years. If one sinner were tried in a second the day of judgment must continue longer than the world has stood—Supposing it to stand seven thousand years. God will not be in haste—duration will not be wanting, eternity will be long enough to settle every thing in the best manner. The day of judgment will, no doubt, be a *long day,* continuing for thousands of years.

Again—It will be a day of great joy to all holy beings. The holy angels have ever been delighted with the glory of God in the plan of salvation. They desire to look into these things.—They rejoice at the repentance of one sinner. And now their desires will be more and more gratified in beholding the *manifold wisdom of God* in the plan of salvation. As the saints come on trial one after another the glory of Christ we may imagine, will more and more appear. There will not be a single Christian in which there will not be something to exhibit the character of Christ. Through the medium of every Christian, angels will admire the Saviour. That is one object of the day of judgment. *Christ shall come to be glorified in his saints, and to be admired in all them that believe in that day.*

The saints too will *be joyful.* They will all know beforehand, the issue of their trial. Many of them will then have been with Christ in heaven for thousands of years. Abraham, Isaac, and Jacob and all who have died in the Lord will have already been assured of heaven, for they have long been with Christ. They have washed their robes and made them white in the blood of the lamb. *They have long been before the throne of God, serving him day and night in his temple.* And their happiness will not be interrupted by the solemnities of the judgment day.

Their bodies will all be glorified bodies, and there will be nothing to interrupt their joy. We can think of but one thing that would appear likely to have this tendency.—It is however thought by some, that a public declaration of all their sins before the whole assembled universe would fill them with such shame as would be inconsistent with a state of complete blessedness. But the sins of many of these saints are recorded in the Bible, and Christians and sinners now read them every day. These glorified spirits cannot but know that many of their foul crimes are left on divine record, on purpose that they might be seen by all who read the Bible, and yet this does not interrupt their joy. The sins of David and Peter and Paul are every Sabbath held up to the view of thousands of congregations, we take as our text, and yet this does not interrupt their songs in heaven. Christians read their sins, and admire the riches of divine grace in their salvation. A clear view of the number and aggravation of their sins, serves to heighten our wonder and admiration of the grace of God. If reading the account of the conversion of these men in the Bible excites so much interest in the hearts of Christians now, much more then to hear them relate the wonderful story themselves.

Nor will it be hard for Christians then to own their guilt and make public confession of all their sins. This is hard indeed to an unhumbled heart, but it will be easy in proportion to our humility. Moses and David and Paul had meekness and humility enough to record their own sins in a book which must be open to the world and read in the most public manner. And this is an evidence of their sincerity and humility which we cannot but admire. What we now so much admire in them, will exist in all Christians, in a far greater degree, at the day of judgment. Destroy all selfishness, and we should be as willing to confess to others, as to have others confess to us—we should be as willing to have our sins disclosed, as the sins of others.

This is already proved by facts which are daily before us. When a Christian brother falls into sin he is unwilling to own and confess it in exact proportion to his want of humility and his want of religion. Even where his sin is already known to the world it is hard in proportion to his want of religion. But there is such a thing as being so far penitent and broken-hearted as to be willing, nay as to be unwilling not to confess their sins. In proportion as the Christian loves God, in the same proportion will he loathe himself. Christ by his sufferings has *condemned sin in the flesh,* and all whose hearts are united to him and pleased with the plan of salvation, will heartily condemn themselves. All who now love Christ, love to own their guilt and confess their sins to him. However humiliating, it makes no difference, the more humbling, the more desirabl;, and the more humble, the more happy is the Christian.

Christians *rejoice in hope of the glory of God.* And his glory is advanced by a confession of those sins, which through boundless grace, have been pardoned. The saints, at the day of judgment, will all be anxious to give glory to God. A sense of the justice and mercy and glory of God will dispel all fear of man. All their anxiety will be to give glory to God, in pardoning such hell deserving sinners. Their wonder and admiration will be so much increased that they will think less and less of themself, and more and more what shall be done to glorify God in their salvation. If others can so admire the wonderful grace of God, in pardoning such sinners, much more may this monument wonder at himself.

At the day of judgment will be given a complete history of the work of redemption. Every particular will be heard and attended to with deep interest; and, as the scene advances, all holy beings will be entertained, and their joy will rise higher and higher from the beginning to the end of that great day.

It will be a day of great terror to the wicked. Every thing which gives joy to Christians will be inexpressibly painful to sinners. Christians rejoice to behold the face of their redeemer; *in his presence is fullness of joy.* But all the wicked tremble at the sight. *Then shall they begin to say to the mountains fall on us, and to the hills cover us. Hide us from the face of him that sitteth on the throne, and from the wrath of the lamb: For the great day of his wrath is come: and who shall be able to stand?*

In the relations which the saints give of their conversion, every thing will be grating to the feelings of sinners. Even now such a relation sounds harsh, it disturbs them, they do not wish to hear it; but at the day of judgment, every thing of this nature will be still more dreadful to every unrenewed soul.

The joy of saints will tend greatly to aggravate their distress. Now the sight of one rejoicing in hope is exceeding painful to one under conviction of sin. But there all sinners will be under conviction— under the deepest conviction of sin. Every hardened sinner will now be under deeper conviction than any ever witnessed on earth. *Behold, the Lord cometh with ten thousands of his saints, to execute judgment upon all, and to convince all that are ungodly among them of all their ungodly deeds which they have committed, and of all their hard speeches which ungodly sinners have spoken against him.* What grief and envy will they feel when former acquaintances shall rejoice while they are in horror? They will then feel as those Christians did not care if they went to hell. They will think it hard that others should feel so joyful when their case is so desperate.

But this is not all. It will be hard for impenitent sinners to confess their sins. How hard is it for an unhumbled heart to fall before God and do it now? How reluctant does he feel to have others think evil of him. How much pains do they now often take to vindicate their characters against the least aspersion. And when known to be guilty how reluctant to own and confess it, even when it is for their credit and interest to do it! But all this reluctance, shame, and remorse of conscience will be greatly increased. All restraint will be taken off, and every heart will now appear in its native deformity. The sinner will be completely selfish and unhumbled.

No such pious motives as operate on the Christian, will sweetly influence his heart. Pious grief and hatred of sin will not make it easy. Love to Christ will not melt his heart or make it easy. The glory of God in pardoning sinners will not do it. The hope or prospect of obtaining pardon does not make it a pleasant duty *now,* much less when all hope of pardon is past. At the day of judgment he must own and confess his guilt, not to display the glory of God in his pardon and salvation; but to display his glorious justice in his everlasting condemnation.—This will be a part of his punishment, that his trial will make it appear to the universe that he deserves no pity. Every thing which in his case, tends to the glory of God, ends *in his shame and everlasting contempt.* The distress and horror of the wicked will rise higher and higher up to the final sentence.

The judgment of the great day is called, *the day of wrath and revelation of the righteous judgment of God.* When every thing is settled and the day of judgment drawing to a close, then the judge will proceed to pronounce the final sentence. *And he shall set the sheep on his right hand, but the goats on the left.* A summary of the final sentence on the righteous and the wicked, the judge has left on record.

This will be the most sublime, joyful, and dreadful scene ever yet beheld. *Then shall the king say unto them on his right hand, Come, ye blessed of my Father, inherit the kingdom prepared for you from the foundation of the world.*—Joy thrills through every pious heart, while this blessed welcome sounds sweetly in the Savior's voice. *Then shall the king say also unto them on his left hand, Depart from me, ye cursed, into everlasting fire, prepared for the devil and his angels.* This sentence will complete the horrors of the damned. Depart from Christ – from heaven and from happiness forever! Depart accursed by the law, and the gospel, and the Savior forever! Depart from the society of angels and all holy beings, with the company of devils and damned spirits into everlasting fire.

The day of judgment will be a day of *great separation. For these shall go away into everlasting punishment, but the righteous into life eternal.* What an awful separation! Many who have long been acquainted, who have lived together in the same society, will now be separated. Many who have walked to the house of God, in company, who have belonged to the same church, and often communed together at the sacramental table on earth, will now part to meet no more forever.

Ministers and people will part. Some who have not been faithful to warn the wicked of his awful guilt and danger, will now turn and go away with the *blood of souls in their skirts.* Others, who, though they have declared the whole counsel of God, have never experienced the power of religion on their own hearts, will loose their own souls. Many who have lifted others into heaven will probably never enter themselves. Those again who have been faithful to their own souls and the souls of their hearers may now enter heaven, while they behold their hearers in multitudes going away never to return.

Members of the same family will now separate. A pious father will now leave his ungodly wife and children while he ascends with Christ.—A pious wife may now leave an ungodly husband to perish in everlasting fire. A pious child will now part with his ungodly parents;, while he ascends to heaven, they sink down to hell. Brothers and sisters too will now part to meet no more forever. The separation at death is nothing compared to that at the day of judgment. *There shall be weeping and gnashing of teeth when ye shall see Abraham, Isaac, and Jacob, and all the prophets in the kingdom of God, and you yourselves thrust out.*

The saints shall all ascend and leave this earth, no more to return. Like the prophet Elijah they shall all ascend—Every one of the saints like him shall be seen mounting up and leaving the world and all it's wicked inhabitants behind to visit them no more. *Then,* saith the Apostle, *we which are alive and remain shall be caught up together with them in the clouds, to meet the Lord in the air: and so shall we ever be with the Lord.*—The great end for which this world was created is answered. The glorious plan of redemption is thus far accomplished—The closing scene of this grand drama has arrived; and the stage of action must now be removed.

About this time the whole material system will undergo a great change. It does not appear from the sacred scriptures that the world will be annihilated. But thus far is certain, that its present form will be greatly changed. Thus the Psalmist, *Of old hast thou laid the foundation of the earth; and the heavens are the work of thy hands. They shall perish, but thou shalt endure; yea, all of them shall wax old like a garment; as a vesture shalt thou change them, and they shall be changed.*

It is believed by many that it can be proved from the word of God that this world will be the eternal abode of all the wicked; where they will be *tormented forever and ever.* It is evident not only that the world will be changed, but that it will be changed by fire. And to this there appears an allusion in the following passages: *And all the host of heaven shall be dissolved, and the heavens shall be rolled together as a scroll: and all their host shall fall down, as the leaf falleth off from the vine; and as a falling fig from the fig tree (Isaiah 34:4). My determination is to gather the nations, that I may assemble the kingdoms, to pour upon them mine indignation, even all my fierce anger: for all the earth shall be devoured by the fire of my jealousy (Zephaniah 3:8).*

The general conflagration is represented as nearly connected with the day of judgment. *Our God shall come, and shall not keep silence: a fire shall devour before him, and it shall be very tempestuous round about him (Psalm 50:3). For, behold, the Lord will come with fire, and with his chariots like a whirlwind, to render his anger with fury, and his rebuke with flames of fire (Isaiah 66:15).* "I beheld

The Second Great Awakening

till the thrones were cast down, and the Ancient of days did sit, whose garment was white as snow, and the hair of his head like the pure wool: his throne was like the fiery flame, and his wheels as burning fire. A fiery stream issued and came forth before him: thousand thousands ministered unto him, and ten thousand times ten thousand stood before him: the judgment was set, and the books were opened" (Daniel 7:9, 10). "For, behold, the day cometh, that shall burn as an oven; and all the proud, yea, and all that do wickedly, shall be stubble: and the day that cometh shall burn them up, saith the Lord of hosts, that it shall leave them neither root nor branch" (Malachi 4:1). "But the heavens and the earth, which are now, by the same word are kept in store, reserved unto fire against the day of judgment and perdition of ungodly men" (II Peter 3:7). When Christ, and all the redeemed have ascended at a distance from the earth, it will then everywhere be set on fire; and kindled by the breath of the Almighty. The Lord Jesus Christ shall be revealed from heaven with his mighty angels, in flaming fire taking vengeance on them that know not God, and that obey not the gospel of our Lord Jesus Christ. Now the heavens shall pass away with a great noise and the elements shall melt with fervent heat, the earth also and the works that are therein shall be burnt up.

This is the day of God; wherein the heavens being on fire shall be dissolved, and the elements shall melt with fervent heat (II Peter 3:10, 11). And so fierce will be the flame that it will burn the earth to its very center. *For a fire is kindled in mine anger,* saith the Lord, *and shall burn unto the lowest hell, and shall consume the earth with her increase, and set on fire the foundation of the mountains (Deuteronomy 32:22).*

But I will not proceed; the scene is beyond description. It is the *Judgment of the great day.*

> "Where now, O where shall sinners seek,
>   For shelter in the general wreck;
> Shall falling rocks be o'er them thrown?
>   See rocks like snow dissolving down.
> In vain for mercy now they cry;
>   In lakes of liquid fire they lie;
> There on the flaming billows tossed,
>   Forever—oh! Forever lost!"

28

The Wicked Standing Before the Judgment Seat

And I saw the dead, small and great, stand before God; and the books were opened: and another book was opened, which is the book of life: and the dead were judged out of those things which were written in the books, according to their works
(Revelation 20:12).

The doctrine of a future general judgment is fundamental to the Christian system. It is inseparable from the existence of God as a righteous moral governor. This world is not the place of final retribution. If we look abroad in the world around us, we often see good men afflicted and bad men prosperous. This inequality loudly proclaims a judgment to come.

It is reasonable to suppose that God will take care to reward virtue and to punish vice. The Bible, however, settles the point beyond a doubt. It gives us many particulars. It describes events solemn and awful. Our Lord himself repeatedly spoke of the event and his Apostles examined it. St. Peter foretells that there shall come in the last days, scoffers walking after their own lusts. To such bold preesumption, the Apostle replied—"The day of the Lord will come."

In Revelation 20:12, as a spectator of passing events, the favored Apostle describes the tremendous scenes of the judgment day. *And I saw,* saith he, *a great white throne, and him that sat on it, from whose face the earth and heaven fled away; and there was no place found for them. And I saw the dead, small and great, stand before God; and the books were opened.* The two prominent things in the text are

I. The universality of judgment and

II. The discoveries which will there be made of the character of the wicked.

No truth is more clearly established than this: that we must *all* stand before the judgment seat. It is established by many passages of the Holy Word. But few are so bold as openly to deny it. Still many make a sort of exception in their favor. One so poor and ignorant sees no propriety in calling him to an account. He thinks he will be judged by a milder rule. To whom little is given, little shall be required. Yet this is not so where means of knowledge are neglected. So none who know their Bibles can make this excuse. The day of judgment then will bring the small as well as the great, the ignorant as well as the learned to trial. Who dare plead his ignorance, which is perhaps the greatest of all his sins, being the parent of all the rest?

Another who has been visited by tedious and severe affliction concludes that he has suffered in this world all that he deserves. A third draws the same conclusion from opposite premises: from his outward prosperity, that the judgment of God is already pronounced in his favor. He expects equal kindness in the world to come. I reply, the worst of men are often found in the best circumstances, and the best in the most adverse. Lazarus and the whole army of persecuted saints suffered their whole lives, while men like Dives and Herod lived in prosperity. Read the account of the rich man who fared sumptuously. Where is he now? Lifting up his eyes in hell. So true is it that all who receive their good things in this life will suffer in the next.

No child of Adam is exempt. High, low, rich, poor, wise or ignorant, prosperous or afflicted—the dead, small and great, must stand before the throne of God.

Consider,

II. The discoveries which will then be made of the character of wicked men.

And the books were opened respects exclusively the wicked. Speaking of the judgment of the righteous it says, *another book was opened which was the book of life.* These expressions are figurative. Books are used as records containing exact accounts of events as they passed, or as containing laws by which the conduct of men is to be tried. The figure is peculiarly plain and striking. It denotes a full and exact manifestation—a preparation for the final sentence.

Objection: Such a minute and complete manifestation of the character of each individual of the vast assembly present cannot be made in a single day.

It is presumption and not arguable to limit the infinite God. The scriptures are explicit—such an examination will be made—scrutinizingly strict, searching, and public. The Son of Man shall come in his glory, then shall he sit upon the throne of his glory: and before him shall be gathered all nations. Every one of us small and great shall give an account to God. Every idle word which men shall speak, they shall give an account thereof in the day of judgment, according to the deeds done in the body. There is nothing hidden which shall not be made known. The Lord will bring to light the hidden things of darkness, and will make manifest the counsels of the hearts. The Scriptures do not tell us how. The *fact* that a full development will be made before God and the assembled world is explicit and cannot be doubted.

Let us be more particular,

1. Their open or public sins will be made more public. What was known only in a neighborhood, a society and town, will then be known to the assembled universe. Then will be fully exposed the character of the worldling; the man who has no treasure but on earth, who has made the world his portion, his God; the sordid worshiper of gold and silver, despising eternal riches, his time, his thoughts, his talents have been devoted to the procuring of a large portion of the dust on which he trod. His base, contracted, groveling soul is seen in all its deformity by the vast assembly before the throne of God.

There is the unjust man, the extortioner in all his dishonesty, fraud, undue advantages, overreaching and oppressions he hath practised—then meet him all the poverty and want and distress which he hath caused to the friendless, the suffering, the widow, and the fatherless.

There appears the devotee of pleasure and amusement, his thoughtless, useless, wicked life, the hours occupied with dress, with idle talk, in idle company, or squandered in the heedless throng of carnal pleasures, his wasted privileges and abused mercies, his contagious and fatal example, his aversion to all serious reflection, and utter disregard of everlasting concerns; thus *he* comes to judgment.

There is the slanderer, who has talked only in calumity and falsehood, who has penetrated the sacred retreats of domestic life—prayed on the peace of families of individuals, of neighborhoods, and found food and life only in miseries he has caused.

There also is the scoffer at religion with all his contempt of that heaven where angels dwell, and of that hell where devils and their associates groan, with all his banters and defiance of the God whose frown is death and all the ridicule thrown on the mercy and grace and love of the Saviour who bled for him. There *he* appears at his final trial.

There is the profane man with all his horrid mass of oaths and curses and blasphemies falling from his lips—the drunkard in all his brutal indulgence, his sense and reason drowned—a self-murderer and murderer of peace and comfort of his family, perhaps of the souls of his wife and children, he stands at the bar of God, a sot, a stupid drunken immortal!

There also will stand the Sabbath breaker. Now it is seen what use he has made of the many Sabbaths that the mercy of God had given him. The man of 20 years of age must give account of hundreds, the man of 40 of more than 2,000, the man of 60 of more than 3,000 Sabbaths wasted and perverted by business, by pleasures, by sloth, without retirement, reading or serious reflection, without prayer, with contempt of every blessing which this day of mercy brings to guilty men.

Here also will be exhibited the character of him who profanes the sanctuary of the living God by sleep, by worldly thoughts, of disregard of the offers of life from the ministers of Christ, contempt of prayers and praises which are offered in the Saviour's name—who week after week comes as a condemned criminal before a righteous Judge, without a thought of his wrath or a wish for his mercy—who month after month turned his back on the broken body of Jesus and spurns all the blessings of his blood.

Such are the characters of multitudes in this world, and such will they appear before God and the vast assembly of the judgment day. Not a single doubt will be found throughout the immense multitude, that such is their real character.

2. Then also will be manifested their more private sins. Nor will these be less in number, nor perhaps less in guilt, than those specified. For the greater part of the sins of wicked men are seen by comparatively few—and if seen, are thought by few to be sins. But at their final trial, every disguise will be stript off, every error of opinion concerning their turpitude will be corrected. Many a man who now maintains so respectable a standing among us for honesty and industry in dealing with others will then be seen guilty of countless undue advantages of the ignorance, or weakness of his fellow men, or artful deceptions and sly overreaching in the hourly business of life—much, very much that passes for strict honesty among men will be pronounced dishonesty and fraud at the bar of God.

There will be seen the companion of wicked men who privately resorts to their midnight feasts, their fraudulent games, and licentious frolics. There will be exhibited the unclean person, the fornicator, and the adulterer. There will the glutton and the sober drunkard, whose God is his belly, whose glory is his shame, be seen in all his bruteishness.

There will appear the caviller against the humbling doctrines of the cross with all his cavils and pretexts and excuses and empty sophistry used here to conceal his hostility to the gospel; the man who attempts to hide his pride, his selfishness, his worldly-mindedness, his evil passions by their garb of external morality—

the man who appears so godly and devout on the Sabbath and other particular occasions, but who lays aside his religion in the business of the day and in the family will be clearly exposed. There will be seen the man who never entered his closet, who neglected the word of God, who never uttered a prayer for his mercy.

There will be seen the master who never instructed his servants, his apprentices, his workmen in the great truths of the gospel, who has emboldened them in sin by living in sin himself. There will be the head of a family who has never acknowledged God in his house, the parent who has never taught his children the fear of God, nor commended them to his love, with their blood in his skirts—That ungrateful child who has neglected or scorned the pious admonitions of a faithful father or affectionate mother.

There will be seen the corrupter of youth, who by his conversation, his writings, or example has seduced their unwary steps into the path of death—There will be seen the hard-hearted wretch who has suffered the hungry to want and who has refused to comfort the afflicted, to defend the persecuted, and to relieve and console the widow, orphan, and fatherless, who ever loved his money better than the church of Christ and souls of men. These and numberless like sins of the wicked known here but to a few even of their acquaintances will all be produced against them when they come to judgment. Every veil will be turned aside, every mask torn off, every work of concealment brought to light.

3. The *secret* sins of impious men will Christ produce against them. And here, my hearers, is a long list which the searcher of hearts only can develop. But the recording angel has been faithful *and the books were opened. The counsels of the heart* with all its corruptions and its crimes it will be laid open and compared with the book of God—destitute of the Christian spirit of love to God or men. Every (minute) transgression. Then the dreadful pain of evil tempers and passions which have lurked within (will be revealed). And when we remember that the Lord Jesus Christ in interpreting: Christ pronounces the lustful look *adultery,* and anger and hatred *murder.*—How will a wicked human heart appear? How with all of its pride and discontent, anger, lust, and malice brought to light? Horrid as the sight might be it will be seen.

But this is not all. A word from him has declared that we are guilty, accursed, ruined, sinners. No reason can be given why the sentence of damnation has not been executed upon us. Thus on the verge of eternal judgment salvation is offered; salvation for us. Salvation!! Oh the glorious sound! Who has heard the glad tidings

The Second Great Awakening

and then not welcomed the message with transport? Who that has heard of the Saviour's love and has not felt his heart melt with gratitude? Alas! it shall be told on the judgment day.

There shall stand that enemy of the cross of Christ, that despiser of the Lord that bought him. A Saviour calls a 1,000 and a 1,000 times, but he has repealed his visits, nor regarded the blessed Spirit which has striven with him from day to day, and from year to year, but perpetually grieved him—the privileges of the Word and the worship of God granted so often but abused to purposes worse than (imagined), the divine forbearance exercised so long but used only as a license to sin, the counsels and warnings and prayers and entreaties cast behind his back, the blood of Christ offered to cleanse him from the pollution of sin, but trampled under foot by men and likewise the angels and the Father, the Son, and the Holy Ghost.— But I dare not proceed. The sum is swelled to an awful amount. Millions of crimes which were not observed or long since forgotten will be brought to light to show the sinner his dreadful guilt and the terror of the wrath which awaits him. But (we) must leave it its catalogue which omniscience alone can unfold. And now, my dear hearers, are you willing to stand before the throne of judgment with such a character? There you must stand and are you still in your sins? Is not death and judgment at the door? Are you still among those to whom it will be said, *Depart from me, ye cursed, into everlasting fire prepared for the devil and his angels?* Still among those who drink of the spirit of the world? Still among the tormented? Shall (the) trumpet summon you to awake and you still slumber on?

Notes on Theology

Proof of the Being of God

Proof 1

1. The existance of things around us.
2. The manner in which they exist.
3. The existance of such a book as the Bible.
4. The universal consent of mankind.
5. The peace of conscience good men enjoy.
6. The stings and lashes of conscience which wicked men feel are proofs of the being of God.

His Attributes Proof 2

Natural	Moral
1. Intelligence	1. Wisdom
2. Omnipotence	2. Holiness
3. Omniscience	3. Justice
4. Omniprescence	4. Goodness
5. Immutability	5. Truth
6. Eternity	

Proof of Scriptures (3)

I. The history of the Bible is a true history.
    1. The history of the scriptures contain not the least marks of forgery and imposture.
    2. They contain a system of truths and duties worthy of God himself.
    3. The writers all agree in foretelling the time, the manner and the circumstances of the same events taking place.
    4. They have recorded their faults, which is contrary to impostors.

The Second Great Awakening

     5. The Apostles have not exalted the character of Christ—his religion, their own virtues, nor reproved their enemies even when they put Christ to death.
     6. Jewish and pagan history record the same facts as contained in the Bible.

II. Doctrinal evidences. Writers were inspired men.
     1. They are wholly superior to all other writers.
     2. They do not speak in their own names; but with a thus saith the Lord.
     3. Their doctrines all harmonize.
     4. The most ignorant writes as truly sublime and correctly as the most learned.
     5. It is unreasonable to suppose that such a number of men all harmonizing, and all sublime should exist in the Jewish nation only unless they were inspired.

  Again from
     1. The Mysteries
     2. The design and contrivence.
          1. The scheme of the scriptures gives all the glory to God.
          2. The plan of the scriptures by Christ.
          3. The nature and the excellency of the commands and precepts.
          4. The harmony of the scriptures.

III. Miscellaneous evidences.
     1. The prophecies which have and are still fulfilling. They were written before the events took place and they have taken place just as they were foretold.
     2. Miracles.
     3. The death and sufferings of Martyrs.
     4. The writings of the scriptures have been faithfully conveyed down to us.

<u>Doctrine of the Trinity</u>

There are three persons in the godhead: the Father, the Son and the Spirit, these three are one God. The Hebrew word Alohim is plural.
1. God said, let *us* make man in *our* image after *our* likeness. And

the Lord said let *us* go down and confuse their language, and who will go for *us*.
2. There are three that bear record in heaven...I John 5:8. The seraphim cried holy, holy, holy. Isaiah 6:3, i.e. Holy Father, Holy Son and Holy Spirit. Baptism name of Father, Son and Holy Ghost.

The Son is God

1. The names - See John 1:1; John 1:14; Isaiah 44:6.
2. The attributes - Rev. 1:8 & 22:13; Heb. 13:8; Matt. 28:18; 18:20; 28:20.
3. The works - John 1:3; Col.1:16; John 5-28-29; 6:40; 11:25.
4. The worship. Heb. 1:6; Phil. 3:3, 10, 11. He was worshiped by a woman of Canaan, by a ruler of the synagogue, a leper—a man born blind—by all in the ship—by the women—and the disciples after his resurrection.

2. The Holy Spirit is God

1. The name. Acts 5:4; Isaiah 63:10.
2. The Attributes. Psalm 33:6; Jer. 23:23-24; Psalm 139:1-12.
3. The works. John 3:5-6; John 1:13.
4. The worship - II Cor. 13:14.

Person is a rational active voluntary being.
Distinction between a created and uncreated person.

1. All created persons are separable in their substance one from the other. But divine persons in their substances are perfectly one and the same and in one another.
2. Different created persons can have only a substance of the same kind, not the same individual one; but divine persons must have each of them the same individual or numerical substance.
3. Every created person is a distinct being in or by or through, not from itself; but all divine persons are and must be one.

A Table showing the harmony of both old and new Testaments respecting the Divinity of Christ.

Old Testament	New Testament
Jehovah Isa. 43:3-11; 43:16. Exodus 3:14.	Who is was and is to come Rev. 1:8; 4:8; 11:17; 16:5; Heb. 13:8.
Jah Psalm 68:8.	I am or he who is John 8:28-58. Rev. 1:8.
Al. Isa. 7:14; 9:6; 44:6.	Al. Matt. 1:23.
Aloah & Alohim or God Job 19:26; Psalm 45:6; Isa. 25:9; 52:7.	God John 1:1; 20:28; Rev. 21:7; Acts 20:28; II Cor. 5:19; Col. 3:1; I Tim. 3:16; Titus 2:13; Heb. 1:8; II Pet 1:1; Jude 1:4.
Sabaoth Isa. 6:5; 44:6; 54:5; Jer. 10:16; 50:34; 51:14.	Sabaoth John 12:37-41; Rom. 9:29; James 5:4.
Shaddai or Almighty Gen. 17:1; Exod. 6:3.	Almighty John 8:56; Rev. 1:8; 15:3; John 1:3.
Jehovah our Righteousness Jer 23:6; 33:16.	Christ our Righteousness Rom. 3:22; 10:4; Phil. 3:9; II Peter 1:1.
Adonai or Lord Ps. 110:1.	Lord Matt. 22:44.
Emanuel Isa. 7:14.	Immanuel Matt. 1:23.
Wonderful Isa. 9:6; 28:29.	Wonderful Matt. 21:15; Acts 2:22.
Councellor Prov. 8:14; Isa. 9:2.	Councellor Eph. 1:11; I John 2:1.

Mighty God
Isa. 9:6; 10:21; 49:26; 60:16.

Mighty God
Matt 11:21; Luke 9:43;
Eph. 1:21; Rev. 7:10-12.

Everlasting Father
Isa. 9:6; Ps. 68:5; Jer 31:9.

Everlasting Father
John 14:9; Rev. 21:7.

Prince of Peace
Isa. 9:6; 45:7; 53:5;
Zech. 9:9-10.

Prince of Peace
Luke 1:79; John 14:27;
Eph 2:14; Heb 7:2.

Anointed or Messiah
Ps. 2:2; 45:7; Isa. 61:1.

Anointed or Christ
Luke 2:11; 4:18; John 1:41;
Acts 4:27; 10:38.

Jesus or Saviour
Isaiah 43:11; 63:8.

Jesus
Matt. 1:22; Luke 2:11;
John 4:42; II Peter 1:1.

Redeemer
Isaiah 47:4; 59:20; Jer 50:34.

Redeemer
Gal. 3:13; Heb. 9:12;
Rev. 5:9.

Shiloh or Deliverer
Gen. 49:10.

Deliverer
Rom. 11:26; John 8:36;
Luke 4:18.

Glory of the Lord
Isaiah 3:8; 40:5; 59:19.

Glory of the Lord
II Cor. 3:18; Heb. 1:3;
Jude 24.

Name of the Lord
Ps. 20:1; Isaiah 29:23;
Micah 5:4.

Name of the Lord
John 12:28; Rom. 15:9.

Word of God
Ps. 33:6; 56:4; 103:20; Isa. 40:8.

Word of the Lord
John 1:1-14.

Arm of the Lord
Ps. 77:15; Isa. 53:1; 63:12.

Arm of the Lord
Luke 1:51.

Angel i.e. one Sent
Gen. 48:15-16; Isa. 63:9; Mal. 3:1.

Angel i.e. one Sent
John 17:3; Gal. 4:4;
I John 4:9-10.

The Second Great Awakening

Elect or Chosen
Isa. 42:1; 43:10.

Wisdom
Ps. 104:24; Prov. 3:19; 8:22.

Prophet
Deut. 18:15.

Priest
Ps. 110:4; Zech. 6:13.

King
Ps. 2:6; 74:12; Isa. 6:5;

Branch
Isa. 4:2; Jer. 23:5; Zech 3:8.

Star
Num. 24:17.

Strength of Israel
I Sam. 15:29; Joel 3:16.

Husband
Isa. 54:5; Jer. 3:14; Hosea 2:20.

Light
Ps. 22:1; Isa. 9:2;.60:19.

Shepherd
Isa. 40:11; Ez.34:28-31;
Zech. 13:7.

Servant
Isa. 42:1; 52:13; Zech 3:8.

Lawgiver
Isa. 33:22; 51:7; Jer. 31:33.

Elect
Matt. 12:18; I Peter 2:6.

Wisdom
Matt. 11:19;
I Cor. 1:23-30; Col. 2:3.

Prophet
Acts 3:22.

Priest
Heb. 4:14; 9:11; 10:21.

King
John 18:36; I Tim. 6:15.
Rev. 17:14.

Branch
Luke 1:78 see margin.

Star
II Peter 1:19;
Rev. 22:16.

Strength
II Cor 12:9;
Rev. 5:12; 12:10.

Husband
II Cor. 11:2; Rev. 21:3.

Light
Matt. 4:16; Luke 2:32;
John 8:12; I John 1:5.

Shepherd
John 10:14; Heb. 13:20;
I Pet. 2:25.

Servant
Matt. 12:18; Phil. 2:7.

Lawgiver
Gal. 6:2; Heb. 8:10;
James 4:12.

Rock
Deut. 32:4; Isa. 8:14.

Rock
Rom. 9:33; I Cor. 10:4.

Physician
Isa. 53:5; Jer. 8:22.

Physician
Matt. 9:12; Luke 4:23; 9:1.

Stone
Ps. 118:22; Isa. 28:16.

Stone
Matt. 21:42; Eph. 2:20;
I Pet. 2:6.

Fountain
Joel 3:18; Zech 13:1.

Fountain
John 6:14; Rev. 21:6.

Keeper
Job 7:20; Ps. 121:5; Jer.32:40.

Keeper
II Tim. 1:12; Jude 1;
John 10:28; 17:12.

To the Father, Son and Spirit. 3 Divine persons in one and the same Jehovah as to the Trinity in unity; and to the one Jehovah existing in 3 persons of Father, Son and Spirit as to the unity in the Trinity; be all Honour, Grace & Glory ascribed by all creatures through all ages. Amen.

Decrees of God

1. God hath fore ordained whatsoever comes to pass.
2. He has decreed the time, manner and circumstances of every events taking place.
3. This is evident from reason and revelation.
4. Perfectly consistent with human liberty. Acts 2:23.

Creation

God executes his decrees in the works of creation, etc.
1. God created all things out of nothing in six days.
2. The Natural creation and Moral creation are 2 things. The Moral creation is the New Jerusalem, the Church of God.
3. God created angels and men. Angels first, etc.
4. God comprehended the whole human race in Adam. He was created holy in the image of God.
5. Angels were made for men, not men for Angels. Angels attend on man, the heirs of salvation.

Providence

1. God upholds all things by the same power with which he created them.
2. They are continually under his directing power.
3. If anything should not answer its end, it would be created in vain.
4. The Divine being works in the natural world by cause and effect.
5. When these laws are counteracted, they are call miracles.

Divine providence as it respects Angels

1. Angels and men are the only moral agents.
2. Angels were under a divine law because they are punished for transgression, and where there is no law there's no punishment.
3. It is not consistent with divine goodness to have his creatures remain always in a state of trial.

Divine providence as it respects Men

1. Man was first upright and holy.
2. He sinned and eternal death was the threatened punishment.
3. Every Sin deserves an infinite punishment.
4. It is consistent with divine goodness to inflict a penalty for sin.
    1. The threatening prevents rebellion.
    2. Expresses the evil nature of sin.
    3. The sacred authority of God and the desert of rebellion against him.
    4. God's hatred and abhorence of sin and sinners.
        1. The death threatened is eternal in opposition to eternal life.
        2. Temporal death not included in the threatening.
        3. Spiritual death not included in the threatening, because it is a moral evil, and moral evil is punished by inflicting natural evil, not punish a crime with a crime. To be dead in this sense is a crime and not a punishment.
            1. Adam was a public head for all his posterity, and as he sinned they

became sinners as is evident from Gen. 1:26. The word man includes all mankind. And further the ground is cursed for thy sake, not for Adam only, but for all mankind as we learn by experience.

The Apostasy of man and the consequences of it.

1. Eve sinned as soon as she harkened to the serpent even before she ate of the fruit and Adam in like manner as soon as he harkened to Eve.
2. The day they ate, they exposed themselves to eternal punishment.
3. Their apostasy was total, they ceased to love God. The Angels who sinned wholly apostalized. In like manner, Man became wholly sinful.
4. All became sinners by Adam's fall. God's constitution.
    1. Evidences, all the evils entaled on his posterity.
    2. The condemnation of all is connected with Adam's sin. By one man sin entered the world and death through sin.
    3. The death of Christ to atone for man proves all sinners.
    4. The scriptures prove all depraved.
    5. By original sin is meant that actual sin which all Adam's posterity commit in consequence of his being constituted their public head.
        1. The corruption of all men is not by less their own sin because it was foreknown and determined that Adam would sin.
        2. It is not less their own because they sin as soon as born.
        3. Not less their own because deeply rooted in their hearts.
        4. Sin is the transgression of the law.
        5. Holiness is benevolence or disinterested love.
        6. Sin is selfishness or the pursuit of self interest.

Redemption

1. All our knowledge on this subject is from scripture.
2. Redemption does not extend to all mankind or the Angels.
3. The redemption of man is the greatest exercise of the goodness of God that ever has or will take place.
    1. Benevolence in bestowing a favour is great in proportion to the merit or demerit of the receiver.
    2. The greater the evil from which it delivers the greater the benevolence.
    3. In proportion to the positive good bestowed.
    4. The greater the expense to purchase salvation the greater the benevolence in giving it.

    5. It is great because offered without money, a free gift.
    6. Work of redemption is the sum and end of all his works.

Humanity of Christ

1. The human nature of Christ is not a distinct person separate from his divine nature.
2. What is true and may be affirmed of either person, Divine or human, may be affirmed of Jesus Christ.
3. These two natures, Divine and Human, remain as distinct as though they were not united.
4. By God's uniting with the human nature does not suppose any change in the Divine nature.
5. The personality of Jesus Christ is in the divine Nature, not in the human.
6. The human nature of Christ is the greatest of all created beings.
7. The human nature of Jesus Christ began to exist when it was created in the virgin Mary, and not before.
8. The human nature of Jesus Christ never became corrupted by sin.
9. Christ taking the human nature did not in the least degrade the divine nature. His humiliation consists in his being born of a virgin—in a manger, etc.

Design and Work of the Redeemer

1. Christ's work was to suffer the penalty of the Law, which

sinners had broken, in his own person, to redeem them from its curse.
2. The sufferings of Christ are the only grounds of the sinner's pardon. Christ bore the penalty.
3. Wrought out the atonement.
4. Applies redemption to the elect.

Regeneration

This, as to the cause, is the work of the Spirit of God.

1. The Spirit of God is the only agent by which the effect takes place.
2. This change is instantaneous.
3. This change is in the will or heart.
4. There are no means which are the cause of this change but is wrought by the immediate energy of the Spirit.
5. The Divine operation is imperceptable by the subject.
6. The grace granted in regeneration is a sovereign, undeserved favour.
7. This change is not in the least inconsistant with liberty.
8. Regeneration is but the beginning of a new life, etc.

Conversion

Regeneration is the cause and conversion the effect. Conversion is carried on through a man's life—turned more and more from sin unto holiness and from the heart grows every Christian grace, which springs from love.

Free agency

We cannot conceive of higher free agency than of acting voluntary. Whatever is prior to, or subsequent on volition does not effect free agency. Man, therefore, is a free agent in this sense only, that he is the subject of volitions.

Disinterested benevolence

1. Self love is selfishness, or a supreme regard for a man's self.
2. Benevolence is wishing well to being in general.
3. There is no distinction between self-love and selfishness.

4. The new heart consists in exercising benevolence, etc.
   1. God is love. God dwells in Christians.
   2. Christ is love, he dwells in Christians.
   3. Christ says, "He who will follow me must deny himself."
   4. St. Paul says that love is the whole of Christian affections. Charity seeketh not her own.
   5. The Law of God proves this, "Thou shalt love the Lord thy God with all thy heart, etc."

Illuminations

1. The heart by nature is depraved, sunk in darkness and depravity.
2. This is moral blindness. "Eyes have they which see not -ears which hear not, etc.
3. They will not see, and none are so blind as they who will not see.
4. To illuminate the heart is to change it.
5. No man can do this.
6. God or the Holy Spirit is the agent.

Saving Faith

1. Faith implies a saving belief in the gospel that Christ is the Son of God and the Saviour of the world.
2. Believing on the name of Christ and receiving him, the same.
3. Eating his flesh and drinking his blood.
4. Calling on the name of Christ looking unto Christ, in the old testament trusting in God, represent saving faith.
3. Love is implied in saving faith.
4. Repentance comes into saving faith - sometimes faith is required of sinners and sometimes repentance as necessary to salvation.
5. It is evident from scripture that the whole of evangelical obedience is included in faith.

Justification

1. The sinner has nothing, nor can have, to render it reasonable to pardon him.
2. God will not show favour to the sinner in pardoning him, so as to disregard his holy law.

3. In Jesus Christ there is righteous enough to deliver the sinner from the curse of the law.
4. In order to be interested in the righteousness of Christ, sinners must be united to him as the members to the body.
5. Sinners who are united to Christ by faith believe in him.
   1. It is impossible according to the reason of things that he who has once broken the law should be saved by it.
   2. If the believer might be saved on being perfectly holy after he believes, yet he is cut off, for no one is holy and cannot be saved by the law on this ground.
   3. All the virtue or holiness a believer has is calculated to lead him to disclaim works and trust to the blood of Christ alone for pardon.
   4. If faith did not unite the sinner to Christ and he justify him by his merits, there can no reason be given why he who believes should be saved, any more than he who does not believe.
6. Men are brought into a justified state by the first act of saving faith.
7. The righteousness of Christ does not become the believers — because:
8. In justifying the sinner his sins are not so blotted out as not to be remembered by God, but only so as never to condemn the believer.
9. Justifying the believer by the righteousness of Christ does not free the believer from being perfectly holy, in his own person—for the law is holy, the commandment holy, just, and good.

Covenant of Grace and Redemption

Comprehends the eternal purpose of the Father, Son and Holy Ghost to redeem fallen man,—fixing the manner of it and everything that relates to it in all its operations, in distinction to the covenant of works, and determining on every individual to be saved.

The covenant of Grace is made between Christ and sinful man. Of Redemption between the Sacred Trinity.

The Second Great Awakening

1. In this covenant all the promises are made to the believers on his first believing, etc.
2. This covenant is call the new in distinction from the former.
3. The covenant of grace has been revealed to man and has been administered in different forms ever since the fall, by it all true believers have been saved from that time to this, nor have been, nor can hereafter be saved in any other way.

Dispensation of Grace

1. Preaching the gospel implies a declaration of the whole system of truths therein contained.
2. Publishing the covenant of Grace does not disannul the law of God, but requires and demands obedience of all to whom it is preached.
3. In preaching the gospel to sinners, nothing is to be required or proposed to be done by them, but faith and repentance or what implies these:
    1. Man while unrenewed is totally depraved.
    2. The obstinacy of man in impenitance does not in the least remove his obligation to repent.
    3. All the law and commands of God respect the heart and there is no duty performed, only as the heart is rightly engaged.
    4. The scriptures do not afford any support to the doctrine, that we must tell sinners to do anything before they repent. See Christ's words and Apostle's.
    5. Telling sinners that they must repent immediately tends to cut them off from works.
    6. Telling them that they can do some good thing before repentance builds them up on works.

Perseverence to the end

1. There is nothing in grace that keeps believers.
2. The perseverence of believers is consistant with their being sanctified only in part.
3. The certain perseverence of believers in holiness does not imply that they will be saved whether they do or not.
4. This does not make their constant care and diligence needless, but necessary.

5. It is far from rendering the use of means unnecessary.
6. This doctrine supposes perseverence unto the end of life necessary to salvation. For he that continueth to the end, etc.
7. This doctrine is abundantly asserted in divine revelation.

Assurance of Salvation

1. This is not essential to saving faith. A person may be a true believer and not be assured that he shall be saved.
2. Assurance of salvation consists in a person's consciousness of the acts of his own heart, that he does believe in Christ; and knowing from reflection that he has attained to those things which imply saving faith, and do accompany salvation which is infallibly connected with it by the promise of God in the covenant of Grace.
3. It is certain that a person may know what the exercises of his own heart are.
4. It appears from scripture that many good men were in fact assured of their salvation.
5. To obtain assurance a person must have all the Christian graces in exercise in so high a degree as to be sure he has saving faith.
6. The believer is wholly dependent on God for assurance of salvation.
7. Assurance of salvation is not common to all believers, many never attain to it, and few or none of those who do, have it constantly without interruption.
8. Every Christian would be constantly assured of salvation if he did not possess so much sin and little discernment, etc.
9. It is the duty of Christians to maintain a constant assurance that they are Christians.

Election - Definition

The doctrine of election imports, that God in his eternal decree has chosen a certain number of mankind to be redeemed—fixing on every particular person whom he will save, and giving up the rest to final impenitance and endless destruction.

Proved

1. Man is entirely dependent on sovereign mercy for salvation.
2. It is infinitely best that God should determine who shall be saved and who not.
3. It is certain from scripture that God has not determined to save all—but only a part.
4. We learn from scripture number of individuals are chosen from among mankind, on whom divine love and sovereign grace are to be displayed in their salvation.
5. The elect are not chosen to salvation because of any goodness in them, or because it was foreseen that they would believe and repent of themselves.
6. The elect are not saved whether they be holy or not.
7. The use of proper means are as necessary to the salvation of the elect as though there were none elected—See Paul's shipwreck and those with him.
8. This doctrine does not represent God as a respecter of persons.
9. No injury is done those who are not elected by electing others to salvation.
10. Salvation may be offered to all men though only a part of them are saved.
    1. Mankind always resist the call unless made willing to accept. Preaching the gospel to all then discovers the obstinacy and depravity of the human heart.
    2. That every one who perishes under the light of the gospel perishes willingly because he would not accept.
    3. The offer of salvation to all discovers to the redeemed the stupidity of the natural heart, and that God made them willing to be saved or they would not have been.
11. The doctrine of election is so far from being a discouraging doctrine that it affords the only ground of hope.
12. Is perfectly consistant with free agency.
13. It is not known to man in this life who the elect are any farther than they are holy.

No man without sin in this life

1. If saints were perfectly holy they would not be so fit to live in this world of sin.

2. It would not be so much a state of trial.
3. Such a state of imperfection and sin is calculated to teach them their depravity—the odious nature of sin - their evil desert, etc.
4. By being in a sinful world they can see a greater contrast between sin and holiness and be led to prize the latter more than otherwise they would.
5. The power, faithfulness, goodness, and truth of the Redeemer are manifest when they could not be in any other way.

Church of Christ

Is found more than 100 times in the New Testament and signifies an assembly of men collected for some special purpose.

1. The visible Church includes all those who name the name of Christ or make a public profession.
2. By the invisible Church we may understand all the redeemed who ever have, or ever will be saved.
3. Sometime the Church is called Militant. Which includes all that will be saved both from the visible and invisible church now on earth, or warfaring on earth.
4. The church triumphant includes all the redeemed now in heaven.
    1. The friend of the Redeemer must profess and actually possess faith.
    2. They must all voluntarily unite to the church.
    3. Jesus Christ is the sole legislator and ruler in the church.
    4. Every person has a right to judge himself what are the laws of his church and what is his duty.
    5. The visible church, in the beginning, was small but has been increasing until now.
    6. The visible church will never be a perfect church on earth.

Public worship

1. The Jewish sabbath was on the 7th day, but the Christians met on the first. The day of Pentecost was a feast of the Jews, celebrated once in 50 days after the passover which was on the 14th day, which is the Jewish sabbath—which was once after every 7. Jewish sabbaths of which always came

on the day after the Jewish Sabbath, on this day the christian church was assembled, and this was the day of Pentecost when 3,000 were added to the church.
2. The christian Sabbath is call the Lord's day. Rev. 1:10.
   1. It is evident that it is the will of God that one day in 7 should be set apart and observed as a sabbath day. The commandment remember the sabbath day proves this.
   2. The 4th commandment does not designate any particular day to be kept holy.
   3. The Jewish Sabbath was not to be perpetual, but we are bound to keep some sabbath always.
   4. There is no proof that the sabbath which God gave to the people of Israel was the same that he gave to Adam.

PREFACE.

THE friends of Dr. Nettleton, especially those of them who were favored with the privilege of listening to those lucid and striking exhibitions of divine truth which fell from his lips in the pulpit, and in private conversation, have expressed deep regret that he did not commit more of his thoughts to writing. The fact that he did'not, is to be attributed to the peculiar circumstances in which he was placed. In the early part of his ministry, while he enjoyed vigor of body and mind, he was almost constantly laboring in revivals of religion, and he was so much occupied in teaching publicly and from house to house, that he had but little time for the use of his pen. He was led to adopt the practice of preaching without writing, and this became his usual and habitual mode of preaching. The consequence was, that he never acquired the habit of writing with facility, and it eventually became rather an irksome employment. He wrote but few sermons, and scarcely any in full. There are very few, if any, of those which are contained in this volume, which were not considerably enlarged by extempore remarks at the time of delivery. And the skeleton's of many of his discourses, if they were ever written, have not been preserved. But still, his manuscripts, few and imperfect as they are, contain many valuable thoughts which ought not to be lost to the world.

A very strong desire has been manifested, in different quarters, that a volume should be compiled from Dr. Nettleton's papers. In compliance with this desire, the present volume is given to the public.

In perusing these sketches, multitudes will be reminded of the solemn period in their history, when these very discourses were to them the power of God unto salvation. They will perceive, of course, that many of them are only outlines of the sermons as they were preached; but they will find in them many things which they will doubtless recollect. Some of these outlines of sermons were found among the manuscripts of Dr. Nettleton. Quite a number of them, however, were taken from his lips, and written at the time, during his last sickness.

It is proper that the reader should be apprized, that what is here exhibited will give but an imperfect view of the character of Dr. Nettleton's preaching; for many of his most impressive sermons, and parts of sermons, were never committed to writing. And besides, there was much in his manner of delivery, that gave interest and efficacy to his preaching, of which nothing can be learned by reading his discourses.

But this volume, if the compiler does not mistake, will be found to be rich in thought, and will be read both by ministers and private christians, with interest and profit.

That the same divine influence which accompanied the preaching of these discourses, may accompany the perusal of them, and bless them to the sanctification of christians, and the conviction and conversion of sinners, is the prayer of the compiler.

EAST WINDSOR, June 1st, 1845.

30

Sinners affectionately entreated to enter on the Christian pilgrimage.

We are journeying unto the place of which the Lord said, I will give it you. Come thou with us, and we will do thee good; for the Lord hath spoken good concerning Israel.—NUMBERS X: 29.

THE Israelites, having been rescued, by the mighty hand of God, from Egyptian bondage, and conducted through the Red Sea, had received the law at Mount Sinai; and being organized by a divine constitution, were about to commence their journey to the promised land. Their tents were taken up,—their tribes marshalled in the prescribed order—and the silver trumpets prepared to give the signal for them to commence their march. The tidings of the departure of Moses out of Egypt, and his intended journey through the wilderness, had reached the ears of Hobab, his father-in-law, who had come from the land of Midian to make a parting visit. At this interesting crisis, Moses affectionately addresses him in the language of the text; "We are journeying unto the place of which the Lord said, I will give it you. Come thou with us, and we will do thee good, for the Lord hath spoken good concerning Israel." Hobab's first answer was, "I will not go; but I will depart to my own land, and to my kindred." Yet Moses could not give up the suit; but with more urgent entreaty, he rejoined ;—" Leave us not, I pray thee, forasmuch as thou knowest how we are to encamp in the wilderness, and thou mayest be to us instead of eyes. And it shall be, if thou go with us, that what goodness the Lord shall do unto us, the same will he do unto thee."

These affectionate entreaties doubtless prevailed, and Hobab, afterward repented, and went; for we read of his posterity among the children of Israel, and of his sharing in the land of promise.

In all this, my brethren, we have an illustration of several things which distinguish the church of God. The whole multitude of believers have been rescued from spiritual bondage. Every Christian has been ransomed from the power of a tyrant far more cruel than Pharaoh. He has been delivered from " the prince of the power of the air"—" the Spirit that now worketh in the children of disobedience"—from " the God of this world, who hath blinded the minds of them that believe not." He has been "turned from darkness to light, and from the power of Satan unto God" —has been " recovered out of the snare of the devil," by whom he was " taken captive at his will." He has been delivered from a servitude to masters far more cruel than the task-masters of Egypt; and a bondage far worse than theirs—the bondage of sin, Satan, and the world. And in the moment of his greatest extremity, when he gave up all for lost— mountains on the one hand, and a howling wilderness on the other—destruction before, and the fell destroyer in the rear, the God of salvation appeared, and showed him a safe and easy passage out of the kingdom of darkness into the kingdom of God's dear Son. " Not by works of righteousness which we had done; but according to his mercy, he saved us, by the washing of regeneration and the renewing of the Holy Ghost." Thus redeemed from the hand of his enemies, and a new song put into his mouth, in common with the people of God, he can now show forth the praises of him who hath called him out of darkness into his marvellous light.

By the voice of God, believers are called to go out from " a world that lieth in wickedness"—to "seek a better country, even a heavenly." Enlisted under the captain of their salvation, they are marshalled as an army with banners, to take possession of the promised rest. And this day, throughout all their hosts, has the silver trumpet of the gospel been sounded, as the appointed signal for them to go forward. And the thousands of Israel are now on their march. " We are journeying unto the place of which the Lord said, I will give it you," is the declaration of the whole church of God on earth. They anxiously desire, and endeavor to persuade others to leave all and accompany them. If they cannot succeed, they must bid them a painful, and solemn farewell. Such are the leading thoughts suggested by the text, which are now to be illustrated, and applied to this assembly.

1. Christians are journeying. They are styled "strangers and pilgrims on the earth"—having here "no continuing city." Long after God's ancient people were settled in the land of promise, the psalmist used this language in prayer to God; "We are strangers before thee, and sojourners, as were all our fathers." Of all the ancient worthies it is said; "These all died in faith, not having received the prom-

ises, but having seen them afar off, and were persuaded of them, and embraced them, and confessed that they were strangers and pilgrims on the earth. For they that say such things, declare plainly that they seek a country." Peter in his epistle to Christians in general, addresses them all under this tender appellation, "Dearly beloved, I beseech you as strangers and pilgrims, abstain from fleshly lusts, which war against the soul." A life of faith, in the sacred Scriptures, is often compared to the journey of the Israelites through the wilderness; and every Christian now on earth, may adopt the language of David, "Hear my prayer, O Lord, and give ear unto my cry; hold not thy peace at my tears, for I am a stranger with thee, and a sojourner, as all my fathers were." And—"Thy statutes have been my song in the house of my pilgrimage." In heart and affections, he forsakes all. "Whosoever he be of you" says our Saviour, "that forsaketh not all that he hath, he cannot be my disciple." The place which he leaves, is the city of destruction. "Arise ye, and depart, for this is not your rest; because it is polluted; it will destroy you with a sore destruction." By faith, the Christian sojourns in the land of promise, as in a strange country—he looketh for a "city which hath foundations, whose builder and maker is God." Heaven is his home. His conversation, his heart, and his treasure are there. With the eye and the heart of a stranger, he prosecutes his journey through the wilderness of this world—"Seeking those things which are above, where Christ sitteth on the right hand of God." Whatever may be cumbersome, or useless, or suited to retard his progress, he will leave, or drop by the way. He will "lay aside every weight, and the sin that doth easily beset" him. To the attainment of this one great end, all his plans are subservient—seeking first the kingdom of God. "By patient continuance in well doing," he seeks "for glory, and honor, and immortality." Though, like the wanderings of the Israelites in the desert, his course, at times, seems retrograde, yet on the whole, he advances towards "the inheritance of the saints in light."

> "Cheerful they walk with growing strength,
> Till all shall meet in heaven at length,
> Till all before thy face appear,
> And join in nobler worship there."

2. Christians desire others, and especially their kindred, to journey with them. "Come thou with us" is the language of their hearts. The common sympathies of our natures alone, would awaken such desires, and much more, the love of God shed abroad in the heart.

But more particularly—they desire

In the first place, that God may be glorified. In this the true Christian chiefly delights. He rejoices in hope of the glory of God. In the conviction and conversion of sinners, God is glorified, both actively and passively. When the news of his conversion reached the ears of the disciples, Paul says, "They glorified God in me." When Peter related the story of the conversion of Cornelius and his household, in the ears of the church, "they glorified God, saying, then hath God also to the gentiles granted repentance unto life." The Psalmist said, "O that men would praise the Lord for his goodness, and for his wonderful works to

3*

the children of men." "O magnify the Lord with me, and let us exalt his name together." His heart was also deeply affected in view of the dishonor cast upon God, by thoughtless sinners around him. "I beheld the transgressors and was grieved."

Again. Christians have a tender regard for the welfare of their unconverted friends.

They see them eager in the pursuit of happiness in paths of disappointment. The pleasures of sense and of sin are but for a season,—unsatisfying, and often attended, and always followed by regret, and the goadings of a guilty conscience. "Even in laughter, the heart is sorrowful, and the end of that mirth is heaviness." The Christian knows from experience the vanity of the world. We have often heard his testimony in language like the following.

> "I try'd each earthly charm,
>   In pleasure's haunts I stray'd,
> I sought its soothing balm,
>   I asked the world its aid;
> But ah! no balm it had
>   To heal a wounded breast;
> And I, forlorn and sad,
>   Must seek another rest."

Sorrow and disappointment, pain and death are the common lot of all; and the hope of the Christian is needful to bear up our spirits under the evils that await us. Poor, indeed, must he be, who has no better portion than this world. With what mingled emotions of pity and grief, does the good man behold his fellow mortal, eagerly pursuing the phantom of pleasure, heedless of the crown of life, suspended within his reach. What a pity that so few should follow the example of Moses, who, "when he was come to years, refused to be called the son of Pharaoh's daughter; choosing rather to suffer affliction with the people of God, than to enjoy the pleasures of sin for a season."

Again—Christians foresee the misery that is coming upon their unconverted friends.

If they cannot be persuaded to leave all their sins, and journey with them, they must linger and be lost. The language of queen Esther expresses their feelings. "How can I endure to see the evil that shall come upon my people? Or how can I endure to see the destruction of my kindred." The language of Paul is also in point. "I have great heaviness and continual sorrow in my heart, for my brethren, my kindred according to the flesh." Notice also, the feelings expressed by the compassionate Saviour, when he beheld the devoted city and wept over it. And

> "Did Christ o'er sinners weep,
> And shall our tears be dry?"

Again—Christians desire the company of their friends in their pilgrimage.

The Israelites had to encounter the dangers of the wilderness, and Moses pleaded for friendly aid. He said, "Leave us not, I pray thee, forasmuch as thou knowest how we are to encamp in the wilderness, and thou mayest be to us instead of eyes." The difficulties and dangers which beset the Christian pilgrim in his pathway to heaven, are many, and often unseen and unexpected. The company and counsel of fellow travelers is mutually beneficial, and always desirable. Travelers to the same country, will inquire for each other—will lay their plans to walk in company, and

agree mutually to assist each other on the way.
"Two are better than one; for they have a good
reward for their labor; for if they fall, the one shall
help up his fellow; but woe to him that is alone when
he falleth, for he hath not another to help him up."
For this reason, pious children will desire the company
of their parents—parents, the company of their children—husbands and wives, brothers and sisters, the
company of each other. Friends who have long been
companions in sin might be mutually helpful in
returning to God.

I observe

3. That to those whom they cannot persuade to
accompany them, they must give the parting hand.

Having tried every method which love and friendship dictate, if they do not succeed, they must not
tarry—they must go and leave them.

My dear hearers, is there nothing in this congregation which resembles the scene which has been described? If there is in reality a revival of religion in
this place, and if there are those who are not subjects
of divine grace, it is even so. How solemn the separation! How affecting, as it respects this world! How
unutterably momentous as it respects the world to
come! When one and another has been led to
inquire, "What must I do to be saved?" and begun
to "rejoice in hope of the glory of God," intimate
friends, observing the change, have sometimes felt a
mournful sadness stealing over their minds. "I have
ost my friend. We have long been intimate—have
visited and sported together often in days that are
past;—but these scenes are over and gone forever.
My friend has now left me to wander alone—gone to

seek a better country. Well, my sober judgment and conscience tell me that he is wise—that he will never lament his choice. "Let me die the death of the righteous." "But what shall I do? A solemn sadness fills my mind, and scarcely can I repress the falling tear at such a parting."

When our friends leave us, and remove only to a distant country, never more expecting to return, how solemn is the hour of separation. It awakens the tenderest feelings of the heart. But, my hearers, such a parting is but a faint emblem of what, in reality, is now transpiring among us. Did you never look forward with deep concern to the separations of the last great day? Have you ever thought of different members of the same family, standing one on the right hand, and the other on the left of the judge? And did you not feel a solemn dread, lest perhaps, you should be found on the left hand? That awful separation, which determines the eternal destiny of every soul, takes place first in our world. It is now taking place in this revival—in this assembly. That change of heart which is necessary to fit the sinner for heaven, must take place on earth, in this life, or never. And a change of heart among sinners now, will, of course, produce a change of views, and feelings and pursuits, which will end in a separation of intimate friends. At such a season, many who feel little or no concern for their own souls, are wont to complain of being neglected by their former friends, who have become the subjects of divine grace. They imagine that those who have embraced the gospel, have ceased to love them.

Let me tell you, they do not love you less, but they

love the Saviour more. They cannot accommodate themselves to your feelings and wishes consistently with their attachment to him. They cannot make you their intimate associates as formerly ; unless *they* change their character, or *you* change yours. With them " old things are passed away, and all things are become new." They have lost their relish for the pleasures of sin—the amusements and vanities of this world. They have set their affections on things above, not on things on the earth. In this sense, they " are dead, and their life is hid with Christ in God." They are no longer "conformed to this world," but "transformed by the renewing of [their] mind." If you will not follow them,—take up the subject of religion and become Christians in solemn earnest, they must, in this sense, forsake you. In such a case, Christ requires them to forsake father, and mother, and wife and children, and all that a man hath, or he cannot be his disciple. A separation of views and feelings, of interests and pursuits, must take place, if you will not accompany them ; or they must die with you in the wilderness, and never enter heaven. If you will not go with them to heaven, do you wish them to drop the subject of religion—to awaken again the terrors of a guilty conscience—to plant thorns on a dying pillow—to barter away the joys of heaven, and go to hell merely to keep you company? Will you urge the wonted affection of a brother, or a sister, or the ties of former friendship ? *Will* you put them on trial of their friendship, their humanity, or their politeness, as some unfeeling wretches have done. That they love you still, their bursting hearts, and streaming eyes, when they speak of you, tell. In their name, and while, as I doubt not, their prayers are solemnly offered for the success of the invitation, I now renew to every one of you the invitation—" Come thou with us, and we will do thee good, for the Lord hath spoken good concerning Israel." " Leave us not, we pray thee—And it shall be if thou go with us, that what goodness the Lord shall do unto us, the same he will do unto thee." He will wash you in the same atoning blood—sanctify you by the same Spirit—He will grant you the same grace—the same peace of conscience, and joy in the Holy Ghost. He will meet you at the same throne of grace—will guide you by the same counsel—and at last, receive you to the same glory.

"And thou my son, know thou the God of thy father, and serve him with a perfect heart, and with a willing mind ; if thou seek him, he will be found of thee ; but if thou forsake him, he will cast thee off forever." Ye children, for whom I travail in birth again—did you know the feelings of a parent's heart— " Come thou with us"—" and my heart shall rejoice even mine." And ye parents too—did you know the heart of a child that has left all for Christ—" He *calls* and I must go. Though I love you none the less, yet I love him more than father or mother. Leave me not, I pray you. I need your help, your counsels, and your prayers. My father, my mother, come thou with us."

And thou, too, my bosom companion—the partner of my sorrows and my joys, " Come thou with us." Let us adopt the resolution together, " As for me, and my house, we will serve the Lord." Though I love you no less than ever, yet I love my Saviour more than all. *Leave me not.*

And ye too, the companions of my youthful days, and companions too in sin; I have seen my folly, and my sport is ended. Often have I invited, and you would never refuse—You too have invited, and I a thousand times have cheerfully complied. One more invitation, and I have done. "Come thou with us." The church on earth invites; and the spirits of just men made perfect; and all the hosts of heaven invite you. "The Spirit and the bride say come; and let him that heareth say come; and let him that is athirst come; and whosoever will, let him take of the water of life freely." If you leave us, the fault will be your own. We desire your company, and pray for your conversion—and all heaven stoops to invite you. If at last you have no part in that kingdom to which we are bound, it will be because you loved the world, and preferred the pleasures of sin for a season.

Thus, in the name of all the subjects of this revival, have I given the invitation to their friends and companions to journey with them;—and I must add, in the name of this church, and in the name of my Lord and Master. And must I leave you here? If it must be so, my hearers, then duty requires me to call even upon your nearest and dearest companions who have commenced their heavenly journey, to stay not a moment for you.

> "Cease, ye pilgrims, cease to mourn,
> Press onward to the prize."

Dry your tears,—and let nothing hinder you from following the steps of your leader. Obey implicitly every command of his. Thwart all the wishes—resist all the entreaties—endure all the frowns—and renounce entirely the society of your dearest earthly companions, RATHER *than neglect the least command of Christ.* To him you are bound by obligations infinitely greater, and ties of affection infinitely dearer, than you can be to them. They never died to save your souls from hell. And his unalterable decision is, "he that loveth father or mother, more than me, is not worthy of me. He that loveth son or daughter, more than me, is not worthy of me." "He that seeketh to save his life shall lose it; and he that loseth his life for my sake shall find it."

Again I repeat it,

"Cease, ye pilgrims, cease to mourn,
    Press onward to the prize;
Soon the Saviour will return,
    Triumphant in the skies.
There we'll join the heavenly train,
    Welcome to partake the bliss;
Fly from sorrow and from pain,
    To realms of endless peace."

But O, my impenitent hearers, I cannot bear to leave you thus. If you cannot be persuaded to accompany your friends, I must remind you that you too are journeying, as fast as the Christian—as fast as the wheels of time can carry you. But whither, ah, whither are you bound?

"See the short course of vain delight,
Closing in everlasting night."

Pursue your present course a little longer, and you

will soon be at a returnless distance from happiness and hope.

> " To day if ye will hear his voice,
> Now is the time to make your choice;
> Say, will you to Mount Zion go!
> Say, will you have this Christ, or no?
> Ye wandering souls who find no rest,
> Say, will you be forever blest?
> Will you be saved from sin and hell?
> Will you with Christ in glory dwell?
> Come, now dear youth, for ruin bound,
> Obey the gospel's joyful sound;
> Come, go with us, and you shall prove
> The joy of Christ's redeeming love.
> Once more, we ask you in his name;
> For yet his love is still the same;
> Say, will you to Mount Zion go?
> Say, will you have this Christ or no?
> Leave all your sports and glittering toys,
> Come share with us eternal joys;
> Or—must we leave you bound to hell?
> Then, dear young friends, a long farewell."

31

The sin and consequences of being ashamed of Christ.

For whosoever shall be ashamed of me, and of my words, of him shall the Son of man be ashamed, when he shall come in his own glory, and in his Father's, and of the holy angels.—LUKE ix: 26.

SHAME is a very powerful passion. Its influence over mankind is universal. It entered the world by sin, and it ought to be exercised towards nothing else. But strange to tell, that very weapon which ought to be turned against sin, is now turned against religion itself.

That some should be frightened into a denial of Christ, is not so incredible. But that any should be *ashamed of him*, whom angels adore, is what we could not have believed without the clearest evidence. But proof is not wanting to establish the fact, that many are now ashamed of Christ. Our Saviour who delivered the warning in the text, was perfectly acquainted with all the secret feelings of the human heart; and sad experience has too often proved the propriety of this solemn warning.

The truth is, the sin is of such a nature, that the sinner is ashamed to confess it. Nor is it incredible that a heart deceitful above all things, should deceive itself. Some may be ashamed of Christ, and yet be ignorant of the fact. Circumstances often reveal the secrets of the heart. Many who flattered themselves that they should be pleased with the advent of Christ, found themselves disappointed when he came. The prediction put into the mouths of sinners by the prophet, was fulfilled. "He hath no form nor comeliness; and when we shall see him, there is no beauty that we should desire him." "He is despised and rejected of men;—a man of sorrows and acquainted with grief; and we hid, as it were, our faces from him."

And thus is it now. Many who have imagined that they should be pleased with a revival of true religion, have found themselves sadly disappointed in the event. It appears so different from what they had expected, that they not unfrequently treat the religion of Christ, as the Jews treated Christ himself. To be deceived in this matter, my hearers, must be fatal; for the Saviour says, "Whosoever shall be ashamed of me, and of my words; of him shall the Son of man be ashamed, when he shall come in his own glory, and in his Father's, and of the holy angels."

I propose
I. To inquire who are ashamed of Christ.
II. Consider the greatness of the sin.
III. Contemplate the consequences of it.
I. Who are ashamed of Christ?

To be ashamed of Christ, it is not necessary that he should appear among us—that he should walk in our streets, enter our dwellings, and converse with us on the concerns of our souls. It is not necessary that we should point at him the finger of scorn, flee at his reproach, or sneer at his warnings. What is done to his disciples, Christ considers as done to himself. It is a remarkable fact, that few, if any will dare to condemn the religion of Christ as such. Their method is, to give to piety some other name, and then to load it and its professors with contempt. All, therefore, who despise and ridicule Christians on account of the strictness of their religion, and their conscientious regard to the duties which it enjoins—who call them precise, superstitious and the like, are ashamed of Christ. By whatever name it may be called, the mask will ere long be taken off, and Christ will say to them, " Inasmuch as ye have done it unto one of the least of these my brethren, ye have done it unto me." Many think, that had they lived in the days of our Saviour, they should have treated him with the utmost respect. All, however, may have a fair opportunity to manifest their feelings towards Christ, by their treatment to his members.

Another criterion, by which we may test our feelings on this subject, is, to inquire how we treat the commands, invitations, warnings, and threatenings of Christ. "Whosoever shall be ashamed of me, and *of my words*," says Christ. Those, then, are ashamed of Christ, and of his words, who are ashamed to be seen reading the Bible. Many who would not be ashamed to be seen reading a romance, would blush to be found searching the Scriptures. No one would blush to be seen perusing a communication from a friend, unless he were ashamed to own an acquaintance with its author. That feeling which leads an individual to neglect, or conceal the Bible, is a sure indication that that individual is ashamed of Christ. Those who despise and reproach others for searching the Scriptures, are, of course, ashamed of Christ, and of his words. And to regard the good or ill will of such, is to join in heart with the enemies of Christ. It cannot be done without paying greater respect to the enemies of Christ, than to Christ himself. All, therefore, who refuse daily to search the Scriptures, simply through fear of what others will think, or say, are ashamed of Christ, and of his words. The same may be said of all who, from similar motives, violate any of the commands of God—such as the duties of religion in the sanctuary, in the family, or the closet. Those who neglect to offer the morning and evening sacrifice, lest the voice of prayer should be heard in their families; and those who refuse to enter their closets, lest their absence should be noticed; are doubtless guilty of this sin.

Again—Those are ashamed of Christ, who are ashamed to have it known that they are anxious for their souls. Other motives may sometimes operate to lead sinners to wish to conceal their anxiety; but that which is the most common, is the one named in the text. How reluctant are they to converse even with Christian friends—still more reluctant are they to be regarded as anxious by the world. *"What will they think? And what will they say?"* "Should I become a Christian, I should hardly know what to do with myself. I should not dare profess religion. I am resolved never to let it be known." Such thoughts as these, often pass through the minds of sinners anxious for their souls; and they are sure indications that in heart, they are ashamed of Christ. When questioned respecting their spiritual trouble, they are ashamed to own it. What other reason can be assigned for their unwillingness to disclose the state of their minds? Do they think it wrong for a sinner to feel the strivings of the Spirit—to see and feel that he is lost? No, my hearers, the reason that they do not disclose their feelings, is not because they think it wrong, or because they think God would be angry with them, if they should tell the truth. The fact is, that though they dread to tell a lie, and dread exposure to the flames of hell, they dread the reproach of wicked companions more than either.

Those who make light of religious anxiety, and labor to divert the attention of others from the concerns of their souls, and drive serious impressions from their minds, are, of course, ashamed of Christ." "Why all this ado about religion?" "I wonder they will be so foolish." Such thoughts are often in the minds of sinners when their companions become anxious for their souls, and are sometimes expressed; and they prove that those who indulge them, are ashamed of Christ.

Again—Those are ashamed of Christ, who are ashamed to confess him before men. Persons may be willing, and even desirous to profess religion, without possessing it. But those who think they are Christians, and yet neglect to make a public profession, merely to escape the reproach of the world, are ashamed of Christ. Mankind are not ashamed to speak, and act in defense of their friends—especially of those whom they highly esteem.

Christianity admits of no neutrality. "He that is not with me," says Christ, " is against me." All who are ashamed to speak for Christ—to appear in defense of his cause, and to confess him before men, are ashamed of him. . . . .

Again—All who are ashamed to celebrate the dying

love of Christ, in obedience to his plain command, "This do, in remembrance of me," are ashamed of Christ. . . . .

Let us consider

II. The greatness of this sin.

And here I would first inquire, how much are sinners ashamed of Christ? The power of this passion, it is true, may be stronger in some, than in others. This, however, is true of all sinners;—they are more ashamed of Christ, than they are of their sins.

I need not say that some who are ashamed of Christ, are not at all ashamed of their ignorance of the Bible, or of their sin in neglecting it. Some, who have only been *suspected* of being under serious concern for their souls, have been offended, and have pretended that they considered themselves slandered. They would sport and jest, and adopt the most silly methods to do away the suspicion, and to show to others how little they cared about God, or Christ, or heaven, or hell. Although ashamed of Christ, they are not at all ashamed of these heaven-daring sins; but even *glory in their shame.*

Would you estimate the strength of this passion, set the greatness of the blessing lost on the one hand, and the littleness of the object gained on the other. Some whose judgment and conscience are well informed, who acknowledge the overwhelming importance of the subject, and who are anxious for their souls, are yet so ashamed of Christ, that they had rather stifle conviction, grieve the Holy Spirit, tell a lie to conceal their feelings, offend God, and expose themselves to the damnation of hell, than—than what?—what mighty object is to be gained?—than to endure the reproach of a wicked companion. Yes, the sinner is so ashamed of Christ, that he will do all this, rather than be pointed at by an enemy of God—a child of the devil—a worm of the dust. Some are so ashamed of Christ, that though God hath commanded, " Come out from among them and be ye separate, saith the Lord ;" yet they dare not obey the command. Though forbidden to walk in the counsel of the ungodly, or to stand in the way of sinners, or to sit in the seat of the scornful; yet they dare do no other, than walk in their counsel, stand in their way, and sit in their seat. They dread the reproach of sinners far more than they do the displeasure of God. When Christ in his gospel invites them one way, and sinful companions another, they immediately begin to inquire, " If we listen to Christ and refuse to listen to them, what will they think? What will they say? Will they not be offended?" But how seldom do they inquire, what will angels—what will the Saviour—what will the omniscient God think?

Why is it, my hearers, that so many are ready to listen to the enticements of wicked companions, and yet profess a respect for religion. It is a fact, as clear as the noon-day sun, that they are far more afraid of offending the devil, or one of his children, than they are of offending the Saviour himself. Though other sinful causes may operate; yet with those whose consciences are at times alarmed, the principal difficulty in renouncing the world, is this; they are ashamed of Christ. And though the motives be ever so strong— though God has declared, that "the companion of fools shall be destroyed ;" yet it makes no difference. Though the mercies of God, and the terrors of his wrath be set in array before them; yet the passion of shame bears them away with the thoughtless multitude, down the broad road to ruin.

Again—Sinners are more ashamed of Christ, than they are of the vilest of characters. How many are ready cheerfully to celebrate the declaration of civil independence in concert with the thoughtless, and even the intemperate, and openly profane; who would be ashamed to unite with Christians around the table of their Lord, who died to emancipate the soul from the bondage of sin and Satan, and to purchase freedom from the pains of hell. With what cheerfulness do thousands celebrate the birth-day of the hero and the statesman, who utterly disregard the dying injunction of the Saviour, "This do in remembrance of me." Hence it appears, that sinners are more ashamed of Christ, than they are of sin, or of sinners. So deeply rooted is this passion in the hearts of the young, that although they might march with courage up to the mouth of a cannon; yet they tremble and are afraid, when pointed at by the finger of scorn.

Many are so ashamed of Christ, that they will never attend in earnest to the concerns of their souls, though urged by all the motives which can be drawn from heaven, earth, and hell. More youth will, in all probability, lose their souls through the influence of this passion, than from any other cause whatever. They will continue to yield, and yield to its influence, until, at last, it may be said, that this, and that youth, were fairly shamed out of heaven.

And now, my hearers, would you see the sin as it is, think of the character of which the sinner is ashamed. Were it of a good man, merely, it would not be so criminal. Were it of his parents only, kind, tender and affectionate as they are, the crime would be small. Were it of the wisest and best man on earth, invested with all the honors of royalty, still the crime would be comparatively small. But it is of the Lord of glory—the Creator of the Universe, whom all the angels of God worship—of him "who is the brightness of the Father's glory and the express image of his person"—It is of *him* that the sinner is ashamed. Measure the crime, by the dignity of his character. Sinner, you are are ashamed of the God who made you!

But this is not all. Think of his love—his boundless compassion for sinners. Think of your vileness—the number and aggravation of your sins; and yet the Saviour has laid down his life for you. "God so loved the world, that he gave his only begotten Son"—And what returns have you made for this unspeakable gift? You have been ashamed of him. Were you justly condemned to die by the laws of the state; and at the awful crisis, should some kind friend step forward and offer to die in your stead; and with his dying breath, request an affectionate remembrance; would not the bare mention of his name, bring tears into your eyes? But what has the Saviour done? Groaned and died under the weight of *all* your sins, to deliver you not from the momentary pangs of death; but from the fire that shall never be quenched. And what returns have you made? You have been ashamed of him. "Scarcely for a righteous man will one die." "But God commendeth his love toward us, in that while we were yet sinners, Christ died for us." How ungrateful to be ashamed of Christ!

Nor is this all. As though it were not enough to

lay down his life, he comes and knocks at your door. "Behold I stand at the door and knock"—And thus he has stood, pleading for admission, until his head is filled with the dew, and his locks with the drops of the night. And all the answer you have made, is, "go thy way for this time." "Depart from me, I desire not the knowledge of thy ways." You have shut the door against him, while wicked companions and sinful thoughts have ever met with a welcome reception.

Let us consider

III. The consequences of this sin.

Those who are ashamed of Christ, are often led into the greatest inconsistencies of conduct. To avoid reproach, they often act against the convictions of conscience. Being ashamed of Christ, and yet ashamed to own it, they are led to act the part of a hypocrite. They wish to treat religion with respect, and at the same time, hold friendship with the world. But this is impossible. "No man can serve two masters." Such duplicity is often detected, and even now, brings with it double disgrace.

But this sin is threatened with a dreadful punishment hereafter. Consider the nature of the punishment. It will be retributive—the nature of the punishment answering to the nature of the crime—Shame rendered for shame. "Of him shall the Son of Man be ashamed."

By neglecting duty, and violating conscience, the sinner may, for the present, escape the reproaches of a sinful world. But all that disgrace which he now so much dreads, and thinks to avoid by shunning duty, will soon meet him with vengeance from another quarter. Every duty thus neglected, will ere long, bring with it double disgrace. Whatever expedient he may now adopt to avoid shame in the path of duty, he cannot escape long. It will certainly overtake him. "The things which shall come upon him, make haste."

Bring this subject, my hearers, home to your hearts. How do you feel when you know that others are ashamed of *you?* Suppose one of your companions should be ashamed to own an acquaintance with you—should blush and hide his face at the bare mention of your name—should flee at your approach—and should bolt and bar his door lest he should be disgraced by your society. To be treated thus by your equal would be trying. To be treated thus by your best friend, would be heart rending. But this is nothing. Christ the friend of sinners, who groaned and died on the cross to save you, will be ashamed of you. O, to have Christ ashamed of you! Let all your friends—Let all the world be ashamed of you—Let them cast out your name as evil—Let them point and hoot at you as you pass along the streets; still it is nothing to the punishment that is coming upon you, if you are now ashamed of Christ. If Christ were your friend, this might be easily borne. It would be nothing. You might even esteem "the reproach of Christ greater riches than all the treasures of" this world. But to have Christ ashamed of you—who can bear it?

Think too of the time when. "When he shall come in his glory." This despised Saviour whom we preach—who stood condemned before the bar of Pilate—whose religion is now despised and trampled under foot by proud, supercilious mortals, will ere long come in the clouds of heaven, with power and great glory. The trump of God shall sound; and the sleeping dead shall all awake; "some to everlasting life, and some to shame and everlasting contempt." "When the Son of Man shall come in his glory and all the holy angels with him, then shall he sit on the throne of his glory, and before him shall be gathered all nations." When you, a poor helpless criminal, shall stand trembling with horror at his bar—when every duty you have neglected, and every word you have spoken against religion, and its professors—when all your secret sins shall be laid open to view—when these, together with all your other crimes shall be brought to light; then the Judge of the world will be ashamed of you.

Think too of the company that will be present. You greatly dread now to be exposed to shame in the presence of your companions. But your whole conduct will be disclosed, and Christ will be ashamed of you in the presence of all your companions—in the presence of this assembly—in the presence of the whole assembled Universe. The Saviour has given you fair warning. "Whosoever shall deny me before men, him will I deny before my Father which is in heaven." Again—"He that denieth me before men, shall be denied before the angels of God." And yet again, "Whosoever shall be ashamed of me and of my words in this adulterous and sinful generation, of him also, shall the Son of Man be ashamed, when he cometh in the glory of his Father with the holy angels." He will then treat you, in the presence of that vast assembly, as you now treat him before the world. Because " I have called and ye refused"—" I also will laugh at your calamity; I will mock when your fear cometh; when your fear cometh as desolation, and your destruction cometh as a whirlwind; when distress and anguish cometh upon you." Then, Christ will be ashamed of you.

I shall close with a short application.

Who among us, my hearers, is ashamed of Christ? Although many may be guilty, perhaps not one in this assembly is willing to acknowledge it. But beware of deceiving yourselves. You may deceive others, and you may deceive yourselves. But you cannot deceive the Saviour. He knows perfectly every feeling of your hearts. As was intimated, you may be ashamed of Christ, and yet be ignorant of the fact. One reason of this ignorance may be, that you are so indifferent to the concerns of your souls—that you think, and speak, and care so little about Christ, that you hardly know whether you are ashamed of him or not. It is not until the conscience is aroused, and the sinner sees and feels that he is in the broad road to ruin, and that he must quit his companions, and turn and flee from the wrath to come—It is not until he is convinced of his bondage to sin and Satan and the world, and begins to think of making his escape, that he sees his heart as he never saw it before. Were you to begin a life of religion now—were you put on trial *this day* to obey the command of God, to come out from the world and be separate, to commence a life of devotion and of self-denial, and to profess Christ before men; and at the same time, were your kindred and friends to reproach and forsake you, and cast out your name as evil—And were this the only alternative, *begin to day, or be lost forever*, then you might see your hearts. We hence see, why so many have hearts ashamed of Christ, and yet know it not. Their awful indifference to the concerns of their souls is such—they think and care so little about the subject, that they know not the wickedness of their hearts.

And now passing by these thoughtless, stupid immortals, I would speak to those, whose consciences are at times alarmed—who feel the strivings of the Spirit, and yet are ashamed to acknowledge it—who are ashamed to renounce the world, forsake their vain companions, and openly espouse the cause of Christ. My fellow immortals, if you have any regard for your souls, no longer be ashamed of Christ. Ashamed to have it known that you feel concern for your souls! I now warn you to beware. In this way, thousands have lost their concern, and lost their *souls*. You cannot be persuaded to forsake your companions, lest you should be accounted serious. While this is the case, I despair of your conversion. "The companion of fools, shall be destroyed." You must either renounce the world, or the Spirit of God will renounce you. "No man can serve two masters." "The friendship of the world is enmity with God. If any man will be the friend of the world, he is the enemy of God." If you cannot bear the reproach of the world, all that you do in religion with such hearts, is mere hypocrisy. You show greater respect for the world, than for Christ. With such hearts, you could not be happy, if admitted to heaven. You are ashamed of the company and employments of the heavenly world. Remaining with the thoughtless world, you are continually violating the dictates of your own consciences. Though you wish Christ to acknowledge you, and perhaps, spend sleepless nights, fearing lest you should be found on the left hand at the last day, yet by your conduct, you are continually denying him before men.

Pause and reflect on your folly. Think of whom you are ashamed. Of him whom angels adore. Of him who died for sinners, and who alone can save you from hell. You are continually denying him—and for what? What do you gain? The good opinion of sinners—the good opinion of those who are soon to awake to shame and everlasting contempt. But nay, you do not gain even that. Let the youth come out from the world—Let him forsake the broad road—Let him return and ask the way to Zion and face a frowning world; and the conscience of every sinner whom he meets, will be constrained to bow and do him homage as he passes. He cannot but approve and admire the choice which he has made. And the scoffer cannot but despise himself for his own cowardice, that he has not courage enough to follow the dictates of his judgment and conscience in a matter of everlasting importance.

Among all who may reproach you, remember there is not even *one* good man. But become the friends of Christ, and you secure the friendship of all good men, of angels, and of the Saviour himself. It is true, you may meet with some ill-natured taunts, and be exposed to bitter reproaches; but what then? Remember these come only from the enemies of God. And will you follow them to destruction, lest you should incur their displeasure? If the fallen angels should ascend out of the bottomless pit, and attempt by every hellish art, to shame you out of religion, must you listen to them? Must you go and join them? Must you fear their displeasure more than the displeasure of Almighty God ?

But if you are still ashamed of Christ, remember a most righteous retribution awaits you. Christ will treat you, as you have treated him; and he will be as much ashamed of you, as you are now ashamed of him. "If we deny him, he will also deny us." In this punishment, there is a fitness which cannot fail to commend itself to every conscience. "With what measure ye meet, it shall be measured to you again." By your conduct you are now deciding the point how the Saviour will treat you when he shall come to judgment.

Finally—Let those who have confessed Christ before men, be careful never to betray his cause. If you are real Christians, you are no longer ashamed of Christ, but you are ashamed of yourselves, and of your conduct in having rejected him so long. Brethren, "If ye be reproached for the name of Christ happy are ye." Choose "rather to suffer affliction with the people of God than to enjoy the pleasures of sin for a season." "Blessed are ye when men shall hate you, and shall separate you from their company, and shall reproach you, and cast out your name as evil, for the Son of Man's sake. Rejoice ye in that day, and leap for joy, for behold your reward is great in heaven; for in like manner did their fathers unto the prophets."

And now let every one adopt from the heart the sentiment contained in the following lines.

> "Jesus, and shall it ever be,
> A mortal man ashamed of thee?
> Ashamed of thee, whom angels praise,—
> Whose glory shines through endless days!

Ashamed of Jesus, that dear friend,
On whom my hopes of heaven depend!
No: when I blush, be this my shame,
That I no more revere his name.
Ashamed of Jesus!—Yes, I may,
When I've no sins to wash away;
No tear to wipe, no good to crave
No fear to quell, no soul to save.
Till then—nor is my boasting vain,
Till then, I boast a Saviour slain;
And O, may this my glory be,
That Christ is not ashamed of me."

32

The Parable of the Lost Sheep.

And he spake this parable unto them, saying, what man of YOU having an hundred sheep, if he lose one of them, doth not leave the ninety and nine in the wilderness, and go after that which is lost until he find it? And when he hath found it, he layeth it on his shoulders rejoicing. And when he cometh home, he calleth together his friends and neighbors, saying unto them, rejoice with me, for I have found my sheep which was lost. I say unto you, that likewise joy shall be in heaven, over one sinner that repenteth, more than over ninety and nine just persons which need no repentance.—LUKE XV: 3—7.

Our Saviour taught much in parables. Some of his parables appear to be true histories. Others are merely supposed cases, intended to illustrate important truth. This mode of instruction possesses many advantages. It is simple, clear, striking and forcible. It always arrests the attention, and serves to fix divine truth in the memory. Whether the parable be fiction, or matter of fact, is not material. A true history may illustrate some important doctrine. A supposition may do the same.

The parable which I have just read to you, was spoken on the following occasion. Many were flocking around the Saviour. "Then drew near unto him, all the publicans and sinners for to hear him." His audience was composed of persons of very different views and feelings. Some were doubtless in tears, desiring to know what they should do to be saved.

They came not to gaze; but they "drew near *to hear him.*" Others, it appears from the sequel of his discourse, had returned home like the prodigal son, and were now rejoicing in hope. Others, it seems, were present with feelings entirely different. They were proud, self-righteous and scornful. These were present for no better purpose than to look on, make observations, and find fault. "And the scribes and pharisees murmured." To see sinners flocking around the Saviour, all attention—some weeping, and some rejoicing, made them angry. They murmured saying, "This man receiveth sinners, and eateth with them." Such was the Saviour's audience. The subject was suited to the occasion. It affords encouragement to penitents; and at the same time, administers pointed reproof to those who stand murmuring.

The parable was spoken in answer to the charge which the scribes and pharisees brought against him; " This man receiveth sinners and eateth with them." Our Saviour did not deny, but fully admitted the charge. He did not attempt to show that the sinners assembled around him, were less guilty than they supposed themselves to be. He admitted that they were lost, and hell-deserving; and this his anxious hearers knew and felt to be true. Nor was our Saviour ashamed to acknowledge, that he made it his great business to seek and to save just such sinners. " This man receiveth sinners, and eateth with them." Very true. You pursue your businesss and I pursue mine. " What man of you, having a hundred sheep, if he lose one of them, doth not leave the ninety and nine in the wilderness, and go after that which is lost, until he find it?" So I profess, says the Saviour, to be the great shepherd and bishop of souls. These have all gone astray. They are lost and have no disposition to return. My errand on earth is "to seek and to save that which was lost." What man of you, having a hundred sheep, if one be missing, would not range the fields and mountains, and call, and seek diligently until he had found it? So I have descended from heaven to earth, on this great errand, "to gather together in one, the children of God which are scattered abroad. "My sheep hear my voice. I know them, and they follow me." (Doubtless some of them were then standing round him, listening to hear his voice.) And now, ye murmurers, what would be your conduct on finding that which was lost? You would publish your success to all around, saying, " Rejoice with me, for I have found my sheep which was lost." " I say unto you that likewise joy shall be in heaven over one sinner that repenteth, more than over ninety and nine just persons who need no repentance."

Here it may be asked, whom did Christ intend by just persons who need no repentance? Some have supposed that he meant *self-righteous persons*. It is indeed true that there is more joy in heaven over one sinner that repenteth than over ninety and nine self-righteous persons. But it does not appear that such were intended. 1. Because they are called *just persons*. The word *just* never means *self-righteous*. 2. Because it is not true, that self-righteous persons need no repentance. They do need repentance. All *men* need repentance, and they must repent or perish. Should it be said, that Christ did not mean that they actually needed no repentance, but only that they felt no need of repentance ; like those whom he describes when he says, " They that are whole need not a physician, but they that are sick. I came not to call the *righteous*, but sinners to repentance." I reply, the interpretation given to this text, is liable to the same objection. It is not true that Christ came not to call *self-righteous* persons to repentance. He did come to call such, and no others. For all are by nature, proud, stubborn and self-righteous. Such was Paul before his conversion. And thousands of such, have, like him, been brought to see their sinfulness, and to bow at the foot of the cross. And 3. There is no joy in heaven over self-righteous persons. Christ is speaking of the great joy there is in heaven over one true penitent. If the comparison is with the self-righteous, it might be expressed thus. There is joy in heaven over one sinner that repenteth. How much ? More than over ninety and nine over whom there is no joy. Such certainly could not have been our Saviour's meaning. Self-righteous persons, therefore, were not intended in the text. It is true the parable was addressed to such. The scribes and pharisees trusted in themselves that they were righteous, and despised others. Our Saviour did not undertake to show them *directly*, that they were guilty, ruined, and lost sinners, and that they must be brought to see this to be their condition, or they could not be saved. His direct object was to convict them of the unreasonableness of their conduct in murmuring at the repentance of others. He takes them on their own ground. Admit that you are righteous, and that these are great sinners. Why murmur at their repentance? Vile as they are, they have souls of infinite value. One soul that is lost, must suffer more pain than all that has ever yet been endured by the whole race of Adam. The past sufferings of all the damned in hell, are not to be compared with the miseries of one soul through the boundless ages of eternity. Is not, then, the salvation of one such soul of infinite importance? Is it not matter of joy on earth to witness one such sinner brought to repentance? Must not such an event touch the heart of every pious man? What heart must that be, which can rejoice at finding a lost sheep, or a piece of silver, but cannot rejoice at the repentance and salvation of a lost sinner? If friends and neighbors assemble and rejoice together, on an occurrence so trifling, how must the friends of the Redeemer rejoice at the repentance of one sinner? On such an occasion, how would the news fly? What conversation—what joy and animation would be witnessed all around? Surely thus it would be with all benevolent beings. If there were any just persons on earth, who had never sinned, and who needed no repentance, they would be the very first to assemble and rejoice together on such an occasion. It is true, there are no such persons on earth. Strictly speaking, "there is none righteous, no, not one." But if there were ninety and nine just persons, who had never committed a single sin; who were never lost, and who needed no repentance, what a group!—what a lovely sight!—such as earth never beheld—And yet, the repentance and salvation of one sinner, is matter of more joy to all holy beings, than the happy condition of the whole ninety and nine who had never been lost. Strange as it may seem to sinners on earth, yet our Saviour declares that this is true in heaven. Whenever Christ finds a lost sinner on earth, and he is brought to true repentance, the holy inhabitants of heaven rejoice together on the occasion. And their joy is greater than over ninety and nine of those holy beings who have never fallen.

The subject suggests the following reflections.

1. Sinners are lost. If they were not lost, Christ would not have come to seek and save them. "For the Son of Man is come to seek and to save that which was lost." And since he has come from heaven to earth, and shed his precious blood to save them, they "will not come to him that they might have life." They are out of his fold, having no part or lot in his kingdom. "He that believeth on the Son, hath everlasting life—and he that believeth not the Son shall not see life, but *the wrath of God abideth on him*." They lie in the open field, exposed to the storm of divine wrath, which is coming upon the world of the ungodly. They are wandering farther and farther from God, and every moment liable to fall into the pit of destruction. They are lost, and yet totally insensible of their condition.

2. Christ knows his own sheep before they are brought into his fold. The good shepherd knows just the number that are missing. If one of them be gone astray, he knows it. Indeed, he would not go after it, did he not know it was gone, and would not, of itself, return. He says, "Other sheep I have which are not of this fold; them also, I must bring, and they shall hear my voice, and there shall be one fold, and one shepherd. He knows who they are, and what are

their names. "He calleth his own sheep *by name*, and leadeth them out." He knows how far they have wandered in the paths of sin and folly. His eye is ever upon them, and follows them in all their wanderings. Is there one more lost sinner in this place to be saved? Where is he? What is his name? Christ knows. Yes—"The foundation of God standeth sure, having this seal, the Lord knoweth them that are his."

3. Christ finds the sinner. He finds him in his sins—careless about his soul—casting off fear and restraining prayer—wandering farther and farther from God, from happiness and from heaven. He often comes upon him by surprise in the midst of his wickedness, and awakens him to a sense of his guilt. He trembles and is alarmed; but he is unwilling to return, and would fain flee out of the Saviour's hand. No sinner will ever awaken himself. Left to himself, not another sinner in this house will ever begin in earnest to seek the salvation of his soul. "The wicked, through the pride of his countenance, will not seek after God." "There is none that understandeth, there is none that seeketh after God." Every Christian knows this to be true in relation to himself. He knows that after he was awakened, that if the Spirit of God had left him, he should have returned to his sinful courses. All who have found the Saviour, will acknowledge that the Saviour first found them. "Since we have known God, or *rather are known of God*," is the language which they are ready to adopt.

This parable may serve to correct a very common mistake among sinners;—and I may add, among some professors of religion. They often think they are seeking Christ, and wonder why they fail of success, when they are actuated only by the fear of hell. They think they are following hard after Christ, and that he is departing from them. They flatter themselves, that if they hold on their way, they shall soon overtake him. They take it for granted that they are *ready* and *willing;* and they are now laboring hard to make Christ willing. But the very reverse is true, as we are taught in this parable. Sinners are departing from Christ, and in order to find him, they must not hold on their way, but stop, and turn. They are all as sheep going astray, and the great shepherd and bishop of souls, is calling upon them to return ; saying, " turn ye, turn ye, for why will ye die." When he finds them, he finds them wandering farther and farther from him. And when they hear his voice it is *behind them,* " saying, this is the way, walk ye in it."

4. How great must be the joy occasioned by the repentance of one sinner. It is contrasted with that over just and holy beings who need no repentance. Joy so great was never occasioned by any other created being, as that occasioned by a repenting and returning sinner. Joy so great, was never occasioned by an angel of light. Gabriel who stands in the presence of God, never occasioned so much joy in heaven. We may number ninety and nine holy angels, and then say, " There is joy in heaven over one sinner that repenteth, more than over these ninety and nine just persons." The creation of the world was a joyful event, when " the morning stars sang together, and all the sons of God shouted for joy." But this is not to be compared with the joy over one sinner that repenteth. The earth itself was created to subserve God's purpose of saving sinners—as a stage on which

to display the wonders of redeeming love to an admiring universe.—"To the intent that now unto principalities and powers in heavenly places, might be known by the church, the manifold wisdom of God." If it be asked, why did the Son of God become incarnate? In the repentance of a lost sinner, you have the answer. "He came to seek, and to save that which was lost." "He came not to call the righteous, but sinners to repentance." Why did the angels announce to the shepherds the news of his birth, and sing "glory to God in the highest?" In the repentance of a lost sinner, you have the answer.

Nor is this joy confined to angels. The Lord himself rejoices. Why did the Son of God leave the bosom of his Father,—condescend to be born in a manger—and to suffer and die on the cross? In the repentance of a lost sinner, you see the glorious object which he had in view, accomplished. For this he bled, and died. Here he sees of the travail of his soul, and is satisfied. This is the fruit of his toil, his shame, his sufferings, and his death. "Who for the *joy* that was set before him, endured the cross, despising the shame." Every Christian, in his turn, has occasioned this joy in heaven.

5. The repentance of every sinner, when first discovered, is the cause of new joy. The joy of angels is most sensibly felt every time one more is added to the company of the redeemed. The ninety and nine already redeemed, seem to be forgotten, when with wonder and joy, they behold their new companion with whom they expect to dwell forever. Could we know, as well as angels do, the reality of a sinner's repentance, we should know better how to rejoice. The

tidings of his repentance, must be received by Christians on earth, with mingled emotions. They "rejoice with trembling." While they delight in each other, the news that a soul is converted to God, excites in them peculiar joy. For a time, they seem to forget themselves and each other. They cannot forbear to assemble, and rejoice together on the occasion. And well they may, for Christ himself rejoices; and he says unto his disciples " rejoice with me, for I have found my sheep which was lost."

6. What must have been the hearts of the scribes and pharisees who stood murmuring, while converted publicans and sinners drew near to Christ, to hear the gracious words which proceeded out of his mouth. While angels in heaven were rejoicing over these sinners, there they stood *murmuring*. What a contrast! Angels, and the Saviour himself, and all holy beings were rejoicing over the repentance of these sinners, but they stood murmuring and finding fault, and saying, "This man receiveth sinners, and eateth with them." How must their conduct have appeared to angels, and to God!

My hearers, had you been present on this occasion, what part would you have acted? Would you have rejoiced at the sight of sinners flocking to the Saviour, and weeping for their sins? Or would you have joined with those that murmured? Bring the subject home to your hearts. How would you like to see sinners flocking to Christ in this place? Are your hearts prepared to welcome a scene like this? Scenes similar to this, may now be in the recollection of many present. At least, you must have heard of the conviction and conversion of sinners--some of them perhaps of your own acquaintance. And how did the news affect your hearts? Did you hear the news with angelic joy, or with sullen sadness? I would put the question to the consciences of all my hearers. How does the subject of the conviction and conversion of sinners affect your hearts? It is a subject in which God, and Christ, and the Holy Spirit, and saints and angels, are all interested. All heaven is moved at the repentance of one sinner. And my hearers, if your hearts are not deeply interested in this subject, it is because you have no claims to the Christian character. Beware of deceiving yourselves in a matter of such infinite moment. If you cannot rejoice in the repentance of sinners, you have none of the spirit of Christ. If you cannot rejoice at the repentance of other sinners, you have never yet repented of your own sins. Your hearts are not right in the sight of God. For those who die with such hearts, there is no happiness, and no heaven hereafter. If such tidings vex the heart, and grate on the ear now, and if you would fain fly from such a scene, whither can you go at the solemn hour of exchanging worlds? Can you enter heaven, and be happy there? Heaven is filled with this joyful theme. There the tidings of the conversion of every penitent on earth will be told. And every saint, and every angel that sings in glory, will proclaim it in loud hozannas around the throne of God and the Lamb. There too, the story of your own repentance must be told, ere you leave this world, or *you* can never join the company of angels and the spirits of just men made perfect.

To all my impenitent hearers in this assembly, let

me say—You have seen what a lively interest angels take in the repentance of *one sinner*. Will there ever be joy in heaven over *your* repentance? Wherever the gospel is preached with the Holy Ghost sent down from heaven, there angels are hovering round to witness the effects. "Which things the angels desire to look into." Yes, angels attend on our worshipping assemblies, to witness the effect of a preached gospel.

> "Invisible to mortal eyes they go,
> And mark our conduct, good or bad, below."

Sinners, these heavenly messengers are now waiting to carry back the tidings of your repentance, to the courts above. And shall they stoop, and gaze, and wait in vain? Have you no tears to shed for your sins?

> "O ye angels hovering round us,
>   Waiting spirits, speed your way,
> Hasten to the court of heaven,
>   Tidings bear without delay;
> Rebel sinners
>   Glad the message will obey."

33

The Parable of the Prodigal Son.

And he said, a certain man had two sons. And the younger of them said to his father, Father give me the portion of goods that falleth to me. And he divided unto them his living. And not many days after, the younger son gathered all together, and took his journey into a far country, and there wasted his substance with riotous living. And when he had spent all, there arose a mighty famine in that land, and he began to be in want. And he went and joined himself to a citizen of that country; and he sent him into his field to feed swine. And he would fain have filled his belly with the husks that the swine did eat; and no man gave unto him. And when he came to himself, he said, how many hired servants of my father's have bread enough and to spare, and I perish with hunger. I will arise and go to my father, and will say unto him, Father, I have sinned against heaven, and before thee, and am no more worthy to be called thy son; make me as one of thy hired servants. And he arose and came to his father. But when he was yet a great way off, his father saw him, and had compassion, and ran and fell on his neck and kissed him. And the son said, Father, I have sinned against heaven, and in thy sight, and am no more worthy to be called thy son. But the father said to his servants, bring forth the best robe, and put it on him; and put a ring on his hand, and shoes on his feet; and bring hither the fatted calf, and kill it; and let us eat and be merry; for this my son was dead and is alive again; he was lost and is found. And they began to be merry.—LUKE XV: 11-25.

It will be my object to give a plain, practical exposition of this parable for the benefit of all whom it may concern.

This is the third parable spoken by our Saviour on the same occasion. The two others show what God does, or the part which he acts, in the recovery of the lost sinner to himself. This is designed to show the criminality of the sinner, and the nature of true conversion. Our Lord always spoke directly to the point, and this parable applies exactly to the persons to whom it was addressed. The younger son represents the persons mentioned in the first verse of the chapter. "Then drew near unto him all the publicans and sinners for to hear him." The elder brother represents the scribes and pharisees mentioned in verse 2d, who "murmured, saying, this man receiveth sinners and eateth with them." The whole is strikingly applicable to the persons to whom, and the occasion on which it was spoken.

Some of our Lord's hearers were then, doubtless, in tears, mourning for their sins. Our Saviour had already assured them, that however the scribes and pharisees might murmur and find fault, yet God and angels were rejoicing over them, provided their repentance was genuine. But how should they know whether their repentance was genuine? On this point, they were doubtless anxious to hear something further. To give them the instruction which they needed, our Lord spake this parable. The history of the prodigal son is a general history of christian experience. In the story as here related, every child of God may trace the outlines of his own history. Then let us follow it, and see its application.

The parable contains two parts, representing the life of the christian before, and at the time of his conversion. Let us, then, consider—

I. The departing prodigal.
II. The returning prodigal.
I. The departing prodigal.

"*A certain man had two sons, and the younger of them said to his father, father, give me the portion of goods that falleth to me.*" His father is represented as kind, tender and affectionate, and yet this son is not satisfied. So God is a kind and tender parent, and yet sinners do not love him. They murmur at the allotments of providence, and manifest little or no interest in those things which concern their eternal peace. Regardless of God and the world to come, they desire a large portion of the good things of this world. And this desire is expressed, not in a humble petition to the Father of mercies, but in the form of an impious demand. "Give me the portion of goods that falleth to me." Such is the language of the sinner's heart, and of his conduct. Whatever may become of his soul, he wishes a large portion of this world; and will murmur and find fault, if his wishes are not gratified.

"*And he divided unto them his living.*"

This represents God's providential dealings towards mankind in this life. He is kind to the evil and the unthankful. He sometimes bestows blessings on sinners with a liberal hand. This he does to try them. His goodness lays the sinner under peculiar obligations to love and serve him. But these obligations are disregarded.

"*And not many days after, the younger son gathered all together, and took his journey into a far country.*"

We see here the disposition of the sinner to depart from God. The prodigal took his journey into a far country, where he thought he should be out of the sight of his father, and where he should feel free from restraint, and be at liberty to follow the inclination of his heart. So sinners, when at a great distance from God, cast off restraints, and go on boldly in sin. They may fear detection from mortals, but they have wandered so far from God, that the thought of his presence does not disturb them. They live "without God in the world."

"*And there wasted his substance in riotous living.*"

Sin is expensive. And sinners use the bounties of providence to no better purpose than to gratify a depraved inclination. All the good things which God bestows upon them are wasted. He feeds and clothes them, that they may go and work in his vineyard; but the language of their hearts is: "Who is the Almighty that we should serve him?" He calls them to engage in the christian warfare, but they go and join his enemies. Instead of laboring to build up, they are laboring to destroy the Redeemer's kingdom. They are employed in the service of Satan, and at the same time riot on the bounties of God's providence. Sinners also waste their advantages for securing eternal life. They are favored with a day of grace—a season for repentance—a precious opportunity to secure an interest in Christ, and to lay up a treasure in heaven. But they will not attend to the concerns of their souls. This precious season of probation is fast drawing to a close, and notwithstanding the kind and melting invitations, and solemn warnings which are addressed to them in the word of God, they persist in the road to death. All the labor and pains taken for their conversion and salvation, so far as they are concerned, are lost; nay, worse than lost, for all their abused privileges will serve as so many weights to sink them deeper and deeper in hell. They have lived so long —and yet nothing is done. They have wasted their privileges. They have heard so many sermons, and yet nothing is done. They have lived so many years, and have wasted them all, and thus they continue to waste the precious day of salvation. A price is put into their hands to get wisdom, but they have no heart to it.

"*And when he had spent all, there arose a mighty famine in that land, and he began to be in want. And he went and joined himself to a citizen of that country, and he sent him into his field, to feed swine.*"

The prodigal was now in a wretched condition—had spent all—was in a land of famine—and began to be in want. But he had too much pride to be willing to return home to his father. He therefore went and joined himself to a citizen of that country, who, deeming him fit for nothing else, sent him into his fields to feed swine. This represents the condition of a sinner beginning to be awakened. He finds himself in a wretched condition. He is entirely destitute—has spent all—is awfully in debt to the justice of God—is in a land of famine—in a world that can give him no relief. He is now invited and entreated to return home to God, and cast himself on his mercy. But his proud heart revolts at such a proposal. He is too stubborn to confess his sin, and ask forgiveness. Nor can he bear the thought of engaging in the service of God. He prefers the service of Satan, the God of this world. Rather than break off his sins by righteousness, he will serve the vilest of masters, and submit to the meanest employments.

"*And he would fain have filled his belly with the husks which the swine did eat.*"

This represents the unsatisfying nature of all sinful pleasures. The sinner may think to find happiness in the enjoyment of the world, but he will not succeed. His soul is ever restless, and nothing in this world can satisfy its boundless desires. He is never satisfied with the past; and the more he indulges his sinful inclinations, the stronger they become. It is just like feeding on husks to satisfy the cravings of hunger. The more the sinner attempts to satisfy himself with sinful gratifications, the more uneasy and miserable he becomes. He plunges himself deeper and deeper in misery at every step. And yet he cleaves to his sins, and would fain satisfy himself with sinful pleasures. But he will not succeed. O, sinner! how shall we convince you of your folly? Look at this wretched prodigal. Go to the field; see him among the noisy swine. See him feeding on husks, when in his father's house, there is bread enough and to spare. See him famishing and just ready to perish with hunger. Go, sinner, and plead with him to return home to his father. Is he not beside himself? Pity him; for die he certainly must, unless prevailed on to return to his father's house. Go, sinner, and tear from him his husks, and show him his folly. If, after all, you cannot persuade him to return to his father—if you must leave him to perish in the field—then, O sinner, if you will not be persuaded to drop your sins, and go home to God as a humble penitent, I must leave you to perish in your own corruptions; for let me tell you, THOU ART THE MAN. There is no other prodigal, but just such a sinner as thyself.

"*And no man gave unto him.*"

We may suppose that when the prodigal became anxious about his condition, he was surrounded by sinful companions, no one of whom would advise him to return to his father. If he made known his distress, they would probably attempt to divert his attention, by offering him some sinful pleasure, which would only increase his torment. At all events, they would do nothing to relieve his wretchedness. And thus it fares with the sinner, when he begins to be alarmed at his awful condition. He is among sinners, who are ignorant of his condition. Not one of them is a friend to his soul. Not one of them will point him to the Saviour, and urge him to return home to God. If he makes known his distress to his sinful companions, they will sometimes mock at his sufferings, or attempt to divert his attention from the concerns of his soul.

"*And no man gave unto him.*"

Nor is it in the power of any man to relieve an awakened conscience. No arm of flesh can help him. And after having looked around on all sides for help, he sometimes begins to think he has not a friend on earth. Thus friendless and hopeless, he is almost ready to sink in despair. He feels that he is lost. .

. . . .

Thus far we have followed the departing prodigal. Let us turn our attention

II. To the returning prodigal.

"*And when he came to himself.*"

This was the turning point. We have here a beautiful representation of the change which takes place in the sinner, when his heart is renewed by divine grace. The expression implies that he had been beside himself, and that he had now come to his right mind. Who are the sinners that will not this day return home to God like the repenting prodigal? The Bible represents them all as madmen—"madness is in their hearts." Such is the infatuation of every impenitent sinner, that he may with great propriety be said to be

10

beside himself. Time will not permit me to enlarge on this point. But I will just inform the sinner, that if he does not this day return home to God, like the repenting prodigal, it will be because he prefers to run the tremendous risk of lying down in hell to all eternity. I would now appeal to the conscience of every one who hears me, whether it is extravagant to say, that the person who is willing to run such a risk, is beside himself.

But to return. The sinner has now come to himself. He views his past conduct with astonishment, and with unfeigned sorrow. He turns his thoughts homeward.

"*How many hired servants of my father have bread enough and to spare, and I perish with hunger.*"

He is now sensible of his folly in departing from his father, and wishes to return. But he knows that he is unworthy to be received. He is ready to say, did ever such a sinner obtain mercy? Will not my father spurn me from his presence? Can I hope to obtain his forgiveness? Vile as I am, I am resolved to try.

"*I will arise, and go to my father, and will say unto him, father, I have sinned against heaven and before thee, and am no more worthy to be called thy son; make me as one of thy hired servants.*"

Never did a sinner adopt a better resolution. Let us examine its import. Every sinner is requested to attend and make the resolutions his own. "*Father, I have sinned against heaven and before thee.*" He had sinned against the God of heaven. It was this that grieved him. Not a word is said by way of excuse. He does not say: Father, I have come to make my apology for what I have done; I hope you will overlook my past conduct, and I will endeavor to do better in future. He does not say : I have exposed myself to punishment. That was not the thing which lay with the greatest weight on his mind; but the thought that he had sinned against God. "Against thee, thee only have I sinned, and done this evil in thy sight." What we have hitherto said of the prodigal since he came to himself, relates to the state of his heart. While he sat musing on his lost condition, all at once he *came to himself.* He began to see how stubborn he had been, and as his thoughts turned on his past conduct, his sins began to rise up to his view. He was almost overwhelmed at the sight. And while he sat mourning and weeping, the thought occurred to him that he had not confessed his sins as he ought. At the same time, he had different views respecting the presence of God. Hitherto he had been regardless of the divine presence. But now he realized that God was perfectly acquainted with all his sins. During his wanderings he little thought that the eye of God was constantly upon him, and that all his secret sins were set in the light of his countenance. But all this, to his shame and confusion of face, this broken-hearted sinner now begins to realize; and he resolves no longer to cover his sins, but to confess them without any reserve.

"*And he arose and came to his father.*"

But his father was not ignorant of what had taken place. He is represented as standing on an eminence where he could see to a great distance, and as anxiously awaiting the return of his son.

"*But while he was yet a great way off, his father saw him, and had compassion.*"

The father was affected with what he saw. He said nothing, but ran. Mercy is swift. But what did he see? And why did he run? Yonder, at a distance you may see him. Come anxious sinners—come careless sinners, all assemble round, and behold this sight. Yonder is something worthy of your notice. Borne down with distress, he has long been a wretched wanderer from his father's house—has squandered his substance—is worn down with hard labor in the service of the vilest of masters—has left all his sinful companions—is coming directly from the field, and from the mean employment of feeding swine—is famished, and just ready to perish with hunger, and has not a friend to help him. Borne down under a sense of his sins, he moves slowly along, while his father hastens to meet him. Ashamed and confounded you see him coming home, just as he is, in all his poverty and rags. In this situation, his father met him, *fell on his neck and kissed him.* What a meeting this! Is it possible? Yes; for it is the compassion of a God. Not a frown is seen on the father's face—Not an angry word drops from his lips.

With what kind reception does the poor brokenhearted sinner meet, who goes home to God just as he is. But a little while since you saw him arise to go to his father that he might make his acknowledgment. But before he has time to carry his resolution fully into effect, he is graciously received. But does he keep back his confession? Listen—what do you hear? "*Father, I have sinned against heaven and in thy sight, and am no more worthy to be called thy son.*" But why this confession, since he is already received to favor? Because, a sense of pardon, so far from lessening, tends only to increase the sorrow of the penitent. He esteems it a privilege to confess his sins. This confession of the prodigal is a striking example of genuine repentance. You will perceive that it was not prompted by a slavish fear of punishment; for his father had already kindly received him. Thus it is with every true penitent. If there were no future punishment, he would still confess his sins with godly sorrow. Though forgiven of God, he will feel that he can never forgive himself. When the prodigal first adopted his resolution, he intended, after confessing his sins, to petition for a low place among his father's hired servants. But before he had time to offer his petition, he was interrupted by his father.

" *But the father said to his servants, bring forth the best robe and put it on him.*"

It will be recollected, that the prodigal son, had been long absent from home. He spent all his substance, and was reduced to poverty and rags. The moment he thought of returning home, he felt ashamed of himself. He could hardly endure the thought of appearing in the presence of his father, in such a mean and tattered dress. But it was in vain for him to attempt to procure a better garment, for he was poor, and had nothing to give in exchange. It was in vain for him to beg; *for no man gave unto him.* Equally vain was it for him to wait, for the longer he tarried, the worse his condition became. O, wretched sinner! He thinks of coming to God, but is ashamed to come as he is. But he must come just as he is, *wretched and miserable, and poor, and blind, and naked,* or he will never come at all.

The longer he labors to establish a righteousness of

his own, the more wretched he becomes. The best robe—the robe of Christ's righteousness, is already prepared. This is the very best robe that was ever wrought; and what is more, it exactly befits the sinner. Clad in this robe, the sinner stands complete in the righteousness of Christ.

"*And put a ring on his hand.*"

A token of friendship—a pledge fitly representing the unchanging, and never-ending love of God to the pardoned sinner.

"*And shoes on his feet.*"

"Shod with the preparation of the gospel of peace." Prepared to run in all the ways of holy obedience.

. . . .

"*And bring hither the fatted calf and kill it, and let us eat and be merry.*"

The satisfaction found in religion, is here represented by a feast.

. . . .

"*For this my son was dead and is alive again; he was lost, and is found.*"

His return was matter of astonishment. Had he actually come out from the grave, where he had long been buried and lost, it would not have been more surprising. The whole scene could not have been more interesting and joyful.

. . . .

Christians, at such a season, have introduced to their society, those who before were the greatest strangers to them. Characters to human view the most unlikely, are often made the subjects of renewing grace.

. . . .

"*And they began to be merry.*"

His sorrow is now turned into joy. Never before did he know what true happiness was. Thus was it with the sinners who had assembled around the Saviour when this parable was spoken. Thus was it when Philip preached in Samaria. "There was great joy in that city." Thus is it in many places where God is now pouring out his Spirit and reviving his work. And thus it will be, wherever sinners are flocking to Christ. "Then shall the lame man leap as a hart, and the tongue of the dumb shall sing." In a revival of religion you may see this parable all acted out.

. . . .

"And they began to be merry."

Here is the joy of the young convert. At this point I must stop; for the sinner can follow me no farther. Do sinners in this assembly wish to know the joy of this prodigal son? You will please to remember one word. If you lose that, I have lost my labor. One word, you will please to remember. If you lose that, you lose all. If you lose that, you lose your souls. *Go ye and do likewise.*

34

The danger of hypocrisy.

Then shall the kingdom of heaven be likened unto ten virgins, who took their lamps, and went forth to meet the bridegroom. And five of them were wise, and five were foolish. They that were foolish took their lamps, and took no oil with them. But the wise took oil in their vessels with their lamps. While the bridegroom tarried, they all slumbered and slept. And at midnight there was a cry made; behold, the bridegroom cometh; go ye out to meet him. Then all those virgins arose and trimmed their lamps. And the foolish said unto the wise, give us of your oil, for our lamps are gone out.—MATTHEW xxv: 1-8.

THE parable, of which the text is a part, was intended to represent, not the state of the world at large, but the visible church, and to teach the danger of making a hypocritical profession of religion. The incidents are taken from the customs which prevailed among the Jews in connection with the marriage solemnity. It was customary for the bridegroom to come, attended by his friends, late at night, to the house of the bride, who was expecting his arrival, attended by her bridesmaids, who upon being notified of the bridegroom's approach, were to go out with lamps in their hands to meet him and accompany him to the house. These were usually ten in number. "Then shall the kingdom of heaven be likened unto ten virgins, who took their lamps, and went forth to meet the bridegroom."

By the kingdom of heaven is meant the visible church. The ten virgins represent professors of religion. The bridegroom is Jesus Christ.

The parable may be applied to the whole church collectively, or to the individual professors of religion. In the former case, the coming of Christ may be considered to be at the day of judgment, when the church, the Lamb's wife, will have made herself ready. In the latter case, the coming of Christ may be considered to be at death. It is in reference to individuals, that I shall at present consider it.

They "took their lamps." This denotes their profession of religion.

They "went forth to meet the bridegroom." This denotes their journey through life, in which they profess to be traveling towards heaven.

"While the bridegroom tarried." His delay denotes the whole term of life.

"They all slumbered and slept." This denotes that spiritual sloth which is too often visible in the lives of christian professors.

"At midnight, there was a cry made; behold, the bridegroom cometh." This denotes the solemn summons made by the sudden and unexpected approach of death.

"Go ye out to meet him." They must go out of time into eternity to meet Christ in judgment.

"Then all those virgins arose and trimmed their lamps." The loud summons of death will arouse from their slumbers both christians and hypocrites, and lead them to inquire whether they are prepared to meet their God.

"And the foolish said unto the wise, give us of your oil." Oil is the emblem of grace in the heart, which constitutes the distinguishing characteristic of the true child of God.

" For our lamps are gone out." But how could they go out, if they had never been lighted, and how could they have been lighted without oil ? Here I pause, and propose to my audience this question. Does not this text prove that real christians may fall from grace, and finally perish ?

That it teaches this doctrine, has often been strenuously maintained. It has been asked, with an air of triumph, "how could their lamps have gone out, if they had never been lighted ? And how could they have been lighted without oil ?"

Let us test the force of this reasoning. If it can be fairly made to appear, that Christ did in this parable, intend to teach that some who shall be finally excluded from heaven, were once real christians, it is a conclusive argument against the doctrine of the saints' perseverance. And the argument will take a tremendous sweep. It will go far towards proving that one half of the whole number of real christians are finally lost. For "*five of them were wise, and five were foolish.*"

But what is the proof that the foolish virgins denote those who were real christians ? It rests solely on their own testimony. "*And* THE FOOLISH SAID *unto the wise, give us of your oil, for our lamps are gone out.*"

The evidence against them rests on the declaration of Christ. He says, "five of them were wise, and five were foolish." Now, if all were christians, then all were wise. The terms wise and foolish are used in the scriptures, to designate the righteous and the wicked. . . . .

But were they not wise when they commenced their journey ? Did they not take oil with them, and afterwards become foolish by suffering their lamps to go

out? This is, doubtless, what they intended to intimate. But what was the fact? Christ asserts that they took no oil with them, and plainly intimates that their folly consisted in taking their lamps without oil. If they had one drop of oil, or one spark of light kindled by the oil of grace, the declaration of Christ cannot be true. Here lies the contradiction. Not that our Saviour contradicts himself; for he never said that their lamps had gone out. He only relates what the foolish virgins say of themselves. The contradiction lies between Christ and the foolish virgins. They would intimate that they had once had religion, and lost it; for say they, "*Our lamps are gone out.*" But Christ says no such thing. He says "they were *foolish, and* TOOK *no oil with them.*" . . . .
. . . .

The only difficulty in understanding this parable, seems to arise from taking it for granted, that what hypocrites and apostates say of themselves must be true, although it contradicts the plain declarations of Christ.

From this parable we learn—

1. That many professors of religion will be finally lost. "The kingdom of heaven"—*i. e.* the visible church, which is composed of those who profess the true religion—is likened unto ten virgins—five of whom were wise, and five were foolish. The church is composed in part of hypocrites, who will never be admitted to heaven.

This solemn truth, our Saviour has most explicitly taught. He would have us all remember it, and take warning. Many who belong to the same church, who profess the same creed, assemble in the same sanctuary, and commune at the same table, will never meet in heaven. In some churches, a majority may be saved. In Sardis, a few names only were found who had not defiled their garments. . . . . . "I say unto you, that many shall come from the east, and from the west, and shall sit down with Abraham, and Isaac, and Jacob, in the kingdom of heaven: but the children of the kingdom shall be cast out into outer darkness."

Will you say that such representations are uncharitable? But shall we pretend to be more charitable than Christ? If, my brethren, you do not suspect danger from this quarter, you reject and set at nought some of the most solemn warnings which our Saviour ever delivered to man. Many will take up with a mere empty profession of religion. "Strive to enter in at the strait gate, for many, I say unto you, will seek to enter in, and shall not be able." "When once the master of the house is risen up, and hath shut to the door, and ye begin to stand without, and to knock at the door, saying, Lord, Lord, open unto us; and he shall answer and say unto you, I know not whence ye are: then shall ye begin to say, we have eaten and drunken in thy presence, and thou has taught in our streets. But he shall say, I tell you, I know you not whence ye are; depart from me, all ye workers of iniquity. There shall be weeping and gnashing of teeth, when ye shall see Abraham, and Isaac, and Jacob, and all the prophets in the kingdom of God, and you, yourselves, thrust out."

This warning is delivered to professors of religion. Of them it is said, " Many shall seek to enter in and shall not be able." Many will stand without, knocking when it will be too late. And may not some of us be found among that number?

2. Persons who appear alike now, may possess characters widely different in the sight of God. "Man looketh on the outward appearance, but God looketh on the heart." No degree of exactness in externals, can determine the state of the heart. "He is not a Jew, who is one outwardly." Our Saviour speaks of some whose outward appearance was indeed beautiful, and yet he compares them to whited sepulchres, within " full of dead men's bones and all uncleanness."

Without a *beautiful* external appearance, we may safely conclude there is no religion. If true religion exists in any church or any individual, there must be outward appearance. The light must and will shine. But where the appearance is the same, there may be a great difference in the sight of God—a difference wide as that between light and darkness—holiness and sin—heaven and hell. . . . .
. . . .

3. It should be our great and constant object to be prepared for the coming of Christ.

All our views and aims, and every thing which we say and do, should have reference to that solemn event. Every moment we should stand prepared to hear the summons, " behold, the bridegroom cometh, go ye out to meet him." This is our business; to be ready now. If we are not, we do not live agreeably to our profession. Brethren, are you prepared to hear the summons? "Let your loins be girded about, and your lights burning; and ye yourselves like unto men that wait for their Lord, when he will return from the wedding." . . . .

4. Real christians, even the very best of them, are never too much engaged in religion. "While the bridegroom tarried, they all slumbered and slept."

There may be a misguided and false zeal. But true christian zeal—humble, holy love to God, can never rise too high. "All slumbered and slept." The Bible is full of complaints of the sloth and lukewarmness of christians, and loud warnings and exhortations to them to awake—to be zealous and repent. Every christian will hereafter look back and reproach himself because his heart was no more deeply and warmly engaged in the cause of Christ. At the hour of death, not one will have to lament that he has labored too hard, and been too much devoted to the service of Christ. At that solemn hour, every child of God will wake up as he never did before. The very moment he meets Christ in another world, he will doubtless blush at his past stupidity. Never will christians be sufficiently awake, till their hearts burn with an angel's flame.

5. We see in what lies the distinction between true and false professors of religion.

Not in the head, but in the heart. "The wise took oil in their vessels with their lamps." Here is something which they *took*, and which the others did not. It is a difference of *hearts*. The one has *oil in his vessel*, the other has not. One is solicitous mainly about his *heart*, that *that* may be replenished with all the christian graces. The other takes up with an empty profession. "He is a Jew, which is one *inwardly*, and circumcision is that of the *heart*, in the *spirit*, and not in the *letter*."

6. We learn from this subject, the true reason why so many professors of religion will be lost.

On this point, there is a difference of opinion. Some say, it is because they once had religion in their hearts, but have since lost it. So said the foolish virgins: "our lamps are gone out." But Christ has given us the true reason. He declares that they were foolish, and "took no oil with them." The reason why so many will be lost, is not because they have lost true religion, but because they never had it. They did not *begin right.* They took the lamp of profession without grace in their hearts. This was their folly. It was their final ruin. None are more likely to fail of salvation than persons of this class. To all such, the Saviour says, " Verily, I say unto you, publicans and harlots go into the kingdom of God before you."

. . . .

My brethren, in application of this solemn warning of our Saviour, what shall I say? Shall I exhort you without distinction, to persevere—to hold on, and hold out to the end? Shall I hold up to the view of all who hear me, that glorious promise, "he that endureth to the end, the same shall be saved?" Alas, my brethren, there is one class of professors of religion, who if they do persevere, if they do hold on, and hold out to the end, will certainly be lost. Such promises are often quoted for the encouragement of all who make any pretensions to religion. But, my hearers, we must sometimes warn you to pause and *examine yourselves.* If you are new creatures in Christ—if you have entered the *strait gate and the narrow way*—then go on— endure to the end and be saved. But if you have only

a name to live while you are dead, you are warned to stop. Let the fatal example of the foolish virgins serve as a warning to you, *now to begin with your hearts.* Suppose the search should be made throughout this congregation—that every heart should now be laid open—and that five out of every ten should be found who have no love to God—no light in them. Awful disclosure! What shall be done? All are traveling on together, and soon will their journey close. Shall they hold on, and hold out to the end? But some have no oil in their vessels. . . . . . .
. . . .
Brethren, are your hearts right with God? Are they replenished with all the christian graces? And do they burn with love to Christ, as you talk together by the way? *Have old things passed away, and all things become new?* If so, then go on—endure to the end, and you shall be saved.

But if your hearts are not thus prepared—stop where you are. Go no farther. "Turn ye, turn ye, for why will ye die?" Go back—for you are on the road to death. Go back, I entreat you, and enter the strait gate and the narrow way. Persevere a little longer—take a few more steps in your present course, and you will be forever too late. Make haste, for the time is far spent, and Christ is at hand. "The coming of the Lord draweth nigh." Haste thee, for the messenger of death is near; and "behold, the bridegroom cometh." Then they that are ready will enter heaven; and the door will be forever shut."

35

The Great Salvation.

How shall we escape if we neglect so great salvation?—HEBREWS ii: 3.

THE apostle had just been speaking of the glorious author of this salvation. He calls him "the brightness of the Father's glory, and the express image of his person." In view of his exalted character, and of what he had done and suffered for the salvation of sinners, the apostle warns us to *take heed;* "For if the word spoken by angels was steadfast, and every transgression and disobedience received the just recompense of reward; how shall we escape if we neglect so great salvation? Which at the first, began to be spoken by the Lord, and was confirmed unto us by them that heard him."

In discoursing from the text I propose to consider
I. In what the greatness of this salvation consists.
II. Who are guilty of neglecting it?
III. The import of the language, "*how shall we escape.*"

I. In what the greatness of this salvation consists.
It is a great salvation.
1. Because it delivers from great and awful punishment. The punishment denounced against the wicked is dreadful in its *nature.* "They shall have their part

in the lake that burneth with fire and brimstone, which is the second death." "The wicked shall be turned into hell, and all the nations that forget God." This punishment will be inflicted by God himself. "Vengeance is mine, I will repay, saith the Lord." When God arises to take vengeance, it will be inconceivably dreadful. "On the wicked God shall rain snares, fire and brimstone, an horrible tempest; this shall be the portion of their cup."

This punishment will be dreadful in its *duration*. The eternal happiness of the righteous, is no more clearly revealed, than the eternal punishment of the wicked. Those who shall be cast into the prison of hell, will have nothing with which to discharge their immense debt to the justice of God; and yet our Saviour has declared, "Verily I say unto thee, thou shalt by no means come out thence, till thou hast paid the very last mite." The duration of this punishment, is set forth in such language as the following—"They shall awake to shame and everlasting contempt"— "To whom the mist of darkness is reserved forever"— "To whom is reserved the blackness of darkness forever"—"Punished with everlasting destruction from the presence of the Lord, and from the glory of his power"—"The smoke of their torment ascendeth up forever and ever." But what decides the point, are these despairing expressions—"Cast into fire that shall never be quenched"—"Where their worm dieth not, and the fire is not quenched"—"Nigh unto cursing, whose end is to be burned"—"Whose end is destruction." If there should ever be a period in eternity when the wicked will be delivered from hell, this language would not be true. It could not be said, "their end is destruction." However long they might suffer in hell, their *beginning* would be destruction, and their end salvation. Abraham said to the rich man, "between us and you there is a great gulf fixed; so that they which would pass from hence to you cannot; neither can they pass to us, that would come from thence." And is not this a great and awful punishment? And is not deliverance from such a punishment, a great salvation?

2. It is a great salvation because it could be effected by nothing short of the death of the Son of God. "Redeemed, not with corruptible things as silver and gold; but with the precious blood of Christ." "Without the shedding of blood, there is no remission"—no not of a single sin—not the blood of a sinner—not the blood of an angel. The mystery runs back to the triune God. Nothing but the precious blood of the Son of God, can atone for sin. Here justice and mercy are gloriously displayed. For when Christ stood in the place of sinners, God did not in the least, suffer his wrath to cool. He said, "Awake O sword against my shepherd, against the man that is my fellow." Surely a salvation, purchased at so dear a rate, is a great salvation.

3. It is a great salvation, because it delivers from the reigning power and dominion of sin. It is not merely a deliverance from punishment, the effect of sin; but a deliverance from sin itself. "The wicked are like the troubled sea when it cannot rest; whose waters cast up mire and dirt." With their present disposition, they would be forever hateful and hating one another—tormented, and tormenting one another, by the rage and fury of their passions. Now it is the

glory of this salvation, that it delivers from the dominion of sin, and sets the prisoner free from all these dreadful evils.

The Christian who now exclaims, " O wretched man that I am," can add, "I thank God, through Jesus Christ our Lord." The author of this salvation, was "called Jesus, because he should save his people from their sins." This salvation is every way suited to those who hate sin, and who desire to be delivered from it as the worst of evils.

4. It is a great salvation, because it introduces those who accept it, into a state of complete holiness and eternal happiness, in the full enjoyment of God, and the society of all holy beings. There they will be adorned with every grace, which can render them happy in themselves, and lovely in the sight of God. " He will beautify the meek with salvation." They will be " accounted worthy to obtain that world." " Neither can they die any more, for they are equal to the angels." " Then shall the righteous shine forth in the kingdom of their father." And they shall sing " Salvation to our God, who sitteth on the throne, and to the Lamb forever and ever."

This, my hearers, is the salvation offered in the gospel. With a sense of the vast importance of the subject, let us inquire

II. Who are guilty of neglecting this salvation?

Need I mention the openly immoral? The covetous, drunkards, swearers, railers, thieves, and all liars, we are assured shall have their part in the lake that burns with fire and brimstone, which is the second death. All who live in open wickedness—all who speak lightly of religion and its professors, are convinced in their own consciences, and need not to be informed that they are guilty of neglecting salvation. Passing by these, I remark, that all who do not comply with the terms on which salvation is offered, are guilty of neglecting it. These terms are repentance towards God, and faith in our Lord Jesus Christ. All, therefore, who do not repent and believe, are, by the living God, charged with the guilt of neglecting the salvation of the gospel.

But is the awakened sinner, who trembles under the fearful apprehensions of divine wrath, and who cries earnestly for mercy, chargeable with this guilt? Christ says, "He that is not with me is against me." It is plain that all who do not repent, whatever else they may have done, shall perish. It is equally plain that all who perish from under the light of the gospel, whatever may have been their distress and their strivings, will be charged with the guilt of neglecting salvation, and of treading under foot the Son of God. It must be remembered, that this is a holy salvation. The name of its author is Jesus. He saves his people from their sins. Whatever sinners may do, for the purpose *merely* of escaping punishment, while they do not long for deliverance from sin, they are still guilty of neglecting the Saviour. "He gave himself for us, that he might redeem us from all iniquity." If, therefore, sinners do not desire deliverance from their sins, they do not desire such a Saviour. What the prophet says is true of them. "He hath no form nor comeliness, and when we shall see him, there is no beauty that we should desire him." All sinners desire to be delivered from punishment, and to be made eternally happy. But if this is all, they do not desire the salvation offered in the gospel; for that is a salvation from sin. Now, my hearers, do you desire this salvation? Is sin odious in itself? Is it your greatest burden, and that from which above all things, you long to be delivered? If so, then you desire the salvation of the gospel; and this salvation shall be yours. But if you do not desire to be delivered from sin, you do not desire the salvation of the gospel; and you do, of course, neglect it. Mistake not your hatred of punishment, for hatred of sin. Mistake not the fear of hell, for the dread of offending a holy God. "Devils believe and tremble." Let no one imagine that he desires the holy salvation of the gospel, while he cannot be persuaded to lead a holy life ; or while his repentance does not flow from supreme love to God. For here that salvation begins, which is to be consummated in complete deliverance from sin, and in perfect love to God and his law. However much the sinner may flatter himself that by his good wishes and laborious exertions, he is seeking salvation, if he does not now repent of sin, he is still under the condemning sentence of God's law, and stands charged with the guilt of neglecting the only method of deliverance.

I proceed to consider

III. The import of the expression *how shall we escape?*

It is an interrogation containing the strongest assertion that those who neglect the salvation of the gospel, shall not escape destruction. Merely neglecting salvation is sufficient to insure this result. Overt acts of wickedness are not mentioned in the text. It does not say, that those only who have been guilty of grossly immoral conduct, shall not escape. All that is necessary to render the sinner's damnation certain, is mere indifference and neglect. He need not scoff at religion, if he will only let it alone, and like Galleo care for none of these things, he will be lost. Those who are saved must strive, and run, and fight, and make great exertions; but to treat religion with neglect, is all that is necessary to destroy the soul.

If this salvation is neglected, all the sinner's schemes to escape, will utterly fail. I know that those who have hitherto neglected salvation, flatter themselves they shall in some way escape. But how will you escape? Do you presume that you shall repent and embrace the Saviour before life closes? But have not your hearts long been hardening under the gospel; and are they not becoming harder and harder every day? What reason have you to suppose you shall hereafter love what you now hate? Have you not great reason to fear, that you will continue to reject the offers of mercy, and die in your sins?

Do you imagine that you may, in some way or other appease the anger of God? But how can you appease his wrath, while you continue to reject the Saviour? God out of Christ, is a consuming fire. He is angry with the wicked every day.

Do you imagine that if you cry earnestly to God for mercy at some future time, he will certainly pity your case, and have mercy on your soul? But how can you presume on his mercy, if you refuse now to listen to his calls? His Spirit shall not always strive with man. Your day of grace is limited. There is a day—an hour—a moment—which if you pass impenitent, you are lost forever.

Do you flatter yourselves that you shall not die suddenly, but shall have sufficient warning of approaching death, to make preparation? But will God in condescension to your desire of continuance in sin, defer the stroke of death, lest you should go down quickly into hell? Those who are now in hell, once thought and felt as you do now. But "he that being often reproved, hardeneth his neck, shall suddenly be destroyed, and that without remedy." "It is a fearful thing to fall into the hands of the living God." How will you escape the solemn hour of death? How will you retain the Spirit, when these bodies shall turn to corruption, and crumble into dust?

The blood of Christ now proclaims mercy to the sinner, but it will shortly cry for vengeance on the guilty soul. "Behold he cometh in clouds, and every eye shall see him, and they also who pierced him, and all the kindreds of the earth shall wail because of him." And how will you escape the dreadful sight, ye murderers of the Son of God? Will you flee from the presence of the judge? Will you escape to the rocks and mountains for shelter; or will you dig into the bowels of the earth, to find a place of concealment? "The hour cometh when all that are in their graves shall hear his voice and come forth." The sea shall give up the dead that are in it. Death and hell shall deliver up the dead that are in them. The judge shall "sit upon the throne of his glory, and before him, shall be gathered all nations." In vain will guilty sinners now call to the rocks and mountains, saying, "Fall on us, and hide us from the face of him that sitteth on the throne, and from the wrath of the Lamb; for the great day of his wrath is come, and who shall be able to stand?" How will you escape? Who will be able to stand?

Do you expect to be overlooked in the transactions of the judgment day? Will you be unobserved in the vast assembly? But how can you escape the omniscient and all searching heart of Jehovah?

Will you resist? Have you an arm like God? Will you raise your feeble arm against omnipotence? How shall you escape?

Now the righteous judge descends. The long neglected Saviour comes. Every eye shall see him. Mercy turns to wrath. Sleeping vengeance now awakes. Rebels once deaf to his call, now shall hear his voice.

> "See the judge's hand arising,
> Filled with vengeance on his foes."

Jesus, whose charming and inviting voice once sounded in the gospel, shall now pronounce their final doom—*depart*. And how will you escape the dreadful sentence?

Horror and despair shall seize their guilty souls. And how will you escape the everlasting fire prepared for the devil and his angels? Now they that are filthy will be filthy still. When ages on ages have rolled away, how will you escape the wrath to come? How will filthy and horrid blasphemers pay the still increasing debt, or pass the fixed gulf, or enter the pure and spotless regions of immortal life?

Once more I entreat you, cast your thoughts forward into a boundless eternity, before you take the tremendous leap into the bottomless pit, and remember that the great salvation is still within your reach. What must be the reflection of that sinner who has lost his soul? "Once I enjoyed a day of salvation—once I heard the offer of pardon; but wretch that I am, I rejected it."

. . . .

He suffers on millions of ages, and then reflects again. "Once I enjoyed a day of salvation. Once, millions of ages back, I remember well the time—it was near the commencement of my being—I was for a moment on trial for eternity. I heard of heaven, and I heard of hell. I was warned to flee from the wrath to come, but I neglected the great salvation.

. . . .

Again, he suffers on millions and millions of ages, and then reflects again. "O, what a precious season I once enjoyed. But alas! it is gone forever. O, that I could once more hear the voice of the Saviour, and the sound of the gospel. But

> "In that lone land of deep despair,
> No Sabbath's heavenly light shall rise,
> No God regard your bitter prayer,
> Nor Saviour call you to the skies.
> No wonders to the dead are shown,
> The wonders of redeeming love:
> No voice his glorious truth makes known,
> Nor sings the bliss of climes above."

I look forward to blackness of darkness forever— Eternity—It is an ocean without a shore. O eternity, eternity!—But stop, my hearers,—Here you are, out of hell. This is the time which thousands will lament for their neglect of salvation, through a long eternity. Awake, sinner. "Behold now is the accepted time, behold now is the day of salvation. Now heaven, with all its glories, is brought within your reach.

"Salvation, O the joyful sound."

Yet a little while, my hearers, and time with you will be no more.

"Seize the kind promise while it waits,
And march to Zion's heavenly gates,
Believe and take the promised rest,
Obey and be forever blest."

36

Self-examination.

Examine yourselves, whether ye be in the faith.—2 CORINTHIANS xiii: 5.

THE Corinthians to whom Paul wrote, were disposed to inquire whence he derived his authority as an apostle; and *to seek a proof of Christ speaking in him*. But he exhorted them to turn their attention to themselves, and examine into their own spiritual state. As there was great danger of self-deception in relation to this momentous concern, this was the most proper employment for them. "Examine yourselves, whether ye be in the faith. Prove your own selves. Know ye not your own selves, how that Jesus Christ is in you, except ye be reprobates?"

The duty enjoined in the text is no less important to us than it was to the Corinthians, and is as binding on professors of religion now, as in the days of the Apostles.

There are two thoughts suggested by the text.

I. A person may be a christian, without certainly knowing it.

II. He who is a true christian may know it.

The first of these propositions is sometimes denied. It is said that the change in regeneration is such, that no person can be the subject of it, without a knowledge of the fact. But if this be true, the direction in the text is needless. It can be applicable to no one. It cannot be applicable to the sinner; for on this supposition, if he does not know that he is a christian, he must be a sinner, of course; and so for him to examine would be useless. It cannot be applicable to the christian, for if he knows that he is a christian, for him to examine would also be useless. Hence, it is evident from the direction in the text, that a person may be a christian without certainly knowing it.

Again—the same truth is evident from the nature of the case. A person must be born again before he can know it; and the method by which he is to ascertain whether he has been born of the Spirit is, to examine the exercises of his heart, and see whether he possesses the fruits of the Spirit.

That a person may be a christian without knowing it, is also evident from the fact, that rules are laid down in the Bible, by which we are to examine and try ourselves. All this would be useless, on the supposition that no one can be a child of God without knowing it.

But it is important here to observe, that we do not assert that a person can be a christian, and yet know nothing about it. He who is a christian has been born again—he has passed from death unto life—he has been called out of darkness into marvellous light. That a person can experience all this, and know nothing about it, is plainly impossible. No person can exercise faith in Christ, repentance for sin, and love to God, without being sensible that a great change has taken place in his views and feelings, respecting divine objects. But whether it is the change which is necessary to prepare him for heaven, he may be in doubt. The person who has experienced no important change in his views and feelings respecting divine objects, should conclude, of course, that he is without God in the world. But if he is sensible that some change has taken place, in order to determine whether it is the change required, he must compare his religious exercises with the rules laid down in the word of God. But notwithstanding a person may be a christian without knowing it, yet, as I proposed to show—

II. He who is a true christian may know it; that is, he may obtain satisfactory evidence of the fact.

This is evident from several examples recorded in the scriptures. Job could say, "I know that my Redeemer liveth." He was assured that Christ was *his* Redeemer. "And that he shall stand at the latter day upon the earth. And though after my skin, worms destroy this body, yet in my flesh shall I see God. Whom mine eyes shall behold, and not another." He felt assured that he should behold Christ for *himself*, as his portion, with his own eyes, in his own body raised from the dead. Paul could say, "I know whom I have believed, and am persuaded that he is able to keep that which I have committed unto him against that day." In respect to his christian race and his warfare, the event was not to him uncertain. "I, therefore, so run, not as uncertainly—so fight I not as one that beateth the air." He could say also, in connection with some of his Corinthian brethren : "For we *know* that if our earthly house of this tabernacle were dissolved, we have a building of God, a house not made with hands, eternal in the heavens." And thus also, the apostle John could say, "Beloved, now are we the sons of God, and it doth not yet appear what we shall be ; but we know that when he shall appear, we shall be like him, for we shall see him as he is." Here, the apostle's assurance is twice asserted. "Now are we the sons of God." And "we know that we shall be like him." Again—"We *know* that we have passed from death unto life, because we love the brethren." "And hereby we *know* that we are of the truth, and shall assure our hearts before him." From these and other passages of scripture, it appears that christians may arrive at the full assurance of hope ; and that some actually have attained to this assurance in the present life. It is a privilege to which all are exhorted to attain. "We desire," says the Apostle, " that every one of you do show the same diligence to the full assurance of hope unto the end." Again— " Wherefore, the rather, brethren, give diligence to make your calling and election *sure.*" And again in the text : " Examine yourselves, whether ye be in the faith." Although the full assurance of hope may not be common among christians, yet we see that it is attainable. We are also taught how it is to be obtained. It is by *self-examination,* and by giving *diligence.* It is owing to the neglect of these, that christians often walk in darkness. It is also owing to the neglect of self-examination, that many are filled with a vain confidence. They are disposed to think well of themselves, and to take things for granted without investigation. Hence they take up with a false and delusive hope—go through life deceived, and at last awake in awful disappointment.

How important it is, that the christian " be ready always to give to every man that asketh him, a reason of the hope that is in him with meekness and fear." And how important that those who are resting on a false hope, should be brought to discover their awful mistake, and to inquire in earnest, *what must we do to be saved?*

The difficulty of settling the important question whether we be in the faith, does not arise from any defect in the rules laid down in the word of God. The evidences of regeneration there stated, are plain and numerous; too numerous to be considered in a single discourse. Some of them, however, it may be proper here to mention.

Love to the moral character of God.
Faith in Jesus Christ.
Repentance for sin.
Love to the duties of religion.
Love to the brethren.

Many others might be mentioned; but let these suffice for the present. Respecting the evidences here enumerated, it may be observed, that they are all *sure.* Each one has the promise of salvation. The person, therefore, who possesses one of these christian graces, is interested in the divine promises. And he who possesses one, possesses the whole; though some may be more clear than others. So also, if a person is destitute of any one of these evidences, he is destitute of all; and it is certain that he is not a christian.

If a person has true love to God, it cannot be said that he has no *faith,* no *repentance,* no *love* to the *duties* of religion, or no *love* to the *brethren.* Now, in the business of self-examination, there may be several difficulties. I will mention two which are perhaps the most common.

The first is, when persons, who are sensible of no real change in their views and feelings, attempt to collect evidence when no evidence exists. Such persons, being ignorant of their own hearts, may, perhaps, be resting in the externals of religion. Here it may be proper to observe, that let the external conduct be ever so correct, if the feelings of the heart do not correspond with the rules of the gospel, it can be no evidence of a justified state. On the other hand, let a person's experience be ever so satisfactory to himself, yet if his general conduct does not comport with the rules of the gospel, this can be no evidence that he is a christian. Works without faith are *dead works*. And faith without works is a *dead faith*. Gospel faith and practice are inseparably connected. Persons may, and often do, for a long time search for evidence when it does not exist. It is not to be taken for granted that the result of every examination will be favorable. Thousands may flatter themselves that they are christians, when they are not. And although in some cases there may be a real difficulty in deciding on which side the evidence preponderates, yet in many cases the evidence against is clear and decisive, and the persons could not fail to see it, if they would look at the subject with candor, and with a sincere desire to know the truth. In such cases the whole difficulty lies in a reluctance to give up an old hope. The individuals concerned are unwilling to believe that their case is so bad. They cling to their old hope, for fear they shall never find a better.

The other difficulty to which I referred, exists in such a case as this. A person is sensible of an important change in his views and feelings, but for want of information, is unable to discriminate between true and false religious affections. He has new views, new sorrows and new joys, and has no doubt that a change of some kind has taken place. But is this the change required? Is it regeneration? This is the question which he finds it difficult to decide. Although it may often be difficult for a person to determine, on the whole, that he is a christian, yet in some cases it might not be difficult for him to determine that he is not. There are certain infallible marks of an impenitent state laid down in the Bible. The following are some. " The works of the flesh are manifest, which are these ; adultery, fornication, uncleanness, lasciviousness, idolatry, witchcraft, hatred, variance, emulations, wrath, strife, seditions, heresies, envyings, murders, drunkenness, revelings and such like : of the which I tell you before, as I have told you in times past, that they which do such things, shall not inherit the kingdom of God." Again. " Know ye not that the unrighteous shall not inherit the kingdom of God ? Be not deceived ; neither fornicators, nor idolaters, nor adulterers, nor effeminate, nor abusers of themselves with mankind, nor thieves, nor covetous, nor drunkards, nor revilers, nor extortioners, shall inherit the kingdom of God." While a person lives in the indulgence of any one sin here enumerated, it will be of no use for him to search for evidence that he is a christian.

Let us now consider the positive evidences of regeneration.

The true christian loves God. " He that loveth is

born of God, and knoweth God." Here is something new—something pleasant and delightful. Now the question is not whether he possesses love of any kind, but whether he loves God for what he is in himself— whether he is pleased and delighted with his moral character, because of its excellence. If this is the case, it will be the language of his heart : " Whom have I in heaven but thee ; and there is none on earth that I desire besides thee." He who has no love to God should conclude that he is a stranger to piety ; for " he that *loveth not*, knoweth not God, for God is love."

Again—the true christian believes in Christ. He receives him as his Saviour and rests alone upon him for salvation. In himself, he is lost and justly condemned to everlasting death, and he despairs of all help from every other quarter. But now the Saviour is unspeakably precious. He sees a beauty in his character, and a glory in the plan of salvation, which fills him with joy unspeakable and full of glory. He counts all things but loss for the excellency of the knowledge of Christ Jesus, his Lord. He is willing to commit his soul, his eternal all, unreservedly into his hands. Of the power and willingness of the Saviour, he has no doubt. The only question with him is, am I willing to embrace him, and trust in him ?

On the other hand, the person who says in his heart, that he would trust his soul in the hands of Christ, if he knew that he would save him—who thinks that he is willing, and that Christ is not ; has no evangelical faith, and no good evidence of an interest in Christ.

Again. The true christian possesses evangelical repentance. " Blessed are they that mourn, for they shall be comforted." Here the question to be decided is not simply, whether a person has sorrow on account of his sins; for there are two kinds of sorrow—selfish sorrow, or the sorrow of the world which worketh death; and godly sorrow which worketh repentance unto salvation not to be repented of. Selfish sorrow for sin, which arises from the fear of punishment, is the sorrow which Judas felt when he had betrayed innocent blood, and the sorrow which the lost spirits in hell will feel to all eternity. But godly sorrow, or true repentance, flows from supreme love to God. It implies hatred of sin, on account of its own odious nature. The true penitent has a broken heart, and this is his language: "Father, I have sinned against heaven, and in thy sight, and am no more worthy to be called thy son." "*Against thee, thee only have I sinned and done evil in thy sight.*" Though forgiven of God, he feels as if he could never forgive himself. The true penitent may sometimes doubt whether his repentance is genuine; but he who has no repentance—no sorrow for sin whatever, need entertain no doubt respecting his spiritual state. He may know that he has no interest in the divine favor; for "except ye repent, ye shall all likewise perish."

Again. The true christian loves the duties of religion. "This is the love of God, that we keep his commandments, and his commandments are not grievous." He loves to read the scriptures, to meditate on divine truth, to pray and to practice all the duties of religion. He feels differently at different times, but that he takes delight in these things, he has no doubt. The only question with him is, whether he attends to these things out of love to God, and a supreme regard to his glory;

or whether it is merely to quiet conscience, and to build up a self-righteousness. He knows, for example, that he must maintain secret prayer, or give up his hope. Now it is proper for him to inquire, whether he does not continue the practice without any love to God, merely to keep alive his hope. If he has grace in his heart, he will " delight in the law of the Lord, after the inward man." It will be the language of his heart: " I esteem thy commandments above gold, yea, above fine gold." If there were no future state, he would be unwilling to give up his present pursuits. He would still love to meet with the people of God, to read and hear his word, to pray and praise.

He would still speak of the glory of the Redeemer's kingdom, and talk of his power. On the other hand, he who does not delight in these things, but uniformly esteems the service of God a weariness and a burden, and more especially, he who lives in the constant neglect of known duty, need not doubt as to his character in the sight of God. He may know that he is in the gall of bitterness and bond of iniquity. For " he that saith, I know him, and keepeth not his commandments, is a liar, and the truth is not in him."

Again. The true christian loves the brethren. " We know that we have passed from death unto life, because we love the brethren." Here is danger of deception. Perhaps no person, whatever may be his character, can help respecting and approving of the christian character. Virtue is certainly preferable to vice. To the truth of this sentiment, the judgment and conscience of every sinner are constrained to give their assent. The person will scarcely be found, who will acknowledge that he prefers a vicious to a virtuous character; or that he loves the sinner, and hates the christian. But although the judgment and conscience may approve of the christian character, and although a person may love christians because he considers them as friendly to him; this is no evidence of regeneration. "If ye love them that love you, what thank have ye? For sinners also love those that love them." But that love which is evincive of the new birth, is entirely different from this. The true christian loves God's children, because they belong to Christ, and bear his image. This is the love of complacency. He delights in their society and heavenly conversation, and "esteems them the excellent of the earth."

Thus, my hearers, I have attempted to lay before you the evidences of a gracious state. Each one of you must examine for himself. No mortal can decide in your case. In this business, every individual must sit in judgment on himself. Deal faithfully with your souls. A false hope is worse than none. A mistake in this momentous concern is awful. Beware of building on the sand, for the trying hour is coming. Our business lies with the heart-searching God. Examine well the foundation on which you rest your hopes of heaven, lest you discover your mistake too late. On whatever foundation you build, remember well—remember all, that you are building for eternity.

37

The Rich Man and Lazarus.

There was a certain rich man, which was clothed in purple and fine linen, and fared sumptuously every day. And there was a certain beggar named Lazarus, which was laid at his gate, full of sores, and desiring to be fed with the crumbs which fell from the rich man's table: moreover, the dogs came and licked his sores. And it came to pass that the beggar died, and was carried by the angels into Abraham's bosom. The rich man also died and was buried; and in hell he lifted up his eyes, being in torments, and seeth Abraham afar off, and Lazarus in his bosom. And he cried and said, Father Abraham, have mercy on me, and send Lazarus, that he may dip the tip of his finger in water, and cool my tongue; for I am tormented in this flame. But Abraham said, Son, remember that thou in thy lifetime receivedst thy good things, and likewise Lazarus evil things; but now he is comforted, and thou art tormented. And besides all this, between us and you there is a great gulf fixed, so that they that would pass from hence to you, cannot; neither can they pass to us, that would come from thence. Then he said, I pray thee, therefore, father, that thou wouldst send him to my father's house; for I have five brethren, that he may testify unto them, lest they also come into this place of torment. Abraham saith unto him, they have Moses and the prophets, let them hear them. And he said, nay, father Abraham, but if one went unto them from the dead, they will repent. And he said unto him, if they will not hear Moses and the prophets, neither will they be persuaded, though one rose from the dead.—LUKE xvi: 19-31.

OUR Saviour had been discoursing to his disciples on the right use of property. He illustrated his subject by the parable of the unjust steward, which teaches us that we must all soon give an account of our stewardship.

We are informed that the "pharisees, who were covetous, heard all these things and they derided him." The language in the original is striking. It expresses the greatest contempt. At length, our Saviour turned and addressed them in the language of the text.

" There was a certain rich man, which was clothed in purple and fine linen, and fared sumptuously every day. And there was a certain beggar, named Lazarus, which was laid at his gate full of sores."

This is sometimes denominated a parable. But though the language is in a measure figurative, it cannot be shown that our Saviour was not describing matters of fact, which had fallen under his own observation.

At all events, the passage was intended to give us a correct view of the invisible world. It was spoken by him of whom it is said, " hell is naked and open before him, and destruction hath no covering."

Here is one who is rolling in splendor—faring sumptuously every day. Here is another, not only poor, but sick—covered with sores—laid at the rich man's gate, that he might excite his compassion—desiring to be fed with the crumbs which fell from the rich man's table. He was satisfied and thankful even for the crumbs. Whether he obtained his desire, we are not informed. He was not only poor and sick, but friendless. He had no one to dress his ulcers, and administer to his necessities. " Moreover the dogs," as being more compassionate than the human beings with whom he was surrounded, " came and licked his sores."

And it came to pass in process of time, that the beggar died. Doubtless death was welcome to him. He had long looked forward to it with joyful anticipation, as the end of sin and sorrow, and the introduction to that glorious rest which remaineth for the people of God.

Nothing is said of his interment. Some poor people, probably, carried him to his grave, there to rest forgotten by the world until the morning of the resurrection. But his soul was carried by the angels into Abraham's bosom. He was a child of God and an heir of heaven. Angels attended him in his last moments, to receive his spirit, and to conduct it safely to the mansions of the blessed.

The joys of heaven are set forth under the emblem of a feast. Abraham is represented as seated at the head, and Lazarus leaning on his bosom. O what a sudden and what a joyful transition. From being the companion of dogs, he awakes surrounded by a guard of shining angels.

"The rich man also died and was buried." When it was told that he was dangerously sick, his numerous friends doubtless felt the greatest solicitude. The most distinguished physicians were employed, and exhausted their skill to restore him to health; but in vain. "Riches profit not in the day of wrath." "No man hath power over the Spirit, to retain the Spirit; neither hath he power in the day of death, and there is no discharge in that war." The rich and the poor alike must lie down in the grave.

He was buried. At the time appointed, his friends far and near doubtless assembled at the house of mourning, to conduct him to the land of darkness. And no doubt some orator pronounced his eulogy, and consoled the mourners with the idea, that he had gone to a better world. In due time, in all probability, a stately monument was erected to his memory, that " he might rot in state." His friends mourned for a season, consoling themselves with the thought that he was happy in heaven.

But the omniscient Saviour informs us that "in hell he lifted up his eyes, being in torments." And what does he see? He "seeth Abraham afar off, and Lazarus in his bosom."

What follows is an interesting dialogue between heaven and hell.

"And he cried and said, father Abraham." He pleaded his relation to the father of the faithful, and doubtless supposed that Abraham would acknowledge the relation. "Father Abraham, have mercy on me, and send Lazarus that he may dip the tip of his finger in water, and cool my tongue; for I am tormented in this flame."

He cried for mercy, whether he ever did before or not. The smallness of the request deserves our notice. He did not ask for a full draught of water; but that he might dip—not his hand—nor his finger—but the tip of his finger in water—barely a single drop—and cool his tongue. His torments were great beyond description. Whether the wicked in the future world will suffer in literal fire or not, their sufferings will certainly be equal to the description here given. He requested that Abraham would send Lazarus. He doubtless regarded him as a benevolent man, and ready to administer relief, whenever it was in his power.

Now, what is the answer to this small request? You hear it from heaven. "Abraham said, Son, remember"—he addressed him in the kindest manner, although he was lost forever—"Remember that thou in thy lifetime receivedst thy good things, and likewise Lazarus evil things. But now he is comforted and thou art tormented. And besides all this, between us and you, there is a great gulf fixed"—fixed by the immutable purpose of God—" so that they which would pass from hence to you, cannot ; neither can they pass to us, that would come from thence."

The answer is two-fold.

1. It was improper that he should receive any mercy. He had received all his good things in his life-time.

2. It was impossible. Between them there was a great gulf fixed. A *great* gulf—an awful separation. There is no passage from heaven to hell, and none from hell to heaven.

And now he sends up another petition. " I pray thee, therefore, Father, that thou wouldst send him to my father's house, for I have five brethren, that he may testify unto them, lest they also come into this place of torment." Despairing of obtaining mercy for himself, he turned his attention to his brethren on earth, who had doubtless consoled themselves with the thought that he had gone to a better world—not because he felt any benevolent regard for the salvation of his brethren : but because he was sensible that their presence in hell would add to his own torment. Sinners who are lost will not wish the society of their companions in hell. And what errand did he wish to send to his brethren ? He knew their sentiments. They may have doubted the existence of such a place as hell. They may have thought that God is not such a being as to torment his creatures in the flames of hell. He did not ask the privilege of going himself, for he knew that that could not be granted; but his petition was : " Send Lazarus that he may testify unto them, lest they also come into this place of torment"—

that he may tell them their brother is not in heaven, but in hell—that no description which they had ever heard of the miseries of the wicked, equals the reality. Or perhaps his brethren may have believed that the wicked will be restored—that in process of time their sufferings will cancel the debt, and they will be admitted to heaven—send Lazarus that he may tell them that there is no passage from hell to heaven—that a great gulf is fixed as firmly as the immutable decree of the eternal God can make it—that those who are once lost, are lost forever. He felt confident that unless something more was done, his brethren would never be saved—that in their present state, and with their present sentiments, they would certainly be lost. This is clearly intimated in his request: "Lest they also come into this place of torment."

And now what was the reply? You hear it from heaven.

"Abraham saith unto him, they have Moses and the prophets, let them hear them." They have all the warnings contained in the Bible, and that is sufficient.

And what is the reply? You hear it from hell.

"Nay, father Abraham, but if one went unto them from the dead, they will repent."

And what is the reply? You hear it from heaven.

"And he saith unto him, if they hear not Moses and the prophets, neither will they be persuaded, though one rose from the dead."

Remarks.

1. Those who die christians go immediately to heaven.

The soul of the believer does not sleep between death and the resurrection. This is evident from the case of Lazarus. He was in heaven while the five brethren of the rich man were living on the earth. It is evident also, from the promise of our Saviour to the penitent thief on the cross. "And Jesus said unto him, verily, I say unto you, to-day shalt thou be with me in paradise." And Paul says," I have a desire to depart and be with Christ, which is far better." And here too, we learn that it is no fancy, that angels invisible to mortal eyes surround the dying bed of the saint, to conduct him to the paradise above.

Christian, you may be nearer to heaven, than you are aware. This night you may wake up surrounded by an innumerable company of angels, and the spirits of just men made perfect.

2. Those who die sinners go immediately to hell. Their souls do not sleep between death and the resurrection. The moment the soul of the rich man left the body, he awoke in hell, surrounded by devils and damned spirits. And this was while his five brethren were still living. "He that being often reproved, hardeneth his neck, shall suddenly be destroyed, and that without remedy." "How are they brought into desolation as in a moment; they are utterly consumed with terrors." "When they shall say peace and safety, then sudden destruction cometh upon them, and they shall not escape."

Sinner, you may be nearer to hell than you are aware. God may say, "thou fool, this night thy soul shall be required of thee."

How suddenly and how unexpectedly the sinner may be lost. "Hell," says one, "is a truth learned too late."

3. We learn from this subject that all sinners will pray, sooner or later.

"The wicked, through the pride of his countenance, will not seek after God." They cast off fear and restrain prayer. They say: " What is the Almighty that we should serve him, and what profit shall we have if we pray unto him ?" But when they are lost they will cry for mercy. The rich man in hell *cried*. He lifted up his voice in awful distress: " Father Abraham, have mercy on me." But it was too late. "Then," says Christ, "they shall call on me, but I will not not answer." It will do no good. They may cry long and loud, but not one drop of the water of life shall descend to those in hell. Not a leaf from the tree of life shall be blown across the great gulf. This, my hearers, is the world where prayer is heard.

> " Where are the living ? On the ground
> Where prayer is heard, and mercy found,
> Where in the compass of a span,
> The mortal makes the immortal man!

Soon it may be forever too late. Sinner, seek the the Lord while he may be found.

4. Those who lose their souls will remember what took place on earth.

"Son, remember." Memory and conscience will now perform their office well. They will remember all the joyful scenes through which they have passed. They will remember all the duties which they have neglected—the Sabbaths and precious privileges which they once enjoyed—all the sins which they have committed, and especially the sins of the tongue. Those who have trifled and made sport of the subject of religion—those who deny that there is any such place as hell—who labor to quiet their own fears, and the fears of others—who say that ministers wish to frighten their hearers—when they get to hell, will wish to come back and unsay what they have said. A great many do before they die. It was thus with Voltaire.

> "The Frenchman, first in literary fame,—
> Mention him, if you please; Voltaire! The same:
> With spirit, genius, eloquence supplied,
> Lived long, wrote much, laughed heartily, and died.
> The Bible was his jest-book, whence he drew
> *Bon mots* to gall the christian and the Jew;
> An infidel in health—But what when sick?
> O, then a text would touch him to the quick."

When he became apprehensive that his death was approaching, he offered his physician, Dr. Tronchin, one half of his property, if he would prolong his life six months. He informed him that he could not live so many days. He replied, "Then I shall go to hell, and you will go with me."

Thomas Paine, too, in his last moments, exclaimed: "O Lord, help me. O Lord, help me. O Christ, help me. O Christ, help me."

All the warnings—all the kind invitations—and all the sermons which you have heard and slighted, you will then remember.

> "The sacred temple's sounding roof,
> The voice of mercy and reproof,
> Regarded never"—

Will then be remembered. And this very discourse to which you are now listening, will hereafter be distinctly recollected, and can never be forgotten.

4. We see what the damned would say, were they to come back to this world.

They could not state what they have seen and felt, better than in the language of the Bible. They could not describe the torments of the lost in better language than they are described in the text. They would call upon their companions to repent, lest they come to the place of torment. This, we know, is the substance of what they would say.

5. We learn that sinners in hell, are not yet entirely convinced of the awful depravity of the human heart. The rich man thought that moral suasion, if increased to a certain amount, would be sufficient to bring sinners to repentance. "If one went unto them from the dead, they will repent." But he labored under a mistake.

Finally. We learn from this subject that our Saviour was a very plain preacher. Never man spake like this man. Some think they should like to hear Christ preach. But while, it is true, that he spoke in the most melting strains to the penitent, it is also true that none ever preached so much terror to the wicked. Who is it that says, "Wide is the gate, and broad is the way which leadeth to destruction, and many there be who go in thereat?" Who is it that says, "Because strait is the gate, and narrow is the way which leadeth unto life, and few there be that find it?" Who is it that says, "Ye serpents, ye generation of vipers, how can ye escape the damnation of hell?" Who is it that speaks of the worm that shall never die, and of the fire that shall never be quenched? Who is it that describes in language inimitable, the solemnities of the last judgment, "Then shall the king say to them on his left hand, depart from me, ye cursed, into everlasting fire, prepared for the devil and his angels?" The discourse before us, of the rich man and Lazarus, is also a specimen. How solemn it would be, if a departed soul should come back from the invisible world, and enter this congregation. Do you wish to hear what such a soul would say? You shall be gratified. The Saviour holds him up, and makes him now speak to sinners in this congregation. He knows all the feelings of every damned soul in hell, and can tell us just what he would say. He hold him up to your view, and permits you to hear him speak. You hear him plead for one drop of water. You hear him beg that Lazarus, or some glorified saint may be sent to warn you. O with what importunity does he press upon you the duty of immediate repentance. "Nay, father Abraham, but if one went unto them from the dead, they will repent."

And now you hear a voice from heaven proclaim—and let it sound in every ear—let it ring in every conscience, "*if they hear not Moses and the prophets, neither will they be persuaded, though one rose from the dead.*"

38

The duty of Fasting, and the manner in which the duty should be performed.

And it came to pass, when I heard these words, that I sat down and wept, and mourned certain days, and fasted, and prayed before the God of heaven.—NEHEMIAH i: 4.

MOURNING and fasting are proper on certain occasions. Nehemiah was a good man, and a zealous and eminent reformer. The cause of God lay near his heart. He resided, at the time to which the text refers, with king Artaxerxes, in Shushan the palace. On a certain occasion, he was visited by some of his brethren from Judah. He made inquiry of the welfare of Jerusalem. "I asked them" he says, "concerning the Jews that had escaped, which were left of the captivity, and concerning Jerusalem. And they said unto me, the remnant that are left of the captivity there in the province, are in great affliction and reproach; the wall of Jerusalem is also broken down, and the gates thereof are burned with fire."

On learning this, Nehemiah was greatly afflicted, and "sat down and wept, and mourned certain days, and fasted, and prayed before the God of heaven."

I propose, in this discourse, to consider
I. The duty of fasting.
II. In what manner it ought to be performed.

I. Fasting in all ages, and among all nations, has been practiced in times of calamity and affliction.

The Jews used often to fast when experiencing the judgments of heaven, and when about to engage in any important undertaking.

Some of their fasts were national. Some less general, were confined to certain bodies of men, and others to single individuals.

The Ninevites, terrified at the preaching of Jonah, proclaimed a national fast. "Jonah began to enter into the city a day's journey, and he cried and said, yet forty days and Nineveh shall be overthrown. So the people of Nineveh believed God, and proclaimed a fast, and put on sackcloth, from the greatest of them even to the least of them. For word came unto the king of Nineveh, and he arose from his throne, and he laid his robe from him, and covered him with sackcloth, and sat in ashes. And he caused it to be proclaimed and published throughout Nineveh, by the decree of the king and his nobles, saying, let neither man nor beast, herd nor flock, taste any thing; let them not feed, nor drink water. But let man and beast be covered with sackcloth, and cry mightily unto God. Yea let them turn every one from his evil way, and from the violence that is in their hands. Who can tell if God will turn and repent, and turn away from his fierce anger, that we perish not."

Thus it was with the Jews in the time of Esther, when all were condemned to die. She proclaimed a fast. "Go gather together all the Jews that are present in Shushan, and fast ye for me, and neither eat nor drink three days, night nor day. I also, and my maidens will fast likewise; and so will I go in unto the king, which is not according to the law, and if I perish, I perish."

No particular time is set apart by Christ or his apostles for the observance of this duty among Christians. Yet the duty is plainly revealed. It is clearly inculcated both by precept and example.

Our Saviour, in his sermon on the mount, gave his disciples directions on this subject.

"Moreover when ye fast, be not as the hypocrites, of a sad countenance; for they disfigure their faces, that they may appear unto men to fast. Verily I say unto you, they have their reward. But thou, when thou fastest, anoint thy head, and wash thy face, that thou appear not unto men to fast, but unto thy father which is in secret; and thy father which seeth in secret shall reward thee openly."

Our Saviour, when reproached by the boasting pharisees because his disciples did not fast so often as they, replied, "Can the children of the bridechamber fast while the bridegroom is with them? But the days will come when the bridegroom shall be taken away from them, and then shall they fast in those days."

We find that the apostles and primitive Christians were in the habit of practising this duty. Paul says, "Approving ourselves as the ministers of God, in labors, in watchings, *in fastings.*" Cornelius said, "Four days ago, I was fasting until this hour, and at the ninth hour I prayed in my house, and behold a man stood before me in bright clothing, and said, Cornelius, thy prayer is heard, and thine alms are had in remembrance in the sight of God." Anna, the prophetess, served God with fastings and prayers, night and day.

II. How ought this duty to be performed ?

Persons may fast, and still not offer to God an acceptable sacrifice. This was the case in the time of Isaiah. They fasted, they afflicted their souls, they lifted up their voice on high, they bowed their heads like a bulrush, and spread sackcloth and ashes under them, and yet the Lord would not accept their services.

"Wherefore have we fasted, say they, and thou seest not? Wherefore have we afflicted our soul, and thou takest no knowledge?" The Lord answers. "Behold in the day of your fast, ye find pleasure, and exact all your labors. Behold ye fast for strife and debate, and to smite with the fist of wickedness. Ye shall not fast as ye do this day, to make your voice to be heard on high."

Some may perhaps think that if they keep the day by abstinence from food, and afflict their souls for the time being, this is all that God requires. But this is a great mistake.

"Is it such a fast that I have chosen? A day for a man to afflict his soul? Is it to bow down his head like a bulrush, and to spread sackcloth and ashes under him? Wilt thou call this a fast, an acceptable day unto the Lord?" A bare outward observance of the day, however strict it may be, is not such a fast as God requires.

Nor is the duty performed by inveighing against the sins of others. To spend our time in scanning the lives of others, and declaiming against their sins, is not what God requires. To talk, and complain of the wickedness of others, is very natural, and very common. It is doubtless our duty to oppose and discountenance sin, wherever we see it. But we must remember that this may be done by the vilest of men, without any desire to reclaim the offender. The good man weeps over the sins of others. He prays for the sinner, and labors to bring him to repentance and reformation.

But to talk and declaim against the sins of others, without feeling any grief or sorrow of heart, and without praying for their reformation, is not what God requires. This is done by the worst of men. To talk of the sins of others with a kind of satisfaction, or to buffet others for their faults, is highly criminal in the sight of God.

To accomplish her nefarious purposes, Jezebel proclaimed a fast, and set Naboth on high among the people, falsely accused, and slew him.

To keep an acceptable fast, we are

1. To humble ourselves for our own sins. Each one must begin with himself, and inquire what have I done? What sins have I committed? This, however humiliating and painful, is absolutely necessary. No one can repent of his sins, till he sees and feels that he is a sinner. Each one must look into his own case and see what duties he has neglected, and in what sins he has indulged. He must take a retrospective view of his past life, and consider the number, and the aggravations of his offences. He must look into his own heart, and think how it must appear in the sight of a holy God.

When you reflect, my hearers, that every act, and every thought of your past life is perfectly known to God, have you no reason to blush—no reason to humble yourselves in his sight? Not to blush and be ashamed at our past sins, is a mark that our iniquity is full. "Were they ashamed when they had committed abomination? Nay, they were not at all ashamed, neither could they blush; therefore shall they fall among them that fall." But he that is truly humbled for his sins, can adopt the language of the prophet, "O my God, I am ashamed, and blush to lift up my face to thee my God, for our iniquities have increased over our head, and our trespass has grown up unto the heavens." "He that exalteth himself shall be abased; but he that humbleth himself shall be exalted." "God resisteth the proud, but giveth grace to the humble." "Humble yourselves, therefore, under the mighty hand of God, that he may exalt you in due time."

2. Confession of sin.

This is always humiliating; but without confession pardon cannot be obtained. Confession is as indispensable in order to obtain pardon, as repentance itself. God requires that we should confess, and that our confession should be according to the nature of our sins.

Some of our sins are of a public nature—some may be national—or we may have sinned as a public body, as a church, or parish, or town. These sins may be generally known; and hence it is proper to assemble, and with united hearts to confess them publicly to God. Thus Nehemiah, as we learn from the context, confessed the sins of the Jewish nation. "And it came to pass, when I heard these words, that I sat down and wept, and mourned certain days, and fasted and prayed before the God of heaven, and said, O Lord God of heaven, the great and terrible God, that keepeth covenant and mercy for them that love him, and observe his commandments. Let thine ear now be attentive, and thine eyes be open, that thou mayest hear the prayer of thy servant which I pray before thee now day and night, for the children of Israel, thy servants, *and confess the sins of the children of Israel,* which we have sinned against thee; both I and my father's house have sinned. We have dealt very corruptly against thee, and have not kept the commandments, nor the statutes, nor the judgments which thou commandest thy servant Moses."

Hear also the confession of the prophet Daniel. "And I set my face unto the Lord God, to seek by prayer and supplications, *with fasting,* and sackcloth and ashes. And I prayed unto the Lord my God, and I made my confession, and said, O Lord, the great and dreadful God, we have sinned, and have committed iniquity, and have done wickedly, and have rebelled, even by departing from thy precepts and from thy judgments. Neither have we hearkened unto thy servants the prophets which spake in thy name to our kings, our princes, and our fathers, and to all the people of the land. O Lord, righteousness belongeth unto thee, but unto us, confusion of faces, as at this day; to the men of Judah, and to the inhabitants of Jerusalem, and unto all Israel that are near, and that are far off, through all the countries whither thou hast driven them, because of their trespass which they have trespassed against thee. O Lord, to us belongeth confusion of face, to our kings, to our princes, and to our fathers, because we have sinned against thee."

This confession included the sins of the whole Jewish nation, kings, princes and all.

And here I would remark, that it is highly proper, in times of spiritual declension, for the members of a particular church to assemble and make a public confession of the prevailing sins of that church, and to renew their covenant with God, and with one another. This should be done with prayer and fasting. Of this we have a striking example recorded in the ninth chapter of Nehemiah. "Now in the twenty and fourth day of this month, the children of Israel were assembled with fasting, and with sackcloths, and earth upon them. *And the seed of Israel separated themselves from all strangers, and* STOOD *and* CONFESSED *their sins, and the iniquity of their fathers. And they stood up in their place, and read in the book of the law of the Lord their God, one fourth part of the day; and another fourth part, they confessed, and worshipped the Lord their God.*"

Some of our sins may be of a less public nature—as wrong feelings, or improper conduct between families, or single individuals, and known only to those. In such cases, the command of God is, "Confess your faults one to another, and pray one for another, that ye may be healed."

Others may be known only to God and ourselves. Here is work for every sinner. It lies between God and your own conscience. Here no friend can follow you, to detect your secret sins, or to bring out your hidden iniquities. Secret sins, and sins of the heart, must all be brought out and slain before the Lord. These are the sins which damn the soul. "Out of the heart," says our Saviour, "proceed evil thoughts, adulteries, fornication, murders, thefts, covetousness, wickedness, deceit, lasciviousness, blasphemy, pride, foolishness."

Some there are, who may indeed appear beautiful without, whom Christ compares to whited sepulchres, which are within full of dead men's bones, and all uncleanness. One single secret sin indulged, and cherished in the heart, unconfessed, and unrepented of, will destroy the soul. "Thus saith the Lord, O Jerusalem, wash thine heart from wickedness, that thou mayest be saved; how long shall thy vain thoughts lodge within thee?" "What! know ye not that your body is the temple of the Holy Ghost? If any man defile the temple of God, him shall God destroy."

That sinner who will not call his own heart to a strict account—who will not accuse and condemn himself, will be accused and condemned of God. "He that covereth his sins shall not prosper." "If we regard iniquity in our heart, the Lord will not hear us." "If we confess our sins, he is faithful and just, to forgive us our sins, and to cleanse us from all unrighteousness." Then "let the wicked forsake his way, and the unrighteous man his thoughts, and let him return unto the Lord, and he will have mercy upon him, and to our God, and he will abundantly pardon." "He that confesseth and forsaketh his sins, shall find mercy."

The difficulty and pain of breaking off from sin may be great. The contest may be long and arduous. But by prayer and fasting the victory may be won. And it must be won, or the soul is lost.

3. A thorough reformation.

It is not that we appear to reform for a day, but that we do it effectually—that we not only repent for the time being, but that we bring forth fruit meet for repentance.

We must do all in our power to repair the injury done to our neighbor, and to the cause of God.

Have any of you been unjust in your dealings? Now is the time to make restitution. Have any of you neglected your duty to the poor? It is the appropriate business of this day to search out the objects of charity, and to supply their wants.

Do quarrels, or unhappy divisions exist between families, or individuals. Let them be settled. In obedience to the divine command, "Execute true judgment, and show mercy and compassion every man to his brother; and oppress not the widow, nor the fatherless, the stranger, nor the poor; and let none of you imagine evil against his brother."

After reproving the Jews for their hypocritical fastings, and their complaints that the Lord would not hear them, God, by his prophet proceeds to describe an acceptable fast.

"Is not this the fast that I have chosen?—to loose the bands of wickedness, to undo the heavy burdens, to let the oppressed go free, and that ye break every yoke? Is it not to deal thy bread to the hungry, and that thou bring the poor that are cast out to thy house? When thou seest the naked that thou cover him, and that thou hide not thyself from thine own flesh?"

He then describes the happy effects which will follow.

"Then shall thy light break forth as the morning, and thy health shall spring forth speedily; and thy righteousness shall go before thee, and the glory of the Lord shall be thy rere-ward. Then shalt thou call, and the Lord shall answer, thou shalt cry, and he shall say, here I am. If thou take away from the midst of thee the yoke, the putting forth of the finger and speaking vanity; and if thou draw out thy soul to the hungry, and satisfy the afflicted soul; then shall thy light rise in obscurity, and thy darkness be as the noon-day. And the Lord shall guide thee continually, and satisfy thy soul in drought, and make fat thy bones; and thou shalt be like a watered garden, and like a spring of water, whose waters fail not. And they that shall be of thee, shall build the old waste places; thou shalt raise up the foundations of many generations, and thou shalt be called the repairer of the breach, the restorer of paths to dwell in. If thou turn away thy foot from the Sabbath, from doing thy pleasure on my holy day, and call the Sabbath a delight, the holy of the Lord, honorable, and shalt honor him, not doing thine own ways, nor finding thine own pleasure, nor speaking thine own words, then shalt thou delight thyself in the Lord; and I will cause thee to ride upon the high places of the earth, and feed thee with the heritage of Jacob thy father; for the mouth of the Lord hath spoken it."

39

Sinners entreated to be reconciled to God.

Now then, we are ambassadors for Christ, as though God did beseech you by us, we pray you in Christ's stead, be ye reconciled to God.—2 CORINTHIANS V : 20.

WERE an ambassador sent from a foreign power with a message to this assembly, every ear would be attentive to hear it. But the message of an earthly sovereign is not what you are now called upon to hear, but a message from the court of heaven. It is addressed to every impenitent sinner. "Now, then, we are ambassadors for Christ; as though God did beseech you by us, we pray you in Christ's stead," that you will listen to the message and comply with its demands, the sum of which is, "be ye reconciled to God."

The text contains a summary of the apostles' preaching, not only to the Corinthians, but to mankind generally. Wherever they went, this was their message to sinners, "we pray you in Christ's stead, be ye reconciled to God."

Let us consider the duty of an ambassador in delivering his message.

His great business is, to publish the treaty of peace, and to set before sinners the terms of reconciliation. In doing this, he is bound inviolably to adhere to the instructions of his divine Master. From these instructions he must not depart in the least degree. He must "justify the ways of God to man." He must hold up the character of God as a holy and righteous sovereign, who claims the love and obedience of all his subjects. He must hold up the character of the sinner as odious in the eyes of infinite purity, as a lost and guilty criminal under the condemning sentence of God's holy law. On the one hand he must bring into view the glorious gospel, with all its melting invitations, and promises of eternal peace and joy. On the other, he must bring into view the broken law, and wrath of God as "revealed from heaven against all ungodliness and unrighteousness of men," and point the sinner to the regions of despair, and never-ending torments in hell. By the mercies of God, he must beseech, and by the terrors of the Lord he must endeavor to persuade men to be reconciled to God.

"As though God did beseech you by us." Here mark the divine condescension. God beseeches. By whom? By his faithful ambassadors. Does God beseech? Then the ambassador is not to deliver his message in the name of a dying man, but in the name, and by the authority of the living God. And thus he must come in the name of God, and deliver his whole message, without regard either to the love or hatred of men. Says the faithful ambassador who penned the words of the text, "Even so we preach, not as pleasing men, but God, who trieth our hearts." "Do I seek to please men? For if I yet pleased men, I should not be the servant of Christ."

"We pray you in Christ's stead." Here again, you will mark the same condescension. Christ still retains his compassion for sinners. He still pleads with them by his ambassadors, who are to stand and plead—beseeching hard-hearted rebels to be reconciled to God. This is their great business. It is all that they can do.

It is proposed

I. To show what is implied in being reconciled to God.

The Scriptures have decided this point with great clearness. It involves whatever is essential to the Christian character.

1. It implies a change from the state of an enemy to that of a friend. All are by nature children of wrath, enemies, unreconciled to God. Hence it is asserted in the context, "If any man be in Christ, he is a new creature; old things are passed away; behold all things are become new." This is essential. Love is the distinguishing characteristic of friendship. Supreme love to God for what he is in himself, is indispensable. "He that loveth is born of God, and knoweth God. But he that loveth not, knoweth not God, for God is love." All, therefore, who have not been born of the Spirit, are unreconciled. They still possess the carnal mind which is enmity against God.

2. Reconciliation to God implies love to his law. This is a perfect transcript of his moral character. Love to God, and love to his law, are, therefore, essentially the same. "O how love I thy law." "I delight in the law of the Lord after the inward man." This is the language of a heart reconciled to God. And the person who is truly reconciled, not only delights in the precepts of the law, but he acquiesces in its penalty. Its condemning sentence appears to him to be right.

3. Reconciliation to God implies a willingness to accept salvation on the terms proposed in the gospel.

The satisfaction which Christ made on the cross, is called a reconciliation on the part of God. This as committed to the apostles, is called the *ministry* and *word* of reconciliation. Now those and those only who are pleased with the plan of salvation, can be saved. The treaty of peace was formed in the counsels of eternity. God claims the right of prescribing the terms of reconciliation, without consulting the notions and feelings of men. That God should act in this manner is both just, and merciful. It is just because God is the offended party, and man the offending party. It is surely improper for the condemned criminal to prescribe to his judge the terms on which he shall be pardoned.

It is merciful, because man, being a sinner justly condemned, has no claims to salvation on any terms whatever.

Hence we find that the Scriptures speak of God's reconciling the world unto himself—not of his being reconciled to the world, or to their plans of salvation. But the fact that Christ has died, and that a way of salvation has been provided, does not settle the question whether the sinner will be saved. If he is displeased with the plan of salvation, and does not freely subscribe with his hand unto the Lord, instead of being saved, he will fall under an aggravated condemnation.

Mankind are naturally opposed to the gospel plan of salvation. Else why is there an enemy to God among all those who have once heard the gospel? Why do not all at once comply with the terms of salvation? Why is there so much opposition to the doctrines of the gospel? This subject explains the reason. Men are unreconciled to God. The fact that the carnal mind is enmity against God, accounts for all this opposition. That persons are opposed to the doctrines which they hear from the pulpit, is no evidence that those doctrines are not true. A previous question remains to be settled. Are these persons reconciled to God? Have they been born again? If not, opposition is to be expected. If the carnal heart is not opposed to the truth, the Bible is not true. Corrupt sentiment will be pleasing to a corrupt heart. Show me a scheme of doctrines with which mankind are naturally pleased, and I will show you one that never came from heaven. The very fact that sinners are unreconciled to God, implies that they are not pleased with the terms of reconciliation. If they were not opposed to these terms, there would be no necessity of beseeching them to be reconciled. They would be reconciled of course.

That mankind are not reconciled to the terms of salvation, is evident not only from the conduct of thoughtless sinners, but of those who are awakened to a sense of their sin and danger. One would suppose that the gospel of reigning grace, and the glad tidings of a Saviour, would be embraced with the utmost readiness by such sinners;—that they would at once individually exclaim in transports of joy, "This is the Saviour I want. This is the salvation suited to my condition." But alas! even the convicted sinner, however clearly he may see his lost condition, and however great may be his distress, will not come to Christ that he might have life. He continues to inquire, "What must I do to be saved?" and the gospel answer, repent, and believe on the Lord Jesus Christ, gives him no relief. His proud heart will not submit to these terms. But let such remember that the terms of salvation will never be altered. The sinner must repent or perish.

Having shown what is implied in being reconciled to God, I proceed

II. To beseech my impenitent hearers to be thus reconciled.

My business now lies directly with the enemies of God; for they only need to be reconciled. An enemy to God! Where can the individual be found, on whom God has fastened this charge? The text takes it for granted that *all* to whom the gospel is sent, are in a state of enmity to God. The king of heaven would not send his ambassadors to his faithful subjects, to beseech them to be reconciled to their friend whom they supremely love. But multitudes who yield some general assent to the truths of the gospel, are not convinced that they are unreconciled to God. Many assert that they never were his enemies, that they were always reconciled to him. If this be so, they are not lost, and Christ has nothing to do with them, for he "came to seek and to save that which was lost."

Numbers who have long imagined themselves at peace with God, have only been at ease in Zion. This was the case of the great body of the Jewish nation, and of Paul himself, who after the straitest sect of their religion lived a pharisee, until he was awakened by the voice of the Son of God, "Saul, Saul, why persecutest thou me?" And of his brethren, the Israelites, he says, "I bear them record, that they have a zeal of God, but not according to knowledge."

It was over the case of such that he wept. "For many walk, of whom I have told you often, and tell you now even weeping, that they are the enemies of the cross of Christ."

And do you, my hearers, plead not guilty? No child of Adam can stand up before his judge, and say, I am innocent. All the subjects of divine grace, were once unreconciled to God, and " were by nature children of wrath even as others." " You who were sometime alienated, and enemies in your mind by wicked works, yet now hath he reconciled."

Have you become reconciled to God? You have seen what is implied in becoming reconciled.

It implies a change from the state of an enemy to that of a friend. Are you conscious of having experienced such a change? Do you now hate what you once loved, and love what you once hated? Do you delight in communion with God? Is it the language of your heart, " whom have I in heaven but thee, and there is none on earth that I desire besides thee?" Or is the thought of a present, holy, heart-searching God, a terror to your minds? Do you cherish the secret wish that there were no God that you might sin without restraint? Do you dismiss, as much as possible, serious thoughts from your minds, that you may enjoy the pleasures of sin undisturbed?

Love to the divine law is another evidence of reconciliation. " If a man love me," says Christ, " he will keep my words." " This is the love of God, that we keep his commandments, and his commandments are not grievous." Do you love God's law, and strive to obey it? Or do you live in the neglect of known duty? Do you murmur at the strictness of the law, and find more delight in forbidden paths, than in walking in the strait and narrow way to life? Do you cast off fear and restrain prayer? Are you ashamed to confess Christ before men? Are you more anxious to secure the friendship of the world, than the approbation of God? If so, there can be no doubt as to your true character and condition. "Whosoever will be the friend of the world, is the enemy of God."

Reconciliation to God, as we have seen, implies also a willingness to accept salvation on the terms which God proposes.

Are you pleased with the terms of salvation? If you are, you have doubtless complied with them. Have you repented and believed in Christ? If not, why? No reason can be assigned but the opposition of your hearts. If you were pleased with the terms of salvation, you would not remain in impenitence and unbelief another moment.

Many, I am aware, express strong desires for salvation, and sometimes say they would give all the world, if they had it, for an interest in the divine favor, while they have never found in their hearts, to feel the least degree of contrition for their sins, or the least degree of love and gratitude to the God who made them, and the Saviour who died for them. Whatever value such individuals may place on a heaven of eternal happiness, they do actually prefer sin to all things else;—and in spite of the offers of eternal life, the calls of a bleeding Saviour, the invitations, commands, and threatenings of Almighty God, they are now forcing their way down to eternal perdition.

Let me ask again, have you become reconciled to God?

To all who do not love God supremely, delight in his law, and render cheerful obedience to its precepts, and who do not acknowledge the justice of its penalty, and weep over their unreasonable transgressions—to all who are not willing to be saved on the humbling terms of the gospel, and to enlist under the Redeemer's banner, and who do not rejoice that Jehovah reigns, I have a message from God. It is a case of life and death to your souls; and as such I beseech you to regard it.

What now is the cause of this enmity between you and God? Has God ever injured you? Has he ever dealt unkindly with you? What have you to allege against his character, against his law, or against this treaty of peace?

Do you ask what God requires of you? The answer is plain. "Be ye reconciled to God." This is what God claims. And from this we cannot depart without entering on forbidden ground. He claims the heart. And from this we cannot depart, without disloyalty to God. Individuals and nations may negotiate a treaty of peace, though the heart be not engaged. An outward reconciliation may be effected, while the heart remains the same. But not so with God. He looketh on the heart. If that be withheld, "to what purpose is the multitude of your sacrifices unto me, saith the Lord?" If the heart be not engaged, however sinners may treat about a reconciliation, their insolence is met with this repulsive demand, "who hath required this at your hand?" Without this, not a step can be taken towards settling your peace with God.

And now all things are ready; and God is inviting and beseeching you to accept his mercy? What is the reply of your heart? Do you not like the terms of this treaty? You are required only to be *reconciled to God*. What can be more reasonable than this? Is it hard that you should be required to love God?—to feel sorrow for sin?—to confess and forsake it? Is this hard? Or is sin so lovely, and so desirable, that it appears hard and unreasonable that you should be required to hate and oppose it with all your heart? Why then will you not renounce it? Is sin so noble a thing in itself, and so desirable in its consequences, that you cannot part with it—that you will lay down your life—your eternal life for its sake? Your love of sin is all the excuse you have, or can have. Or will you plead your *inability?* What! cannot be reconciled to God! Cannot feel sorrow for sin! Cannot cease to rebel against the king of heaven! What an acknowledgment is this! Out of thine own mouth, wilt thou be condemned. If, indeed, you are so opposed to God, that you cannot feel sorrow for sin, this is the very reason why you ought to be condemned. The harder it is for you to repent and love God, the more wicked you are, and the greater will be your condemnation.

God himself is beseeching you to be reconciled. And why do you not obey? Have your pride and stubbornness risen to such a pitch, that you will not do the most reasonable thing, though God beseeches you?

In the name of God I come to beseech you to *be reconciled*. Why will you stand out against the will of heaven? You are on the side of his enemies. The prince of darkness, ever since his first rebellion, has been attempting to rear his kingdom within the limits of Jehovah's empire. But how feeble are all his attempts. "He that sitteth in the heavens shall laugh. The Lord shall have them in derision." "For he hath prepared his throne in the heavens, and his kingdom ruleth over all." Why then will you continue this unequal contest with your God? He is the rightful Sovereign of the Universe, and claims a throne in every heart. You are under infinite obligations to him as your Creator and constant preserver, and are therefore bound to obey him.

God possesses all excellence in himself, and on this account he deserves the supreme love of all his rational creatures. It is the duty even of the fallen angels to love him, for their rebellion has not cancelled their obligations. While God is on the throne, all his enemies, whether on earth, or in hell, will be forever criminal for not loving him, their torments notwithstanding. For on what principle, can the prince of darkness justify his conduct in maintaining eternal war with the king of heaven? But while you continue unreconciled to God, you virtually justify all the rebellion of wicked men and devils. And are you willing to be the apologists of the devil and his angels?

Again—consider what God has done for your salvation. The gift of a Saviour was not an act of justice to our world. Sinners had no right to demand the blood of the Son of God to atone for their guilt. Why then should he come to our world with a message of peace? Why not take on him the nature of angels, and extend pardoning mercy to those of them who had fallen? Though this has not been done, they are not justified in continuing in rebellion against God. No more would man have been justified, if Christ had never died.

But let us suppose that Christ had left the race of Adam, and gone down to redeem the fallen angels; should we not have been astonished at the mercy of God to them? And had those rebels mocked and insulted the beloved Son of God, and in their hellish rage had stripped him, crowned him with thorns, nailed him to the cross, and put him to death, would you not have thought this to be heaven-daring wickedness? What depravity, think ye, would this conduct have manifested to the Universe?

Be astonished, O ye heavens! This Saviour has concluded a treaty of peace for rebellious man, and now sends this message to you, " *Be ye reconciled to God.*"

In his name I plead. You may now disregard the voice of a dying fellow mortal. Let him be forgotten. But will you not hear the voice of God? "*Hear O heavens, and give ear O earth, for the Lord hath spoken!*" His commanding voice to every sinner present, is, " *Be ye reconciled to God.*" Have you not continued long enough in your rebellion? Have you not long enough resisted his call? And will you now again turn away from him that speaketh from heaven? Will you not hearken to the voice of the heavenly charmer?—your bleeding Saviour? Have you no repentance—not a tear to shed for the sins which nailed him to the cross?

O what amazing love invites! "He is the brightness of the Father's glory, and the express image of his person"—and is he unworthy of your love?

He is the delight of the Father—his only begotten and well-beloved Son, in whom he is well pleased—and is he unworthy of your love?

He is the lamb of God—the light of the heavenly world, and receives the homage of angels and glorified spirits—and is he unworthy of your love?

When from his exalted throne, he beheld the miserable enemies of God, sitting in the region and shadow of death; he left the bosom of his Father and with the keys of death and hell at his command, passed by the fallen angels, opened the prison-doors of rebel man, and lighted up his dreary abode with rays of celestial hope—and is he unworthy of your love?

Admiring angels, eager to bear the news of his entrance into our world, announced to the shepherds the birth of their incarnate God, and sang "glory to God in the highest, and on earth peace, and good will to man"—and is he unworthy of your love?

He was a man of sorrows, and acquainted with grief—He knew no sin, neither was guile found in his mouth—yet he was treated as a stranger and an outcast—as one unfit to live. The world knew him not. "Foxes have holes, and the birds of the air have nests," but your Saviour "had not where to lay his head." He was esteemed as less worthy to live than the vilest robber. Barabbas may live, but he must die. He was stoned, and found no rest in his passage through this world. He was falsely accused, unrighteously condemned, scourged, arrayed in a purple robe, crowned with thorns, a vast multitude of feeble worms hailed him with acclamations of mock homage, they spit upon him, smote him with the palms of their hands, and nailed him to the cross. There he yielded up the ghost. But he arose from the dead, and ascended to his throne of glory, from which he now invites you to his arms, and beseeches you to accept the salvation which he has purchased with his blood—and is he unworthy of your love?

"If any man love not our Lord Jesus Christ, let him be anathema maranatha."

I must close my feeble entreaties, and leave the event with God. This is, perhaps, the last time that I shall speak to you, in the name of God, on this side of the eternal world.

Sinners, must I leave you where I found you, unreconciled to God? Your business is not with a fellow mortal. I have done; and the whole remains to be settled between God and your souls. However hard you may think of this message, it is not mine. God beseeches—God commands your compliance *now*. And will you raise your feeble arm to oppose? God is on the throne; and have you an arm like God? However opposed you may be, yet God is on the throne, and what can you do? God is on the throne, and will dash his enemies in pieces like a potter's vessel.

Before I close, I must remind you, that with some of you this may be the last call—the last offer of peace which God will ever send you. But a different message will soon arrive. You will shortly hear again from your offended Sovereign. Before the setting of the sun, the messenger of death may be despatched with a commission to drag some guilty soul to his dread tribunal. He may now be even at the door.

By the mercies of God, and by the terrors of his wrath—by the joys of heaven and the pains of hell—by the merits of a Saviour's blood, and by the worth of your immortal souls, I beseech you, lay down the arms of your rebellion; bow and submit to your rightful Sovereign. Oppose, and still he will reign. "*For God hath set his king upon his holy hill of Zion,*" and hath sworn by himself that unto him every knee shall bow.

Once he has descended with a message of peace and good will to men. But shortly, he will be "*revealed from heaven with his mighty angels, in flaming fire, taking vengeance on them that know not God, and that obey not the gospel of our Lord Jesus Christ; who shall be punished with everlasting destruction from the presence of the Lord, and from the glory of his power.*"

40

The Government of God, matter of rejoicing.

The Lord reigneth, let the earth rejoice.—PSALM xcvii : 1.

THE simple truth contained in these words, is, that it is matter of rejoicing that God governs the Universe. I shall not spend time, at present, in showing what is implied in the government of God. I shall barely state, that he exercises absolute control over both the natural and moral world—that he " worketh all things after the counsel of his own will," and that no event great or small ever takes place which is not included in his eternal purpose, and which is not made to subserve his ultimate designs.

My present object is to show that it is matter of rejoicing that the Lord thus reigns.

I am aware that it is not thus regarded by wicked men. There is no doctrine to which the natural heart is more bitterly opposed, than that of the absolute sovereignty of Jehovah.

Wicked men are willing that God should govern the natural world—that he should regulate the motions of the planets, order the vicissitudes of day and night —of summer and winter—of seed time and harvest, and perform his pleasure in the animal, vegetable, and mineral kingdoms. They do not object to the doctrine of God's decrees, so far as it relates to the natural world merely. But when we speak of the government of God over the moral world, the enmity of the heart is roused. " What! does God reign over moral agents?"

All the objections which I have ever heard against the doctrine of decrees, or election, may be reduced to this one. If God operates on the hearts of men, and determines their actions, how can they be free? Though the objection is stated in different forms, yet the whole difficulty is resolved into this. My hearers, am I bound to obviate this difficulty? Does it lie against none but those who hold the doctrine of God's decrees? We will drop the doctrine of decrees—How is it then? Does God operate on the hearts of men, or does he not? If not, then we must not pray that he would do it. . . . .

No person can pray for himself without admitting that God can operate on his heart, and yet he be free. *" Turn thou me, and I shall be turned"*—*" Turn us O God of our salvation"*—*"Draw us and we will run after thee"*—*" Create in me a clean heart, O God, and renew a right spirit within me."* These prayers are found in the Bible. But persons ought not to have prayed in this manner, if God could not answer their prayers without destroying their free agency. Ought we to pray that God would destroy our freedom?—that he would make us machines? This no one will pretend. How then can we pray that God would work in us that which is well pleasing in his sight, if as the objection supposes, he cannot operate on our hearts without destroying our freedom. I would ask the objector, how he can pray for himself consistently with the views which he maintains? Can he deem it right to pray that God would do, what he believes God has no power to do?

No person can pray for others without admitting that God may operate on their hearts, and yet they be free.

It is a doctrine clearly taught in the scriptures, that a change of heart is absolutely necessary to prepare sinners for heaven. " Except a man be born again he cannot see the kingdom of God." We are also taught that God is the author of this change. " Born, not of blood, nor of the will of the flesh, nor of the will of man, but of God." But if God cannot operate on the hearts of men without destroying their freedom, then we ought not to pray that God would renew the hearts of sinners. Surely we ought not to pray that God would convert men into machines. However wicked mankind may be, we cannot pray that God would stop them in their career of sin, because he cannot do it without destroying their freedom. When sinners have proud stubborn and rebellious hearts, we cannot pray that God would make them humble, submissive and obedient; because he cannot do it without converting them into machines.

When sinners are invited to Christ, they all with one consent begin to make excuse. And Christ declared, " ye will not come to me that ye might have life." Sinners are then in awful condition. They will not come to Christ, and God cannot make them willing without destroying their freedom. What shall be done? It will be of no use to pray for them. Nor is it proper to pray for them; for surely we ought not to pray that God would do what he is unable to do.

We have dropped the doctrine of decrees, and the same difficulty still remains. The grand objection which is urged against the decrees of God, lies with equal force against the duty of prayer. If it be true that those who hold the doctrine of decrees, make men machines, it is equally true of those who pray. "Therefore, thou art inexcusable O man, whosoever thou art that judgest; for wherein thou judgest another, thou condemnest thyself; for thou that judgest, dost the same things."

Now whether we can see *how* God operates upon the hearts of free agents, or not, it makes no difference. We know but very little of the *mode* of divine operation. The question is, does God govern "all his creatures and all their actions?" Does he govern the actions of wicked men and devils?

No, says one—he cannot do it without destroying their freedom.

No, says another—he cannot do it without becoming the author of sin.

My present object is *not* to prove the doctrine that God does reign over all his creatures; but to show that it is a desirable thing—and that if he *can* and *does* thus reign, it is matter of rejoicing; and that if he does not thus reign, it is matter of mourning and lamentation.

If indeed God cannot govern human beings without destroying their freedom, or becoming the author of sin, and if he must resign his dominion over them, or let them alone, the Universe is truly in a melancholy condition. Let us for a moment contemplate the condition we are in. Cast your eyes abroad and see how the wickedness of men prevails. The adversary of souls goeth about as a roaring lion seeking whom he may devour. What then shall be done? God cannot govern these beings it is said without becoming the author of sin. The church of Christ is truly in a lamentable condition. What will become of the church we know not, for the devil has come down with great wrath. He will do all he can to destroy the kingdom of Christ on earth. He will do all he can to destroy heaven itself. What shall be done? We live under a government which can afford us no protection. Wicked men and devils are let loose upon us. They have entered the dominions of Jehovah, and are fast subverting his kingdom. Nothing can be done. The work of desolation must go on through eternity, for God cannot control the actions of his creatures without destroying their freedom, or becoming the author of sin. Thus my hearers, you see the condition we are in. It is gloomy and awful beyond description. And is it so? Must God forever look with regret and grief upon his creation, because he cannot stay the work of ruin carried on by his rebellious creatures?

That wicked men and devils very much need a governor, one who can control them at pleasure, you must, I think be convinced. And why then do you object to the absolute supremacy of Jehovah? Is not God qualified to reign?

He is infinitely wise. He knows perfectly what is for the best. There can be no objection to his government on this ground.

He is infinitely good. He is disposed to do every thing in the best possible manner. In this respect he is qualified to reign.

The only question relates to his power. But his power is as infinite as his wisdom and goodness. All things are possible with him. All his creatures are the workmanship of his hands—and has he made creatures whom he cannot govern? No, my hearers, the Lord reigneth. "He sits on no precarious throne." "He doeth according to his will in the army of heaven, and among the inhabitants of the earth, and none can stay his hand, or say unto him what doest thou?"

> "Rejoice, the Lord is king;
> Your God and king adore,
> Mortals give thanks and sing,
> And triumph ever more.
> Lift up the heart,
> Lift up the voice,
> Rejoice aloud
> Ye saints, rejoice.

41

Christ standing at the door.

Behold I stand at the door and knock; if any man hear my voice, and open the door. I will come in to him, and sup with him, and he with me.—REVELATIONS iii: 20.

THE text is the language of Christ. The methods which he adopts to secure attention to what he has to say, are many and interesting. He condescends to adapt himself to the language and practice of mortals.

"Behold I stand at the door and knock." This language is suited to rouse and attract attention. Who is he?—Where is he?—At what door does he stand?—At the door of thy heart, O sinner. Though invisible to mortal eyes, he is here, whether you regard it not.

He knocks. But how?

By his word——by a preached gospel——by the admonitions of conscience——and by the strivings of his Spirit. Nor is this all.

He *calls.* "Unto you O men, I call, and my voice is unto the sons of men." He calls by all the invitations of mercy contained in the Bible. "Whosoever will, let him take of the water of life freely." "Come for all things are now ready." Open unto me—open unto me, is the language of Christ.

He threatens. "Because I have called, and ye

refused—I also will laugh at your calamity." "Wo unto them when I depart from them."

"If any man hear his voice"—What is it to hear his voice? To pay a respectful attention to his word—to listen to a preached gospel—But this is not all. Hearing in the language of the text, implies obedience. "Incline your ear, and come unto me; hear, and your soul shall live."

"And open the door"—And what does this imply? Alas! it implies that the hearts of sinners are closed against Christ. They are closed

By prejudice.
By pride.
By unwillingness to receive the Saviour.
By excuses.
By unwillingness to see their lost condition.

Effort to prevent conviction, is an effort to exclude Christ from the heart. Thus sinners fortify their hearts, and make them as strong and stout against Christ as possible.

To open the door to Christ, my hearers, implies a willingness to see and feel what sinners you are. Painful as may be the sight, you must be willing to see it.

Again—to open the door to Christ, implies a willingness to turn out every opposing enemy. There are many idols lodged in the sinner's heart. With none of these, will Christ consent to dwell. If you love any object more than you love him, you are none of his. Search, then, every corner of your heart, and turn out every opposing enemy.

Again—to open the door to Christ, implies a willingness to confess the very worst of your sins, and to forsake them. "He that covereth his sins, shall not prosper; but whoso confesseth and forsaketh them shall have mercy."

"I will come in to him"—And what does this mean? It is a glorious promise that he will set up his kingdom in the heart of the sinner. And will God in very deed, dwell with men on earth? It is even so. Said one to our Saviour, "How is it that thou wilt manifest thyself to us and not unto the world?" He said, "If any man love me, my father will love him, and we will come and make our abode with him." Thus the strong man armed is overcome, and Christ sets up his kingdom in the heart of the sinner, who is translated from the kingdom of darkness into the kingdom of God's dear Son.

"And I will sup with him, and he with me."

It is with the sinner a joyful time. As when the prodigal returned, there was great rejoicing.

Reflections.

The text is introduced by a note of admiration. "Behold!"

Behold then, 1. The greatness of our Redeemer. He is every where present. And is it so?—that he knocks at the door of a sinner's heart here—of another's there—and of another's there? And is it true that he meets with two or three of his disciples assembled here—and with others assembled there, and in different and distant parts of the world at the same time? And is that true which he said on earth, "even the Son of Man, which is in heaven?" He must then fill heaven and earth at the same time. And O, what can those do, who deny the omnipresence of the Saviour?

He calls, "Come unto me all ye that labor and are heavy laden, and I will give you rest;" but if he is not omniscient, where shall they find him? They have no Saviour to go to. But, my friend, say not in thine heart, who shall ascend unto heaven to bring him down—or descend into the deep to bring him up—He is nigh thee—He is every where present. Sinners need not leave their seats, but only open their hearts, and he will take possession.

2. Behold the depth of Christ's condescension. The high and lofty One who inhabiteth eternity, dwelling in the high and holy place, condescends to take up his abode in the hearts of men. He comes not to the palace;—but to poverty and wretchedness—to sinners, and to those who have long rejected him—to those who have been ashamed of him. He does not knock at the door of his friends merely, but at the door of his enemies. He knocks at the door of the vilest of sinners.

> "When the Eternal bows the skies,
>   To visit earthly things,
> With scorn divine he turns his eyes,
>   From towers of lofty kings.
> He bids his awful chariot roll,
>   Far downward from the skies,
> To visit every humble soul,
>   With pleasure in his eyes.

O, the depth of his condescension! Is it possible! And will he stoop so low, as to take such vile sinners—heirs of hell—and make them the sons of God—heirs of God, and joint-heirs with Christ to an eternal inheritance?

3. Behold the extent of his willingness to receive

sinners. The sinner sometimes says, I am willing to receive Christ, but he is not willing to receive me. But what says the text? "Behold I stand at the door and knock." Does not this imply his readiness and willingness to come in? Nor is this all—He calls, open unto me—open unto me. Nor is this all—He says, "if any man hear my voice and open the door, I will come in." He positively declares that he is willing. Nor is this all—you may say, I am such a great sinner—I have rejected him so long, that he will not receive me now. But what says the Saviour? "If *any* man hear my voice"—vile as he may be, if he is on this side of hell—" if *any* man hear *my* voice and open the door, I will come in to him, and sup with him, and he with me."

If you are not now a Christian, permit me to say that you have never yet heard his voice, nor opened the door, nor been willing to receive him. You have never complied with the invitation in the text. The Saviour is ready and willing, but you will not come to him that you might have life.

4. Behold your danger. The Saviour *stands* at your door. He does not sit. He stands ready to enter or ready to depart. How long would you stand at the door of your neighbor, asking for admittance, if he should bar and bolt you out? And how long has Christ stood knocking? Even till his head is filled with the dew and his locks with the drops of the night. But he will not stand long. There will be a last knock. The Saviour can do without you; but you cannot do without him. He may say, as he once said to the Jews, "I go my way. Ye shall seek me, and

shall die in your sins." How often "*I* would," and "*ye* would not." "Behold your house is left unto you desolate."

I repeat, sinner, there will be a last knock at the door of your heart.

"Behold a stranger at the door,
He gently knocks, has knock'd before,
Hath waited long, is waiting still,
You treat no other friend so ill.

O lovely attitude, he stands,
With melting heart and loaded hands,
O matchless kindness, and he shows
This matchless kindness to his foes.

But will he prove a friend indeed?
He will, the very friend you need;
The friend of sinners—yes, 'tis he,
With garments dy'd on Calvary.

Rise, touched with gratitude divine,
Turn out his enemy and thine,
That soul-destroying monster sin,
And let the heavenly stranger in.

Admit him ere his anger burn,
His feet departed ne'er return;
Admit him, or the hour's at hand,
You'll at his door rejected stand."

42

Religion the only Source of True Happiness.

(ADDRESSED TO YOUTH.)

Happy is the man that findeth wisdom.—PROVERBS III: 13.

ALL mankind desire and seek happiness. The great inquiry is, " Who will show us any good?" But happiness keeps at a distance, and they are subject to continual disappointment. My young friends, if you have not yet found happiness in the enjoyment of the world, you are too late—you have lost your chance—you may give up the pursuit.

But try once more, and in another way.

> " I tried each earthly charm,
> In pleasure's haunts I stray'd,
> I sought its soothing balm,
> I asked the world its aid.
> But ah! no balm it had,
> To heal a wounded breast,
> And I forlorn and sad,
> Must seek another rest:
> My days of happiness are gone,
> And I am left to weep alone."

There is one source of true happiness. "Happy is the man that findeth wisdom."

True religion is denominated wisdom. And why? Because mankind despise it. The proud and haughty sinner looks down upon it with contempt, as a thing beneath his notice. But God regards it as the height of wisdom; and he would rescue it from this degradation by pronouncing it wisdom.

It is also called wisdom, because it is the highest wisdom of man to attend to the concerns of the soul. Wisdom in a worldly sense, consists in selecting the most important object, and adopting the best means to secure it—in laying a plan for time, which there will be no reason to regret. But wisdom in the text, is, laying a plan for eternity which will never be regretted. Sin is called folly, because although sinners affect to be wise, they will hereafter be constrained to alter their opinion, and to curse their folly to all eternity. The time will never come, when those who secure an interest in Christ, will regret it. They will not regret it on a dying bed. They will not regret it at the day of judgment. They will not regret it to all eternity. No one was ever heard to say, and no one ever will be heard to say, at the close of life, I am sorry that I have attended to the subject of religion. Let me die the death of the sinner, and let my last end be like his. This was never said. But directly the reverse has always been matter of fact. The sinner who now despises the subject of religion, will on a dying bed, and at the judgment day, curse his own folly for having neglected the concerns of his soul; and thus the sober judgment and conscience of all in heaven, and all in hell, will declare that sin is the greatest folly, and that religion is the highest wisdom. Hence it is calling things by their right names.

Or if, in the text, wisdom means Christ, as some suppose, it amounts to the same thing. Happy is the man that findeth wisdom; and happy is the man that findeth Christ. One cannot be found without the other.

> " Happy the man who wisdom gains,
> In whose obedient heart she reigns;
> He owns, and will forever own,
> Wisdom and Christ, and heaven are one."

I have selected this topic because the young often regard religion as a gloomy subject. But the reverse is true. Religion is not gloomy; but it is gloomy to be without it. This subject may be presented to advantage by contrast.

How gloomy must be the state of those who delight in nothing but what God forbids. All their pleasures are forbidden pleasures. With what stings of remorse, they must be accompanied. What a miserable portion this. And how gloomy the condition of those who have no other.

Sickness, and sorrow, and pain are the common lot of all, and no feeling heart could wish to interrupt the little joys of the present life, if there were no other.

How gloomy the state of those whose sins are all unpardoned. They are like prisoners under sentence of death, and every moment liable to be called forth to execution. "He that believeth not is condemned already, and the wrath of God abideth on him." " Because sentence against an evil work is not executed speedily, therefore the hearts of the sons of men are fully set in them to do evil." O what miserable sport. They know not but the next moment they shall be hurried into eternity.

How gloomy the state of those who receive all their

good things in this life. They have no title to heaven—no Saviour to go to. How gloomy the state of such an one on a dying bed. He has spent all his life in sin, and the day of salvation is now drawing to a close.

> "The work, the mighty work
> Of life, so long delayed,
> Repentance yet to be begun,
> Upon a dying bed."

On the other hand, how happy the man who delights in those things which God commands—who can say, " O how love I thy holy law." Religion is his amusement. "Her ways are ways of pleasantness, and all her paths are peace." He is pleased with the Bible—with its doctrines and precepts. He is pleased with the people of God. They are the excellent of the earth. He is pleased with the Sabbath, and with the ordinances of God's house. "I was glad when they said unto me, let us go into the house of the Lord."

How happy the state of those whose sins are pardoned. " Blessed is the man whose transgressions are forgiven, and whose sin is covered."

How happy the man who has God for his friend. Let all the world be against him, if God be for him, it is enough.

How happy the man who suffers all his evil things in this life. A few more pains, and his sufferings will be over. He may say, "I have fought a good fight, I have finished my course, henceforth there is laid up for me a crown of righteousness, which the Lord the righteous judge shall give me at that day."

> " What matter whether pain or pleasures fill
> The swelling heart one little moment here ;
> From both alike how vain is every thrill,
> While an untried eternity is near.
> Think not of rest, fond man, in life's career,
> The joys and griefs that meet thee, dash aside
> Like bubbles; and thy bark right onward steer,
> Through calm and tempest, till it cross the tide,
> Shoot into port in triumph, or serenely glide."

The last enemy is about to be slain. "O death where is thy sting ? O grave where is thy victory ?"

> " E'en now before we rise
> To that immortal state,
> The thoughts of such amazing bliss,
> Should constant joys create.
>
> The men of grace have found
> Glory begun below,
> Celestial fruits on earthly ground,
> From faith and hope may grow.
>
> Then let our songs abound,
> And every tear be dry,
> We're marching through Immanuel's ground,
> To fairer worlds on high."

We come then to the conclusion that religion is not a gloomy subject, and that the reason why it appears gloomy to you, is a consciousness that you do not possess it; and that if you were to die in this state, you must be lost forever. This is proved from the experience of all under conviction of sin. The distress of those who were pricked in the heart on the day of Pentecost, was not owing to their religion, but to the fact that they had no religion. But when their hearts were changed, and they found the Saviour, O how happy they were. They *gladly* received the word.

And so it was with the trembling jailor. He *rejoiced* in God. And so when Philip preached in Samaria, "there was great joy in that city." And so it is in our day. We have the testimony of thousands of youth, that religion is not a gloomy subject, but that it is awfully gloomy to be without it.

But suppose it were not so. It is absolutely necessary to the salvation of the soul; and what are the trials of a short life compared with a miserable eternity?

43

The Backslider Restored.

Restore unto me the joy of thy salvation, and uphold me by thy free Spirit. Then will I teach transgressors thy ways; and sinners shall be converted unto thee.— PSALM li : 12, 13.

THIS passage of Scripture reveals to us the method which God usually employs in commencing a revival of religion. He first revives his work in the hearts of his people, and thus prepares them to pray, and to labor successfully for the salvation of their fellow men.

This prayer of David carries back our thoughts to that period in his history, when, after having seen his lost condition, he was brought up out of the horrible pit and the miry clay, and his feet were set upon a rock, and a new song was put into his mouth, even praise unto our God. It was then that he first experienced the joy of God's salvation; and having lost it by falling into sin, he penitently and earnestly prays that it may be restored.

In treating of this subject it is important to discriminate between that joy which is spiritual, and that which is natural. All religious joy is not the joy of God's salvation. There is the joy of the hypocrite, which is but for a moment. Job xx: 5. The stony ground hearers received the word with joy. They rejoiced prematurely, and having no root in themselves, they endured only for a time.

Sinners may flatter themselves without any good reason, that their sins are pardoned, and be filled with joy. Their joy may arise to a high degree, and be accompanied by the warmest expressions of gratitude, and by great zeal in the external duties of religion. Thus a criminal, under sentence of death, understanding, through mistake, that he is pardoned, is filled with transports of joy, and cannot find words to express his gratitude to his sovereign for his kindness and mercy. But when he discovers his mistake, his joy vanishes, and all his love and gratitude to his supposed benefactor, disappear at once. In like manner, the self-deceived sinner, who rejoices only in his own fancied safety, has no love to the character of God, no delight in holiness, and no joy in the contemplation of divine objects. All his regard centers in self. If he only can be safe, he cares not what becomes of God, or his glory, or the interests of his kingdom. But the joy of God's salvation is not a selfish joy. It results from the exercise of the Christian graces, and consists in the delight which the renewed soul takes in contemplating the objects of holy affection, without reference to self, or self-interest.

God's salvation, is not a salvation from punishment merely; but a salvation from the power and dominion of sin. Christ was called Jesus, because he should *save his people from their sins.* "Out of Zion shall come a deliverer, *who shall turn away ungodliness from Jacob.*" "Unto you first, God having raised up his Son, Jesus, sent him to bless you, *in turning away every one of you from his iniquities.*"

The first joy of the new born soul does not arise from the belief that his sins are pardoned; for his sins are not pardoned until the love of God is shed abroad in his heart. He can, of course, have no evidence that he is pardoned, until he finds himself rejoicing in the contemplation of the divine character. The joy of God's salvation may be realized, when the individual has no idea that his sins are pardoned. The renewed soul while contemplating the loveliness of Christ, and other divine objects, forgets himself, and his mind is absorbed in the delightful contemplation of these objects.

This joy of God's salvation, may, for a season, be lost; not only by falling into open and scandalous sins, as in the case of David; but by the indulgence of secret sins; or by becoming cold, formal, or negligent in the performance of duty.

When the Christian loses the joy of God's salvation, all his spiritual consolation departs, and he is filled with sore distress. It was so with David. The pains of hell gat hold upon him, and he found trouble and sorrow.

And what must the backslidden Christian do, that the joy of God's salvation may be restored? He must consider from whence he has fallen, and repent, and do his first works. Like the Psalmist, he must confess his sins, and turn from them unto God. He must obtain this joy as he did at first, by repentance and faith in Christ. God is ready to forgive those who come unto him with broken and contrite hearts. "Turn O backsliding children, saith the Lord." "I will heal their backslidings. I will love them freely."

When the Christian is thus restored, he will be like one converted anew; and he will be more humble and watchful than he was before. He will also be more sensible of his dependence on divine grace, and will look to God to keep him from falling. Thus David prayed that God would not only restore unto him the joy of his salvation, but that he would uphold him with his *free Spirit—free* in two senses.

1. Because the gift of the Spirit is gratuitous. And
2. Because by the operations of the Spirit the sinner is liberated from the bondage of corruption.

"Then," the psalmist says, "will I teach transgressors thy ways, and sinners shall be converted unto thee." The best preparation for usefulness in ministers, and in Christians, is the possession of a right state of heart. The spirit which they manifest, they will be likely to diffuse around them.

To teach transgressors God's ways, is to teach them not only their duty and their sinfulness, but the ways in which God deals with his sinful creatures, in bringing them into a state of favor with him. Thus David could say, "when I kept silence, my bones waxed old through my roaring all the day"—"I acknowledged my sin unto thee, and mine iniquity have I not hid. I said I will confess my transgressions unto the Lord, and thou forgavest the iniquity of my sin."

This whole subject is strikingly illustrated in the history of Peter. Think of the warning which Christ gave him, and of his confident assurance that he should not deny his master. Think of his unhappy fall, and of his deep and bitter repentance. Now witness his preaching on the day of Pentecost, and the remarkable success which attended his labors. God had restored unto him the joy of his salvation, and upheld him by his free Spirit; and he taught transgressors God's ways, and sinners were converted unto him.

44

Total Depravity.

And God saw that the wickedness of man was great in the earth; and that every imagination of the thoughts of his heart, was only evil continually.—GENESIS vi: 5.

THE object of this discourse will be to illustrate and establish the doctrine of *Total Depravity*.

The doctrine does not imply that all men are equally wicked. There are evidently degrees of wickedness. It shall be more tolerable for the inhabitants of Sodom, than for those who reject the gospel. The servant that knew his Lord's will, and did it not, shall be beaten with many stripes; but he who knew not his Lord's will and did commit things worthy of stripes, shall be beaten with few stripes. In hell all will be totally depraved, and yet all will not be equally bad.

This doctrine does not imply that men are as bad as they can be. "Evil men and seducers shall wax worse and worse." And all the finally impenitent will wax worse and worse forever. The longer sinners suffer in hell, the more will they deserve to continue there.

This doctrine does not imply that men are not free moral agents. They possess all the faculties which are essential to moral agency—reason, judgment, memory, will, and affections. If they were not free moral agents, they could not be the subjects of moral depravity. To say, therefore, that total depravity is inconsistent with free agency is absurd. If it is, there can be no such thing as sin or blame in the Universe. For if total depravity annihilates free agency, then partial depravity destroys it in some degree. So far as an individual is depraved, so far he is not free, and of course, not blame-worthy.

This doctrine does not imply that men are destitute of conscience. The question is sometimes asked, is there not something in man which tells him what is right and what is wrong? Undoubtedly there is. If man had not a conscience, he could not be a sinner. But it is one thing to know our duty, and another to love it, and to do it. The more clearly a person sees his duty, the greater is his guilt if he does not perform it. Conscience will exist in hell. It is the worm which never dies. And who doubts that the lost spirits in hell are totally depraved?

But positively—by the doctrine of Total Depravity is meant, that all men, by nature, are destitute of love to God, and consequently wholly sinful—or to adopt the language of the text, that every imagination of the thoughts of their heart, is only evil continually. The truth of this doctrine appears

1. From direct passages of scripture. The text is decisive. The language is very striking. Suppose it were affirmed of Gabriel that every imagination of the thoughts of his heart was only holy continually. Could any one doubt that this language was intended to affirm that Gabriel was perfectly holy. . . . .
. . . .
2. From the doctrine of regeneration. Men must

be born again—they must pass from death to life—
"You hath he quickened, who were dead"—If the
heart were not entirely depraved, this change would
not be necessary. . . . .
. . . .
3. From the distinction which the scriptures make
between the saint and the sinner. "Every one that
loveth, is born of God." This declaration implies that
all unrenewed men are destitute of love to God, and
of course totally depraved. . . . .
. . . .
Should the sinner say, there certainly is some goodness in myself; I would answer, your testimony cannot be admitted. You are a party concerned. Suppose that it does not seem to you that you are totally depraved. You may be blinded by self-flattery. Your character may appear very differently to the omniscient God. "That which is highly esteemed among men, is abomination in the sight of God." Mark the words of the text. "And *God saw* that the wickedness of men was great," &c. Psalm xiv. Rom. ii: 9—12. . . . .
. . . .
4. From the experience of every Christian. Look back, my brethren, to the time when you were under conviction of sin. Were you not brought to see that there was no good thing in you? Did not God treat you as if you were totally depraved, by refusing to hear and answer your prayers? Did you not find that you were not only destitute of love to God, but that your hearts were enmity against him? When others were taken and you were left, how did you feel? And

when you began to love God, were you not conscious that you had never loved him before? . . . . .

If this doctrine is true, conviction and conversion are necessary; and when persons begin to love God, it will be all new. And so we find it in revivals. So it was with Paul. " I know that in me, that is, in my flesh dwelleth no good thing."

Thus, the experience of Christians perfectly harmonizes with this doctrine. But if the doctrine were not true, the young convert might say, I have indeed experienced a great change, but it is nothing new. I always felt so. I always loved God. . . . . .
. . . .

Finally.—From the experience of every sinner. When Adam had sinned, he was afraid, and hid himself from the presence of the Lord. So children when they first learn that God is present, are afraid, and disposed to hide themselves. This shows that they are totally depraved. If there was any love to God in their hearts, they would be pleased with the idea of God's presence. They would love to pray to him, and to converse about him. . . . .

Let me appeal to the experience of impenitent sinners. Do you love to pray? Do you love to meditate and converse on the subject of religion? Why is it that all the motives which are presented to your minds, are insufficient to induce you to comply with the terms of the gospel? Why do you not repent? Do you say, you cannot? Then certainly you are totally depraved. If you had the least love to God, you could not help repenting. Think against who you have sinned. What a heart must that be that can feel no contrition for sin committed against such a glorious being? Think of the love of Christ in dying for your sins, and in offering you salvation without money and without price. Surely if this is not sufficient to melt your hearts, they must be harder than adamant.

Think of the threatenings of eternal death. If you can venture on in sin in view of these threatenings, how amazingly obdurate must be your hearts. . .

Perhaps some one will say, if these things are so, it will do no good for me to attempt the service of God, and I will do nothing. To such an one, let me say, you express the very feeling of a totally depraved heart. If you had any love to God, you would not stop to inquire whether it would do you any good to serve him. You would delight in his service, and esteem it a privilege to serve him. . . . . . .
. . . .

If any of you, my hearers, do not believe that you are totally depraved, let me put your feelings to the test. You know that it will be your duty to enter into your closets to pray this night. If you love God, you will esteem it a privilege to do so. If you find your hearts opposed to this duty, and neglect it, or attempt it with great reluctance, you will know to-morrow, that you possess just such hearts as have been described.
. . . .

45

The ways in which sinners cover their sins.

He that covereth his sins shall not prosper; but whoso confesseth and forsaketh them, shall have mercy. —PROVERBS xxviii: 13.

It is natural to all men to attempt to cover their sins—as natural as it is to commit sin. When Adam was called to an account for eating the forbidden fruit, he attempted to throw off the blame from himself, by saying, "the woman whom thou gavest to be with me, she gave me of the tree, and I did eat." And when the woman was called to an account, she said, "the serpent beguiled me, and I did eat." And it is remarkable, that children sometimes show the ingenuity of the serpent, in attempting to cover their sins.

The first thing, if possible, is to deny the fact. But when the fact cannot be denied, the next thing is to excuse and palliate their sin.

I will mention some ways in which sinners attempt to cover their sins. I shall confine my remarks to some of the ways in which they excuse themselves for neglecting the subject of religion.

One pleads that he has no time to attend to the subject.

Another says, I would become a Christian if I could, but I cannot.

Another cloaks his sin under the failings of professors of religion. He will not become a Christian, because there are so many hypocrites in the world.

Another says, I did not make my own heart, and how can I be to blame.

In these and many other ways, the sinner attempts to cover his sins.

But he shall not prosper. He shall not succeed. He shall fail of the object which he has in view.

If his object is to appear well for the time being, he will fail. It would have been better for him to have said nothing.

Does he plead want of time. How must such an excuse appear? Cannot find time to attend to the concerns of his immortal soul! He can find time to attend to other things infinitely less important. And he must find time to die.

Does he plead that he would be a Christian if he could, but cannot? What an excuse is this! Do you, O sinner, really believe what you say? Is it so? Can you not repent of your sins? Can you not feel sorrow that you have sinned against God, and against Christ? What a heart must yours be! Is your heart so hard and obdurate, what, then, are your prospects? Can you go to heaven with such a heart? "After thy hardness and impenitent heart, *treasurest up unto thyself wrath against the day of wrath.*"

Again. Do you believe that God is such a being, that he will condemn you for not doing what you have no power to do? He has declared, that except you repent you must perish. And is it true that you cannot repent? Then your state must be dreadful.

But would you be pleased if others should tell you

the same? Would you not be offended if ministers should tell you that you are condemned to eternal death for not doing impossibilities?

Does the sinner excuse himself for neglecting religion, because there are so many hypocrites in the world? What an excuse is this! Suppose, my hearers, there are hypocrites who are going down to hell. Is this a reason why you should neglect religion, and destroy your own souls? I am aware, that the failings of professors of religion, give great occasion to the enemies of the Lord to blaspheme. But remember, that those who take occasion to blaspheme, are the enemies of the Lord. If you excuse yourselves and reproach religion because Christian professors disgrace their profession, remember that you proclaim to all the world, that you are the enemies of the Lord.

Does the sinner plead that he did not make his own heart? What an excuse is this! Suppose your neighbor should injure you, and should plead in his justification, that he did not make his own heart; would you be satisfied with such an excuse? Are you the only being who did not make his own heart?

The principle involved in this excuse, if true, will exculpate every sinner in the universe. All the fallen angels may plead that they did not make their own hearts.

Suppose a number of men in a boat. By some means, one of them gets overboard. He exclaims, how came I here? No matter, says one of his friends, let us help you into the boat. No, says he, there is an important question first to be settled; how came I here? We cannot tell, says his friend. There are different ways in which you may have got where you are. You may have jumped overboard—or you may have been thrown overboard—or you may have fallen overboard in your sleep. But take hold of this rope. No—he replies, if you will not tell me how I came here, I am determined to drown.

Is it the sinner's object to become a Christian; he will fail. No one ever did, or ever will, become a Christian by covering his sins. One reason why persons are sometimes long distressed, and obtain no relief is, that some secret sin is covered. "When I kept silence, my bones waxed old, through my roaring all the day."

Is it the sinner's object to quiet his conscience, he *may* not succeed. Sinners often plead excuses which their consciences tell them are not valid. If they succeed in quieting their consciences, they will certainly destroy their souls. "He that being often reproved, hardeneth his neck, shall suddenly be destroyed and that without remedy."

But if those who cover their sins will not prosper now, what will they do on the day of judgment, when "God shall bring every work into judgment, with every secret thing, whether it be good, or whether it be evil!"

The sinner who covers his sins, is only attempting to conceal one crime by the commission of another, and is thus continually making his condemnation more and more just.

But "whoso confesseth and forsaketh them." Here is a term of pardon. Confession of sin is as much a term of pardon, as faith and repentance, and has the same promise. Ps. xxxii: 5.—1 Kings viii: 47—Jer. iii: 12, 13—Job xxxiii: 27, 28—1 John i: 9.

But it is not sufficient for the sinner to confess his sin in words. The text says, " Whoso confesseth, and forsaketh them." The sinner has to deal with the heart-searching God. If he does not break off his sins by righteousness, he cannot be saved. He must bring forth fruit meet for repentance.

"Shall have mercy"—who does not need mercy? What a sweet and joyful sound! O, how reasonable the condition. If the sinner had one right feeling in his heart, he would esteem it a privilege to confess and forsake his sins, whether he was ever to receive mercy or not.

The language of the penitent is,

> " Welcome, welcome, dear Redeemer,
> Welcome to this heart of mine,
> Lord, I make a full surrender,
> Every power and thought be thine—
> Thine entirely,
> Through eternal ages thine."

46

The example of Esau, a warning to sinners.

Lest there be any fornicator or profane person as Esau, who for one morsel of meat sold his birth-right.—HEBREWS xii: 16.

THE conduct of Esau is adduced by the apostle to illustrate the danger of sinners who reject the gospel of Christ. The story is this. "Esau came from the field, and he was faint. And Esau said to Jacob, feed me with that same red pottage, for I am faint. And Jacob said, sell me this day thy birth-right. And Esau said, behold I am at the point to die, and what profit shall this birth-right do to me?" We cannot believe that he was on the point of starvation in his father's house. The meaning is that he would forego no worldly gratification for the sake of spiritual blessings. Life is short, and I am determined to make the most of it. "And Jacob said, swear unto me this day. And he sware unto him, and he sold his birth-right unto Jacob. And then Jacob gave Esau bread, and pottage of lentiles, and he did eat and drink, and rose up and went his way. Thus Esau despised his birth-right."

The birth-right included a double portion of his father's substance, together with supreme authority in the family. But this was not the most important part. It included a prophetic blessing, with which were connected great spiritual privileges. These were the things which Esau despised—and on this account he is denominated by the apostle, a profane person. And this is what gives the passage so much point in illustrating the conduct of sinners in selling the blessings of the gospel.

What do they sell?—How?—For what?—The consequences.

1. What do they sell? All the blessings purchased by the blood of Christ, and offered to men in the gospel—pardon of sin—peace of conscience—joy in the Holy Ghost—and a title to an eternal inheritance among the saints.

" 'The Lord said unto Abraham, lift up now thine eyes, and look from the place where thou art, northward, and southward, and eastward, and westward. For all the land which thou seest, to thee will I give it, and to thy seed forever." This was only a type of those blessings which are presented to the sinner in the gospel—a crown—a kingdom—an inheritance incorruptible, undefiled, and that fadeth not away. All these things are offered in the gospel.

2. How?—By resisting the strivings of the Spirit. All these blessings are intimately connected with the strivings of the Spirit, by whose influence alone, the sinner is made meet for the inheritance of the saints in light.

Now the sinner like Esau, may be unwilling to forego the pleasures of sense. He may set a higher value upon them than upon the salvation of his soul; and for the sake of securing these pleasures, he may resist the Holy Ghost, and seal his everlasting doom. " If ye live after the flesh, ye shall die."

3. For what does the sinner sell the blessings of the gospel ? Not for value received ;—but for mere trifles—one morsel of meat—a momentary gratification, he parts with the joys of heaven. It may be for the sake of present ease—or for a title of worldly honor—a puff of noisy breath—or perhaps for the sake of obliging a companion, who is the enemy of God— or for the sake of indulging some beloved lust.

In the indulgence of these pleasures, the conduct of the sinner may be attended by the stings of conscience. It is true, no one expects to complete the bargain. But many do it. Temptation comes, and conviction goes.

Now I would ask the sinner to consider well *for what* he is about to part with heaven. Count the cost. " Thus saith the Lord, ye have sold yourselves for nought." O, for what trifles sinners sell their souls. Lysimachus, king of Thrace, suffering under extreme thirst, offered his kingdom to the Getæ, for the means of quenching it. His exclamation, when he had drunk, is very striking. " Ah! wretched me, who for such a momentary gratification, have lost so great a kingdom." How applicable this to the case of him who, for the momentary pleasures of sin, parts with the kingdom of heaven.

4. The consequences. " Afterwards, when he would have inherited the blessing"—My hearers, there is an afterwards. O, if there was not, we would not trouble the sinner. Forty-five years *afterwards* when Esau would have inherited the blessing, he was rejected. How different now are his feelings. The story is related in the 27th chapter of Genesis. When he found that God in his providence had given the

blessing to Jacob, though it was in accordance with his own voluntary conduct, how did he then feel? When he heard the words of his father, he cried with a great and exceeding bitter cry. O, how great, and exceeding bitter will the cry of the sinner be, when it is forever too late to retrieve his loss. He said to his father, "Bless me, even me also, O, my father." But he found no place of repentance. He could not induce his father to change his mind, though he sought it carefully with tears. So it will be with the sinner. On the judgment of the great day, he will cry, Lord, Lord, open unto me, but the door will be shut.

Reflections.

1. What great consequences are sometimes connected with little circumstances. For one morsel of meat—for the indulgence of one sinful appetite or passion, under certain circumstances, heaven is bartered away.

When the sinner is anxious for his soul, one word of contempt dropped in his ear—one sneering look, may occasion the loss of his soul—his absence from one interesting meeting of inquiry, may terminate in the loss of his conviction, and the loss of salvation. How great the danger of the sinner! "If the righteous scarcely be saved, where shall the ungodly and the sinner appear?"

2. What a solemn thing it is to live. The sinner is on trial once for all.

> "Let us not lose the living God,
> For one short dream of joy,
> With fond embrace cling to a clod,
> And fling all heaven away."

47

The sinner slain by the law.

For I was alive without the law once, but when the commandment came, sin revived, and I died.—ROMANS vii: 9.

THE time to which Paul alludes in the text, is doubtless the time when he was on the way from Jerusalem to Damascus—when he was struck to the earth, and remained three days without sight.

We will consider

I. The life which Paul lived.

II. The death which he died.

I. He lived what many regard as a very moral life. "My manner of life from my youth, which was first among mine own nation at Jerusalem, know all the Jews, which knew me from the beginning, if they would testify, that after the straitest sect of our religion, I lived a pharisee." This was regarded very much to his credit.

He appears to have been very conscientious.

"And Paul earnestly beholding the council, said, men and brethren, I have lived in all good conscience until this day."

He was also sincere. "I verily thought" he says, "that I ought to do many things contrary to the name of Jesus of Nazareth."

He was very zealous. "I am" he says, "verily a man who am a Jew—brought up in this city at the feet of Gamaliel, and taught according to the perfect manner of the law of the fathers, and was *zealous* toward God, as ye all are this day."

"I profited in the Jew's religion above many mine equals, being more *exceeding zealous* of the traditions of the fathers."

If any man could assert a claim to heaven on the ground of his own righteousness, Paul could do it. "If any man have whereof to glory, I more—as touching the righteousness of the law, blameless." So far as external conduct was concerned, he regarded himself, and was regarded by others as blameless.

But notwithstanding his zeal and activity in religion, he had no true knowledge of his own heart, and no right principle of action. He was alive without the law. The law of God reveals the great principles of right moral action. Of these, he was perfectly ignorant.

When he says that he was without the law, the meaning cannot be, that he had no Bible. He was doubtless better acquainted with the contents of the Bible than most of his brethren; for he was taught according to the perfect manner of the law of the fathers. He had the best of advantages. But although he was acquainted with the letter of the law, and could probably repeat from memory much of the Bible; yet he was totally ignorant of the spirituality and extent of the law.

II. The death which he died.

Of course he did not mean that he died a natural death, for he was then alive.

The language implies that he found himself under sentence of death; for he says, when the commandment came, sin revived, and I died. He found himself under the curse of the law. "Cursed is every one who continueth not in all things written in the book of the law to do them."

Again—He found himself destitute of all spiritual life. "To be carnally minded is death; but to be spiritually minded is life and peace." The language which he so often uses in his epistles on this subject, he knew to be true from his own experience. "Dead in trespasses and sins."

Again—All his self-righteous hopes were slain, and he felt that he was utterly lost.

Reflections.

1. Many think themselves to be Christians when they are not. They have not been under conviction of sin. They have not seen and felt that they were condemned, and that they were dead in trespasses and sins.

2. We see the importance of preaching the law. No sinner can see and feel his need of pardon and salvation, until he sees that he is lost—none are convicted of sin without a knowledge of the law—"By the law is the knowledge of sin." "I had not known sin but by the law." None can feel their need of Christ, till they feel that they are condemned. It is true that sinners may be greatly distressed, and have great fears of hell without conviction. Hence the need of preaching the law that sinners may see their need of pardon and salvation.

3. Sinners that are under conviction, realize that they are waxing worse and worse. Thus it was with

Paul while under conviction of sin. He doubtless, at that time, saw more of his heart than ever before. Had there been any good thing in his heart, he doubtless would have discovered it. But he does not say, when the commandment came, the good principle revived, and I lived; but sin revived, and I died.

And thus sinners now under conviction complain that they are waxing worse and worse. We need not contradict them, for it is true, whether they realize it or not.

4. Gospel preaching will distress sinners more and more, while unreconciled to God.

They often complain that ministers destroy all that they have been doing. Painful as it is, it must be done. Should a sinner find relief under any sermon, without a change of heart, he may know either that he has not understood the preacher, or that the preacher has not done his duty.

5. The sooner sinners die in the sense of the text, the better.

Sinners under conviction sometimes say, it seems as if you would kill me. They must be killed. They must be slain by the law, before they will be made alive by the gospel.

48

Causes of alarm to awakened sinners.

Now when they heard this, they were pricked in their heart, and said unto Peter, and to the rest of the apostles, men, and brethren, what shall we do?—ACTS ii: 37.

WHAT ailed these men? This was the language of distress.

After the resurrection of Christ, he continued forty days with his disciples, speaking to them of the things pertaining to the kingdom of God. Among other things, he gave commission to his apostles to go into all the world, and preach the gospel to every creature; at the same time enjoining them to begin at Jerusalem. Obedient to their Lord, they retired to an upper chamber, where abode the apostles, and held a meeting for prayer. "These all continued with one accord in prayer and supplication, with the women, and Mary the mother of Jesus, and with his brethren." The number of the disciples was about one hundred and twenty. This prayer-meeting could not have been established more than about ten days; for Christ ascended on the fortieth day, and the day of Pentecost was on the fiftieth day after his crucifixion. The feast of Pentecost was appointed to celebrate the giving of the law on mount Sinai, and it is remarkable that it occurred on our present Sabbath morning.

"When the day of Pentecost was fully come, they were all with one accord in one place"—with united hearts, praying for the descent of the Holy Spirit. "And suddenly, there was a sound from heaven, as of a rushing mighty wind"—This mighty agent is an emblem of the Spirit of God. Invisible to mortal eyes, we hear the sound as it sweeps over fields and forests, and lays all prostrate before it. Though we may not be under its influence, we can hear the sound, and witness the effects. And so it is when the Spirit of God is sent to subdue the hearts of rebels. The effects in the latter case, can no more be doubted, than in the former. "The wind bloweth where it listeth, and thou hearest the sound thereof, but canst not tell whence it cometh, nor whither it goeth; so is every one that is born of the Spirit."

"And there appeared unto them cloven tongues, like as of fire, and it sat upon each of them"—a parting flame in the shape of tongues—a fit emblem of that flaming zeal with which the gospel was to be preached in different languages through the world. "And they were all filled with the Holy Ghost, and began to speak with other tongues, as the Spirit gave them utterance." It being the feast of Pentecost, Jerusalem was filled with people. There were dwelling there, devout men from every nation, speaking not less than seven or eight different languages, besides different dialects of the same language. Now when these strange appearances were noised abroad, a great multitude came together, and were confounded, because that every man heard them speak in his own language.

These strangers, not the apostles, proclaimed the miracle. "They were all amazed, and marvelled, saying one to another, Behold are not all these which speak, Galileans? And how hear we every man in our own tongue, wherein we were born?" "And they were all amazed and were in doubt, saying, what meaneth this?"

"But others mocking, said, these men are full of new wine."

At this interesting crisis, "Peter standing up with eleven, lifted up his voice," and preached the first gospel sermon under the new commission of our Saviour. He in the first place repelled the insinuation that they were drunken. In the next place he referred them to an ancient prediction of the very events which were transpiring before them. He then applied the subject. "Ye men of Israel, hear these words. Jesus of Nazareth, a man approved of God among you by miracles, and wonders and signs, which God did by him in the midst of you, as ye yourselves know; him being delivered by the determinate counsel and foreknowledge of God, ye have taken, and with wicked hands have crucified and slain; whom God hath raised up" &c.

In all which they did to the Saviour, they only fulfilled some ancient prediction, and did it with wicked hands. They did not strike a stroke which did not fulfill the determinate counsel of God.

> "And while by Satan's rage he fell,
> He dashed the rising hopes of hell."

Peter in his sermon connects the counsel of God, and the free agency of man. And if his hearers could not understand that they might with wicked hands fulfill the counsel of God, there was no way in which he could prove to them that Christ was the true Messiah.

To prove that God had raised Christ from the dead, he next quotes the 16th Psalm, and comments upon it, showing that it refers to the resurrection of Christ. He then presses home the argument. "Therefore, let the house of Israel know assuredly that God hath made that same Jesus, whom ye have crucified, both Lord and Christ."

At this point, the Spirit of God set home the word with power upon the consciences of the hearers. "Now when they heard this, they were pricked in their heart, and said unto Peter, and the rest of the apostles, men and brethren, what shall we do?" They saw and felt their danger. The phraseology is peculiar—"They were pricked in their heart"—the effect corresponding with the instrument used. "The word of God is quick and powerful, sharper than a two edged sword." This is the sword of the Spirit. A stab in the heart is fatal. "The letter killeth." "When the commandment came, sin revived, and I died."

I would here remark, that in genuine conviction there is something peculiar. It is not simply alarm, or fear of hell. The word of God comes with power to the conscience, and shows sinners their true character and condition. It was so with Peter's hearers. This was what ailed them.

I propose to state some of the principal grounds of alarm to the awakened sinner.

1. He realizes that he is condemned by the divine law. He knows that he has broken the law in times and ways to him innumerable; and that not a single sin is pardoned. He knows that he has no interest in the atonement of Christ, and that there is no other way of escape from the curse of the law. "He that believeth not the Son is condemned already, and the wrath of God abideth on him."

Again—he realizes that the punishment to which he is exposed, is eternal. Not until the sinner sees himself condemned, does he realize how he shall feel at the hour of execution—Now he is convinced of sin, of righteousness and of judgment. Now he dwells with awful solemnity on the eternity of hell torments. The more he reflects, the more rational he becomes, and the more he is alarmed.

Again—he realizes the awful uncertainty of human life. He knows that he has no security of a single day. He is aware that the God in whose hand his breath is, he has not glorified, and that he has a right to cut him down at any moment. He perceives that his soul is in jeopardy every hour. When he lies down at night, he knows not but before morning he shall awake in hell, where the worm dieth not, and the fire is not quenched.

Again—he realizes that pardon is uncertain. . .
. . . .
Again—he realizes that it is altogether uncertain how long the Spirit will strive. He knows that he has resisted his strivings, and that God may justly at any moment take his Spirit from him. He may, perhaps, be conscious of having resisted the Spirit in former years. He knows that many have been given up of

God, and that some younger than himself, have been cut down in their sins, and called to their last account.

Again—he is convinced that he shall never do any thing to better his condition short of repentance. The sinner partly awakened, often flatters himself that he shall do something to recommend him to God. But when his self-righteousness is demolished, he sees the sinfulness of all that he has done. He sees that the motive, the principle of action, is wrong; and he is persuaded that he never shall do any thing with his present feelings, acceptable to God.

Again—he realizes that he is altogether without excuse for not repenting and believing in Christ now. This is generally the last stage of conviction. When *He*, the Spirit of truth, is come, he shall convince the world of sin, because they *believe not on me*.

Finally—he is convinced that if he does not repent now, he never shall. Those who are not brought to this state of mind, will, in all probability drop the subject, and like Felix look for a more convenient season. But those who are under thorough conviction, do not expect to find a more convenient season. They conclude that this is their last call. And until the sinner is brought to this conviction, there is no hope of his conversion.

But, my hearers, it is one thing to hear the account of those who are pricked in the heart, and under conviction, and quite another thing to feel it.

> "I saw the opening gates of hell,
> With endless pains, and sorrows there,
> Which none but they that feel can tell,
> While I was hurried to despair."

I do not pretend that every awakened sinner goes over precisely the same ground. But these are the common grounds of alarm to awakened sinners. Have you, my hearers, felt that out of Christ, you were justly condemned by the divine law? Have you felt that you were altogether without excuse for not repenting and believing in Christ immediately?—that there was no difficulty in your way, but a criminal difficulty? If you have not felt these things, you have not come to Christ.

And now, I have no occasion to ask my hearers, how do you like this statement? For I have only been stating matters of fact. It is what hundreds and thousands have felt.

We see from this subject,

1. That it is no new thing for persons to be under conviction. It was so on the day of Pentecost, under the preaching of Peter. But some one will say, we are not to expect such things now. The age of miracles is past. True, the age of miracles is past—but the age of preaching the gospel is not past. It was not the miracle, but the preaching of Peter, which was the means of awakening his hearers. "*When they heard this, they were pricked in their heart.*" And this is the genuine effect of a preached gospel. It must be the same in all ages; and the more nearly the effects resemble those on the day of Pentecost, the greater is the evidence that they are genuine.

2. It is no surprising thing that sinners should be under conviction. If what has been said is true, that the sinner is condemned to eternal death, and every moment in danger of being lost forever, it is not surprising that he should be alarmed. It is amazing that

any sinners should remain stupid. And here permit me to ask, are there any who are listening to my voice, who begin to feel that they are condemned, and that not one of their sins is pardoned? If out of Christ, let me tell you, your fears are not without foundation. You are condemned, and O that you might realize it more and more.

Again—do any of you begin to fear that you are exposed to eternal punishment? If out of Christ, your fears are not without foundation. It is even so; and O that you might realize it more and more.

Again—do any of you begin to realize the uncertainty of life? Do you tremble lest you should be suddenly cut down by the stroke of death, and hurried into a miserable eternity? If out of Christ, your fears are not without foundation. You are in just such danger. You know not what a day may bring forth. And O that you might realize it more and more.

Again—do any of you begin to fear that you never shall be pardoned. Let me tell you, your fears are not without foundation. It is yet an awful uncertainty whether your sins will ever be pardoned. And O that you might realize it more and more.

Again—do any of you fear that the Spirit of God may cease to strive with you? Your fears are not without foundation. There is great danger that the Spirit will cease to strive. Many who were as anxious as you are, have gone back to stupidity, and have lost their souls.

Do any of you begin to realize that you shall never do any thing to better your condition short of repentance? It is a correct conclusion. You never will. If you have any thing to do before you repent, I beg that you will make haste, and do it soon; for after all, you must repent or perish.

Do any of you begin to realize that you are altogether without excuse for not repenting now? It is even so. Hardness and impenitency of heart are awful sins in the sight of God.

Do any of you begin to feel that if you do not repent now, you never shall? This, in all probability, is a correct conclusion. If you now resist the Spirit, and turn back to stupidity, there is the greatest reason to fear that you will slumber on in impenitence, till you perish.

I perceive that all my hearers are going to be under conviction of sin. It may not be to-day—or to-morrow. Perhaps it will not be in this life. O, that it might be. How much better to be awakened now, while pardon is offered, than when the day of grace is past.

But those who are not convinced of sin now, will be hereafter. They will be convinced of all their sins; and it will be conviction that will be succeeded by no conversion; but will last forever. "Behold the Lord cometh with ten thousands of his saints to execute judgment upon all, and to *convince* all that are ungodly among them, of all their ungodly deeds, which they have ungodly committed, and of all the hard speeches which ungodly sinners have spoken against them."

> "Sinners, awake betimes, ye fools, be wise,
> Awake before this dreadful morning rise,
> Change your vain thoughts, your crooked works amend,
> Fly to the Saviour, make the judge your friend;
> Lest like a lion, his last vengeance tear
> Your trembling souls, and no deliverer near."

49

The burdened sinner invited to Christ for rest.

Come unto me all ye that labor and are heavy laden, and I will give you rest. Take my yoke upon you, and learn of me, for I am meek and lowly, and ye shall find rest to your souls. For my yoke is easy and my burden is light.—MATTHEW xi: 28-30.

AFTER our Saviour had been preaching in different places for some time, very few seemed to take much interest in his preaching. At length he lifted up his voice in a strain of awful solemnity, wo, wo, wo—and it broke like a peal of thunder over the cities of Chorasin, Bethsaida, and Capernaum, because they repented not. He then raised his eyes, and thanked his Father in heaven, that this was not true of all. There was another class to whom he now turned with a voice of welcome, like that on the judgment of the great day; "Come ye blessed of my Father," &c. He says, "Come unto me all ye that labor and are heavy laden and I will give you rest."

I propose to consider,

I. The characters here addressed.

They *labor* and are *heavy laden*. In some sense all men labor, but not in the sense of the text. They seem to care little about their souls; but they labor to obtain the pleasures of sin, and vanities of this world. They are like the troubled sea, when it cannot rest. Persons of this description are thus addressed in the

Bible, "Wherefore do you spend your money for that which is not bread, and your labor for that which satisfieth not? hearken diligently unto me, and eat ye that which is good, and let your soul delight itself in fatness."

Those who are addressed in the text, are of a different class. They have lost all their interest in the objects of time and sense. All their anxiety respects the salvation of the soul. They are said to labor. Those who are under deep concern for their souls, will not be idle. They feel that something must be done. They generally commence by laboring to build up a righteousness of their own. "Being ignorant of God's righteousness, they go about to establish their own righteousness," as the most probable method of securing their salvation. And thus they often continue for a long time, laboring and toiling, but without success.

They are said to be heavy laden—borne down under a sense of their sins, which are like a heavy burden. They find no rest, day nor night. And their burden often increases continually. These are the characters particularly addressed in the text.

And who is the person that speaks? Not a mere man—not an angel. No created being can save the sinner. It is the Lord Jesus Christ, who came from heaven to earth, and shed his own precious blood.

"Neither is there salvation in any other." This is the great errand on which he came from heaven to earth. Here in the text, he seems to fulfill the prediction uttered by the evangelical prophet. "In that day, there shall be a root out of Jesse, which shall stand for an ensign to the people; to it shall the gentiles seek, and his rest shall be glorious."

"*I will give you rest*"—rest from all your self-righteous efforts—rest from the burden of sin. "Return unto thy rest, O my soul."

Rest to the body after toil, after laboring under a heavy burden, is sweet; but rest to the heavy laden soul, is infinitely more desirable.

Rest implies cessation from warfare—from the fruitless contest in which the sinner is engaged. He lays down the weapons of his rebellion. "Therefore, being justified by faith, we have peace with God, through our Lord Jesus Christ." "We who believe do enter into rest."

"*And I* WILL GIVE *you rest.*" The sinner will never do any thing by which to purchase pardon and salvation. He has nothing to give in exchange—nothing but a poor sinful soul.

> "Lo, glad I come, and thou blest Lamb,
> Shalt take me to thee as I am;
> Nothing but sin I thee can give,
> Nothing but love shall I receive."

But the sinner lingers, hoping that he shall grow better—that he shall do something to recommend him to favor. But this can never be, for so long as he refuses to come to Christ, he will surely wax worse and worse.

> "Let not conscience make you linger,
>   Nor of fitness fondly dream;
> All the fitness he requireth,
>   Is to feel your need of him.
> This he gives you,
>   'Tis his Spirit's rising beam.

> Come ye weary, heavy laden,
>   Lost and ruined by the fall,
> If you tarry till you're better,
>   You will never come at all.
> Not the righteous,
>   Sinners, Jesus came to call

"*Take my yoke upon you.*" What does this imply? It implies that the sinner must be henceforth employed in the service of Christ. He has heretofore been employed in the service of sin; henceforth he is to yield himself unto God, as one that is alive from the dead, and his members as instruments of righteousness unto holiness.

"*And learn of me.*" He must abandon all his self-righteous plans, and carnal wisdom, and learn at the feet of Christ all the doctrines and duties of religion. He must also imitate the example of Christ, and possess his spirit.

"*For I am meek and lowly in heart.*" This is the character of the Saviour who knew no sin, and the character which all who will enter heaven must finally possess. How directly opposite to the character of proud, stubborn, rebellious sinners.

"*Meek and lowly in heart.*" Thus the sinner is required to come to Christ. We have sometimes heard of sinners coming up to the terms of salvation. In the text they are called upon to come down to the terms of salvation—to be meek and lowly in heart.

"*And ye shall find rest to your souls.*" The sinner will no longer be like the troubled sea when it cannot rest. He finds peace. The exercise of the christian graces is pleasant and delightful.

"*For my yoke is easy.*" The service of Christ, when

contrasted with the service of sin, is easy. The sinner often refuses to come to Christ for fear he shall have to be employed in his service; and indeed, it would be irksome and galling, with an unrenewed heart; for "no man can serve two masters." But all who have tried the service of Christ, can testify that it is easy—that wisdom's ways are ways of pleasantness, and that all her paths are peace.

"*And my burden is light.*" Christ has a burden to place upon the sinner who comes to him. It may be a burden of affliction. He may be called to part with father or mother, or he may be called to suffer shame and reproach in the cause of Christ. "If any man will live godly in Christ Jesus he shall suffer persecution." But the burden will be light—light in comparison with the burden of sin—light in comparison with what those endure who have lost their souls, and whose consciences will torment them forever for rejecting Christ.

I know not how better to illustrate this subject than by a comparison which I have seen in the book of an ancient author. "I look around creation for an illustration of this text. I see a bird walking with folded wings, which he carries as a little burden on his back. But he is not willing to part with his burden. For the burden which he carries, often carries him. 'So they that wait on the Lord, shall renew their strength; they shall mount up with wings as eagles; they shall run and not be weary; they shall walk and not faint.'"

50

The necessity of regeneration no matter of wonder.

Marvel not that I said unto thee, ye must be born again.—John iii: 7.

It will be the object of this discourse to show that it is no marvellous thing that sinners must be born again.

If there is any cause of wonder in this, it must arise from the fact, that sinners now love God so well, that it appears strange and marvellous, that they should need to love him any better.

It has sometimes been said that sinners would not be happy, if taken to heaven without a change of heart. My object will be to prove the truth of this declaration. This may be done, by ascertaining the nature of the happiness of heaven, and that in which the sinner now delights.

What then is heaven?

1. It is a holy place—a place of spotless purity. There is no sin there. There shall in no wise enter into the new Jerusalem, any thing that defileth, neither whatsoever " worketh abomination, or maketh a lie." The son of man shall send forth his angels and they shall gather out of his kingdom *all things that offend, and them that do iniquity.*

2. Heaven is a place of ineffable glory.

It is the place where God in a special manner manifests himself. It is represented by the apostle John under the figure of a most beautiful and magnificent city. There is no temple therein; for the Lord God Almighty and the Lamb are the temple of it. And it hath no need of the sun, neither of the moon to shine in it; for the glory of the Lord doth lighten it, and the Lamb is the light thereof.

3. The inhabitants of heaven are holy.

There is an innumerable company of angels, and of the spirits of just men made perfect. There are Abraham, and Isaac, and Jacob, and all the patriarchs and prophets, and apostles, and all the saints who have finished their earthly pilgrimage, now made perfect in the image of their Saviour—clothed in white robes and palms in their hands. And there too is God the Judge of all, and Jesus the Mediator of the new covenant.

4. The employments of heaven are holy.

Angels and glorified saints are constantly employed in the service of God. "They serve him day and night in his temple." "I beheld, and I heard the voice of many angels round about the throne, and the beasts and the elders, and the number of them was ten thousand times ten thousand and thousands of thousands, saying with a loud voice, worthy is the Lamb that was slain to receive power, and riches, and wisdom, and strength, and honor, and glory, and blessing." "The four and twenty elders fell down before him that sat on the throne, and worship him that liveth forever and ever, and cast their crowns before the throne, saying thou art worthy, O Lord, to receive glory, and honor, and power; for thou hast created all things, and for thy pleasure they are, and were created." In such employments, the happiness of heaven consists.

Now are sinners prepared, without a change of heart to enter upon the holy employments and enjoyments of the heavenly state? Are they conformed in the temper of their hearts to the character of God? Do they delight in his service? Is it their meat and drink to do his will? What saith the scripture? "The wickedness of man is great in the earth, and every imagination of the thoughts of his heart is only evil continually." "The hearts of the sons of men are fully set in them to do evil." "The carnal mind is enmity against God." "The natural man receiveth not the things of the Spirit of God, for they are foolishness unto him; neither can he know them, for they are spiritually discerned."

In what do wicked men delight? "They take the timbrel and harp, and rejoice at the sound of the organ. They spend their days in wealth, and in a moment go down to the grave. Therefore they say unto God, depart from us, for we desire not the knowledge of thy ways. What is the Almighty that we should serve him, and what profit shall we have if we pray unto him?"

But let me appeal directly to the consciences of my impenitent hearers. What are the employments in which you delight? Do you delight in the service of God? Do you love to study his character, and to contemplate his perfections? Do you love to search the scriptures, and to offer up prayer and praise to your great creator? Do you love to converse on the things of the kingdom of God, to labor to promote the interests of Zion? What employment would you prefer, if you could have your heart's desire ? And what company do you choose ? The disciples of Christ ? Or those who take no interest in the things of religion ? Do you esteem the saints, the excellent of the earth, in whom is all you delight ?—Or are the precious sons of Zion, who are comparable to fine gold, esteemed by you as earthen pitchers, the work of the hands of the potter ? Is there any thing in heaven suited to your present taste? Suppose heaven were now opened on your view, and you were permitted to look in. What would you see there to attract your hearts? Or suppose that this night your souls should be released from their clay tenements, and should be conducted by some guardian angel into the immediate presence of God and the Lamb. Suppose you should see the saints, clothed in white robes, surrounding the Redeemer's throne, and crying, holy, holy, holy, is the Lord Almighty;—Would you not be ready to exclaim, is this heaven?—Is this that place of happiness of which I have so often heard ? There is nothing here which suits my taste. My companions are not here. There are no employments here such as I delight in. I cannot live here. Let me go back to earth whence I came. After such a sight, you would forever despair of entering heaven without a great change of heart. I ask you now my impenitent hearers, are you not convinced that with your present feelings, you could not be happy in heaven ? Marvel not then, that Christ has said unto you, ye must be born again.

This subject furnishes a criterion by which to test our hopes of heaven.

All men hope to go to heaven when they die. But all have not a well grounded hope. Hope implies the

30

desire and expectation of some future good. To be well grounded, there must be a correspondence between the state of the heart, and the object of hope.

Do you hope to go to heaven simply because it is a place of happiness? If this is all, you have no good reason to hope. The wicked as well as the righteous desire to be happy. Do you see any thing in heaven suited to make you happy?

Do you hope to go to heaven because it is a refuge from the ills of time, and from the pains of hell? If this is all, you have no reason to hope. It is true, heaven may be endeared to the saints, as a refuge from the miseries of the present and the future world; but this is not a distinguishing characteristic of the Christian hope.

Again—Do you hope to go to heaven, on account of the company which is there? Do you desire to join the society of angels, and of the spirits of just men made perfect? If so, your hope is well founded. Heaven is yours. But be not too hasty. If you really desire to join the society of heaven, you will delight in the society of God's people now. You will feel a peculiar attachment to the saints. You will esteem them the excellent of the earth. Is it so? Are they your chosen companions?

Again—Do you hope to go to heaven because Christ is there? If so your hope is well founded. This was the hope of Paul. He had a desire to depart and be with Christ. But be not too hasty. If you really desire to dwell with Christ in his kingdom, one thing is true. You love him now. He is precious to you, and you count all things but loss for the excellency of the knowledge of Christ Jesus you Lord. If you can say, whom have I in *heaven* but thee, you can add, there is none upon *earth* that I desire beside thee. Is it so?

Again—Do you hope to go to heaven on account of the employments of the heavenly world? If so your hope is well founded. But be not too hasty. If you are prepared to enter on the employments of heaven, you love God's service now. You are able to say, " O how I love thy holy law." " I delight in the law of the Lord, after the inward man." " I esteem all thy precepts concerning all things to be right." Is it so with you?

Again—Do you hope to go to heaven because it is a holy place—because there is no sin there? If so your hope is well founded; but then remember, if this is really so, you hate sin now, and long to be free from it. It is your ardent desire to be ·perfectly conformed to the image of your Saviour. If this is your real desire, it will eventually be gratified; and you may say,

> "O glorious hour, O blest abode,
> I shall be near and like my God,
> And flesh and sin no more control,
> The sacred pleasures of the soul."

51

The nature and reasonableness of Evangelical Repentance.

And the times of this ignorance God winked at; but now commandeth all men every where to repent.—ACTS xvii: 30.

THE text is a part of Paul's discourse before the Athenian philosophers. The times of ignorance to which he alludes, were the times of heathen idolatry. The phrase "winked at," does not mean that God, of course, overlooks the sin of ignorance. It is not the meaning of this, or of any other text in the Bible. The servant who knew his Lord's will and did it not, shall be beaten with many stripes; and the servant who knew not his Lord's will, and who committed things worthy of stripes, shall be beaten with few stripes. They that sin without law, are not saved, but perish without law. It was not their sin, but their ignorance, or the times of this ignorance that God overlooked. Because they did not like to retain God in their knowledge, he gave them up—he made no further efforts by raising up prophets to warn them. No commission had been given to preach the gospel to all nations. Even our Saviour when he first commissioned the twelve apostles, said "go not in the way of the gentiles, and into any city of the Samaritans, enter ye not. But go rather to the lost sheep of the house of Israel." But now a new commission had been given. The antithetic form of expression shows this. The times of this ignorance God winked at, but the times have altered. God now commandeth all men every where to repent.

> " No more the sovereign eye of God
> O'erlooks the crimes of men,
> His heralds are despatched abroad,
> To warn the world of sin."

Paul now appears at Athens, acting under this high commission. The text is the application of his discourse.

The great object of gospel preaching is to bring sinners to repentance. The subject though common is very important; for without repentance, there is no pardon nor salvation. So long, therefore, as there is one sinner out of Christ, so long it will be necessary for ministers to preach repentance.

I propose to consider,

I. The nature.

II. The reasonableness of evangelical repentance.

I. The nature.

Repentance implies that we are sinners. The gospel without ceremony addresses all men as sinners. The command to all now to repent, is proof positive that all are sinners. This is generally admitted. But something more is necessary. Repentance implies conviction of sin. Without conviction no sinner ever did, or ever will repent. But conviction itself is not repentance; nor is it necessarily connected with it. Conviction may rise to the highest degree—the sinner may see and feel that he is lost—he may be for a long time in this state, and still his heart be as proud and stubborn as ever. This hundreds and thousands have felt. It was so with Peter's hearers on the day of Pentecost. Although pricked in the heart, Peter did not say, "poor mourning souls"—taking it for granted that they were penitent. But he presumed the contrary; and urged upon them the duty of immediate repentance.

Repentance implies confession of sin. "I acknowledged my sin unto thee, and mine iniquity have I not hid." The sinner who has long refused to retire to confess his sins to God, will now be constrained by the power of conscience to cry for mercy. And those who do not confess their sins, may know that they have never repented. "He that covereth his sins, shall not prosper." But the sinner may be constrained by the power of conscience to confess his sins—he may do it often, by day and by night—he may cry long and loud for mercy, and after all, never repent. His heart may be as proud and stubborn as ever. This hundreds and thousands have felt. They have lost their concern and have shown that their hearts were never broken for sin. All that I have stated the sinner may experience, and yet never repent. What then is repentance?

It implies not only conviction and confession, but forsaking of sin. "Whoso confesseth and *forsaketh* his sins, shall have mercy." Unless the sinner breaks off his sins by righteousness, however much he may confess them—however much he may be distressed on account of them, he is not sincere, and God will not accept him.

Repentance implies loathing of sin. "I have heard of thee by the hearing of the ear, but now mine eye seeth thee, wherefore I abhor myself and repent in dust and ashes." "And then ye shall remember your ways, and all your doings wherein ye have been defiled, and ye shall loathe yourselves, in your own sight, for all your evils, that ye have committed."

Repentance implies sorrow for sin, because it is committed against God. "Against thee, thee only have I sinned." "Father I have sinned against heaven and before thee." And against Christ. "And they shall look on me whom they have pierced, and shall mourn for him as one mourneth for his only child; and shall be in bitterness, as one is in bitterness for his first born." Repentance is godly sorrow—or sorrow arising from love to God. The penitent feels a sweet pleasure mingled with his sorrow.

> "Let humble, penitential wo,
> With painful, pleasing anguish flow,
> And thy forgiving smiles impart
> Life, hope and joy to every heart."

II. The reasonableness of evangelical repentance.

Are there any present who have not repented—what I have here to say, will be addressed to you.

That repentance is your most reasonable duty, is evident from the fact that the law which you have broken is most reasonable. Also

From the fact, that sin is odious in itself. How reasonable that you should feel sorrow for that which is so odious in the sight of all holy beings. If you were required to feel sorrow for some good conduct, it might seem hard; but it is only because you have done wrong, that you are required to repent. Your sins have been committed against God, whose character is infinitely lovely, and is it not reasonable that you should repent.

Your sins have been committed against Christ who died for sinners—and is it hard that you should be required to feel sorrow for sins which have contributed to nail the Saviour to the cross? What a heart must that be which does not melt in view of a Saviour's dying love?

It is no more than you require of others—parents of children—you of your neighbors. When they injure you, you feel that they ought to repent. And how is this? Are you of more consequence than your Maker?

Christ and his apostles preached that men should repent; and God now commandeth all men every where to repent. Remember this is not my command, but God's; and whether we urge it or not, it will be binding upon you. . . . .
. . . .

Whose duty is it to repent? The text answers. *All men, every where*—the high and the low—the rich and the poor—the learned and the ignorant. The king must come down from his throne, and sit in sackcloth—the anxious sinner, however distressed—the thoughtless sinner, however hard and stubborn may be his heart, all are commanded to repent.

When is it their duty to repent? Doubtless it is their duty to repent, when God commands them to do it. And what says the text? *God now commandeth all men every where to repent.* If it is not the duty of the sinner to repent now, it never has been his duty, and it never will be. If we cannot urge immediate repentance, we cannot urge it at all. If the sinner finds it hard to repent to-day, it will be harder to-morrow. The longer he delays, the greater will be the number of his sins, and the harder will be his heart. And my hearers, if you cannot repent now, you never can. Do not misunderstand me. I do not say you never will. But you have no good reason to think you ever shall.

Paul preached the duty of immediate repentance; and has thus set an example for all other preachers of the gospel. Surrounded by rows of Athenian philosophers, with wonderful adroitness he says, " As I passed by and beheld your devotions, I found an altar with this inscription, ' To the unknown God.' " Having selected his text, he begins, " Whom, therefore, ye ignorantly worship, him declare I unto you." " God who made the world, and all things therein"—It was as though he had shot ten thousand suns into chaos.

. . . .

With awful solemnity, he pressed home the subject, "God now commandeth all men every where to repent, because he hath appointed a day in which he will judge the world in righteousness by that man whom he hath ordained; whereof he hath given *assurance* unto all men, in that he hath raised him from the dead." Just as surely as Christ was raised from the dead, so surely, " all who are in their graves shall hear his voice and come forth; they that have done good, to the resurrection of life; and they that have done evil, to the resurrection of damnation."

Mark the effect of Paul's discourse. It divided his audience into three parts.

Some mocked.

Others said, we will hear thee again of this matter. But some clave unto him.

Here were the scoffers—the doubters—and the believers. A number believed, among whom was Dionysius the Areopagite, and a woman named Damaris. To the honor of divine grace their names are recorded.

O, what a preacher was Paul!

> "There stands the messenger of truth—there stands
> The legate of the skies—his theme divine,
> His office sacred, his credentials clear.
> By him the violated law speaks out
> Its thunders; and by him, in strains as sweet
> As angels use, the gospel whispers peace."

By all the solemnity of the judgment day, I entreat you, my hearers, immediately to repent.

> "Together in his presence bow,
> And all your guilt confess;
> Accept the offered Saviour now,
> Nor trifle with his grace.
>
> Bow, ere the awful trumpet sound,
> And call you to his bar,
> For mercy knows the appointed bound,
> And turns to judgment there."

52

God's Spirit will not always strive.

And the Lord said, my Spirit shall not always strive with man.—GENESIS vi: 3.

THAT God should give his Son to die for this rebellious world—that Christ should consent to assume our nature, and suffer in our stead—and that salvation should be freely offered to the children of men, is an exhibition of astonishing mercy. And that all with one consent, should begin to make excuse, and refuse to accept of offered mercy, is proof of astonishing depravity. We should naturally expect that God would do no more for such ungrateful creatures. But he has given his Holy Spirit to strive with them. This may properly be styled God's last effort with sinners.

On this blessed influence, every preacher of the gospel must depend entirely for his success. Without this influence, no sinner will ever be brought to embrace the Saviour. Though he may listen to a preached gospel, he will listen in vain. He will continue to reject the counsel of God against himself, till the day of grace is past.

We will consider
    I. The fact that the Spirit does strive with men.
    II. The fact that he will not always strive.
    III. The consequences of his ceasing to strive.

I. That the Spirit does strive with men is evident from the whole tenor of the gospel. Every one who prays, admits the fact, that the Spirit has access to the minds of men.

But what is the object of the Spirit's strivings? Not to make men free moral agents; nor to make it their duty to repent and believe the gospel. If they were not moral agents, they would not be sinners, and would not need the strivings of the Spirit. But he strives with men to convince them of sin. It is just as natural for men to conceal and cover their sins, as it is to commit sin. They love darkness rather than light. Every one that doeth evil, hateth the light, and will not come to the light, lest he should be brought under conviction.

The Spirit comes to demolish the excuses of sinners— to destroy their self-flattery, and to show them their lost condition. He commonly commences by troubling the conscience in view of some overt act of sin. Then he lays open to the sinner the plague of his own heart.

The Spirit strives with men, not merely to show them their guilt and danger; but to show them their need of a Saviour, and to incline them to come to Christ. When they see their need of Christ, they are unwilling to come to him. "Ye will not come to me that ye might have life." "No man can come unto me, except the Father which hath sent me draw him." Now the Spirit comes to draw reluctant hearts. If it were not for this awful reluctance of the sinner to come to Christ, this drawing would not be necessary.

The language of the Bible in relation to this subject, is very striking. It is martial language. "The weapons of our warfare, are not carnal, but mighty through

God to the pulling down of strong holds; casting down imaginations, and every high thing which exalteth itself against the knowledge of God, and bringing into captivity every thought to the obedience of Christ." All this is the work of the Spirit, and without his agency, none will be saved.

Some may, perhaps, think they shall come to Christ, if the Spirit ceases to strive with them. But this is a delusion. They will certainly persist in sin, as they have heretofore done, till they awake in the world of despair.

I will mention some tokens of the Spirit's strivings.

When the Spirit strives, the sinner loses all interest in the concerns of time. The world is seen to be vanity. He has no relish for its pleasures. The noise of mirth fills him with distress. A dreadful sound is in his ears. Every thing is shrouded in gloom. As the poet expresses it :

> " Darker and darker still, the darkness grew,
> . . . . His interest in life,
> In being ceased. . . . .
> The blue heavens withered; and the moon, and sun,
> And all the stars, and the green earth, and morn
> And evening withered; and the eyes and smiles
> And fears of all men and women withered;
> Withered to him; and all the Universe
> Like something that had been, appeared; but now
> Was dead, and mouldering fast away."

When the Spirit strives, the sinner is filled with fear and trembling. However courageous he may have been, he is now afraid to be alone. He is afraid of God, and is ready to say in the language of the psalmist, "Whither shall I go from thy Spirit? Whither shall I flee from thy presence?"

When the Spirit strives, the sinner is troubled about that great change of heart which the Scriptures teach him he must experience, or he cannot be saved. He is troubled about beginning to pray. He knows it is his duty to worship God, and yet his proud heart resists the conviction. When the Spirit strives with the sinner, there is an awful struggle between his conscience and his heart. His conscience pleads for God, but his heart still cleaves to sin.

Let us consider,

II. The fact that God's Spirit will not always strive with man. This is clearly asserted in the text. Some have tried to flatter the sinner that there is little or no danger of the Spirit's ceasing to strive. But the text speaks a different language. "And the Lord said, my Spirit shall not always strive with man."

How long the Spirit will strive with any individual, we cannot tell. With some he strives longer than with others. Some *live* longer than others. In this God acts as a holy Sovereign. He has a right to cut off the sinner at any moment, and put a period to his day of salvation. And though the sinner may continue to live, it is by no means certain that the Spirit will continue to strive with him.

The Bible speaks of some who were given up of God. "Ephraim is joined to idols, let him alone." Our Saviour addressed his hearers as if some of them were given over of God. "If thou hadst known, even thou, in this thy day, the things which belong to thy peace—but now they are hid from thine eyes."

Many are given up because they receive not the

love of the truth that they might be saved. "For this cause, God shall send them strong delusion that they might believe a lie, that they all might be damned, because they received not the love of the truth, but had pleasure in unrighteousness." "Wo unto them, when I depart from them."

The sinner may be given up while young. He may have done such despite unto the Spirit of grace, as even in youth, to be given over to a hard heart, and a reprobate mind. "Turn you at my reproof," said Christ. "Behold, I will pour out my Spirit unto you. I will make known my words unto you." Then he adds, with awful solemnity, "Because I have called, and *ye refused*——then shall they call upon me, but I will not answer; they shall seek me early, but they shall not find me."

But how do sinners resist the strivings of the Spirit?

Sometimes, by rushing into thoughtless company, and into scenes of amusement. This they may do through ignorance, not knowing that the Spirit is striving with them. They are, not unfrequently, advised to this course, by ministers and parents who do not believe in conviction and conversion. In this way, they sometimes succeed in banishing their religious impressions;—and sometimes these things only increase their distress. Not unfrequently they are advised to journey, to divert their minds, and in some instances, medical aid has been sought. So it was in former times. The celebrated Dr. Darwin was often called to prescribe in such cases, but he could do nothing for the relief of his patients. He called the disease " Timor orci"—the fear of hell; and although he was an infidel, he acknowledged that he could prescribe nothing better than the gospel of Christ. For although the patient had lost all his interest in the concerns of this world, he said he might be cheered by the prospect of a happy immortality. Poor Darwin— O that he could have known from experience the value of his own prescription.

Sinners resist the Spirit by postponing the subject of religion, like Felix, to a more convenient season—by self-righteousness—by an unwillingness to see the worst of their case—by refusing to retire from the world to confess their sins to God—and by being ashamed of the subject of religion.

Let us consider,

III. The consequences of the Spirit's ceasing to strive.

When the Spirit has departed, the sinner may be cheerful. . . . . He may feel little concern for the salvation of his soul. . . . . . . He may even laugh, and make sport of the subject of religion. . . . . . He may listen to a preached gospel—to the most solemn warnings, and to the most melting invitations;—but it will be all in vain. He will slumber on in impenitence till he awakes in hell, and his soul is lost forever.

53

Salvation for the lost.

For the Son of man is come to seek and to save that which was lost.—LUKE xix: 10.

THE incarnation of Christ, his doctrine, miracles, sufferings, death, resurrection, and ascension to heaven, are topics familiar to you all. What astonishing truths? And yet heard, O with what indifference!

Suppose, my hearers, that you had never heard this until this evening—that you were now assembled for the first time to hear this interesting story that " the son of man is come to seek and to save that which is lost;" with what interest would you listen? Here I am reminded of a fact related by one of our early missionaries.

"As I sat in my window," he says, "I saw the heathen assembling from all quarters—each one running with all his might, and taking the shortest course to the place of worship, to hear the wonderful story how that the son of man had come to seek and to save that which was lost. As I entered the place of worship, I found it crowded with the young, who had outstripped the aged and decrepid, that were lingering about the doors and windows. As I commenced reading the trial of our Saviour before the bar of Pilate, every eye was fixed, and every ear intent. As I advanced, the interest increased until I arrived at the passage 'It is finished, and he bowed his head and gave up the ghost.' At this point, every individual involuntarily dropped upon his knees."

Or suppose that it was not true that Christ had come, and that you had now assembled for the first time to learn that the whole Christian world had been under a mistake—that he had not come to our world, but had gone to some other world—that the Bible by some means had been dropped into our world—that its contents were true, but not in application to us—that Christ had gone to some other world to seek and to save that was lost. How would you now feel?

Some would doubtless cry out. Who can dwell with devouring fire? Who can dwell with everlasting burnings? It would indeed be solemn, you say; but it is not so. Christ has come to our world, and we may set our hearts at rest. But remember although Christ has come, all out of Christ are lost.

My object will be to show in what sense sinners are lost.

A thing may be lost past recovery;—or it may be lost, and afterwards found.

1. The sinner is condemned by the law. He is under sentence of death—as really so, as the criminal who has heard his sentence from the lips of his judge. "Cursed is every one who continueth not in all things written in the book of the law to do them." Should the sinner die and go to judgment as he now is, he would find himself condemned for every failure of perfect obedience to the divine law. Thus he is lost —or dead in point of law.

2. The sinner needs pardon. This is implied in what has been said under the last head; but I name it distinctly because every sinner who needs pardon, is of course condemned already; and no sinner ever did, or ever will, in earnest plead for pardon, who does not see and feel that he is lost. All those passages in the Bible which show the sinner's need of pardon, imply that he is lost.

3. The sinner is invited to Christ for life. "I am come," said Christ, "that they might have life." He that believeth on the Son, hath everlasting life, and shall not come into condemnation, but is passed from death unto life." Sinners are invited to Christ that they may receive life. And Christ says, "ye will not come unto me that ye might have life?" Now it is clear, that none but those who are under sentence of death, and are destitute of spiritual life, are invited to Christ for life. The offer of life, is proof positive that all to whom the offer is made, are lost. The gospel offer, "Whosoever will, let him take the water of life freely," is made to those, and those only who are spiritually dead.

4. That the sinner is lost, is evident from the inquiry, "What must I do to be saved?" Every sinner who makes this inquiry sincerely, feels that he is lost. And when the sinner comes to Christ, from that very moment he is saved. When the prodigal returned, his father said, "This my son was dead, and is alive again;—was lost, and is found."

The occasion on which our Saviour uttered the text, reveals the same truth. He entered and passed through Jericho. And Zaccheus sought to see him, and could not for the press, because he was little of stature.

And he ran before, and climbed up into a sycamore tree to see him. When Jesus came to the place, he said to him, "make haste, and come down, for to day I must abide at thy house. And he made haste and came down and received him joyfully."

Others seeing what had taken place, murmured. But Zaccheus gave evidence of supreme attachment to Christ. He received the Saviour joyfully, and made ample restitution to all whom he defrauded. "And Jesus said unto him, *this day is salvation come to this house,* for as much as he also is a son of Abraham." Then follow the words of the text. "For the son of man is come to seek and save that which was lost." We here learn what our Saviour means by this declaration. He sought and found Zaccheus. And whenever a sinner comes to Christ, with equal propriety it may be said, "This day is salvation come to this house." "For the son of man is come to seek and to save that which was lost." Every time a sinner comes down and receives the Saviour joyfully the text is fulfilled.

But there are some who have never felt that they were lost. And what does this prove? "If our gospel be hid, it is hid to them that are lost." Their case is truly deplorable. They are lost and know it not.

Reflections.

1. We see why it is, that sinners say so little about the Saviour. They do not feel that they are lost. "They that are whole, need not a physician, but they that are sick. And Christ came not to call the righteous, but sinners to repentance."

2. We learn from this subject why ministers preach the gospel. Although Christ has come and laid down his life for sinners, they all with one consent, refuse to come to him for pardon and eternal life. The business of ministers is to show them their lost condition, and to urge them to come to Christ for life. This is the reason why Paul, and the other apostles preached the gospel to sinners;—and this is the reason why missionaries are sent into all parts of the world to proclaim the gospel.

3. We learn what is the genuine effect of a preached gospel. Sinners begin to feel that they are lost, and to enquire what they must do to be saved. Until this is the case, no sinner will come to Christ. So it was under the preaching of Peter. His hearers were first pricked in the heart, and then like Zaccheus, they received the word gladly. And thus it is now wherever the gospel is preached with the Holy Ghost sent down from heaven.

4. Were sinners in this house to realize their true condition they would immediately begin to inquire what they must do to be saved.

There is one other sense in which the sinner is lost. He is wandering farther and farther from God. Were you lost in a natural sense, would you not cry for help? I will here mention a fact related by Burder.

"It was in the dead of a cold winter's night, when the snow fell thick and heavy, that a gentleman was awaked by the sound of a human voice. He arose and lifted the window, and heard distinctly uttered, in a piteous tone, these words, LOST, LOST, LOST. It was a child who had been sent on an errand and lost his way. He discovered his danger, and cried for help, and happy for him, he was found." But this is nothing in comparison with the state of the sinner. He is lost in a sense infinitely more solemn; and God has sent his messengers to call " turn ye, turn ye, for why will ye die."

Let it ring in your ears when you go from this place, and through the silent watches of the night, when you awake in the morning, and through the day at every turn, LOST—LOST—LOST—until you come to Christ.

But should you not wake to see the light of the morning, where are you? You will then feel what was intimated at the commencement of this discourse. You will wake up, in that world where Christ never died for sinners, in awful despair. Alas! you will say, this is the world of despair, where the gospel was never proclaimed. Christ never came to this world to seek and to save that which was lost; but to yonder world whence I came. You may feel all this before to-morrow's light shall dawn. O how solemn.

> "In vain for mercy now they cry,
> In lakes of liquid fire they lie;
> There on the flaming billows lost,
> Forever, O forever lost."

PLANS OF SERMONS,

AND

BRIEF OBSERVATIONS ON TEXTS OF SCRIPTURE.

Sir, we remember that deceiver said, while he was yet alive, after three days, I will rise again.—MATTHEW xxvii: 63.

Notice.

1. The prediction. The chief priests and pharisees remembered it, talked of it, and told it to Pilate. Hence Christ must have declared it openly. The most unlikely event on which to practice deceit.

2. What a happy circumstance that they did remember it. Now they had an important object before them. If they could retain him three days in the tomb, a complete triumph would have been gained. The stone must be *sealed*, and be guarded by a band of soldiers. They no doubt expected to assemble on the fourth day and to examine the seal in triumph. They expected to break it and to show that the body was there. If they had not *remembered*, they might have said after Christ's resurrection, strange that we did not think of his prediction. Then we might have guarded the sepulchre. But this they could not say, for they had taken every precaution to prevent the possibility of fraud. But he could not be kept in the

grave. How striking that text, "whom God raised from the dead, because it was not *possible* for him to be holden of it."

Reflections.

1. The enemies of religion will be sure to remember, and to tell every thing which they think will work injury to the cause of Christ.

2. God will make even the wrath of man to praise him.

3. All Christ's predictions will certainly be fulfilled.

And for this cause, God shall send them strong delusion, that they should believe a lie; that they all might be damned who believed not the truth, but had pleasure in unrighteousness.—2 THESSALONIANS ii: 11, 12.

1. Some errors are damnable. "He that believeth not shall be damned." What errors? Generally such as prevent conviction of sin, and a sense of the justice of God—such as deny the necessity of regeneration, and such as break the force of the divine threatenings.

Objection. Cannot God convert those who embrace these errors?

Answer. Yes, if he has not declared the contrary. But does he? God can cause a crop to grow without seed. But does he? "God cannot lie."

2. Speak of the delusion.

It is strong delusion—not to be removed by argument, or any means which man can employ. God sends it.

Objection. God will not send delusion upon his creatures.

Answer. He says he will. And we know he has done it. " He hath blinded their eyes and hardened their hearts."

How? By sending them false teachers, and giving them opportunity to hear smooth things.

Why ? There may be many reasons. The text specifies one. *For this cause,* " God shall send them strong delusion"—because they " *believed not the truth, but had pleasure in unrighteousness.*" When sinners try to believe against the convictions of conscience— when, because they do not love the truth, they labor continually to find arguments against it, they are in peculiar danger of being given up to judicial blindness.

3. The punishment. Those who are sincere in fatal error, are in a most fearful condition.

Inferences.

1. We see the equity of the punishment. Sinners choose to be deceived, and God gives them their choice.

2. We see the danger of the sentiment, that it is no matter what a man believes, provided he is sincere. A man may be sincerely wrong, as well as sincerely right. He may be in the road to hell, and sincerely believe that he is in the road to heaven. "There is a way that seemeth right unto a man, but the end thereof is the way of death."

3. Persons may *firmly* believe a lie. They may trust in it, and even venture their souls upon it. This is evident both from the word of God, and from observ-

ation. The fact that persons die in the full belief of certain doctrines, is no conclusive proof that those doctrines are true.

4. We see the danger of entertaining loose sentiments. A man is as much accountable for his belief on moral subjects, as he is for his practice. No man's character is better than the sentiments which he embraces. It is sometimes said, a man has a right to think as he pleases. But he has no more right, in the sight of God, to think as he pleases, than he has to act as he pleases.

5. Let the subject be applied in a way of self-examination. Let me ask you, my hearers, how came you by your present sentiments? Were you obedient to first suggestions of conscience? If there has been a struggle in your minds, was it with conscience against sin, or with inclination and sin against conscience? If you have in your minds a doubt whether the principles which you have adopted will stand in the hour of trial, I entreat you to pause and reflect. If you wish to be safe, dare to be faithful to your souls, and shun with horror that treachery to your best interests, which would impel you to sacrifice the peace of eternity to the quiet of a moment. Let the light of truth, however painful for the present, be admitted in its full force, and whatever secrets it may discover "in the chamber of imagery," while it unveils "still greater and greater abominations," shrink not from the view, but entreat God to search you and try you.

If you do not like the duties of religion, and if you wish to believe a lie, you may take the following course. Labor to obtain arguments on one side, and stop your ears to arguments on the other side—refuse to hear every thing which crosses your prejudices—disbelieve the warning in the text; and there is no doubt you will succeed in blinding your minds and hardening your hearts. God will help on the work. He will send upon you a strong delusion that you may believe a lie.

So then it is not of him that willeth, nor of him that runneth, but of God that showeth mercy.—ROMANS ix: 16.

Doctrine.

The conversion and salvation of sinners is owing entirely to the sovereign mercy of God.

I. Establish the truth of the doctrine.

II. Inquire why it is so.

The truth of the doctrine appears,

1. From what the Bible says of the character of sinners. Carnal—none seek God—will not come to Christ—hate the light—dead in trespasses and sins.

2. From what the Bible says of the author of regeneration. "God who commanded the light to shine out of darkness"—"of his own will begat he us"—"born not of blood, nor of the will of the flesh," &c.—"not by works of righteousness which we have done," &c.—"we are his workmanship."

3. From what the Bible says of the inefficacy of means. "Who then is Paul?"—"I have planted and Apollos watered."—

II. Why is it so?

Not because the atonement is not sufficient for all men.

Not because salvation is not offered to all.

But it is not of him that willeth nor of him that runneth, because
Sinners always will wrong, and always run wrong.

Reflection.

The state of sinners is worse than they are apt to imagine.

The case of the two thieves.—LUKE xxiii: 39-43.

Consider

I. In what respects they were alike.
II. In what respects they differed.
III. What made the difference.
They were alike.
By nature—both descended from Adam.
They were both Jews.
They lived under the same laws.
They were both thieves.
They were detected in their crimes.
They were condemned.
They were crucified.
They both saw the Saviour.
They both reviled him. Matt. xxvii: 38. Mark xv: 32.
They were both condemned by God's law.
They both deserved eternal death.
They were both about to be launched into eternity.

II. In what respects were they unlike? One differed from the other in the following things:
He was convinced of sin.
He felt the justice of his condemnation.

He feared God.
He declared the Lord's innocence.
He prayed.
He believed God.
He was not ashamed to confess his faith in Christ.
He was submissive.
He loved the soul of his fellow sufferer.
He reproved his sin.
He was an heir of heaven.

III. What made him to differ from his companion?

Nothing that he had done—not morality—no acts of charity. But

Grace—wondrous grace. He might have said, "By the grace of God I am what I am."

Remarks.

1. This subject exhibits strikingly the sovereignty of God. One taken and another left.

2. Let none take encouragement from this subject to postpone religion to a dying hour. Of all the cases of conversion recorded in the Scriptures, this is the only instance mentioned of repentance at so late an hour.

3. How interesting the thought, that our Saviour in his dying agonies, should be dispensing pardon, and fixing the destinies of immortal beings.

> "He that distributes crowns and thorns,
> Hangs on a tree and bleeds and groans,
> The prince of life, resigns his breath,
> The king of glory bows to death."

Come see a man which told me all things that ever I did.—JOHN iv: 29.

1. The duty of preachers. It is to tell sinners their hearts. "He told me" &c.

2. Preaching which discloses the hearts of sinners, is likely to be remembered. It will be remembered and conversed upon, while other preaching, and other things are forgotten. "She saith to the men of the city, he told me" &c.

3. The preacher who tells sinners their hearts, is not likely to want for hearers. The invitation will be given, "Come see the man" &c.

4. The conversion of one sinner is likely to be followed by the conversion of others. The invitation "Come" &c. was complied with, and a great spiritual harvest followed.

Surely the wrath of man shall praise thee; the remainder of wrath thou shalt restrain.—PSALM lxxiii: 10.

All kinds of wrath—

That God will cause the wrath of man to praise him, is evident,

1. From the perfections of God. The wisdom, goodness, and power of God will all lead him to do it.

2. From facts recorded in the Bible—*e. g.* the story of Joseph, and the crucifixion of Christ. David was kept back by Abigail, but attributes it to God. It is an important and desirable truth, that God should cause the wrath of man to praise him, &c.

Inferences.
1. The doctrine of decrees is true. If God overrules, and restrains the wrath of men and devils, so as ultimately to praise him, then he has determined to do it, and all objections against the doctrine of decrees fall to the ground.
2. The safety of God's friends. Esther vi: 13. "Begun to fall," &c.
3. The folly of opposing God. "Who hath hardened himself against him and prospered?" "No wisdom, nor understanding, nor counsel against the Lord."

If we had been in the days of our fathers, we would not have been partakers with them in the blood of the prophets.—MATTHEW xxiii: 30.

1. Sinners may mistake the character of their own feelings. [The Jews.] At the foot of Sinai, said, would do so—soon made a calf. Peter—I will not deny thee—disciples—command fire—"Ye know not what manner of spirit ye are of." Hazael—dog. 2 Kings viii: 13. Heart deceitful—who can know it? Herod said he had been desirous to see Jesus, &c.
2. Sinners may think that they are better than others, when they are in heart opposed to true religion. Text.
3. Sinners may do much, and profess great respect for religion, when they are totally opposed to true religion. Text—Build the prophets' tombs, and hate the prophets' doctrine.
4. When sinners say they were never opposed to

God, it is no evidence against the doctrine of total depravity.

5. If they never have seen that they were totally depraved, they have reason to fear they are still ignorant of their hearts, and have never yet been thoroughly awakened. Text.

Words betray hearts—when they most seek to cover their hearts, they most expose them—what they did.

1. Built anew, at their own expense, the tombs, &c.
2. Protested against the murder of the prophets.

"If we had been in the days of our fathers," &c.— we had never consented to the silencing of Amos—the imprisonment of Micaiah—the putting of Hananiah into the stocks, and of Jeremiah into the dungeon—the stoning of Zechariah, and the mocking of the messengers of the Lord—no—not they. They would sooner have lost their hands, or their lives. What, is thy servant a dog? And yet at this very time, they were plotting against Christ, to put him to death, to whom all the prophets gave witness. They would have heard them gladly—and yet were filled with wrath against Christ. See their enmity—"Ye are witnesses against yourselves." Verse 31. Their own words and works prove what they are—so now.

Inferences.

1. If mankind may mistake their own character, then the doctrine of total depravity may be true, though they universally deny it. Jews no love to Christ.

2. We see a reason why sinners, when awakened, find themselves to be much worse than they had ever imagined themselves to be.

3. We see why sinners act worse in certain circumstances, than they ever imagined they should.

For let not that man think that he shall receive any thing of the Lord.
JAMES i : 7.

What man ? The man who does not ask in faith.

1. Mankind are prone to think they shall receive answers to their prayers, though they do not ask in faith.
2. This is a mistake.
3. We are bound to correct the mistake. We must not let them think so. If they do, they will act accordingly.

And they all with one consent began to make excuse.—LUKE xiv : 18.

Much as unrenewed men may differ in other respects, there is one thing in which they are all agreed. When invited to come to Christ, they all with *one consent*, begin to make excuse. They do not say, in plain terms, that they will not come. But they plead some reason to justify themselves in refusing to come.

That we may view this matter in a clear point of light, let us look at the parable of which the text is a part.

A certain man made a great supper, and bade many ; and sent his servant at supper time, to say to them that were bidden, come for all things are now ready.

The servant faithful to his orders, delivered his message to one. He said to the servant, *I have bought a piece of ground, and must needs go and see it.* You know it is our duty to take care of our worldly interests. This I am bound to do; and this I trust, is a sufficient reason for declining the invitation. *I pray thee have me excused.*

The servant goes to another, and receives a similar answer. *I have bought five yoke of oxen, and I go to prove them. I pray thee have me excused.* He goes to a third. He pleads a different excuse. *I have married a wife, and therefore, I cannot come.*

At length the servant begins to expostulate with them. He speaks of the expensive entertainment which his master has made. He tells them that there is sufficient for all who will come, and that every thing is prepared in the best possible manner. *All things are now ready.* My master is liberal. The invitation is free. Whosoever will, may come and take without money and without price. Thus he attempts to allure them.

Finding no success, he tries a different method. He attempts to alarm their fears, by pointing them to the consequences of a refusal. He informs them that his master will be displeased, and that fearful consequences will follow. This also proves ineffectual. Perceiving that no considerations which he can present to their minds have any influence to persuade them, the servant at length speaks in plain terms— you are all so opposed to my master, that not one of you ever will come, unless my master comes and brings you. On hearing this, one of the persons invited becomes angry, and begins to dispute with the servant. Did you not tell us, says he, that we are freely invited, and that whosoever will may come?

I did, replies the servant; and so it is. You are all freely invited. Nay, you are commanded to come, and threatened with a fearful punishment if you do not come. But since my master has made such large provision, he is determined that it shall not be lost.

And as all my arguments prove ineffectual, and I cannot persuade one of you to come, he has determined to exert his own power on a certain number, and make them willing.

Then your master is partial, and does not give us all an equal opportunity to come to the feast.

The servant replies, you just now acknowledged that all were freely invited, and that whosoever will, may come. Have you any reason to find fault, because you are left to your own choice? Will you find fault even if my master has not determined to make you willing to come?

The other replies, I do not believe your master has determined to make any willing. I believe that all are left to their own choice.

Why then, replies the servant, do you not come? If no special power is necessary to make you willing, why do you stand making excuses? Why do you not come now? I tell you again, you are so opposed, that you never will come, unless my master exerts his power to make you willing. And there is but one way for you to prove my declaration false; and that is to come. Now contradict what I say, by coming of your own accord. I call upon you to do it; and again repeat the assertion that you never will do it unless my master makes you willing.

But instead of coming to the feast, he stands disputing with the servant. How discouragingly you talk. You tell us, if your master has not determined to make us willing, we never shall be willing. Is not this a discouraging doctrine?

If it is discouraging, the servant replies, to hear that my master has determined to make some willing, and to leave others to their own choice, let us suppose that he has not determined to make any willing, but to leave all to their own choice. Is this more encouraging?

He now pleads another excuse. He says, if your master has not determined to make me willing to come to the feast, I cannot come. How can I?

This, replies the servant, is giving up the point. If you cannot come, unless my master makes you willing, then what I said is true; that you never will come unless he makes you willing. And remember, your opposition is all that hinders. You labor under no other inability.

But, says the other, if your master has not determined that I shall come, I cannot, and I am not to blame.

It is your duty to come, says the servant, whether he has determined to make you willing or not. Thousands who have been invited, have never come; nor has my master made them willing; and he has punished them for not coming. And thus he will deal with you, and I leave you to settle the matter with him.

And when his disciples James and John saw this, they said, Lord, wilt thou that we command fire to come down from heaven, and consume them, even as Elias did? But he turned and rebuked them, and said, ye know not what manner of Spirit ye are of.—LUKE ix: 54, 55.

What a lesson of instruction is this to all the disciples of Christ. If the warm-hearted disciples, James and John, in vindicating the cause of their divine master, might lose a good temper, and indulge a bad one how does it become others to take heed. James and John were certainly on the right side—on the side of religion, and the side of Christ. In this they were right. Well might they feel a holy indignation. But with this, they unwittingly suffered a bad spirit to be intermingled, for which they received a solemn rebuke. What a lesson of instruction is this to the ministers of Christ, who are sent to cities, towns, and villages, as messengers before his face to call upon the people to open their houses and their hearts to receive him. Should they meet with a repulse, through prejudice and pride and unwillingness to receive the Saviour, this may well grieve their hearts; but in vindicating the cause of Christ, and urging sinners to receive him they must not forget the solemn caution, " take heed to thyself." The example of the two ardent disciples, is recorded for their instruction and warning. In the ardor of their zeal, there may be something noble, but still they may lack the meekness and gentleness of Christ. The case before us is truly affecting. That which many have commended as bold and heroic in the cause of religion met with the divine rebuke, " Ye know not what spirit ye are of." While ministers are faithful to deliver their whole message, whether men will hear, or forbear, let them look well to the Spirit by which they are actuated.

And he said unto another, follow me. But he said, Lord, suffer me first to go and bury my father.— LUKE ix : 59.

The circumstances of this case, seem to have been peculiar. The person who was called upon to follow Christ, was in deep affliction. His father was dead.

Lord, I will follow thee, but suffer me *first* to pay the last tribute of respect to a deceased parent.

How many in similar circumstances, resolve to attend to the subject of religion. How many when called to stand by the sick and dying bed of a father, a mother, a brother, a sister, or some dear friend, resolve that they will attend to the subject of religion. They sigh, and are ready to exclaim, " let me die the death of the righteous and let my last end be like his." Or it may be they are summoned to hear the warning voice of such as have neglected the concerns of their souls, and slighted all the calls and melting invitations of the Saviour, while in health. The very sight itself, or even the tidings of the death of kindred and friends, checks the spirit of worldliness and vanity, and says impressively, " Be ye also ready." Thousands under these circumstances, have felt the littleness of earth with all its concerns, and have resolved that they will attend to the great concerns of the soul. But unhappily, as the case before us, their very afflictions prevent an *immediate* attention to the subject, and thus the call of infinite mercy, is neglected to their eternal undoing.

And there are diversities of operations but it is the same God which worketh all in all.—1 CORINTHEANS xii: 6.

Religion is the same everywhere, but there is a diversity of manner in which persons are brought to experience religion. Diversities of operations but the same result—all are brought to possess the same Spirit—all children of God—all members of Christ—

all possess his image, and of course resemble each other.

Difference in the following respects:

1. As to time of life, when converted.

Some old—some young, third, sixth, ninth and eleventh hour.

2. As to means of conviction.

Some by hearing a sermon—reading the Bible—some other book—alarming providences—word dropped by a friend—by seeing others anxious—seeing others joyful—hearing of the conversion of others—by their own wickedness—a thought suggested by the Spirit without any apparent means.

3. As to the clearness of evidence of conversion.

Some sudden and very clear—others less clear and gradual—like the rising light of the morning.

6. As to growth in grace.

Some bring forth a hundred fold—some sixty—some thirty.

Reflections.

1. Others not a perfect standard of trial for us.

Word of God.

2. There is in the church a beautiful vanity.

Like flowers in a garden.

" Let us get up early to the vineyards."

Let us all be careful to possess the graces of the Spirit —and to grow in grace.

I thought on my ways, and turned my feet unto thy testimonies. I made haste and delayed not to keep thy commandments.—PSALM cxix: 59, 60,

The Psalmist here gives an account of his conversion.

Apply it to sinners.

1. Think on your ways. Duties neglected—sins committed—their number and aggravation—thousands of sins have been forgotten—God remembers all.

3. Think of the end of your ways.

How short your course—increased velocity—near to death—end of these things is death—how solemn!—how will thine heart endure?—O that you were wise.

4. Think on *your* ways—not be forever thinking and talking about the sins of others. This is very common—what folly to be thus employed.

5. Turn your feet. No use to think unless you turn—turn to God—all by nature traveling the wrong way. Turn ye, turn ye—turn your affections from the love of sin.

6. You must make haste and delay not.

Say not suffer me first to go and bury my father—or to bid farewell. If you delay—

Business will crowd in.

Temptations will increase.

Sins will become more numerous.

Heart will become more hard.

By becoming familiar with awful subjects they will lose their effect upon you.

The Spirit will cease to strive.

And death may come. Lose no time. Zaccheus, make haste. Felix—escape for thy life.

Who will rise up for me against the evil doers? Or who will stand up for me against the workers of iniquity?—PSALM xciv: 16.

This is the language of Christ.

I. The grounds of this appeal.

II. What can be done.
III. Reasons for compliance.
I. Grounds &c.
1. Christ has a moral kingdom in this world.
2. In building up his kingdom, he makes use of human instrumentality.
3. Much yet remains to be done. But a small part of the world yet belongs to the kingdom of Christ.
II. What can be done?
1. Give up yourself.
2. Pray for the peace of Jerusalem.
3. Make personal efforts for the advancement of Christ's kingdom.
4. Contribute of your substance.
III. Reasons for so doing.
1. Christ claims your service.
2. He has a right to it.
3. If you do not render it, you will be ranked among the workers of iniquity, and will be destroyed.

Application.

"Who will rise up?" Who?

When once the master of the house is risen up, and hath shut to the door.—MATTHEW xiii: 25.

The house heaven.
I. The door of heaven is opened.
By whom? Rev. iii: 7, 8. "'These things saith he that is holy, he that is true, he that hath the key of David, he that *openeth* and no man shutteth," &c.
How? By his sufferings and death.
For whom? " Who gave himself a ransom for

all." "Tasted death for every man." "We thus judge if one died for all."

II. The door will be shut.

When? At death—when the Spirit ceases to strive.

By whom? By Christ the master of the house.

How long will it be shut?

Forever. He that is holy—holy still. He that is filthy—filthy still.

When the door is shut some will be shut out, and some will be shut in.

If it should now be shut, where should we be found?

Reflections.

1. How happy those who will be shut in.
2. How wretched those who will be shut out.

Agree with thine adversary quickly, while thou art in the way with him, lest at any time the adversary deliver thee to the judge, and the judge deliver thee to the officer, and thou be cast into prison; verily I say unto thee, thou shalt by no means come out thence till thou hast paid the uttermost farthing.—MATTHEW v: 25.

1. God is the sinner's adversary—adversary at law.
2. Sinners are now on the way to judgment.
3. The sinner is called upon to agree with his adversary—but two ways of settling a controversy—by compromise, or by the yielding of one of the parties, In this controversy, the sinner must yield.
4. What sinners do, must be done quickly.

Motives to agree quickly.

1. God is a powerful adversary. "What king going to make war." "Let the potsherds"—"Who ever hardened himself against God and prospered?" "Can thine heart endure, or thy head be strong."

2. The cause will certainly come to trial, " We must all stand before the judgment seat of Christ."

3. The sinner dying unreconciled to God will certainly be lost.

4. Once lost, he will be lost forever. Uttermost farthing.

5. " Lest at *any time*—in health—in youth—while anxious or stupid—in the midst of wickedness—awake or asleep—at *any time* the sinner is liable to be arrested."

Turn ye, turn ye, for why will ye die ?—EZEKIEL xxxiii: 11.

Death what ? Not natural death, or the death of the body—God never asks sinners why they will die in this sense—and in this sense they will die, whether they turn or not.

There is a death beyond the grave.

Turn—Implies that sinners are departing from God. To turn is to repent—to turn the affections to God.

Why will ye die ?

Not because God delights in your death. " As I live, saith the Lord," &c.

There is usually some one sin which occasions the sinner's death—that is, some one sin which he is unwilling to give up.

The young ruler was *sad* when Christ told him *to sell all*. Herod could not part with Herodias. There is generally some *right eye* which the sinner is unwilling to pluck out.

1. One will die because his heart is engrossed with worldly cares.

2. Another, because he is ashamed to have it known that he is anxious.

3. Another, because he is unwilling to give up at some sinful companion.

4. Another, because he is unwilling to leave his profession.

5. Another, because he is unwilling to pray in his family.

6. Another, because he is unwilling to confess Christ before men.

7. Another will lose his soul by talking about others.

8. Pride of consistency will keep some out of heaven. They fear that if they commence a religious life they will not hold out, and so will not begin.

9. Some will lose their souls by spending their time in caviling at divine truth.

10. Others will perish in consequence of cherishing some secret sin, known only to God, and their own consciences.

MISCELLANEOUS REMARKS.

What answer would you give to the question, how can I repent, or believe, or love God, or become a Christian?

I would answer according to the character of the querist. If he does not believe the doctrines of grace, I would take occasion from his inquiry, to endeavor to convince him. I would say to him, your question, if sincere, implies that you would repent if you could. If you cannot, then there is no hope in your case, unless the doctrine of election is true.

If he does believe the doctrines of grace, I would endeavor to show him the justice of his condemnation. I would say, if you cannot repent of sin, and love God, what a desperately wicked heart you must have. Out of your own mouth you will be condemned.

I would also endeavor to show him his insincerity. I would ask him, will you do what I tell you? Will you break off your sins, and perform the duties of religion? If not, you would not become a Christian, if you could.

Special Grace.

It is sometimes affirmed that the Spirit of God operates equally at all times.

To this I have the following objections.

1. It destroys all encouragement to prayer; for it supposes that the Spirit of God operates just as much where there is no prayer, as where there is.

2. It places on a level a faithful and unfaithful ministry; for it takes it for granted that those who preach error, or who do not preach at all, will be equally successful with those who take heed to themselves and to their doctrine, and who are abundant in their labors.

3. It admits that there is just as much religion where the gospel was never heard, as where it is faithfully preached; as much in Hindostan as any where else.

4. It is contrary to the experience of every Christian. He knows that the Spirit has striven more with himself at some times than at others.

5. It supposes that all men are equally sinful, or equally holy; or that if there is a difference, man makes it.

6. It is contradicted by many plain texts of Scripture, such as the following: " Turn ye at my reproof, *behold I will pour out my Spirit unto you.*" " 'Tis time to seek the Lord *till he come,* and rain righteousness upon you." " Sensual, *having not the Spirit.*"

Those texts which speak of a change of heart, wrought by the Holy Spirit. "Except a man be born of water *and of the Spirit.*" " *The Spirit quickeneth.*"

Those texts which speak of sinners as given up of God. " My Spirit *shall not always strive* with man."

7. It saps the foundation of true religion. It places Christianity on a level with heathenism or infidelity. The person who maintains this opinion, virtually confesses that he knows no more about vital piety, than an infidel or Hindoo.

Thoughts on Revivals.

Against revivals many objections are urged. It is said they are mere excitements which have in them nothing of the nature of true religion, and that they ought not to be ascribed to the Spirit of God. In support of these allegations is alleged,

1. Their suddenness, and the fact that such numbers profess to be converted in so short a time.

Answer. The influences of the Spirit are compared in the Scriptures, to the rain. "He shall come unto us as the rain, as the latter and the former rain unto the earth." Would you object to the rain, and say it cannot be rain, because it sometimes comes suddenly, and in so many drops? We are given to understand that a nation will be born in a day.

2. The great distress which exists in revivals is urged as an objection against them.

Answer. It is not religion, which causes the distress, but a conviction of the want of it. Is it surprizing that sinners should be distressed, when they are brought to realize that they are exposed to eternal destruction? When a person's body is in pain, he is in distress; and his friends often sigh and weep. And is the soul of less consequence than the body? Are heaven and hell trifles? Were not sinners pricked in the heart on the day of Pentecost? And was not the jailor of Philippi distressed when he fell down before Paul and Silas?

3. It is said that persons are only terrified by alarming preaching.

Answer. Why were they not terrified before? They have often heard the same truths. They have heard, perhaps for years, the most alarming preaching, and remained unmoved. Why are they alarmed now, if they are under no influence from on high? Besides, the very same truths which fill sinners with alarm, often after a season, fill them with joy unspeakable and full of glory. How is this to be explained? Does the same preaching, of itself, cause in the same mind, sorrow and joy?

But have not sinners reason to be terrified? When persons have no fear of God before their eyes, it is a mark of great depravity. Was not Felix terrified under the preaching of Paul?

If the results witnessed in revivals, are the result of human influence only, believing what I do of the nature of these results, I should feel under obligation to awaken all my hearers. I should not expect to be saved myself, if I failed to do it. Are you willing to grant that ministers have so much power? Are they able to change the enemies of God into his friends?—to cause them to love what they hated with perfect hatred?

But the objection might have been made against the revival on the day of Pentecost, as well as against modern revivals. It might have been said, that the people were terrified—that Peter frightened them.

4. It is said that what we witness in revivals is all the effect of sympathy?

Answer. What begins them? Are the first cases of awakening to be attributed to sympathy? But it not unfrequently happens that numbers are awakened about the same time, without any knowledge of each other's feelings, or of the awakening of any other individuals.

But suppose sympathy does have an influence, after a revival has commenced; cannot God make use of it as a means of promoting the work, as well as any other means? The psalmist says, "Many shall see it and fear, and shall trust in the Lord." When sinners see others anxious for their souls, it is to them powerful preaching, and God can bless it to their conviction and conversion.

5. It is said that it is all enthusiasm.

Answer. If the distress of sinners is greater than the case demands, then call it enthusiasm. But if the sinner is in danger of losing his soul; not to be distressed, is blockish stupidity. Is it rational to brave the terrors of the Almighty, and to slumber on the brink of eternal perdition?

6. It is said, the sudden joy manifested in revivals, is irrational, and cannot be the effect of divine influence.

Answer. What shall we find to answer these expressions in the Bible? "The peace of God that passeth all understanding"—"Rejoicing with joy unspeakable and full of glory"—"All joy and peace in believing"—"called out of darkness into marvellous light"—"having the day star arise in our hearts." Would not a criminal, who should be reprieved on his way to the gallows, rejoice? Besides, were not the same effects witnessed in the days of Christ and the apostles? Did not Zaccheus come down from the tree and receive Christ joyfully? Did not Peter's hearers on the day of Pentecost, receive the word with joy? When Philip preached in Samaria, was there not great joy in that city?

7. It is said many who are zealous for a season, turn back, and become worse than before.

Answer. True. And so it was in the time of Christ. "Many went back and walked no more with him." Does this prove that Christ had no true disciples? It was so likewise in the days of the apostles. John says, "They went out from us, but they were not of us; for if they had been of us, they would, no doubt, have continued with us."

That the objection may be valid, it must be shown that all who profess to be the subjects of revivals, apostatize. But this cannot be shown. There are precious fruits that abide.

8. The question is sometimes asked, if revivals are the work of God, why do they not exist among other denominations, and why am not I taken?

Answer. This objection lies with equal force against the Christian religion. Not more than one-fifth part of the world is evangelized. Jews, Mohamedans, and Pagans might say, if yours is the true religion, why does not God convince us of its truth?

But revivals do exist in other denominations. All evangelical denominations have been favored with them in a greater or less degree.

If I were to find serious, praying people generally opposed to revivals, and all the impenitent and profane in favor of them, it would alter the case. But praying people pray for them, and rejoice in them.

They are doubtless the work of God, or the work of the devil. If they are the work of the devil, I believe all will acknowledge that there is more praying, and more apparent religion in the devil's kingdom, than there is out of it.

To all who oppose revivals, I would say, beware lest you be found fighting against God.

On Professing Religion.

Objection. I know it is my duty, but I have many fears that my hope is not well founded, and what shall I do?

Answer. It is your duty so to live, that you will not doubt. Your difficulty is a common one. We know how to feel for you, but we must be plain. Your difficulty is occasioned by your sin.

Objection. I am afraid that I shall do wrong—that I shall eat and drink unworthily.

Answer. It may be so. But is it not strange that any one should have conscientious scruples against obeying a plain command of Christ? Are you afraid to obey the Saviour? If you are really conscientious, you might well say, I am afraid I shall do wrong if I neglect to confess Christ before men. This you ought to say and to feel. You cannot neglect a known duty and be innocent. Is it not astonishing to see persons who are seriously disposed, making a righteousness of their disobedience to the command of God? They hope that they are Christians, and yet refuse to obey a plain command, lest they should sin.

Objection. My relatives oppose my making a profession, and threaten to turn me out of doors; and what shall I do?

Answer. You have a good opportunity to try your heart, and to ascertain whether you are willing to give up all for Christ.

The duty of being tender of the character of ministers.

A minister's usefulness depends very much on the good opinion that his hearers entertain of him at the time of his preaching or conversation. Prejudice is an effectual bar to conviction. If this cannot be removed, the heart is inaccessible. What cannot be answered by argument, will be repelled by prejudice. Hence the miracles of our Saviour instead of producing conviction, drew upon him the foulest reproach. In the case of Stephen's hearers, although they could not resist the Spirit and wisdom by which he spake, they could accuse him of blasphemy. If they could not answer his arguments, they could assert that they knew him to be a very bad man.

Resolved, with repect to my brethren in the ministry, in regular standing, I will be careful not to say, or insinuate any thing which may tend to destroy their usefulness among their hearers; but will use my influence to make them respected and beloved by them.

My feelings have often been wounded by the complaints of people about their minister; and I have been much pleased and gratified, when I have seen persons take the part of their pastor.

Decrees of God.

Objection. The decrees of God destroy man's free agency.

Answer. The reverse is true. God has decreed that man shall be a free moral agent. Is not man a free agent? Yes, you will say. How came he to be a free agent, unless God decreed that he should be so? If you are a free agent, God has made you such, and if he has made you such, he decreed to make you such. You are a free agent of *necessity*, and you cannot help being free. You can no more cease to be a free agent, than you can annihilate your soul. You are obliged to act as you please, and you cannot act in any other way. If you do not believe it, make the experiment. Try, try hard for five minutes, to do something which you do not choose or wish to do.

If you say this destroys freedom, then you adopt the sentiment that you cannot be free, unless you have the power of choosing to do something which you do not wish to do.

The doctrine of Election.

Although there may be difficulties in admitting this doctrine, there are greater difficulties in denying it.

If it is not true, then Christians make themselves to differ from sinners. There is certainly a difference; and if Christians make themselves to differ, then a new heart is not the gift of God. But if God makes the difference, he determined or decreed to do it from eternity; for all his determinations are eternal. He is the same yesterday, to-day, and forever. What he once chooses, he always chose. We cannot ascribe the difference to God, without attributing it to his eternal purpose. And what objection can there be to this? If God has changed your heart, he determined to do it, and why not determine to do it from eternity, as well as the moment before it was done? If it was a good determination, what difference does it make to you, whether it was formed in time or in eternity?

If this doctrine is not true, then we may say to sinners, why have you not become Christians? God has done as much for you as he has for others. If you had been as faithful as I have, the Christian may say, you might have been Christians long ago. By your own confession, you have not done as much as that vile wretch who never did any thing, till a short time before his conversion.

Objection. If I believed this doctrine, I should be an infidel. I had rather be an infidel than believe it.

Answer. What kind of argument is this? What does your dislike prove? Do not sinners hate the truth? Is not the carnal mind enmity against God? If you hate it, as you say, then you have reason to think that your prejudice will prevent you from examining with candor whether it is true. It seems, indeed, that according to your own confession, you are determined not to believe it, whatever evidence there may be of its truth. It is not for want of evidence that this doctrine is contained in the Bible, that any reject it. One half of the evidence would be sufficient, were not the heart set against it.

Objection. But if I am not elected, I cannot be saved. How can I?

Answer. 1. What then will become of you if the doctrine is not true? If it is not true, you are not elected of course. If it is not true, none are elected. Is it any evidence that the doctrine is not true, that you cannot be saved without it? But continues the objector, if I am not elected, I cannot be saved. How can I?

Answer. 2. Precisely in the same way that you can, if the doctrine is not true. Tell me how you can be saved on your own plan, without this doctrine, and I will tell you how all the non-elect can be saved. Tell me how any sinner can be saved on your own plan, when none are elected, and I will tell you how all may be saved on my plan, when a part only are elected.

But if I am not elected, I cannot be saved, continues the objector. How can I?

Answer. 3. Sir, you do not mean as you say. You mean that you can be saved without the doctrine of election. For if this doctrine is not true, you are not elected, of course. And still, you think you can be saved, if you are not elected.

You, who do not believe this doctrine, who maintain that none are elected till they believe and become Christians, of all men, ought never to say, if I am not elected, I cannot be saved. If I am not elected how can I be saved? is a question, which all who deny the doctrine of election, are doubly bound to answer. For on their plan, this is the awful condition of every impenitent sinner.

Those who deny the doctrine of election, do not suppose that it lies at the foundation of all hope, as to the salvation of men. They suppose that any or all may be saved as well without, as with it.

If mankind are so good, and so well disposed, that they can and will become Christians without being elected, very well. I have certainly no objection to your undertaking. If you will repent, and believe, and be born again without being elected, then commence the work immediately. But if I have no such opinion of the goodness of my heart,—if I choose to join with Paul, and attribute my faith, and repentance, and new heart to God alone—if I choose to trace all up to God's electing love, and say, "Blessed be the God and Father of our Lord Jesus Christ, who hath blessed us with all spiritual blessings in heavenly places in Christ Jesus, according as he hath chosen us in him before the foundation of the world"—"Who hath saved us, and called us with a holy calling not according to our works, but according to his own purpose and grace which were given us in Christ Jesus before the world began"—why should any one complain ?

But if I am not elected, I cannot be saved. How can I ?

Answer. 4. I do not know. That is for you to answer, who deny the doctrine. My object has been to show that if there are difficulties in admitting the doctrine, there are still greater difficulties in rejecting it.

Sinners who cannot get along with the doctrine of election, uniformly plead that they cannot get along without it.

If mankind were good enough to become Christians without being elected, then I acknowledge that this doctrine would not be necessary. That it is the duty of sinners to become Christians without being elected, I agree. But that sinners are disposed to do their duty, is not admitted.

Perseverance of the Saints.

It is said that Judas became a devil after the sop, and not before; for would the devil enter into a devil? Ans. The devil did enter into a thief, for so Judas was called, at least, six days before the devil is said to have entered into him.

Infant Depravity.

If infants sustain the same relation to the moral government of God, as brute animals, then they can no more be the subjects of prayer, of regeneration, of redemption by Christ, or of salvation, than brute animals.

Those who deny that infants are sinners, have devolved on them the Herculean task of defending the justice of God in bringing suffering and death upon millions of beings who are perfectly innocent. Those who admit the doctrine of infant depravity, have no difficulty on this subject.

How old must a child be, before he can be said to belong to the human race? When a child dies, how old must he be, before it can be said of him, that his death was *by sin?* in other words, before he can be considered as included in the following declaration of the apostle? "By one man, sin entered into the world, and death by sin, and so death passed upon *all men* for that *all have sinned.*"

The influence of self-interest on human belief.

To believe against personal interest, requires an honest heart. Without it, the mind will exert itself to evade the truth. It often requires but little evidence to lead to the adoption of a pleasing sentiment; while the most conclusive evidence fails to produce conviction of an unwelcome truth. *E. g.* The word everlasting when applied to the future punishment of the wicked, is by some explained to mean always a limited duration; but when applied to the future happiness of the righteous, it is readily admitted to denote endless duration. I know not that the latter was ever questioned. If a man were to undertake seriously to prove, that the word everlasting when applied to the happiness of the righteous, denotes only a limited duration, and when applied to the punishment of the wicked means an endless state of being, he would be pronounced a fool. And yet he would act no more irrationally than the man who adopts the opposite course of reasoning, by which so many profess to be convinced.

Hence we should exercise great caution in receiving doctrines which are pleasing to the natural heart; and equal caution in rejecting doctrines to which the natural heart is opposed.

Prayer.

Objection. I have a wicked heart, and it is an abomination for me to pray with such a heart.

Answer. Granted. It is so. But what then? Is

it not an abomination to neglect to pray? And do you think that God will accept of one abomination, in excuse for another?

Objection. What shall I do then? You tell me I must neither neglect to pray, nor pray with an impenitent heart. You leave me no choice. I expose myself to the curse either way.

Answer. This statement is not correct. There is a course left for you to choose, and that is, to pray as God commands you. Why are you not willing to do as he commands? It is true you have no choice between neglecting prayer, and praying with an impenitent heart. The path of duty is plain.

Objection. If to neglect prayer is sin, and if to pray with an impenitent heart is sin, I wish to know which is the greatest sin?

Answer. Why do you ask such a question as this? What right have you to be balancing sins, to see which you shall choose, when your duty is plain before you? It is of no consequence to you to have this question answered. To neglect prayer, or to pray with an impenitent heart, is abomination to God. Either course leads to hell. Of what consequence is it to the poor soul who is determined to walk in one of them, to know whether they are of equal or unequal length, when they both lead with equal certainty to destruction? Your duty is plain. You must pray with a penitent heart, or be lost.

Objection. But I cannot pray with a penitent and believing heart. I do not possess such a heart; and I cannot change my heart.

Answer. Do you mean to plead your wicked heart as an excuse? Will God who commands you to love him, excuse you from performing this duty, because you hate him? You say you have no heart to pray aright. What a confession is this! This is the very thing for which you are to blame. Will you plead your sin—your desert of condemnation as an excuse for disobeying God? Do you think God will accept such an excuse?

Objection. The ground you take, leaves only one way for the sinner, and cuts off all hope of safety in any other.

Answer. This is the very thing I aim at. To cut off all hope of safety in your present course, is the grand object I have had in view. The ground I have taken is, that obedience, and that only, is acceptable to God; and that we cannot expect safety in any other way. There is not a principle more clearly taught in the Bible, than that it is the duty of all men to love God, and to worship him in Spirit and in truth.